Planets in Love

Other Para Research Publications:

Astrology, Nutrition and Health
by Robert C. Jansky

Huna: A Beginner's Guide
by Enid Hoffman

Planets in Aspect: Understanding Your Inner Dynamics
by Robert Pelletier

Planets in Composite: Analyzing Human Relationships
by Robert Hand

Planets in Transit: Life Cycles for Living
by Robert Hand

Planets in Youth: Patterns of Early Development
by Robert Hand

John Townley

Planets in Love

*Exploring Your Emotional
and Sexual Needs*

Para Research
Rockport
Massachusetts

International Standard Book Number: 0-914918-11-7

Edited by Margaret E. Anderson
Type set in 9 pt. Paladium
Printed by Nimrod Press
Bound by Stanhope Bindery

Published by Para Research, Inc.
Whistlestop Mall
Rockport, Massachusetts 01966

Manufactured in the United States of America

First Printing, February 1978, 6,000 copies

To Janie,
for giving me
such a loving start

Contents

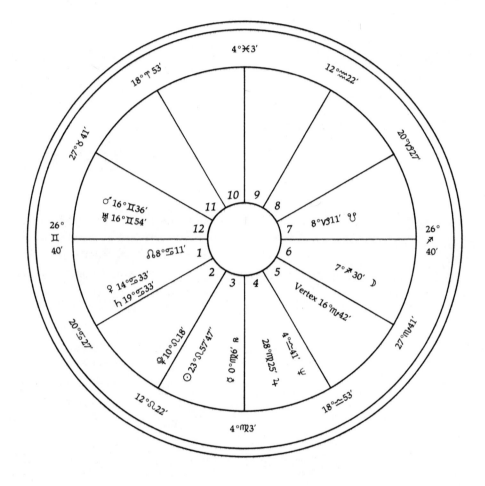

Natal chart of John Townley
August 17, 1945
1:56 AM E.W.T.
Washington, D.C.

Foreword

More than any other human experience, love is the theme underlying all our written and oral communication. It is the emotional and spiritual food that nourishes the soul and gives us the space to expand in the universe. The experience of love is both personal and cosmic; it includes caring, energy and affection, and encompasses the strength and power that is embodied in the pyramids. Love is communicated and made real to us through its expression in words and deeds as well as in sexuality. An infinite and invisible force, love passes through us to others and back again to the extent that we open ourselves to it.

How does astrology figure in? An accurately drawn birth chart is a measuring device that reveals how much love the individual accepts, how far he or she goes in giving up the self in love and how long it will take for the inner consciousness of love to awaken.

Planets in Love is not a book to be read from beginning to end in one sitting. Rather, it is a guide in the ongoing process of exploration and discovery of one's sexuality. The theoretical portion of the book, which is written especially for those who are serious in their study of astrology, offers fresh and original insights into the realms of sexuality and astrology. In these first four chapters, John Townley presents a clear and coherent framework, showing how the planets, signs, houses and aspects reflect the various stages of human sexuality. His theoretical structure of the factors of the natal chart is well conceived, thought-provoking and worthwhile for practicing astrologers who have an opportunity to apply the principles in clinical and experimental settings. Chapter Four presents a cross-section of love and astrology through three fascinating case studies that illustrate his principles.

The 550 delineations presented in the main body of the book can be valuable catalysts for couples who want to open up their communication about sexual and emotional needs. Lovers and marital partners can enrich their relationship by reading and discussing together the significance of their personal delineations. Townley's style of writing is refreshingly witty, injecting the merriment of the leprechaun with the wisdom of the serpent; the combination provides an unabashed look at our strengths and talents as well as our most laughable traits and embarrassing quirks in romance. His delineations are delightful to read and titillating to think about.

Planets in Love is not all-encompassing; it does not convey how or why we relate to others in nonromantic contexts, as in relationship between parents and children or friends. It also does not explore the topics of sexual preference and identification. While his delineations do allow ample room for individual needs for variety and for experimentation in sex, Townley does not specifically discuss the psychology or ramifications of nonheterosexuality, except to acknowledge its existence and to mention it within the context of his study of sado-masochism in the appendix. The delicate and morality-laden issues that confront us in homosexuality and even transsexuality are of vital concern to the current generation. There are no easy answers to the difficult and pressing questions that come up for each of us in this regard; ultimately the answers must be sought after and discovered within the individual.

I am in basic agreement with what this book represents, and I congratulate John Townley and Para Research for having produced and published it. The idea and the energy for *Planets in Love* grew out of their shared interests and talents, which have come together in this dynamic and exciting work that is guaranteed to blast the lid off the "eighth house" secrets of sexuality in astrology. *Planets in Love* sheds new light on that which has long remained in the dark recesses of the psyche and which is now ready for illumination.

As every astrologer knows, that which is conceived and born in time and space carries with it the imprint of the celestial sphere at that moment. *Planets in Love* reflects the present—the regenerative process that is being experienced in relationships (Pluto in Libra), the awakening of new consciousness in sexuality (Uranus in Scorpio), the need for responsibility for our creations and love expressions (Saturn in Leo) and the dissolution of outdated codes of morality by which we have judged ourselves and others (Neptune in Sagittarius).

I loved it!

Amy Shapiro

Chapter One

Developmental Stages

There are many ways to love and to be in love. The type of love that we will be exploring in this book is the love that the adult man or woman shares with another person.

The act of sharing physical love is broadly known as sex. But sexuality is far more than the physical union of male and female. Sexuality is the regenerative urge within each adult human being that draws us into relationships with those who can "bear fruit" with us. This fruit may take the tangible form of children or the intangible form of creative energy, or *prana*, that allows us to approach life with renewed vigor and enthusiasm.

In attempting to analyze human sexuality, some researchers have tried to categorize sexual behavior by defining boundaries between sexual and nonsexual activities. In clinical studies like those conducted by Kinsey and more recent researchers, sex has been defined in very physical terms by listing a number of genitally oriented actions that are intended to lead to orgasm. The purpose of these studies is to quantify data in order to arrive at some statistical conclusions.

In order to delve more deeply into the motivations behind specific kinds of sexual activity, more subjective psychological studies are necessary. While such studies may not deliver the mass of reliable statistics that large-scale clinical laboratory experiments will yield, long-term analysis of a single patient can provide much more understanding about a specific problem or drive that may be common to many individuals. One must be cautious, however, in making generalizations based on single case studies. One of the "catch-22's" of generalizing from an individual case study is that, in most cases, the person has come to the attention of the psychologist in the first place because he or she is suffering from sexual problems, and therefore the client is not necessarily representative of the population at large.

A third approach to the study of sexuality and love relationships, which combines some elements of the first two, uses the researcher-involved method of investigation pioneered by Masters and Johnson. In that approach, extensive clinical measurements of physical sexual responses are analyzed to find out how these responses are related to the individual's underlying motivations, desires and fears. To date, this method has provided the most realistic definitions of sexuality, and the treatments for sexual dysfunction resulting from these studies have been more successful than any previously attempted methods of remediation.

But the concepts of love and sexuality extend far beyond the bedroom, the psychiatrist's office or the laboratory. Love is an overwhelmingly strong motivating force. Our behavior may be motivated by fear of losing love or by prejudice toward someone whom we are afraid to love, which may cause inner conflict, as does social pressure against a person who loves or has sexual relations with someone outside of their social milieu. These conflicts in love can become so great as to cause both psychological and physical harm to the individuals involved. It is all very well for a clinician to arrive at a positive, clear-cut definition of physical sexuality, but it is something else entirely to make that definition work in an individual's daily life. Expressing love in a healthy creative manner requires understanding of the influence that love has on us and the influences that our lives have on love.

Scholars in nearly all areas of the humanities have applied their skills to this subject, often giving us a splintered picture, with each area of study having its valid application, although each one is necessarily so structured that it often excludes other, equally valid approaches. The moralist or theologian presents us with a spiritual view, aiming to help the individual elevate his or her awareness of sexuality. With this approach, balance is important, for unless the individual achieves a truly profound understanding, a moralistic view of sexuality may serve only to thwart an otherwise healthy sexual expression.

With the recent social-political movements for sexual liberation for women and for nonheterosexuals, heretofore private aspects of human relations have been taken out of the realm of intimacy and placed before the public to be viewed in the light of political doctrine. These movements are aimed, of course, at supporting change in the way that society values (and devalues) its members, based on their sexual status.

The fields of anthropology and sociology have also contributed perspectives on sexual behavior and patterns of human relations. Through anthropology we gain awareness of comparative cultural behavior patterns, putting ourselves in the context of the larger human existence on earth. Sociology analyzes human sexual relations as they reflect and shape the social order, helping us to see ourselves as integral members of the societal organism.

All of these studies have as their goal helping the individual to achieve self-understanding and at the same time to fit in with the world around him. Can any area of study encompass all of these splinter views of human sexuality? Or must the individual be an expert in a dozen or so different fields in order to arrive at a reasonable understanding of his or her own sexuality? I believe that astrology can effectively encompass all aspects of this monumental subject with very little conflict. Certainly, no other system so completely satisfies our Western need for specifics, since it is organized in such a way as to describe every kind of human action and quality in sexual terms, and at the same time allows such vast amounts of room for the Eastern realms of transcendental thinking.

More than any other philosophy, science or belief system, astrology is capable of painting a detailed picture of the individual from birth to death, describing each inclination—sexual and otherwise—using a language that involves the female and male principles: yin and yang, the receptive and creative principles. Every sign, planet, house and aspect can be discussed in this context, and thus the symbols of astrology can be used to describe reality in a subtle yet broadly sexual fashion.

Let me further clarify, astrologically, the meaning of these sexual indicators. In astrology the concepts of masculinity and femininity have nothing to do with men and women per se, but refer to the active and passive principles that operate throughout the cosmos. Every man and every woman is an amalgam of active and passive forces in varying degrees of tension and interplay, with the tension, or disequilibrium, providing the basis for human sexual motivation. Our Western social illusion that a man should have no feminine qualities and that a woman should have no masculine qualities is completely contradicted by astrology, as well as by the evidence of reality.

This approach to understanding sexuality allows us to consider the individual as a dualistic being, whose character is attuned to all of creation. Although in scientific terms we tend not to associate inanimate objects and natural forces with sexuality, we can, nevertheless, see that symbolically the ocean (water) and the earth, which provide us with food, are of the feminine polarity: maternal and nurturing. Conversely, the winds of the atmosphere (air) and the charge of electrical impulses and combustion (fire), which provide us with motion and change, are masculine in polarity. Thus, the four elements or temperaments—fire, earth, air and water—are conclusively masculine or feminine in nature. By looking at the number of planets in your chart that are in fire signs (Aries, Leo, Sagittarius) and air signs (Gemini, Libra and Aquarius), you will see how much creative, masculine or yang energy you possess. The number of planets in your chart in earth signs (Taurus, Virgo and Capricorn) and water signs (Cancer, Scorpio and Pisces) indicate the degree of receptive, feminine or yin characteristics you possess. Of course, these emphases will be affected by the house positions of planets in your chart. For example, a person with mostly earth and water planets but with Mars and the Sun in angular houses, particularly the first or tenth, will project and express his or her masculine qualities much more than you might expect from examining just the sign gender breakdown.

Just as the signs are associated with a gender, each of the houses and the planets is also associated with either a receptive or creative principle. On the next page is a table listing the traditional gender assignments, which will help us to understand the somewhat flexible balance that exists in astrology.

Because the system is holistic and self-balancing, it is not radically altered when another planet is found or a new fact about the solar system is discovered. Astrology was a complete system before Uranus, Neptune and Pluto were known to exist; the discovery of these bodies only adds richer detail to the picture of human evolution. Indeed, there is room for even more planets to complete the astrological sign rulerships by gender, although the ones we have serve quite well. A glance at the above list of rulerships reveals that in some instances a newly discovered planet would be more appropriate, specifically for the Taurus/Libra and Gemini/Virgo double rulerships of Venus and Mercury. Many astrologers have suggested substituting certain asteroids as the rulers of Libra and Virgo, but until that change is accepted (or new planets are discovered and assigned rulerships), we will get along with the present system.

While the zodiacal signs and their corresponding houses are easily divided into creative and receptive polarities, the planetary energies are not always so accommodating. Libra, for instance is an airy, and thus masculine, sign, which makes Venus a less than ideal ruler. In this case, we have a sign whose function is to balance polarities, a process which must necessarily be active and aggressive, but the planet assigned to it is all love, beauty and attracting in nature, not at all desirous of confrontation or open warfare. Venus is appropriate as the ruler of Libra because it desires reconciliation and harmony; the inconsistency of the rulership lies in Venus' desire to avoid the loss of personal comfort that may be necessary in order to bring about the balance.

Similarly, the qualities associated with Virgo are so specific that of the currently known planets, only Mercury could rule it, even though Mercury does not share the feminine characteristics associated with the earth element of Virgo. In this case, Mercury is an appropriate ruler of the Virgo function of accountability and discrimination, which requires great mental fortitude. Virgo's job is to seek clarification of detail so that

Table I
Gender Assignments
Masculine
active, yang

Planet	*Sign*	*House*	*Other Points*	*Aspects*
Sun	Leo	Fifth	Ascendant	Opposition
Mercury	Gemini	Third	North Node	Square
Mars	Aries	First		Inconjunct
Jupiter	Sagittarius	Ninth		
Uranus	Aquarius	Eleventh		
Venus	Libra	Seventh		
(Pallas, Juno)				

Feminine
passive, yin

Planet	*Sign*	*House*	*Other Points*	*Aspects*
Moon	Cancer	Fourth	Midheaven	Trine
Mercury	Virgo	Sixth	South Node	Sextile
(Ceres, Vesta)				Semisextile
Venus	Taurus	Second		
Saturn	Capricorn	Tenth		
Neptune	Pisces	Twelfth		
Pluto	Scorpio	Eighth		

Bisexual
Vertex
Conjunction

everything may be put in its proper place. In mythology, Mercury has always been the messenger of the gods, the bearer of news, a function that is essentially objective and noninvolved. In Virgo, however, Mercury must do more than pass on information as it does in Gemini; it is called upon to exercise categorical and inductive reasoning. These functions are a bit more weighty and sophisticated than we think of Mercury as able to handle.

This seemingly contradictory situation can be resolved if we understand that the planets are not innately connected to the signs but are assigned to them for convenience because of similar characteristics. The whole question of rulerships, detriments, exaltations and falls is one that many astrologers are struggling with because of the delicate nature of passing qualitative judgment (good and bad) upon certain planetary positions. Houses, signs and planets do function independently of each other, and although each class can be divided into masculine and feminine categories, they cannot be rigorously equated with each other across classes. It is better to look at rulerships as showing similarities in style that help to trace the influences in a horoscope (as in studying the flow of planetary energies through dispositors) rather than as fixed assignments that are innate to the structure of astrology.

In the human character, the planets represent basic motivations. The signs represent the forms those motivations take, varying in expression from individual to individual. The houses represent the areas of life in which the individual expresses those motivations, working out his needs and life lessons through the various circumstances and opportunities presented to him. Lastly, the planetary aspects represent the interplay among the various drives and motivations, causing conflict and challenge in the individual. The meanings of the individual planets are discussed in greater detail in Chapter Two, and the meanings of the signs and houses are discussed in Chapter Three.

In addition to their masculine or feminine attributes, each of the planets may also be discussed as symbolically representing stages of life growth. If we divide the ten planets into five pairs, each pair having a *creative* planet and a *receptive* planet, we can learn much about our basic human character as we move from birth to death through five stages of development and awareness. The planetary pairs and their corresponding stages here presented also provide a picture of our sexual development in a more literal sense. These stages are sequential to some extent, but they overlap at many points and should not be considered rigid divisions.

Sun and Moon: Primal Stage

The two most important planets in the horoscope, also known as the luminaries, the Sun and Moon, symbolize the archetypal principles of male and female, the creator and the creation, the father and the mother. It is of these two principles that we are conceived, as man and woman unite to generate new life. At birth the infant is closest to its source, having just left the mother's womb of protection, not yet touched by worldly knowledge. The infant's cry is primal, demanding that its needs—for food, warmth, dryness and comfort—be met. This is the classical oral stage. We all begin in a helpless state, completely dependent upon others to take care of and nurture us. The Moon in the chart shows how well the newborn's needs are met. It also represents the infant's response to the world, taking in food by sucking and beginning to structure its world by passive observation. The Sun relates to the active principle within the primal stage which is evident in the spontaneous and uncontrived actions of the infant, who expresses life without inhibition. The Sun represents the egocentric child in all of us, going out into the world as if all activity revolved around the self. These are fundamental modes that form the core of the personality. They have a strong effect on the individual's sexuality, particularly if any of his or her needs are denied or thwarted at this stage of development.

Venus and Mars: Physical Stage

As the child develops, he or she becomes very aware of the physical body's energies and needs. Along with the Ascendant and the Midheaven, Venus and Mars represent the modifying experiences of early childhood, the effects of which continue into later life. During this phase of youth the individual achieves control over the body, learning about the eliminative functions, the genitals and sexual differentiation, a basic step toward achieving sexual identity and orientation. This is the classical anal stage. Venus in the chart shows one's capacity to give and accept love, which starts very early in life by learning to share what one has with others. In this respect, the young child growing up is tremendously influenced by the values of others, the virtues of Venus being instilled in the child throughout the early years. If beauty and kindness are appreciated by those around the child, the child will come to value those qualities. If affection is expressed to the child, the child will become an affectionate person later in life, easily expressing love to others. Venus is also very connected with our sensory apparatus—particularly our ability to taste and to touch. It is through the senses that we are first stimulated to learn, since we most want to learn about that which activates our desires.

Mars in the chart represents the urge to act, to be independent and self-sufficient. But, of course, along the road to independence there are many obstacles. Mars gives one the drive to go on and to meet challenges head on, confronting opposition and, if need be, fighting to overcome one's fears. Mars is the instinct to survive and to be felt by others as an influence on the world. Where Venus is our capacity to receive what the world has to offer, Mars is our ability to generate activity and make an impact on others. In the context of love and sexuality, Mars is virile and male, ready to lead and to conquer. How Mars is situated in the chart shows how courageous and potent the individual—man or woman—is in all areas of life.

Jupiter and Saturn: Social, External Stage

This stage of development extends from middle childhood through early adulthood and represents social encouragement and restriction of the individual's behavior. Jupiter functions through the judgment of right and wrong. Saturn requires the individual to be responsible for the consequences of his or her behavior. During this stage of development, the individual's sexual attitudes are shaped by external pressures through experiences and by specific teachings, either verbally or by implication, about sexual morality. This stage determines how free the individual is to express the previously formed sexual identity. How well one is able to adjust to the social pressures and promptings of this period determines one's later motivations for or inhibitions against social development. Jupiter is usually a beneficent influence in the chart. Where it is placed indicates where life will open doors to the individual. In love, Jupiter shows the area of life in which the individual can usually be trusted to provide strength, comfort and understanding. Saturn, a traditionally "malefic" planet, shows where in life the individual needs to work to supply what is needed. In a relationship, and in love, the placement of Saturn indicates the area of life in which the individual experiences need and in which he or she is most sensitive to the opinion of others, particularly those in authority. Saturn is the celestial schoolmaster, and as such neither encourages nor discourages love, but asks that it be looked upon as just another means of learning about life.

Uranus and Neptune: Spiritual, Internal Stage

Once the individual has become aligned with the sexual mores of his or her society, he has earned the freedom and the right to go beyond convention, to make inner discoveries and to reach out for patterns of thought and behavior that add meaning to life. These urges may become active at any time from adolescence through middle adulthood; they gain in importance throughout life. At this stage sexuality becomes a vehicle for experiencing freedom and transcendence. Here the individual's learned (Saturn) responses can become ritualized so as to seem either magical or imprisoning. Uranus represents the evolutionary drive to feel that one is within the context of a changing, growing world. In order to achieve that awareness, the individual may choose to break away from the norm and experiment with behavior and relationships that are not sanctioned by society. If the person has already become aware of himself as an evolving individual, then his behavior in love will merely not conform to accepted standards, although it needn't cause any disturbances to others.

With Neptune, the individual must experience the vast ocean of love that is God, or divine. This can come through the realization that the loved one is a reflection of all that is divine within the universe, for whom no sacrifice is too great to make. Neptune encourages selfless love within the individual, who comes to feel that life has value only if there is willingness to lose it for a cause. The wisdom that is gained through Neptune does not come easily. More often than not, the individual falsely adores another for nonexistent virtues and attributes. This leads to great disappointment in love when the cloud passes, but it is important to understand that nothing in the universe that truly belongs to us can be taken away. Under the influence of Neptune we are forced to let go of what we thought we possessed, only to find out that perhaps it wasn't what we needed after all. Neptune's place in the chart shows where the individual's "escape hatch" or release valve is hidden. In relationships Neptune shows how receptive the individual is to involvement with someone who releases that valve and aids in the escape from "reality." This escape can take any number of forms, from music and religion to drugs and alcohol. Neptune rules the "lost and found" department of life. As such it often attracts us to relationships in which we can either "be found" or can "save another's soul."

Mercury and Pluto: Structural Stage

This odd combination of planets represents the opposite ends of a sexual spectrum. Mercury, essentially nonsexual in nature, represents the separative and individuating principle that structures the perceptions of the mind. Mercury shows its strongest effect during the early childhood learning period when the mind must assimilate vast amounts of information. Relative to sexuality, Mercury enables the individual to concretely express the primal, physical, social and spiritual realms through the act of sex itself. It is the mechanical awareness of who-what-where-when-and-how that cares for every last detail. Pluto, on the other hand, represents the dissolution of those very rational structures, ultimately resulting in death or transformation. Mercury is associated with a sexual technique as a goal in itself, around which the other areas of learning must be tested. Pluto gives the individual the awareness that we essentially are not our bodies—that the body is only the vehicle through which life flows. Impersonal and unattached, Pluto represents the regenerative urge, which can do without sex for its own sake, needing sex only for the sake of continuing the species. Because Pluto is such a powerful planet, its influence can give the individual a sense of actually becoming a channel or vehicle. This sense can be quite productive if the person has great integrity. However, it can be extremely dangerous if the individual's ego needs are so great as to erase respect for others' needs and others' lives. Specifically, the strongly Plutonian person may see himself as a chosen vehicle for delivering destiny's blows and/or promises to those around him. Misuse of power is the danger with Pluto, sexually as well as otherwise.

If a person has a particular sexual blockage or problem, it is often possible to find its source by looking at the more difficult planetary aspects in the natal chart, which may suggest the areas of learning and development that have given rise to the problem. The signs and houses involved in these difficult aspects may further illuminate the problem and suggest how it may be alleviated.

If you are interpreting the chart for sexuality you must keep in mind that the sexual slant is provided largely by the observer rather than the observed. To an astrologer whose interest or research lies in the area of sexuality, a particular planetary aspect may seem to have much sexual meaning; however, the individual may express that influence in some very different area of life, with only a slight effect sexually. So much is determined by the individual's conditioning and experience, that unless the astrologer knows the person well, he can say only that the aspect has an implied sexual meaning rather than a definite effect. Any aspect holds a wealth of potentials, both sexual and nonsexual, and it is not wise to make explicit statements about an individual's sexuality as it is shown in the natal horoscope without having more information about the person's life.

However, information about sexual potential in itself can be of great value, particularly if you are studying someone who is quite repressed sexually, because it can indicate directions that may lead to more free and enjoyable sexual expression.

Although I mention some rather specific sexual inclinations in connection with some horoscope factors, these are not certainties. An astrologer would be unwise to mention them to a repressed person, because the suggestions might be offensive. Very often a person's strongest desires and inclinations are the most heavily repressed, and if the astrologer is too specific, he may unleash energy that is too powerful to handle.

For this reason, I have confined these specifics to the introductory chapters on the planets, signs, houses and aspects, which are written for the astrologer, while the delineations in the second half of the book are more general, for astrologers and non-astrologers alike. This division serves two purposes: first it avoids stereotyping and perhaps offending the non-astrologer who looks up his or her aspects for instant self-analysis and second, it affords the astrologer two different views of the same material. The delineations are cued to counseling clients, while the descriptions here present the various horoscope factors from a sexual and emotional viewpoint.

By drawing a symbolic parallel between planetary pairs and human growth, we are following the primary tenet of astrology: that an individual's basic personality structure is set at birth and that it develops accordingly throughout life. While there is at present no physical basis for this assumption, as there is for Newton's laws of motion, there is a vast array of observations about personal styles and events, which has lent practical credibility to astrology. In this respect astrology is similar to other systems that attempt to explain sexuality, such as psychology and sociology, which likewise have no physical basis but are aggregations of observation and prediction.

But while other systems deal with sexuality in fragments, the symbolism of astrology can effectively cover the whole field. In great detail, astrology is able to tie the whole picture of sexuality together in a way that other disciplines cannot. The immediate test of this assumption remains its application to individual cases, with necessary changes being made as experience warrants. This is, after all, how the other sciences have evolved. Because we have so much information available to us about sexuality, thanks to Freud and others, astrologers today should find it much easier to determine the applicability and relevance of its symbolism to everyday life.

In order to test the relevance of astrology, its full symbolism must be understood and meticulously applied, because to treat either astrology or sexuality superficially will not yield any meaningful results. As the behavioral sciences lean more and more toward holistic explanations of human behavior, many more people are seriously testing the effectiveness of astrology. In the process, it is being subjected to vindication in some areas and necessary modification in others where it does not pass the test of reality. I have conducted an extensive study of astrology in relation to one particular area of sexual behavior, sado-masochism. The results of my study are presented for the reader in the appendix (page 351).

In looking at sexual and emotional needs through the lens of astrology, it is wise to keep in mind that dogma has no place here. In order to constitute a system, the basic symbolism must remain intact, but its specific applications are subject to continual change as society changes. Only when an astrological principle is proved through repeated personal or experimental results can it be depended upon, and the older the principle, the more it should be tested. If we keep these reservations in mind, astrology can be a useful and enlightening tool for exploring the inner realms of sexual expression through observation of other people as well as through one's own personal experience and growth.

Chapter Two

Planetary Energies

The Sun, Moon and planets are the backbone of the horoscope, whether we are considering sexuality or any other area, because they delineate the basic structure of the personality. They show which aspects of one's character are strong and reliable, which are fragile or excitable and how the previously mentioned stages of growth have strengthened or weakened the individual's ability to deal with the world.

The influence of any one planet is seldom felt in its pure form, because it is usually combined with the qualities of other planets through mutual aspects or through sign and house position. Nonetheless, the planet's basic influence remains the same, although modified by its relationships with other factors in the chart.

Sun

The Sun reveals a person's innermost being, the central force around which all else revolves. Like the actual Sun in the universe, the symbolic Sun in the horoscope is the central guiding force in our lives, dictating the purpose or focus that all other activities must be directed toward. Since the Sun is the point of reference, it is the "I am" of the chart, the point of individual identification. With respect to sexuality, the placement of the natal Sun, along with that of the Moon, shows the extent of one's overall confidence and the strength of one's sexual identity as a male or female. The Sun is very important to a person's sexuality, not in the specific details of sexual style, but in the overall approach to sexuality and whether it is natural or forced. In love and sexuality, the Sun exudes a quality of warm, wholesome, childlike innocence and healthy fun.

Since the Sun is one of the yang, or projective, planets in the chart, the qualities of the sign that the Sun is in will be expressed assertively throughout the individual's life. The Sun sign shows the quality of life force that the individual radiates out into the world and the kind of attracting or magnetic power that he or she has over others. For example, an individual with the Sun in Leo will exert a very powerful influence over others because Leo is a positive, fixed fire sign. The Leo individual must be able to shine in love and express the natural steady warmth that this sign represents. A person whose Sun is in Pisces, on the other hand, will have a somewhat mystical life, merging the ego with a sense of universal oneness and divinity. Pisces is a feminine, mutable water sign, which signifies that the ego is dissolved in the vast ocean of life. The Pisces Sun expresses love by selflessly giving to the partner, which can be quite "other-worldly."

The house that the natal Sun is in shows what life activities are most important to the individual and therefore are the strongest priorities. In love, it may be through the activities indicated by that house that the individual shines to a mate, being proud of his or her accomplishments in that area. Because the activities associated with the house that the Sun is in, as well as those of the house where Leo is on the cusp, are so vital to the individual, it is crucial that a partner in love allow the individual to express himself or herself through those activities. Otherwise both the person's ego and the relationship will suffer. For example, the person whose Sun is in the tenth house will expect others to appreciate his or her career accomplishments above and beyond all else. This individual is proud of the ability to rise in life to a position of authority over others, and expects respect and admiration from a partner. Conversely, a person with the Sun in the fourth house gains a sense of importance by his or her own internal standards, seeking privacy and intimacy in life, inner peace being of prime importance. This person needs a mate who can appreciate this inner life, who will not try to push the person into competition.

Reinforcing aspects to the Sun usually indicate an easy-going and confident person who approaches sex in a loving manner based on inner security. This applies only to the individual's active approach to sexuality, unless other factors, such as the Moon, which indicate responsiveness, are similarly reinforced. It is quite possible, therefore, for a person to be very confident when taking an active (Sun) role in lovemaking, but to be hesitant or suspicious in a passive role. In any case, the person with a strongly reinforced Sun can positively resolve even the harshest aspects between the middle and outer planets, while someone with hard aspects to the Sun may take many years to derive the potential benefits from easy aspects elsewhere in the chart. For someone with a well-aspected Sun, sex can have the frivolity and grace that we associate with the Garden of Eden. But if it is poorly aspected, the childlikeness can become infantile and demanding because of the person's desire to return to the more egocentric and self-satisfying state of childhood, although that is not a realistic option.

Easy or hard aspects to the Sun may reflect how wanted the person was as an infant, whether the parents looked upon the child as a gift from God or a burden from the devil. Because the Sun is closely tied with the will, it is natural for the child to internalize the parents' feelings about having produced the child. Simply stated, the child, even in earliest infancy, can sense whether or not it has been born into a family that is proud to have it as their newest member. When an infant is not wanted, that basic sense of rejection is transmitted and incorporated into the child's developing self-image, which carries over into adulthood. Thus will the child see his or her worth as an individual, for better or for worse.

Difficult aspects to the Sun generally indicate lack of confidence in sex, as well as in other areas of life. Often the individual unconsciously overcompensates for his or her insecurity with aggressive or pushy behavior. By forcing another's will into submission, the individual thus obtains a false sense of strength and mastery. The Sun in inconjunct aspect is most likely to bring about this type of behavior, as the inconjunct is associated with frustration that is linked to obscure sources. The most debilitating aspect is the square, of course, because it clouds or impedes the natural energy of the Sun, replacing the vital force with dissatisfaction and self-reproach, preventing the person from taking positive, decisive action. In the long run, however, squares prod the individual into achieving quite a bit of conscious control over the issues or area of life indicated by the other planet involved in the square. Experiences in life force this individual to learn moderation.

The Sun is very important to the success of an affair because it shows how free the person is to express his or her individuality. When the Sun has supportive aspects, there is no problem. But with strong squares to the Sun, the individual may create possibly insurmountable tension because the conflict is so basic that change is improbable.

Moon

The Moon represents the individual's receptivity and responsiveness to the environment, and as such, it is a key to understanding sexual responsiveness. The Moon is said to govern the emotions, but this is a question of definitions. If emotions are thought of as only those feelings that one has in response to an outside stimulus, then the Moon is the appropriate ruler. And, like the predictable turn of the tides, we can be sure that our emotions will change course daily and hourly in response to whatever is happening in the subjective world of our environment. But emotions such as inspiration, pride and love do not necessarily fit that definition, because they may be generated within the individual with no apparent outside stimulus. Thus it is best to think of the Moon as the primary body of response.

The Moon represents our ability to respond to another's needs as well as our own. To be able to care for and nurture others is a mark of emotional maturity, and aspects to the Moon show how the individual responds to others' needs, whether instinctively or under inhibition.

The Moon is also that which becomes habitual in our lives, through the process of continual repetition. Each of us has our peculiar quirks or habits of personality that may be either endearing or intolerable to a mate. These traits are shown by aspects to the Moon, and knowing exactly how these aspects work can help the person make conscious what is unconscious. Otherwise, the responses are likely to remain mechanical and reflexive, as though the individual is not responsible for them.

In traditional astrology, the Moon is said to be more important than the Sun in a woman's chart. That may have been true in earlier times, when women were always cast in the role of being responsive rather than assertive. But today we recognize that women are not confined to a passive role, any more than men are confined to an aggressive role. Both men and women reach their fullest potential only by expressing and experiencing both their Sun and their Moon principles. In practical terms, this means getting in touch with our subconscious needs for security, safety and protection, which operate in all of us throughout our lives, whether we acknowledge it or not.

The sign that the Moon is in determines the quality of the individual's emotional responsiveness. For example, the Moon in Gemini makes for a kind of emotional hypersensitivity because of the speed at which flighty Gemini moves. However, this sensitivity is not very deep; it is a surface response to circumstances and to people, which can seem quite humorous or immature to others. The Moon in Scorpio, by contrast, makes a person capable of having the most intense reactions to others without necessarily showing these reactions in obvious or open ways.

The house that the Moon is in natally indicates the area of life where the person moves almost unconsciously, so that those activities are part of the daily and habitual routine.

The individual operates very effectively in that area through sheer repetition, attracting experiences that will enhance that area of life. Often the issues that are tied to that house are ones that the person has been conditioned about since early childhood, so there is a very strong pattern of response that is difficult to break. For example, a person with the Moon in the sixth house is a voracious worker, taking great pleasure in his or her capacity to accomplish innumerable small tasks. In a love relationship, this could be nice if the partner likes to be "looked after," since this person will automatically respond to any of the loved one's bodily or personal needs. However, this can become a problem if the partner is very independent and doesn't like to be helped unnecessarily.

A well-aspected Moon enables the individual to glean pleasure from experiences that might cause another person to complain or feel incomplete. Such reinforcement of the Moon also makes the individual less likely to be aggressive. Because he or she feels sure of an appropriate and satisfying response from others, defensive measures seem unnecessary. For example, someone with a well-aspected Moon in Sagittarius can respond to upsetting situations with a laugh, while someone with an afflicted Moon in Cancer is likely to draw back in anxiety from a lover's friendliest advance.

Difficult aspects to the Moon may lead to insecurity and even to emotional or sexual dysfunction. As a defense mechanism, such a person may become caustic or critical, attacking others verbally or emotionally to forestall attack. The form of defense depends on the other planet, with Mercury creating a smokescreen of verbiage; Mars, argumentativeness or anger; Saturn, undermining criticism, and so on.

The relationship between the Sun and the Moon in the chart is quite important in determining whether there is a dichotomy between a person's active approach to love and his or her feelings in response to love from others. Easy aspects between the Sun and Moon give the person a feeling of substance and reliability that survives hard angles from even the outer planets.

If the Moon is stronger than the Sun in an individual's chart, he or she should take a primarily responsive role in sexual situations. Or, if the Sun is the stronger, the primary role should be active. This is not to say that someone with a weak Sun should abandon the active role for the passive, but that he or she can successfully adopt the passive role as necessary, thus making the best use of strong points in the personality. Not surprisingly, a Sun-Moon opposition creates a definite split between the manner of approach and of response, while the square creates a lack of confidence.

Mercury

Mercury is the mental space we live in. Broadly speaking, it is our thinking apparatus as well as our speaking ability. It is our ability to communicate our ideas to others and to apply a method of intelligent inquiry to the problems that life offers us. Because Mercury is a highly rationalizing planet, its role in love is limited, since we think of love as something that must be experienced and shared from the heart rather than the head. But certainly, we can and do talk about love, and we think and write about love, as this book testifies. Therefore, Mercury can be a good key to understanding how well the individual can communicate, verbally or in writing, his or her needs, desires or intentions toward another person.

Although Mercury is not usually considered a highly sexual planet, it has a critical effect on a person's ability to find enjoyable forms of sexual expression. Mercury governs one's mental comprehension of the sexual act and its implications, which provides the basis for a variety of enjoyable sexual techniques. Mercury rules the hands in the physical body, and thus one's manipulative skills—obviously a necessary factor in successful foreplay and sexual communication. Hand-holding, stroking, petting and caressing are all sexual expressions of affection that Mercury rules.

The sign that Mercury is in at birth qualitatively affects the way one thinks and communicates. If Mercury is in Aquarius, for example, the individual can express the most abstract and altruistic concepts to a lover and can discuss the relationship within the context of a larger whole. Mercury in Sagittarius is a speculative thinker, one who wants to project the outcome of a relationship before it even gets off the ground.

The house that natal Mercury is in shows the issues that most occupy the person's mind and about which the person keeps well informed. Mercury in the third house, for example, is an individual who is mentally stimulated by practically everything and everyone nearby. Never at a loss for something to talk about, this individual wants to know as much about a potential lover as he or she can learn, and is equally willing to disclose any and all personal background information to an interested lover.

Mercury's position in the chart also shows how nervous the person is likely to be. A well-aspected Mercury indicates someone who can put a partner at ease in a sexual encounter by helping him or her talk out any anxieties about sexual involvement. Since Mercury rules thought, an overactive Mercury (through angularity and having a number of aspects) can mean an individual who thinks love rather than makes love!

If Mercury is well aspected, the person is able to use ideas inventively to confirm a positive view of sexuality and to prevent sexual stagnation or boredom. A poorly aspected Mercury, however, can repress a person's imagination or, depending on the aspected planet, cause the imagination to split away from reality and take impossible approaches to sex, which results in frustration. Or it may detract from physical enjoyment by analyzing the sexual experience as it occurs.

Mercurial problems arise only if the chart indicates a person whose mind plays too great a role in determining the time, place or style of sexual expression, not giving the body and emotions enough freedom of movement or choice. In many other areas of life the body is necessarily the servant of the mind for reasons of comfort and survival, but for the same reasons, in sex the mind must be the servant of the body, and the mind should be willing to take that role.

One of Mercury's most endearing traits is that it rules our ability to laugh at ourselves and to see the lighter side of life. A strong Mercury can give the individual the ability to look upon sex, and all of life, with a touch of wit. If Mercury is weak, however, this wit can turn into biting sarcasm or cynicism, which can turn off a partner faster than a cold shower. Learning when not to talk is an important lesson for such a person.

More than with the other planets, the favorableness of a Mercury aspect depends on the house and the sign Mercury is in natally. If it is bogged down in Taurus, a harsh aspect can get it moving, but if Mercury is in Gemini, it needs an aspect that will slow it down and bring it back to earth.

The relationship between Mercury and Uranus in a chart is quite important, because this has a strong influence on one's sexual inventiveness. A harsh relation between the two can indicate fruitless and unsatisfying experimentalism, while an easy aspect leads to a wealth of delightful innovations that keep one's sexual expression interesting. The Mercury-Venus relationship is also important, because it can give rise to a host of satisfying and enlightening sexual desires, particularly if the planets are conjunct.

Probably the most debilitating afflictions for Mercury come from aspects to Neptune, which tend to diffuse sexuality and sometimes even eliminate it as a source of enjoyment or creativity. A soft Neptune-Mercury aspect indicates a dreamer, often with a passive imagination, while a hard aspect creates unreal fantasies that cannot be fulfilled. Of all the aspects, the conjunction is probably the most favorable, because it provides the motivation to make dreams come true.

Venus

More than any other planet, Venus takes us to the heart of what this book is all about: love, that life experience that defies intellectualizing. Venus is appropriately named our sister planet, for we know that love is indeed the tie that binds. Venus's position in the chart shows where, what and how easily we love—not in the mercurial sense of sexual technique, but in the emotional sense of finding personal satisfaction through emotional involvement. This involvement need not be limited to sexual relationships. On the contrary, there is so much of life to love that Venus gives us an appetite for all kinds of involvements.

Venus' role in sexuality is more clearly understood by the word sensuality. Our appetite for food is stimulated by an attractive plate and delicious aroma, and in that sense Venus indicates the kind of "dish" you are to a prospective lover, whether you are male or female. Venus is our awareness of all that is beautiful within and around us, and as such, represents the proverbial honey that attracts the bear. The key word for understanding Venus in a sexual context is desire, and since desire is essential to any successful sexual experience, the position and aspects of Venus are critical. Without practical and realizable desire, there can be no sexual fulfillment.

Venus' sign placement shows in what way the person experiences love and how he or she is loving. In Virgo, Venus is bound to seek perfection, wanting so much to be thought of as the perfect mate. This can go to an uncomfortable extreme, so that the individual misses out on much of the simple pleasure and beauty of a relationship because he or she is too busy analyzing it. Venus in Libra, however, indicates a person for whom sharing love is second nature. This person wants wholeheartedly to please others and to be as attractive as possible in all regards.

The house that natal Venus is in indicates the area of a person's life where good things come easily through one's own desires and values. If it is in the first house, for example, a person has a most pleasing appearance and presentation that will win many good things in life because the individual values himself or herself highly. Others find it very easy to let these people have their way because they are so charming and pleasant to be with.

Almost any conjunction of Venus with another planet is ideal for romantic intensity of the highest order, unless both planets are in hard aspect with other planets in the chart. Even a Venus-Pluto conjunction, although sometimes problematic in its insatiability, gives sexual need great intensity and also provides great release. Of course, intense sexual expression is not best for everyone. If the rest of the chart indicates a more diffuse style of sexual expression, such intensity may be difficult, because the rest of one's personality is not prepared for it.

Any harsh contact to Venus gives an unusual flavor to sexual desire, although it may not be anything strange, except with Uranus. One's desire may not come at the same time as the opportunity to express it, as with the Venus-Mars square, or sexual desire may be tied to the need to dominate or to be dominated, as with the Venus-Pluto square. In any case, with these aspects, in order to have deep sexual satisfaction, one must first settle the characteristic interference from the planet making the hard aspect. Even benefic bodies such as Jupiter can have this effect to a certain extent, making the flow of desire irregular or causing too much or too little desire for the available source of satisfaction. Older texts often mention that hard Venus aspects lead to sexual abnormality or perversion, but that depends on your definition of perversion. Those aspects may lead a person to desire some rather circuitous and not always satisfying forms of sexual expression, but Venus aspects are not likely to lead to the more harmful "perversions" involving unwilling partners, as hard aspects to Mars can. Usually any harm that results from a difficult Venus aspect is to the individual rather than to those around him. Certainly this is likely when the rest of the chart is full of difficult or frustrating aspects.

Otherwise, these aspects are more likely to lead to sexual eccentricity or desires channeled into unusual forms of expression, which may have more positive enjoyment value for the individual than mundane forms. This kind of expression can often be traced to early learning patterns in which more secondary satisfactions were substituted for the primary object of the infant's desires. However, there is nothing innately harmful in such eccentric forms of expression.

Mars

Mars represents the sexual and aggressive drives that allow us to act on our desires (Venus) to actively pursue what we want. In its purest expression, Mars represents impulse propelled into action, always going forward into new territory. It is the fearless and unbridled animal instinct within us all that assures our survival on this planet. In sexuality, Mars represents our energy trigger and supply. Its placement indicates whether the individual has a smooth and uninterrupted flow of energy or whether it is blocked for a time and then released too strongly, and whether the person tires easily.

The sign placement of Mars influences the nature of one's aggressive and sexual drives, describing the manner in which the person acts. If Mars is in a fire or air sign—the masculine signs—the individual will not have much trouble expressing his or her drives. In the feminine signs, water and earth, Mars is a more domesticated animal, often waiting for external circumstances to be "just right" before acting on impulse. For example, Mars in Aries moves at a moment's notice, fearlessly going after the object of desire. This placement makes the individual short on patience and high on impulse. This is a no-beating-around-the-bush person who wants sex hot and exciting, though not necessarily enduring. In a less aggressive sign, like Cancer, Mars can tire quite easily unless the mood is just right and the person feels sure of acceptance. Here the individual might turn his or her aggressive drives inward, choosing not to risk rejection from a potentially hostile partner. Because of the maternal nature of Cancer, this individual will express sexuality by being very protective of a mate, often using food and shelter as symbols of love.

Mars' natal house shows the area in life where the person acts out assertively. In sexuality, this can mean that the person is likely to "make a move" in romance when involved in activities relating to that house. For example, Mars in the eighth house is highly secretive about his or her intentions, choosing to initiate sex when it is probably least expected or anticipated. This is a very manipulative placement for Mars, one in which the individual plays on the responses of others in making his or her moves. By contrast, a person with Mars in the second house is far less mysterious, setting about doing what he or she wants without too much concern for how others will respond. This is a persistent placement for Mars and indicates that the individual is likely to initiate a sexual encounter when he or she feels comfortable, with everything that could be wanted readily available.

If there are difficult aspects to Mars, they should be worked out through active expression of the energies, even if that causes an immediate problem or temporary inconvenience. These are not problems that can be solved intellectually or passively but, as in other Mars endeavors, such as sports, by active practice. The problems connected with Mars aspects are mainly of two kinds. The first involves sexual rhythms that are not matched with a partner's. A Mars-Jupiter conjunction, for instance, may describe a person who is eager for more when a partner has had enough. On the other hand, hard aspects from Saturn may make a person's energies low or intermittent, so that a partner is left wanting. The best solution to this problem is a simple explanation, so that the partners can either come to an understanding and adapt, or they can separate.

Difficult Mars-Saturn aspects are usually associated with problems of sexual dysfunction such as impotence or frigidity, but that may not always be the case. If a client is experiencing such dysfunctions as a recent phenomenon, look to the transits for indications of emotional insecurity or ill health, the two basic causes of this problem. Knowing how long the condition can be expected to last should relieve the client's anxiety somewhat. But, more importantly, the astrologer may want to recommend that the client see either a medical doctor or a qualified professional psychotherapist for further help if the chart indicates a health problem or long-term psychological problem. In any case, an astrologer should never suggest to a client that certain aspects in his chart might cause impotence, because the suggestion can either bring on the problem or make it worse by causing the client to believe that the problem cannot be overcome.

Hard aspects, including the conjunction between Mars and Uranus or Mars and Pluto, give sexual expression an explosive quality that may cause problems, because most people do not enjoy violence in lovemaking. In some extreme cases, if the energies of these aspects are repressed too long or too thoroughly, they (along with some Mars-Saturn and Mars-Neptune aspects) can lead to criminality. That is rare, but these energies should be expressed regularly to keep them from building up excessively. One way to accomplish that is through controlled bedroom fantasy fulfillment with the scenario spelled out and limited ahead of time, so that the energies are expressed without doing physical or emotional harm. If a sexual outlet is not found for these energies, the result is usually anger or aggressiveness, both of which may be destructive to the relationship.

Jupiter

A key word for Jupiter in the context of love and sexuality is *trust*. Trust is what allows us to provide and to accept comfort and support in a relationship, and to a degree, gives us the courage to look ahead rather than back into the past. Jupiter also represents our positive learning patterns in love, our ability to see ahead of time just where a relationship is likely to lead. It is our sense of judgment about life, which is inspired by the faith that the future will bring what we hope for. The sign that Jupiter is in describes how the individual's judgment operates. In a mutable sign (Gemini, Virgo, Sagittarius or Pisces), for instance, the person's judgment is specific to each changing circumstance, and the person is likely to seek out all possible sources of back-up information before passing judgment. In a fixed sign (Taurus, Leo, Scorpio or Aquarius), however, the individual is likely to hold fast to certain key guiding moral principles, which will not waver with changing circumstances. With Jupiter in a cardinal sign (Aries, Cancer, Libra or Capricorn), a person, in judging the correctness or incorrectness of a situation, feels that he or she must set a precedent. In each new situation, this person weighs the evidence and arrives at the most suitable conclusion, which may change as new evidence arrives on the scene.

In romance, the sign Jupiter is in shows how well the individual can judge the merits of risking involvement with that person, whether the relationship is likely to be a wise investment. If natal Jupiter is in Leo, for instance, the person wants to know if this relationship is likely to bring pleasure and fun. If that does not seem likely, he or she will not feel comfortable or relaxed with the partner, knowing that the relationship will not measure up to his or her expectations. By contrast, someone with natal Jupiter in Capricorn is interested only in a long-term relationship that is reliable and practical. This person has a very pragmatic view of life and will seek a mate who offers some measure of worldly status or promise.

Jupiter tends to expand and heighten the area of life governed by the house that it is in, showing where the individual stretches out and seeks to multiply what he or she has. It represents the area of life in which others give abundantly to the individual because of his or her own generosity. In the twelfth house, Jupiter graces the individual's life with spiritual and/or psychological insight, which he or she may then offer to others. This placement gives the person an abiding and transcendent trust in a divine guiding plan that will see him or her through any difficulties that arise. In the seventh house, Jupiter indicates a person who is likely to attract a very understanding, broad-minded and implicitly trusting partner because of the individual's own fairness and honesty in relating to others.

Jupiter tends to increase or exaggerate the energy of any planet that it aspects. A well-aspected Jupiter usually indicates an uninhibited and sexually creative person who may have a very liberating effect on a partner, inspiring trust and confidence in the individual's good judgment. The Jupiterian person often appears in love as a guiding, almost fatherly figure, pointing out the way at each step.

Hard aspects to Jupiter indicate problems caused not by malice but by thoughtlessness, often based on behavior patterns that won approval at an earlier stage of life, but that are no longer desirable or appropriate. Usually, reminding the individual of that inappropriateness is the most effective treatment. A person with Jupiter in hard aspect, particularly the square, tends to go overboard and will lack a realistic sense of when to stop pursuing whatever may (or may not) be at the end of the illusory rainbow. This individual makes a sport of love, as if it were there only for the challenge and the risks. But, just as love is pursued relentlessly, once caught it loses its appeal entirely, for the individual is always looking ahead to newer challenges.

In weighing the effects of Jupiter, one should also carefully consider the position of stabilizing Saturn. A strong Saturn can tone down and regulate even the most bombastic Jupiterian tendencies, but if Saturn is weak by aspect or sign, even with a well-aspected Jupiter, the person may have a hard time being moderate in his or her involvements. Aspects of Jupiter to Mars expand one's energy; Jupiter-Venus aspects, one's needs and desires. Jupiter with Mercury gives the individual a broad sexual imagination that can help when a partner is hard to please.

Basically, Jupiter does act as a benefic influence in the individual's life, and those areas of the chart touched off by Jupiter can be used to help ease and relax the person who feels very inhibited in sex. Because it is easiest to project a positive expression through Jupiter contacts, the astrologer can suggest that the individual use those contacts to help loosen up other inhibiting aspects. In this way the lid is gradually pried off sexual repression with a minimum of anxiety and emotional stress.

The other problems that are likely to show up with Jupiter afflictions are uncoordinated timing and too much egotism, particularly when Jupiter is in conjunction with or in hard aspect to the lights. These aspects may make a person quite thoughtless of a lover out of sheer excitement, which is a sure way to lose a sensitive partner. The best way for the individual to counter this tendency is by keeping a mental checklist of a partner's needs in love, and double-checking it often.

Saturn

Saturn is the planet of limitation and discipline, and when viewed in the context of sexual and emotional experiences, it represents inhibitions that are learned in middle childhood and adolescence. Specifically, as the individual passes through puberty and learns about the possible and real consequences of having sexual relations, an understandable caution or fear about having sex is instilled in the consciousness. Saturn also dictates to the individual what is socially acceptable in the context of sexual relations: the proper time, place and amount, as well as the type of partner who will be sanctioned by "society." These often rigid standards for sexual behavior can be extremely repressive and may have to be overcome in order for the individual to derive guilt-free pleasure from sexual encounters.

However, Saturn is also the regulatory mechanism within each of us that tells us when enough is enough, and these inhibitions, like a good alarm clock, should not simply be cast aside. Because Saturn does rule time, the issues governed by the house that Saturn is in take more time to work out than other issues in one's life. Age is a crucial factor in successfully resolving these issues, for where Saturn is concerned, the lessons become easier to learn as we get older. Saturn's sign position begins to date the individual, since Saturn spends about two and a third years in each sign. Often it is the position of Saturn by sign that separates older and younger siblings with respect to family responsibilities, seniority and disciplinary measures. These early structuring experiences with authority remain an integral part of the native's character, molding him or her as a member of society at large.

Saturn assigns to each person a life task represented by the sign it is in. In relationships, this means that in the area of life ruled by Saturn's sign, the individual has a sense of having to get a job done that no one must interfere with. For example, if natal Saturn is in Aquarius, the person feels responsible for living strictly what he or she knows to be true, not compromising the truth for anyone else's sake. Thus, a prospective partner should be ready to respect this person's need to be highly principled, or the relationship will fail. If Saturn is in Virgo, however, the native feels responsible for making the absolute best use of his or her time, seeing to it that life continues to run in an orderly and systematic fashion, and this person requires a potential mate who is quite conscious of maintaining high standards of health.

The house position of Saturn is most likely to indicate an area of difficulty for the individual early in life, but later it may become the area in which the person takes the greatest pride because of his or her accomplishments here, often motivated by those initial life problems. For example, if natal Saturn is in the fifth house, the person may have found self-expression quite difficult as a child. Perhaps the parents taught that it was wrong to enjoy yourself. But later in life this person might actually make a business out of pleasure or creativity by mastering some leisure-time activity such as chess or directing in the theater. Saturn in the fifth is not an easy placement for love, however, because this same tendency makes the individual likely to demand complete control and authority in an affair. For this reason the individual might choose to have an affair with a much older or much younger person, where the great difference in age allows the individual to manipulate the partner, knowing exactly what needs to respond to for which purposes.

A well-aspected Saturn stabilizes the areas governed by the aspected planets and has a desirable bracing effect on the entire personality. In this case the individual will be viewed by others as reliable and practical in love, as someone who shows respect and consideration for the partner's needs.

The most common effect of hard aspects to Saturn, especially with the lights, is a deep lack of confidence in one's ability to perform sexually or to be desirable to a partner. This is often the result of some childhood experience with parents, other elders or peers that convinced the native of his or her worthlessness, an attitude that extends into adult life. In order to make sexuality enjoyable and fulfilling, this attitude must be unlearned and the idea of self-worth established. Hard Saturn aspects may lead to coldness in love, serious sexual repression or even excessively negative sexual expression. Repression can be alleviated to some extent by making creative use of the individual's positive Jupiter aspects, as previously discussed in the Jupiter section of this chapter.

But it is much harder to deal with the actively negative sexual expression that may be brought on by difficult Saturn aspects. In many cases it is better to devise a way to turn this kind of expression to advantage than to try to eradicate it. Only if active and harmful hostility is generating the negative expression, as may happen with Saturn-Mars aspects, should one make a real effort to change it completely.

Actively negative Saturn behavior patterns are hard to unlearn because they are quite enjoyable. This is unlike repression, which merely helps the individual avoid the pain of what he or she subconsciously fears, which has no pleasurable advantages at all. The sado-masochistic desire to be dominated by another person or to be treated cruelly in some fashion can develop into an awesome pathway for expressing pleasure, one that is difficult to extinguish or abandon in favor of others that would be more positive but less familiar.

This kind of negative expression can be turned to one's advantage if it is formalized and ritualized so as to specifically heighten sexual arousal in both partners. In that way the Saturn effects may be channeled into enjoyable, if offbeat, expression in the bedroom. Otherwise these negative emotional needs may find more harmful expression in everyday life, as these sado-masochistic tendencies become part of the fiber of the individual's nonsexual exchanges with others. Formalizing the negative behavior patterns, however, can bring about eventual character change, because it forces the individual to become at least more aware of these personality traits and possibly to be motivated to seek help in exploring their roots in childhood.

Uranus

Of all the planets that we use in astrology, Uranus must certainly be the most exciting in all realms of life's activities. Just as Uranus astronomically is outside of Saturn's orbit, so too Uranus symbolically represents our ability to go outside of the limits of social convention and order to find freedom in other realms of experience and expression, sexual or otherwise. For this reason, Uranus's placement in the chart represents the area where the individual is not bound by past structures of reality. In sexuality, this means involvement in unorthodox relationships and behaviors that do not conform to society's dictates.

If Uranus is quite prominent in the chart, the individual should not try to adhere to a perfectly regular, predictable life. He or she is easily bored unless something new is always happening and cannot be held down or possessed in a sexual bond unless it is a continuing adventure. This person does not necessarily change partners continually for variety, but he or she certainly desires quite a bit of sexual experimentation. This person needs a partner who is amenable to continuing sexual change and development.

As with Neptune and Pluto, Uranus' natal position by sign clearly places the individual within the context of an age group, since Uranus spends roughly seven years in each sign. This placement therefore says something about the individual's identification with his or her peer group and how that peer group makes itself known to society as a new and vital generation. In love, two people born with Uranus in the same sign will have an unspoken agreement about the ideals of their generation. If the Uranuses are in adjacent signs, then the younger partner may have a sense that he or she is blazing a new trail, which is an extension of the path prepared by the older partner. If the age difference is great enough for the Uranuses to be two signs apart, both individuals will have Uranus in either masculine or feminine signs, indicating that they support each other in their respective individual searches for truth and freedom.

The house where Uranus is at birth varies, of course, from hour to hour and is quite specific to each person. Therefore, Uranus' house position tells a lot about how the individual expresses the ideals of that generation and where he or she takes liberties. In a relationship, the house position of Uranus simply shows where the person is not bound or restricted. If Uranus is in the fourth house, for example, the person may not care to settle in one spot permanently. If Uranus is in the tenth house, the person wants a career that offers a great deal of freedom, but not necessarily stability. These are aspects of the person's character that a partner can do little about.

A Uranus aspect tends to make the area it activates more unusual and sexually explorative. Depending upon the individual's surroundings, this can be exciting and pleasant or a source of conflict with others. In a relatively free environment, Uranus has a very positive influence on sexuality, stimulating the mind and body and certainly preventing sexual boredom. In a more repressive situation, the individual may be considered odd or sexually freakish, which can result in great emotional harm because of peer pressure or ridicule. Homosexuality, which is often said to be associated with Uranus, is a good example of this. In the right conditions it can be a rewarding lifestyle, as the homosexual is usually more experimental than the average heterosexual person. But in a repressive climate, the harsh opinions of others may result in guilt and self-hatred.

When Uranus is in easy aspect, the individual's originality is usually channeled sexually into accepted and nonoffensive practices. This individual can make the sex act a real sharing, because he or she always wants to know how the partner sees the sexual experience and in what way it could be improved upon.

Hard aspects of Uranus, however, often make the person want to break away from pressuring influences. This means that others must give the native more freedom and tolerence to keep this energy from being turned to destructive ends. Uranus in hard aspect does not necessarily imply unusual sex practices; its only influence may be to make the individual's expression in the areas it affects too sudden or abrupt. This is particularly true with aspects of Uranus to the Sun, Mars and Jupiter, which can make one's sexual style quite overwhelming and in need of toning down, so as not to put people off. A Uranus contact with the Moon or Venus, on the other hand, often means that the individual, although not unusual himself, may be attracted to people who are personally or sexually unusual.

27

Neptune

Elusive and illusory Neptune defies any single definition, since by its very nature, Neptune dissolves whatever appears to be solid and defined. *Humility* is the key word for Neptune in matters of love, for this is what Neptune has to offer us. In a highly materialistic society, such as our western culture, it is difficult to embrace the concept of humility, since it has nothing at all to do with competition, status or self-satisfaction—quite the opposite. Neptune's gift to us is the compassionate heart, but it takes many disappointments, losses and sacrifices before we are ready to accept this humble gift. It is really the gift of our own humanity, but there is great suffering and sorrow along the way to reaching this magnitude of lovingness, and the road is paved with tempting illusions of every sort. Neptune's position in the chart indicates where the individual has to give up something of personal value in order to make room for something greater and more divine.

Even more than with Uranus, the sign position of natal Neptune places the individual within the context of a larger whole. Because Neptune spends roughly fourteen years transiting each sign, huge masses of people are born sharing that placement. It is interesting to compare the amount of time Neptune spends in a sign with that same span of time in human life. Specifically, it takes approximately fourteen years for the human organism to mature to the point of puberty, when he or she is capable of reproduction and therefore of carrying on the human race should that generation die. To some extent, this is symbolic of the meaning of Neptune, which asks the individual to find a worthy cause to believe in and make some sacrifice for, perhaps even the sacrifice of life. It is no secret that bearing and raising children requires great unselfishness and sacrifice by the parents. That is what Neptune asks of us—unselfishness and sacrifice. Neptune is also closely tied to one's belief system about God. Those with Neptune in the same generational sign are likely to share a common belief system, which underlies that generation's contributions to coming generations.

Neptune's house position in the natal chart indicates where the individual has something to give away in this lifetime; through the matters associated with this house the individual learns how to serve the needs of others. Neptune in the ninth house, for example, gives the person a cosmic view onto the world, although he or she may be unable to define exactly what that view is. What is given to others here is a sense of faith in the future and a belief that there is always a new dream worth dreaming. Because the ninth house is the third house from the seventh house, indicating the partner's relatives, Neptune here may require the native to make some sacrifice concerning in-laws.

Neptune aspects have a generally debilitating effect on one's physical sexual expression on several levels. First, they tend to diffuse sexual specificity and make one less intense, so that a possibly sexual relationship becomes a platonic affair, which may seem quite spiritual. This is most likely to happen when Neptune is in easy aspect, although it may also give the individual a smoother approach to the areas governed by the aspect.

Second, because Neptune is associated with ideals and expectations, its aspects can be quite crippling to sexual endeavors by making sex goal-oriented and thereby robbing it of spontaneity. In hard aspect, especially the inconjunct, the individual's expectations may be way ahead of the ability to fulfill them, resulting in continual disappointment.

Third, since difficult Neptune aspects tend to cause confusion and error, they may hamper sexual expression by causing misunderstanding about a partner's assumptions or goals. The individual may be very anxious about sexual performance, not knowing where he or she stands. That person should be encouraged not to give up but to double-check every message and hint from a partner so that decisions are made not on the basis of assumptions but with a firm knowledge of a lover's needs and demands.

Deliberate deception may also occur with hard aspects to Neptune, especially if the Moon or Mercury is involved. Often the person feels that it is easier to reach a goal by lying than by patiently staying with the truth. Indeed, the individual is often not even aware of altering reality to suit the needs of the moment, so that fact should be pointed out tactfully.

The remedy for Neptune difficulties is for the individual to attempt to stick with practical possibilities, even if they don't seem as potentially satisfying as more idealistic dreams. But reality does provide some immediate pleasures, which can lead to further enjoyment and growth. The Neptunian person must learn to take life as it comes, flowing with it without judgment, perhaps by relying on a partner who is more realistic. Very often a Neptunian personality finds it easier to have faith and trust in someone else than to have enough self-confidence to go it alone.

Pluto

If we could conceive of a deep, deep planetary well of life energy from which is pumped our invisible supply of life force, that would be analogous to the symbolism of Pluto. What pumps this supply, very simply, is desire—the desire to channel our lives in a creative way. This desire for creativity may often be expressed in a way that appears to be very destructive. This occurs when the individual is unable to raise his or her desire nature high enough to allow it to be transformed by light. When we get bogged down by our desires we can be used by them, as with lust and greed, rather than using them for the benefit of ourselves and of the planet as a whole. A key to understanding the nature of this well of life that desire calls forth is to accept the fact that we are more than what we seem to be on the surface of our lives. While we need to be able to function on the surface through the material dimension, our lives must also move in an evolutionary direction, and we must recognize that all desire has this basic regenerative quality behind it.

One word that we often use with reference to Pluto is *power.* Power is desire in action, channeled through the individual to cause change on earth. It is easy to misuse power or to use it irresponsibly, without being conscious of its effects. However, no man or woman on this planet can "get away" with irresponsibility, for sooner or later the boomerang always returns to the sender.

Like Neptune, Pluto spends a generational period of time transiting each sign of the zodiac, characterizing a whole wave of earth's population as it passes through a sign. Like a wave, Pluto's effect in any sign is to carry us forward and beyond our present stage of human existence to a new level of awareness. This kind of evolutionary growth is quite remote from the average interaction between two people in a personal love relationship. Only those who are channels of the forces of evolution will fully use the potential of Pluto. For everyone else, the sign placement of Pluto exists in their reality only as background scenery that they are scarcely conscious of.

Unless Pluto is prominent natally by being in an angular house or by aspect, its house position is not likely to have much effect in the individual's life except as transiting planets aspect it. By and large its house position indicates those affairs that must change or transform the person by first becoming merged in consciousness with those issues, then experiencing a process of decay and rebirth. The full implications of this concept are not easily grasped by the intellect.

In sexuality, as in all else, Pluto is a planet of extremes and can grant a person either the greatest sexual security or awful and debilitating fears, depending upon its aspects and the planets it is contacting. In reinforcing aspect, it has tremendous stabilizing power. In trine to the Moon, for instance, Pluto can make an individual quite unflappable, no matter how threatening the situation. This aspect greatly increases one's patience and tolerance, based on deep faith that everything will work out all right.

Pluto conjunctions are probably the most sexually exciting, because they lend tremendous intensity to any area that they touch. The quality of the planet conjoined is intensified tremendously. A Pluto conjunction with Venus, Jupiter or the Moon, for instance, can raise sexual desire and fulfillment to almost religious intensity. A Pluto-Mars conjunction should be watched, because it can slip into physical domination of a partner, which can be enjoyable, but only if both partners agree on it. A Pluto-Saturn conjunction creates a tremendous capacity for soul-shaking sorrow which, although not pleasant, seems to be quite cathartic and rejuvenating.

The hard aspects of Pluto are the most debilitating, however, and the individual must go through a difficult and lengthy period of self-confrontation in order to get rid of their unhappy effects. They create an almost unspeakable terror that at its core is the fear of death and the unknown. Most often this can be traced to childhood fears of destruction, fears that became attached to situations, feelings or people, which perpetuate the fear long after the cause has vanished.

In later life, however, this fear is seldom expressed literally, because it is too threatening for the average adult. Fortunately or unfortunately, society does not consider it proper for an adult to be so riddled with fear. Therefore the fear is transformed into a compulsive need to control people or situations in some way, depending on the planet or planets that are contacted. With Mars, the people needs to have physical control; with the Moon, emotional control, and so on, based on the irrational fear of destruction if this control is lost or relinquished.

Altering this pattern is difficult, and the attempt is not always successful. One way is for the person to channel these inclinations into ritualized and agreed-upon games of sexual control in the privacy of the bedroom, which can take some of the tensions out of everyday life. As the individual becomes more aware of his or her tendencies to demand control, there is at least the possibility of deeper self-exploration, which can get to the root of the problem. At worst, this method gives the individual an interesting sexual outlet and relieves some of the pressure in other areas of life.

The Ascendant

The sign that is rising at the time of birth, its decanate ruler and degree, and the placement of its planetary ruler have much to do with love and sexuality, for we need to be able to relate to another person through the vehicle of our physical bodies. The combined influence of the Ascendant and the above-named factors shows how comfortable the individual is in her or his body, and whether the individual is able to use the body as a means to an end: enjoyment of life and love. The Ascendant is thus important in the overall discussion of sexuality because it describes the appearance of the physical body and one's general external presentation.

A well-aspected Ascendant makes the native physically attractive, so that it is not difficult to find potential partners. However, no matter how attractive a person is on the surface, it is important that appearance be integrated with the rest of the personality, so that what is up front is consistent with what is out of sight. If the person's real personality does not live up to the impression given by the external image, as indicated by the Ascendant, every new relationship will end in disappointment. That person must learn to play down physical beauty and not use it to win in sexual competition with others, for in the end the results will be counterproductive. Rather, this person needs to work at bringing out some of the finer aspects of his or her personality so that people will know there is substance behind the facade.

On the other hand, an individual who has difficult aspects to the Ascendant may be less attractive physically, and at first he or she will find that looks are a barrier to sexual relationships. But once a relationship is established, it can grow in a rewarding and realistic fashion, because it is based on inner qualities rather than external good looks. Discrepancies between looks and personality may account for the shifting love affairs of the "beautiful people" as opposed to the more lasting relationships of people who may be less attractive outwardly.

Hard aspects to the Ascendant may also mean that certain aspects of one's character are mismatched. Hard aspects from Mars, Jupiter or Uranus, for example, may make the outer personality seem very active or restless, even though other factors of the chart indicate inner restfulness or security. Conversely, a calm exterior, as shown by trines and sextiles to the Ascendant, may mask an agitated personality underneath. It is necessary to weigh all of the various horoscope factors before making any judgments.

If the individual is self-aware, the image projected by the sign and aspects of the Ascendant can become consistent with the inner personality. Being truthful to one's self is the best way to make meaningful contact with a desired partner, and for that, one needs quite a bit of self-study. This can be done on one's own to some extent, but it is also very helpful to get the candid opinions of friends so that one's external presentation or inner personality can be effectively modified.

The Midheaven

Because the Midheaven is at the height of the chart, it symbolically represents the heights to which we aspire in life. Normally, we view the Midheaven only in the context of a life calling, as in career direction or job objectives. As such, it is not central to the understanding of active sexuality, unless, of course, one's profession is tied with one's sexuality in some fashion. This can go beyond the obvious profession of prostitution to include any career in which a reputation for sexual prowess is important, as in popular screen acting, pop music, sports, fashion and cosmetics.

However, it is worth considering the Midheaven in this context, because sexual reputation can affect other areas of one's private life, as can any type of reputation. This is most clearly seen during adolescence, when reputation may shape one's later sexual direction. Hard aspects to the Midheaven may harm a person's reputation so much that the individual, because of external pressure, adopts the very habits that the gossips have ascribed to him or her. This applies especially to high-school students, who get the reputation that "they do" or, perhaps worse, "they don't." Trying to live down this reputation, or live up to it, can be traumatic.

The best thing to do about this type of problem is for the individual to take steps so that future rumors will be nipped in the bud. Some people naturally attract idle rumors, and if that problem is not explained to a partner, it can cause unnecessary friction, because the partner doesn't know whether or not to believe others' stories about the person.

Even a very well-aspected Midheaven can be troublesome, because the individual may have an exaggerated reputation for sexual prowess or desirability, which may be difficult to live up to when put to the test. Persons who have such a reputation should be very modest if they want to avoid situations in which they must prove themselves.

Except in these cases, the Midheaven has less influence on sexuality than other factors in the chart. Any illusions about a person because of reputation are quickly dispelled by the first sexual encounter and are subsequently of little importance to either partner. The Midheaven is critical only when one's social interaction is shaped by strong prejudices or expectations based on an extreme reputation, as might happen with a Hollywood sex symbol who equates social prominence with sexual desirability.

The Vertex

In and of itself, the Vertex is an asexual point, but because it signifies critical events in an individual's life, it may be important in sexual involvements. Its manifestations can be seen more clearly in synastry or through transits than in the natal chart, unless the Vertex is natally conjoined by a planet that colors its effects. A turning point in life is likely to occur with a major transit to the Vertex, although it may not be recognized as a turning point until long afterward. Thus, a sexual experience that has a lasting effect on the personality may take place under such a transit.

More noticeable, however, is the role of the Vertex as a point of contact between the charts of partners who have a strong involvement. Very frequently in a strong relationship, the Vertex of one partner conjoins one of the lights in the other's chart. When an important sexual experience has a profound effect on a person, the Ascendant or one of the personal planets of the affecting partner is often found to touch the Vertex of the partner thus affected. Although it is usually difficult to know whether a relationship is profoundly important until after it is completed or at least substantially developed, a Vertex contact is a significant clue that something major is happening, even if it isn't apparent on the surface.

If the Vertex is in the fifth house, the important event is much more likely to be sexual and therefore particularly intense, or it may pertain to other fifth-house concerns, such as recreation; when it is in another house, that is less likely. If a natal planet falls on the Vertex, the events indicated are more specifically connected with the area ruled by that planet. In that case the overall life direction is significantly colored by it, which makes it much easier to judge whether the event is sexual in nature.

The North Node

Like the Vertex, the lunar nodes are not specifically sexual, but they are often associated with personal commitments involving sexual partners. They are divided into active and passive, north and south, but their effect is so general and pervasive that they are only incidentally sexual. Essentially, the North Node is concerned with commitment to new responsibilities and involvements of any kind: financial, creative, personal or sexual.

If a new sexual involvement begins during a transit to the North Node, the relationship is likely to be more permanent or at least longer-lasting than originally conceived or even desired. Emotional responsibilities seem to crystallize around an event that occurs at such a time, and somehow it hangs on even though it was not planned as more than a passing enjoyment. Circumstances may conspire to cement the situation in some way, perhaps through pregnancy or unexpected repercussions from another partner. One should think twice before entering a relationship under such a transit unless it is definitely worth staying with and exploring.

This applies not only to transits to the North Node in the individual's chart but to planets in a partner's chart that touch the North Node of the other chart. In that case the partner is likely to become a responsibility or even a burden. Or if a love relationship flowers, it will become a positive, long-range commitment, but the person whose North Node is contacted will bear the main weight of responsibility for the relationship.

The South Node

Like the North Node, the South Node is most important to our discussion by transit or when contacted by another's chart. The difference is that while the North Node is active and undertakes responsibility, the South Node is passive and collects reward or punishment, depending on the situation.

One should avoid becoming involved with someone whose chart shows Mars, Saturn or Pluto conjoining one's South Node; unless great care is taken, that partner will be troublesome, even if unintentionally. On the other hand, a partner with positive planets (Sun, Jupiter, Venus) conjoining the South Node in the first chart may be very helpful, either on purpose or simply by happenstance. In either case, the relationship is not necessarily sexual, but when it is, it is likely to be quite intense.

Much has been written about the lunar nodes and sometimes the Vertex as points of contact for karmic undertakings and payoffs. Contacts to these points do give a relationship a fated, inexorable quality. If the individual is to stay in control of the situation, he or she must be keenly aware, making decisions consciously rather than being swept along by feelings. It is particularly easy to lose control in a highly charged emotional situation, which may be indicated by sexually relevant nodal contacts, so one should be especially wary of them. This is not to say that such relationships should be avoided, because some can be fine and rewarding, but some are very difficult. Simply keep in mind that the relationship will be important in some way and make judgments accordingly.

Chapter Three

The Signs
Houses and Aspects

In this chapter we discuss the three other horoscope factors that astrologers traditionally use when delineating a chart—signs, houses and aspects. Our goal in examining these factors is to offer a romantic and/or sexual interpretation of them as they apply to the individual. It is helpful to remember that in any chart, something that is true and significant will be shown in several different ways. Thus all the factors must be examined and synthesized before passing judgment. This is the case in any realm, sexual or otherwise.

The Signs

First we will look at the twelve signs of the zodiac, whose positions around the wheel of the chart give direction and order to the individual's life. The Ascendant is the first point of visibility in the chart, as one moves clockwise toward the Midheaven and around the rest of the chart along the Sun's apparent daily path. The signs of the zodiac follow a logical sequence from Aries to Pisces around the chart, showing where we begin and end our own personal cycle of experience.

To a large extent, the twelve signs of the zodiac also describe how the planetary energies are operating in the individual's life. The sign that a planet occupies either strengthens or weakens the planet's intensity, in much the same way that wearing a particular outfit or color affects how a person feels and looks. It is important, when discussing these influences with a client, to help the person see how much he or she chooses particular kinds of behavior and attitudes and how these choices can be changed if there is discord and tension. But change is effective only if there is conscious desire for it and deliberate effort to make it. The astrologer can be a source of great encouragement in this regard, helping the person to see positive alternatives to his or her current mode of behavior or direction of energies.

Aries

Because Aries is the first sign, we literally begin our cycle of experiences with Aries, no matter where it is. The house ruled by Aries on the cusp represents the area of life in which the individual applies forward and aggressive energy to make new beginnings. If Aries is on the eleventh house, for example, the person is assertive in friendships and takes the role of leader in a group. It is important for this person to be a friend to others, and that drive is sure to color all relationships. Because Aries is a cardinal fire sign, planets in Aries, whether basically active or passive, show more active and assertive qualities here. This can be an asset or a liability, depending on the planet and its aspects.

37

When normally passive planets such as the Moon, Venus or Saturn are in this sign, the individual's sexual needs and tastes are clarified, and he or she is less likely to be too hesitant or indecisive. With Venus in Aries, a person can make his or her sexual needs known quickly so that they can be satisfied. The Moon in this sign means that the person can react quickly to a situation and either pursue it or get out of it. Even Saturn here, which if harshly aspected may mean that a person has a grating effect on others, can be helpful by allowing the person to make dislikes known to a partner instead of suffering in silence.

The difficulty with having planets in Aries is that these energies may be expressed too quickly, so that some of the more relaxed and subtle possibilities of an affair are missed. While an ultimately satisfying relationship can start off quite slowly and mature in time, the Arian tendency is to write off any relationship that does not deliver total enjoyment right away.

Restraint is usually needed especially when there are active planets in Aries, so that the individual can weather the slow and difficult periods in an affair and avoid rushing to a climax without sufficient build-up. Slowing down is easier said than done, however, and some very Arian people may be most compatible with a partner who likes sex with a minimum of foreplay. Too much forced slowing down can result in a shortage of energy from having to hold back physically and emotionally.

Strongly Arian individuals derive a great deal of pleasure from brief but intense love affairs, and they don't usually cling to relationships once they are over. Such people may seem shallow, but they are just more intense than subtle.

The effect of any planet in Aries is highlighted and made immediately noticeable. In the long run it may not be an important influence, but it is likely to be the first personality influence that others experience and deal with.

Taurus

Because Taurus is a very magnetic sign, its influence is one of drawing in or attracting, rather than going out and getting. This magnetic quality is quite powerful; it can be compared to the earth's gravitational pull, which keeps all of the earth's possessions hugged tightly to the surface. Taurus is similarly possessive and in relationships acts almost as if any partner whom the individual holds near and dear is actually a possession.

The house position of Taurus in the chart represents the area of life where the person places value; he or she wants to acquire the things indicated by that house. If Taurus is on the cusp of the ninth house, for example, the person wants to hold on to the horizons of the world and may do this by collecting tokens and souvenirs from his or her travels. A perfect gift for this person from a loved one would be something that comes from far away, perhaps an object representing a foreign culture or a treasured book that will take the person on an adventure.

The effects of any planet in Taurus are felt strongly in relationships, but not necessarily right away. Undesirable manifestations caused by hard aspects to these planets can be quite difficult to eradicate, not only because Taurus is stubborn and intransigent, but also because it is nonverbal. A partner's simplest and most convincing arguments are thus ineffective in promoting change. If harsh aspects are troublesome, experience is a much better teacher than argument or analysis.

In the past, having planets in Taurus was thought to help a love relationship, because this sign is quite romantic and sexy in a down-to-earth way. In recent years, however, changing definitions of sexuality have made the sweep-them-off-their-feet brand of love seem rather old-fashioned. In the Aquarian Age, a satisfying, complete relationship requires many more qualities than just those of Taurus.

Frequently, people with planets in Taurus tend to ignore the detailed and intellectual aspects of sex, which can be a problem. Taurus is a gut-level sign that does not fantasize or intellectualize sex very well, and with Mercury, Mars or Jupiter in Taurus, the person may have some difficulties with sexual expression. There is little that can be done to change the person's nature, so the effort should be to find partners who do not make heavy technical or intellectual demands but who communicate sexually in a nonverbal, down-to-earth manner.

On the other hand, well-aspected planets in Taurus indicate an individual who is very reliable and trustworthy, qualities that can enhance and support a relationship. The heart-to-heart warmth and earnestness of this sign usually has very positive effects, and a planet such as Saturn can use some warming up.

A heavy Taurus influence in a chart tends to make the individual monogamous or at least inclined to long-term relationships. Dependable sexual expression outweighs many other factors for that person, and the warmth and security of knowing that there is someone to love and be loved by, keeps the individual from being tempted by more exotic but less regular forms of sexual expression.

Gemini

Gemini is the sign of curiosity and communication, and in the area of sexuality, Gemini often tends to over-intellectualize, sometimes to such an extent that the emotions are denied expression.

The Gemini goal in lovemaking is fantasy fulfillment, exploring a variety of techniques and making sex an endless playground of ways to have fun. However, communication tends to remain intellectual and verbal, for gut-level intuition by itself has little meaning for Gemini.

The house that is ruled by Gemini indicates the area of life that the person is extremely curious about, with an unquenchable thirst for gathering and distributing information. If Gemini is on the cusp of the fifth house, for example, the person will experience an affair from a reporter's point of view more than a lover's, observing it "play-by-play" and providing the lover with a running commentary!

Similarly, the expression of any planet that is in this sign must also be verbal and intellectual. If Saturn is here, limits must be agreed on verbally, not merely understood.

With Venus here, desires are made known verbally rather than through body language; in fact, the desires may be so complex that they cannot be expressed in any other way. With Mars in Gemini, a person's physical sexual technique may be highly developed, with specific, but perhaps variable, fantasy scenarios arranged ahead of time.

Physically, Gemini tends to be interested in total bodily sensuality rather than focusing just on genital sex, which may be part of the reason why this sign is not considered very passionate. Gemini likes to spread out, both physically over the entire body and emotionally in elaborate webs of fantasy. There is no less enjoyment or intensity than with the other signs, it is just more widely dispersed.

This tendency lends the Gemini person a delicacy of touch and technique that gives and requires much sensitivity in loving, and this influence does not respond at all to a heavier approach. If one could assign an astrological home for tickling as an erotic art, it would have to be Gemini.

This approach to sexuality is ideal for many, but certainly not for everyone, because it lacks the firmness and intensity that characterize the weightier signs, such as Scorpio. However, if there are extremely intense aspects to planets in this sign, such as Mars and Uranus together, their influence is retained, although it may be lightened by the nature of Gemini.

In fact, any harsh aspect is softened here, because it finds release in mental tasks and so does not cause as many sexual conflicts or frustrations as in a less adaptable sign. Sexual tensions can be absorbed in fantasy and defused in the imagination during sex so that it is not necessary to give them direct physical expression.

Cancer

Cancer's basic motif is internalized activity, like the crab that retreats into its hard protective shell and burrows backward into a hole in the sand. That is how the person with a strong Cancer emphasis in the chart tends to behave in romance. The cardinal mode that this sign belongs to implies the urgency of Cancer's desire to have his or her needs met, yet the Cancerian person has great difficulty expressing these needs openly.

The house that is ruled by Cancer represents the area of life in which the individual feels the need to build a protective fortress that offers shelter from the world. The person is most defensive when anything threatens the security of the issues indicated by that house and clings tight to keep those things safe from harm. For example, the person with Cancer on the seventh house cusp mothers the marriage partner and others in general, because he or she needs to be needed by other people. This person tries to keep marriage very private and intimate, wanting to protect the partner from any and all of life's hardships. Needless to say, someone with this placement of Cancer is bound to meet some conflict, because a partner is unlikely to be able to satisfy this need for emotional security and still grow as an individual.

Sexual difficulties are more likely to occur with planets in Cancer than with planets in most other signs, especially if a person is single and has not established secure pathways of communication with a long-term partner. This situation can develop into a classic double bind in which lack of closeness makes communication difficult, and lack of communication makes it almost impossible to achieve closeness. This can lead to denial of gratification, causing a great build-up of sexual pressure, and the person may eventually become emotionally traumatized.

When a person has one of the lights or the Ascendant in Cancer, the problem is more personal. With Mars, Venus or Mercury in this sign, especially if they are harshly aspected, the individual has some difficulty involving controlled or repressed expression. The middle and outer planets will be colored but not dominated by Cancer.

Once established in a secure love relationship, a strongly Cancerian person becomes a most loving and faithful partner, lavishly expressing affection and devotion. In fact, in return for security, that person may give up much more freedom than is desirable or fair. This kind of trade-off can become destructive and can lead to extreme jealousy or paranoia if it goes too far, particularly if the person also has hard Pluto or Neptune aspects. Like the clinging vine, the Cancer type seems to "grow on you."

In the past, when there was less freedom of sexual expression, the Cancerian nature was more positive, representing the nurturer and protector, the keeper of the home and the emotions. Today, however, society encourages more independent sexual expression, and people with strong planets in Cancer are less able to relate to or express the present freedom.

It is not that Cancer is incapable of expressing emotion—quite the opposite: there is so much emotion that it is difficult to express it clearly unless definite channels of communication have been established. Once the lines of communication are open, a person with planets in Cancer is the most assertively caring and loving partner, particularly if the planets are well aspected. The relationship should be stable, however, not an affair in which expectations change frequently.

Leo

Like the lion, the king of the jungle, Leo is the natural lord and ruler of the chart, giving the person dominance and control over the affairs of the house it rules. If Leo is on the cusp of the fourth house, for example, the person wants a home that is a palace, full of decorative touches that give it an air of royalty and class, no matter how humble a cottage it really is. Because Leo's will prevails here, the person clearly wants to have final authority over all domestic matters, which requires great tolerance and respect from other family members.

Since Leo is the natural ruler of the fifth house, in a very broad sense it is a sexually positive sign. Its sexuality is warm and playful and may even be dominating, but a person with a strong Leo emphasis is generally not fixated on sex and is also not inclined toward the more unusual and intense forms of sexual expression.

At this time, there is one major exception to this statement. Because Pluto was in Leo from 1938 to 1957, people of that generation are quite likely to have a conjunction of Pluto with another planet in Leo. Depending on the planet making the conjunction, such an aspect heightens either a person's sexual compulsiveness or his or her emotional pressure. But the Pluto influence is likely to be expressed as a general need for control over personal situations rather than as a directly sexual compulsion.

The general effect of Leo is to make sex nonspecific, to apply it broadly to all aspects of life, so that there is no clear, recognizable distinction between sexual and nonsexual activity. This can mean that sexuality is integrated into one's life so that innocent gestures in everyday activities have a playful sexual connotation, and active physical sex is likewise colored by images and references to everyday life.

On the other hand, if there are afflictions to planets in Leo, sexuality may become a constant issue, so that everything in life takes on sexual connotations, which can be tiresome to those who are less preoccupied with the subject.

Leo's pride can also cause problems with sex. If the Leo planet is not afflicted, the person has a positive attitude about the body's accomplishments in lovemaking. If there is an affliction, particularly with the lights or Mars, the person may have great anxiety about sexual performance, which can result in sexual dysfunction.

Leo is a creature of habit and not very interested in specific sexual techniques, perhaps repeating the same experience many times, which a partner may find boring. In that case, the partner should introduce new ideas in such a way that the native's pride is not injured. Flattery will go a long way when coaxing a Leo type to venture into new or unfamiliar areas. Leos like to feel that they are strong and that others depend upon them for assistance.

Virgo

The task of Virgo, the last of the first six personal signs, is to account for all the unfinished business and loose ends left by Aries through Leo. As such, whatever house is ruled by Virgo shows where the individual "tidies up" in life, meticulously repairing and completing whatever needs it. If Virgo is on the third house, for example, the person is very analytical in speaking, choosing each word with exactness, so that the information communicated will be precise and accurate. This kind of precision is also expressed in the person's questions to others; Virgo wants to get the full story of any incident with no detail missed.

Virgo can be the most repressed or the most sexually expressive of the signs, mainly because of its unwavering specificity. A Virgo person has quite specific standards, which can either enhance sex or rule it out entirely. For instance, the individual may have the attitude that "I won't do it unless it's just right." If the definition of "just right" is too detailed or demanding, it will never happen. Even though the individual is at fault for making the rules too strict, he or she blames the outside world for the problem, especially if the Virgo planet is in square aspect with another planet, which is debilitating.

On the positive side, Virgo is a sign of service, which means that a strongly Virgo personality takes great pleasure in making a partner as comfortable as possible and attending to the loved one's every need. Virgo tries not to overlook any detail and can be fastidious about getting the task done just right, whether that involves sex or any other activity. Also another positive aspect of Virgo is that the individual may have a talent for devising elaborate sexual fantasies, which can lead to hours of pleasure with the right partner. Because the details are so important, the person should spell them out verbally to a partner, so that nothing is omitted. In that way, even the most fragile fantasy will be successful.

However, the individual must guard against becoming obsessed with the details of a fantasy, so that the partner becomes merely a tool for fulfilling them. The players should be in control of the game, not the other way around.

If the Virgo planet is harshly aspected, especially by Saturn or Neptune, the individual must try to avoid insisting on impossibly high standards. A partner should point out when the person seems overly insistent on having everything just right, because too much picky criticism can kill the loving feelings between two people. Both partners must discuss their desires and standards, perhaps even writing them down so there will be no misunderstandings.

Virgo's specificity may also be manifested in fetishism, so that the person attaches unusual sexual meaning to particular actions or objects, such as items of clothing. There is no great harm in this, and it can heighten sexuality unless it becomes an obsession so that the person is unable to obtain sexual fulfillment in any other way. For most people, however, it is just one facet of a lively sexual imagination.

Libra

Libra is never dull in a relationship; it is always trying to improve the relationship or make it more beautiful and satisfying. Depending on the planet that is in Libra, the improvements may be emotional, or they may be in changing the physical surroundings of love to make more pleasure available on every level. Libra's infuence may not, however, be conducive to a stable emotional life, since there is constant pressure for change, which can be either helpful or harmful, depending on the kind of change.

The house where Libra is found natally shows the area of life where balance in relationships is needed. In that area the person tends to swing from one point of view to another in order to be fair and equitable. For example, if Libra is on the cusp of the sixth house, the person's attitudes toward health and work are constantly changing, because of changing demands by others. This person is likely to work artistically and handle people with diplomacy and tact. This person may also see relationships as being vauable only within the context of work; love must serve some useful purpose.

If there are hard aspects to planets in Libra, the person may introduce changes in a restless, compulsive way, which robs the relationship of its stability. Change for the sake of change can be quite destructive, because it interrupts or confuses the flow of communication between partners. Or the person's insistence on equality may be overdone or applied inappropriately, so that the situation devolves into a battle for control to correct a supposed imbalance. Any relationship needs to grow and evolve, and well-aspected Libra planets can be very helpful by making the individual an instrument of change in a positive way. And he or she will try to balance the other partner, so that the affair is not one-sided.

43

In a troubled relationship that requires painful adjustments, however, a person with strong Libra planets can attack the problems persistently and forcefully to bring needed changes, especially if the partner needs a shove to get moving or to admit that there is a problem.

Libra planets also intensify the effect of any opposition aspects in a chart, not just those that involve Libra, because the swinging, rearranging quality of the opposition is related to the qualities of Libra. The opposition and the sign tend to reinforce each other, causing the extremes to be greater, especially if there are difficult aspects to the planets in Libra.

Ruled by Venus, Libra is not a sexually charged sign. Here the importance of sex is as a form of communication rather than as an end in itself. The individual may look at sex as an indicator of compatibility, but it is not always an accurate indicator, because there may be physically caused sexual problems that do not reflect the emotional health of the relationship.

Scorpio

Scorpio represents either the "fight to the finish" that follows the Libran "confrontation with the enemy" or the passionate embrace and consummation that follow Libra's dance of love. Scorpio's location in the chart represents the area of life in which a person is somehow physically entangled in the lives of others, through material resources or sexuality. It is where one's assets and resources are interrelated with other people's, the final outcome being the regeneration of that which belongs to each one. If Scorpio is on the cusp of the tenth house, the person might make a career of this concept by becoming involved with taxes, insurance or the funeral industry. This person takes his or her career very seriously, allowing no one to interfere with its progress. With Scorpio here, one's career would be one's passion, and vice versa.

Scorpio has always been considered the sexiest sign and, in a strictly physical way, it is. Any planet in Scorpio plays a significant role in sexuality and direct sexual expression. It may take time to find an appropriate and satisfactory channel for this expression, however, because Scorpio also represses and thus intensifies the effects of any planets here.

The image of Scorpio is of smoldering passion rather than carefree sexuality. This sign has a compulsive force that is often fueled by inner tension and then released explosively. Because of this inclination to hold down inner forces until the pressure is very great, a person with a strong Scorpio emphasis in the chart may be destructive or violent, especially if there are difficult aspects to the more forceful planets, such as Mars. In that case the individual should plan on frequent sexual expression so that pressure and tension do not build up to a destructive level.

In addition to sex, Scorpio is associated with death, if only of the ego, sexuality being seen as an irresistible force that sweeps away the boundaries of individuality in a transcendent union. The identification of sex with death is actually a very logical primal interpretation. As biologist Lyall Watson has observed, until sexual differentiation began at a cellular level, there was no biological death and decay as we know it. As long as reproduction was accomplished by simple cell division, the original organism did not die, but divided again and again into countless generations. When sexual reproduction at the cellular level began, two cells united to produce a third cell, then the two parent organisms separated and, in many cases, perished soon afterward. This more sophisticated means of propagating species brought death into the world for the first time and also introduced the connection between sex and death.

At the highest level this symbolic association of death or loss of self with sexual union can be tremendously uplifting or transcending. When Scorpio planets are in hard aspect, however, the individual may bring this association down to a less creative level, so that death becomes a willful drive for personal dominance, with the power to destroy one's own self or another. If the reality of death is not faced and accepted, it may become a source of fear for Scorpio, which then breeds a compulsive need to control circumstances and people to prevent the feared symbolic destruction. This need for control is one of Scorpio's less desirable traits. Just as the scorpion eventually stings itself, bringing about its own demise, so does the individual with a heavy Scorpio emphasis hurt himself in the end.

Sagittarius

The robust and nonspecific quality of Sagittarius does not favor detailed sexual expression or intricate fantasies. Instead, a Sagittarian person expresses sexuality through valued friendship and spontaneity. The Sagittarian physical expression of sexuality is more enthusiastic than that of any other sign, except perhaps Leo, and pleasure is found as much in energy of expression as in elegance of manner. If there is a strong Sagittarius influence, the individual should find partners who are similarly spontaneous; otherwise, neither partner will get what is desired.

The sexuality of Sagittarius is highly adventurous, seeking out any new form of sexual expression that promises excitement and challenge. Once a relationship has been explored and no longer has the excitement of something new, it's time to go on to the next adventure. This approach is quite different from that of people influenced by other experiment-oriented signs, such as Gemini or Virgo, which may cling to a specific experience long after the novelty has worn off. This difference may cause problems between partners if one wants to stay with a particularly satisfying sexual experience and the other is bored and wants to move on.

The house that Sagittarius rules in the natal chart indicates where the individual expresses this optimism and spirit of adventure. If Sagittarius is on the cusp of the twelfth house, for instance, the native seeks out excitement and adventure by exploring his or her own inner psyche and by helping others who are less fortunate, who are in need of moral or physical assistance.

If the person has planets in Sagittarius that are well aspected, he or she is likely to be very tolerant and eager to please as long as the favor will be reciprocated. With harshly aspected planets, the person may egotistically insist on getting his or her way or, on the other hand, lose confidence and not know which way to turn. In either case, the relationship becomes unequal or dependent, and the natural flow of spontaneous communication, which so well suits this sign, is blocked.

The Sagittarius person is not particularly verbal about love, because the love he or she seeks is not detailed or premeditated. But this sign, more than others, allows the individual to fully understand detailed internal concepts of love, where others sometimes lose their way.

Capricorn

Crusty Capricorn strives to rise to the heights of human endeavor in all realms, sexual or otherwise. The location of Capricorn, a sign of mastery and initiation, in the chart represents the area of life where the person seeks to attain mastery and can therefore be a teacher, someone who shows others the way. Capricorn rising, on the cusp of the first house, for example, means that the individual expects to master the physical body and may test its strength and endurance by subjecting it to difficult physical labor or other tasks that require the body to work very hard.

Capricorn is credited as being the least overtly sexual sign, its main effect on sexuality being to channel it in directions indicated by other factors in the chart. If there are supportive aspects to planets in this sign, the individual will have a good sense of timing and of how far to go before pleasure crosses the bounds of consideration for others. In any social context, this awareness is a valuable asset, for it earns the person admiration and respect.

With hard aspects, however, the Capricorn influence can be sexually destructive in several ways. Planets with difficult aspects in Capricorn can inhibit sex excessively or entirely, cutting off one's natural expression and forcing the energies to find channels of release that may be unsatisfactory or unhealthy. This can often be traced to heavy parental or social repression in childhood, which may require therapy and/or painful introspection to work out. Although the chart can indicate the possibility of such problems, it is certainly not within the realm of the astrologer who is not trained in psychotherapy to attempt to treat them; he or she can only encourage the person to seek professional treatment.

Another effect of hard aspects to planets in Capricorn is that sex may become negatively objectified and used in bargaining for favors, position and affection. That may be a harder problem to deal with, because the individual's initial rejection of sexuality has been turned to short-term profitable ends, so there is less motivation to change it. The person uses sex for personal power or control in much the same way as someone with hard aspects to Scorpio planets, but without Scorpio's desire for sexual satisfaction.

Again, with hard aspects to planets in Capricorn, the individual may experience failure in love or sex because of negative experiences caused by insecurity or by too-high expectations. When this happens a few times, the person is likely to give up on love as a bad bet.

On the other hand, well-aspected planets in Capricorn can indicate a person who is very loyal and committed in relationships, so that he or she can hang on through hard times and achieve a truly stable love. A person whose chart has a lot of Capricorn can bank the fires of love so that they don't burn out too quickly but develop into a long-term relationship.

Aquarius

Aquarius is a highly intellectual sign that chooses to relate to others cerebrally rather than emotionally. A sign of the brotherhood and sisterhood of humanity, Aquarius is essentially concerned with how the individual relates to the greater whole of society: one's peers.

Where Aquarius is in the natal chart shows the area of life in which the person identifies with others, usually in the context of a group of friends or a large organization. For example, a person with Aquarius on the cusp of the second house might enjoy sharing what he or she has with good friends, valuing friendship above all else, and may even find ways to earn an income in collaboration with friends and associates. However, personally, this individual would be very detached from materialism, except as a means of continued existence on the planet. He or she might be very concerned with how one's personal resources affect our planetary resources.

Aquarius is not a very physically sexy sign, but it is one of the more experimental signs, though often in a rather clinical way. While Gemini experiments because it enjoys the mechanisms involved, Aquarius does so to add yet another possibility to the whole question of sexuality. Hard aspects to planets in Aquarius can turn this attitude into a shallow, flighty dilettantism without deep commitment at any point. The person tends to treat a lover as an interesting object rather than as an involved partner.

A strongly Aquarian person may be very self-conscious and find it hard to be close to another person, who may interpret the lack of intimacy as lack of love. However, this distant attitude is usually just a normal characteristic of this sign, and the individual may express love in other ways, through thoughtfulness and friendship rather than intuition or physical passion. There is the potential for much loyalty, but it is a general loyalty, not to one relationship alone. Because Aquarius is a pluralistic sign, the person can engage in several sincere affairs at once, and this sincerity makes jealousy less likely to be a destructive force.

In fact, the Aquarius person does not allow one relationship to interfere with another, since that wouldn't seem fair. Even in a single commitment, equality is of the utmost importance, as it is with Libra. But because Aquarius is more static than Libra, the person may insist upon permanently assigned areas of responsibility and credit in a relationship.

Although it is ruled by Uranus, in the long run Aquarius is rather conservative. Experimentation is seen as a means to arriving at an overview of the subject rather than as an end in itself. Aquarius is capable of complex intellectual gyrations, but not usually those that have heavy sexual overtones. Instead, sexuality has a cumulative impact, reinforced by the building of friendship and intellectual intimacy.

Pisces

Where Pisces is found in the horoscope shows where the individual lets go, releasing any claim to the matters indicated by that house. Thus the person is able to use those affairs to escape from the involvements, responsibilities and debts incurred by the other eleven signs. It is where the individual surrenders the will, allowing the forces that be to have their way. If Pisces is on the cusp of the eighth house, for example, the person easily lets go of anything that belongs to others and is quite likely to see death and sex as means to dissolving the ego into a state of bliss and unity with God.

Pisces is the most loving and giving of the signs, but it is not highly erotic in a strictly physical sense. Because Pisces is very intuitive and empathetic, sexuality is geared to a more ethereal form of expression. A person's sexual energy may be diverted into highly charged platonic relationships in which there is little or no physical sexual expression, but with a similar pattern of flow and release in the exchange of love. When physical sex does enter the relationship, it is as the result of established mental and spiritual communication rather than the other way around.

Because Pisces is so giving and therefore vulnerable to exploitation, hard aspects, especially the square, to planets in this sign are particularly difficult sexually. Unselfish impulses tend to be misdirected, and the individual may be misused by an ungrateful lover. This increases the person's sense of worthlessness and martyrdom, which makes him or her even more vulnerable to further exploitation.

In this respect, difficult aspects to Pisces planets lead to a certain kind of masochism or of sadism in defense against mistreatment, which can cripple a person's approach to life. With Pisces it is much harder to be an equal partner in a relationship than to be a slave or master. If there are sadomasochistic tendencies, the person should crystallize them specifically in bedroom role-playing, where the energies can do less harm than in daily life. With care, such scenarios can be played out without harm to either partner, but if these feelings are repressed, they will leak out in other areas and cause trouble for all concerned. In fact, Pisces can express the most highly charged physical sexuality in fantasies of this kind.

The person who has a strong Pisces emphasis must learn how much to give and when to say no. That is a hard line to draw, particularly if there are hard aspects, because the desire to show love by giving, sexually and otherwise, is strong. Another problem that may arise, especially with the inconjunct, is that the person romanticizes love and expects too much spirituality from sexual contact. When such demands are made of sex, there is necessarily disappointment.

The Houses

We now turn to the twelve houses of the horoscope and their significance within the context of love and sexuality.

The houses are viewed in the same counterclockwise order as the twelve signs of the zodiac, and the significance of each house is closely tied with that of its associated sign. Thus, since Aries is the natural ruler of the first house, the first house qualitatively resembles Aries, and much of what we have said earlier about Aries applies also to the first house.

The main difference between the influence of the signs and that of the planets and houses is that the signs describe the strengths and weakness of the planets that are "in" them. A person's approach to the affairs of a given house is also described by the sign on its cusp. The houses represent the settings or scenes within which the play of life occurs, where the planets move and express themselves through their signs and aspects in various circumstances and environments.

The First House

The first house is a house of beingness, and of one's awareness of the physical body as a vehicle for and a projection of the spirit. The sign on the cusp of the first house, the rising sign, says a lot about how the personality is presented to others. It describes the physical appearance, mannerisms and gait. For example, a person with Virgo rising is fastidious about his or her personal appearance and is meticulous to the last detail to make just the right impression. For this person, cleanliness and good grooming are high priorities. These are qualities which can be either highly attractive or repellent to a partner.

Planets in the first house usually have the most immediately noticeable influence, so supportive or difficult aspects to these planets influence the first impression that a person has on others, thus making it either easier or more difficult for the person to find partners. Conjunctions or stelliums here are quite powerful regardless of which planets are involved, because of their noticeable presence and magnetism. An individual with the Sun or Moon here may even be too powerful a personality and thus a less desirable partner.

Hard aspects to planets in the first house, particularly to the lights and inner planets, can often be traced to childhood, when negative behavior patterns were learned and persisted, even though inappropriate, later in life. Square aspects can either cripple one's assertiveness (Saturn) or make one overly assertive (Mars or Jupiter), which the person is usually not aware of. The inconjunct usually indicates that the person doesn't know "when to stop" in the area of life ruled by that planet.

In sexuality, planets in the first house generally make the person play games of influence and dominance. For that reason, the individual's overall impact on the loved one is more important than the form or quality of sexual expression. These people are inclined to express their sexuality through role-playing for intentional effect rather than through spontaneous lovemaking. The strength of this influence, of course, depends on the relative importance of the first house in the chart; the more involved it is with the rest of the chart, especially by hard aspect, the more important is the effect.

The Second House

The second house represents a person's natural resources. It shows how materially wealthy or poor the person is and how he or she obtains financial sustenance. The sign on the cusp of the second house indicates how the person values and spends money. For example, Gemini on the cusp of the second makes a person curious about money and interested in buying intellectually stimulating things.

Because the second house either adds to or takes away from one's physical and financial security, its effects on a love relationship are only indirectly sexual, to the extent that one associates love with money. If there are difficult aspects to planets in this house, the person may have financial problems that prohibit offering a partner monetary stability.

A chart with many planets in the second house indicates an individual who is very concerned with worldly affairs and related values. If the planets are well-aspected, indicating financial stability, the person is likely to have a substantial home and family.

The Third House

The third house can have an important effect on love relationships, because it governs the individual's ability to add interest and variety to sexual expression. In addition to ruling verbal communications, the third house also rules short writings, letters and notes of love, which may be a favorite pastime for the individual with planetary activity here. The sign on the cusp of the third house indicates the content and quality of the individual's communications with others. For example, with Scorpio on the cusp of the third house, the person is quite secretive about what he or she knows and may use information to manipulate others, for better or worse. This placement also indicates that sex is likely to be a favorite topic of discussion and interest.

If there are several planets in the third house, the person may intellectualize sex beyond the point of enjoyment or turn it into a complex mental exercise, ignoring the body's most basic needs. This may be a problem if the partner is more down to earth and bored by such intricacies. But if the partner has a lot of Gemini or Virgo, the couple can enjoy endlessly detailed fantasies without repetition or boredom.

The third house has a certain capacity to sexualize ideas and objects, such as a partner's suggestions or clothing. That is the motivation behind the continual changes in fashion, whose purpose is to decorate the body and enhance its physical attractiveness. Difficult aspects to planets in this house may overemphasize this tendency to the point of fetishism, or sex may become so intellectual that all physical pleasure is lost.

With supportive aspects, the third house allows the individual to use mind and body together creatively, bringing variety and substance to sexual expression. In that case, sexual pressures can be relaxed through fantasy fulfillment, so that they are not expressed through inappropriate or harmful actions in other areas of life.

The Fourth House

The fourth house is quite important to the issues of love and sexuality because it describes in part the individual's early upbringing and how the individual sees himself, which profoundly affects one's sexual development. The sign on the cusp of the fourth house natally shows what dominant characteristic or quality the individual identifies with internally. For example, with Taurus on the cusp of the fourth house, the person sees himself or herself as a physical and sensory being who is very aware of the demands of the body and the material world. This can be either pleasant or burdensome, depending upon the planets in Taurus in this house and the aspects they are involved in.

A strong fourth house gives the individual a strong self-image, so that he or she can readily bounce back from any difficulties. A strong fourth also inclines the individual to develop long-lasting and creative relationships, because he or she feels secure internally and can operate effectively as a person from that stable foundation. Hard aspects to planets here may mean that parental conditioning had a negative effect on the person's ability to be at peace with his or her own sexual identity, which can make relating to people of either sex difficult. It would be hard for this individual to survive disappointment without emotional injury.

Usually the home that an adult creates is a re-creation of the childhood home, so aspects to planets in the fourth tell about both homes. Weak or restless aspects to planets in this house, such as the inconjunct, may not mean that there are problems of sexual identity, but simply that the individual is not settled, either sexually or geographically. That person will have difficulty with a partner who demands reliability and stability, for that will cause emotional injury to both.

The Fifth House

Traditionally this house rules children and offspring in general. Given this background concept, it is easy to see that the fifth house is closely tied with the forces of love and creative self-expression. The sign that rules the fifth house shows one's approach to affairs of the heart, whether open or closed, impulsive or cautious. For instance, if the person has Libra on the fifth, he or she expresses love and creativity in a very refined and artistic manner, wanting love affairs to be beautiful partnerships that are colorful and romantic.

The fifth house has a very enjoyable influence on sexual expression, and positive aspects here give the person an open, healthy attitude toward sex. The sexual style is not likely to be extremely intricate or associative, especially if the house is heavily tenanted or well aspected. Sex is considered a form of recreation and pleasant communication rather than a transcending or ego-releasing experience.

Hard aspects in the fifth may overstate this playfulness to the point of licentiousness (Jupiter) or inhibit sexuality (Saturn). If well aspected, Jupiter makes for more freedom of sexual expression, and Saturn channels it carefully.

Usually, however, sexual abnormalities are not indicated by the fifth house; the causes are more likely to be found in the first, third or fourth.

The Sixth House

Like all the even-numbered feminine houses, the sixth has an indirect effect on sexuality through the personality and the resulting lifestyle. The natural house of Virgo, the sixth house is where a person's life runs with a certain regularity of detail. These characteristics carry over into one's sexual expression as either security or a tendency to boredom, depending on the individual.

The sign on the cusp of the sixth house indicates how the person orders and organizes his or her personal life to take care of whatever has to get done. For example, with Pisces on the cusp of the sixth, the person romanticizes day-to-day activities, often dreaming about what should be done rather than doing it. Mundane concerns can thus take on a disproportionate significance, which may lead to confusion and anxiety about small matters. With such a disorganized lifestyle, this person is likely to joyfully put aside the cumbersome chores of daily life for the more elusive pleasures of love, a trait that can be most inspiring, although unrealistic.

The sixth house also involves teaching and learning in the sense of acquiring skills that make life run more smoothly, and if it is heavily tenanted, the individual may approach sex quite systematically, covering every base in order to be thoroughly informed and able to operate efficiently. There may also be a natural talent for passing on one's practical knowledge about sex to the less experienced.

If there are difficult planetary aspects associated with the sixth house, the individual may look for and attract either student/teacher relationships, positively, or servant/master relationships, negatively. If the latter is the case, it is better and more gratifying to fulfill these tendencies by acting out these sexual fantasies with a partner. Squares to planets in this house indicate difficulty in learning from sexual experience, with repeated errors and adjustments necessary before attaining success and satisfaction.

The Seventh House

Above the horizon and opposite the first house, the seventh house represents the individual's experience of the not-self, or others. This house is of great importance in this discussion because it represents the individual's need for and demands of a complementary partner. The sign on the cusp of the seventh house determines the kind of life mate the individual is likely to attract. With Sagittarius on the cusp, for example, the person is challenged through marriage by a partner who is either broad-minded and philosophical, on the higher side, or carefree and irresponsible, on the lower side. Sagittarius is half horse and half human, meaning that the marital partner either runs away, looking for greener pastures elsewhere, or finds sufficient challenge and adventure within the marriage scene to stay with it.

The significance of this house must not be overlooked when judging relationships. The planets in this house and their aspects tell a great deal about what the person has to learn through relationships. If the seventh house is heavily tenanted, the partner's role is emphasized; the planets here often describe the ideal, and sometimes the real, partner for that person. Depending on the planets and their aspects, the effect can be creative or destructive. An outer planet in the seventh may mean that the individual expects a great deal of the partner, either realistically, if it is well aspected, or unreasonably, if it is in hard aspect.

Pluto or Saturn expresses the desire for a dominating partner, while Jupiter or the Sun indicates the desire for someone who is fun-loving or creative. Whether the planets seem good or difficult, however, it is the aspects that tell the story. If Jupiter is badly aspected, the individual may be attracted to a pompous buffoon, while a well-aspected Saturn may mean attraction to an older and wiser partner.

In general, a well-fortified seventh house helps establish a secure and emotionally equal relationship. If planets here are in hard aspect, there may be an imbalance in the relationship, or the individual may be drawn to an unsuitable person. In that case, the individual must learn a great deal through difficult experience before being able to maintain a satisfactory relationship.

The Eighth House

The eighth house is known as the house of death and sex and regeneration. Because it is linked to Scorpio, the eighth house has dark or mysterious qualities. It is also known as the house of secrets, and sexuality and death are often considered topics inappropriate for open parley or discussion. The sign on the cusp of the eighth house shows how the individual handles sexuality. For instance, Capricorn on the cusp of the eighth house represents a person who is quite serious about his or her sexual needs and who expects a partner to work toward sexual fulfillment in an almost structured or ritualized manner. For this person, sex can take on a sense of status or accomplishment, as if the adequacy of one's sexual performance is always being tested.

Because the eighth house is rather secretive, it has an obscuring effect on sexuality. If there are many planets here, the individual will probably be attracted to older or somewhat enigmatic partners. The hidden nature of the eighth house environment makes the energies of any planets that are in it a bit more difficult to understand. It may be wiser to take the person's actions at face value than to look for hidden meanings.

Well-aspected planets in the eighth enable the individual to intuitively understand sexual mysteries without emotional stress or disappointment. But difficult aspects here mean that journeys into the unknown will have many pitfalls, and the individual should stay in familiar, predictable territory. This applies not to sexual experimentation but to sexual adventures in which the outcome is unknown and where there is no turning back when the situation goes awry. There is always some emotional or even physical risk in such excursions, and those who have difficult aspects in the eighth should avoid them.

The Ninth House

The ninth house determines how innovative and adventurous the individual is in exploring new directions in life. The sign on the cusp of the ninth house shows what fields these explorations may cover, sexual or otherwise. For example, with Aries on the cusp of the ninth house, the person tries just about anything that is new and that offers some promise of excitement and adventure. For this person life is worth living only insofar as it is a challenge and a risk.

With a well-supported ninth, the individual can range freely in sexual expression without being tied down by outmoded ideas. Also the individual can choose the most profitable paths of exploration and pursue them effectively.

Difficult aspects here may inhibit sexual exploration for reasons that seem rational but that have no logical basis, especially with Saturn or Neptune. Or the person may want to explore, but the paths chosen may lead to embarrassment instead of pleasure.

The kind of exploration indicated by this house is not in specific techniques but in the basic concepts of and approaches to sexuality. A heavily tenanted ninth house lessens the interest in detailed sex scenarios, because they get in the way of the overall picture of love.

The sexuality generated by the ninth house often has a more emotional than physical impact, such that the partners can change roles endlessly without ever having to change the basic techniques.

The Tenth House

The tenth house is concerned more with the effects of one's career and reputation on a relationship than with the relationship itself. At the zenith of the chart, the tenth house describes the heights of achievement that we strive to attain in this lifetime. It is where we look up to others who are in authority over us and work to attain mastery over the material world through a career or vocation. The sign on the cusp of the tenth house describes how the individual views his or her climb to the top and indicates what field of work is most appropriate. With Aquarius on the tenth house, for example, the person may pursue a career in the occult or in some area relating to social reform.

If there are many planets in this house, the individual may actively pursue a career or a reputation, with sexual expression taking second place. With good aspects, these two goals can work together in a positive way, the best example being a couple who work as a team in their career, making time for both sex and work, with neither drive frustrated by the other.

But if there are hard aspects here, the individual may become sexually involved with a working partner in such a way that working together becomes difficult and sex impossible. Or the person's work is so demanding that there is little time or energy left for sex, which can lead to frustration or sexual dysfunction. Another possibility is that sexual expression has a negative effect on the person's career, through scandal or neglect of work that must be done.

The matters represented by the tenth house do not reflect the individual's basic sexual style, but one's style is shaped by external pressures to some extent, and this house shows how well that style will adapt to those pressures.

The Eleventh House

This house indicates the individual's opportunities to meet desirable partners and to make long-lasting friends both in and out of sexual relationships. If this house is heavily tenanted, the individual will be very concerned about a potential partner's style, making judgments on that basis without really getting to know the other person. If a potential partner is not up to the individual's standards, the relationship will end before it has really begun.

This trait can mean establishing relationships with the finest partners, or it can mean missing some desirable diamonds in the rough, depending on the aspects involved and the original judgment. Once a relationship is established, the individual will continually upgrade it and improve the partner's style. Again depending on the aspect, this may result in ever-increasing enjoyment, or it may ruin what was good because of meddling.

In general, an active eleventh house means that the native has many close friends, whether or not they are lovers. With good aspects, friends provide good times and support; with difficult aspects, friends may be a source of disappointment and betrayal at critical moments.

The Twelfth House

The last of the houses, the twelfth is the proverbial closet that holds all the skeletons from the incomplete experiences of the previous eleven houses. The sign on the cusp of the twelfth house shows what kind of debris may be waiting for disposal in the psychological storehouse of the past. For example, if Cancer is on the cusp of the twelfth, the person has domestic attachments that await severance.

The twelfth house is usually thought to bode no good to anyone in sexual experiences. The planets here and their aspects may indicate early mistakes in love that lead to difficulty or disappointment. With Mars and Uranus in the twelfth, the individual might marry in haste, with disastrous results; with the Moon and Saturn, a very desirable lover might get away because the individual hesitates or is unwilling to make a commitment.

However, if the person is able to learn from mistakes, the twelfth house offers some of the deepest and most exciting sexual experiences, because it represents the elements of sexuality that have been most completely hidden and repressed. Careful exploration of that realm can be fascinating and can lead to a wealth of inner understanding and unexpected pleasure.

If there are difficult aspects, the person should go slowly and cautiously, because there will be pitfalls, and his or her judgment will not be so practical. With supportive aspects, however, the journey into the subconscious regions of sexuality will be easy and profitable, and unknown instincts may unexpectedly surface at just the right time to turn a problem into a delight. In any case, the matters indicated by the twelfth house should be treated with care and respect, not only as potential hazards but also as sources of inner revelation.

The Aspects

We now turn to the aspects and how they influence our feelings of love and sexuality. Aspects represent energy flowing between planets and modifying the effects of any single planet. The so-called "hard" or "difficult" aspects are usually squares, oppositions and minor aspects such as the semisquare and sesquiquadrate. The inconjunct, or quincunx, is by no means an easy aspect, but neither is it hard. It is, however, a major aspect that complicates life to an uncomfortable degree until the person shifts position.

The easy or supportive aspects are the sextile and trine, and sometimes the conjunction, depending on the planets involved. Because they are easy aspects, the person doesn't have to work to overcome any obstacle except the inertia that these aspects bring. Minor supportive aspects include the semisextile and the quintile. We will discuss here only the six major aspects: conjunction, sextile, square, trine, inconjunct and opposition.

The Conjunction

This aspect is neither difficult nor supportive necessarily; it simply intensifies the effects of the planets involved. If the chart shows too much intensity, this may be an affliction, but in an otherwise mild chart, the conjunction may be helpful.

In sexuality, however, the conjunction can be considered an asset, because it heightens one's energy, even when the planets combined are opposites, such as Jupiter and Saturn. When sparks fly, there is likely to be sexual excitement as well.

Only when a conjunction is in the twelfth house or is involved in hard angular aspect does it have unfortunate implications, for then the individual must be careful that the intensity is not directed in a harmful or unsuitable direction. Pockets of intensity in the chart must be given an outlet, because if they are suppressed, they will create such great pressure that when the urgency and desperation are finally expressed, the outcome will not be pleasant.

The Sextile

This is a mild, supportive aspect, indicating matters that come naturally for the individual. It does not indicate major points of strength, just areas that are not likely to cause trouble, although they should not be ignored. Like a car that is in good working condition, a sextile will run smoothly with regular care, but if neglected it is likely to develop problems or fall into disrepair. Sextiling planets always provide support to help solve problems brought on by difficult aspects in the chart.

The Square

The square is doubtless the most difficult aspect in the chart to handle, particularly if there is more than one. It tends to create errors that compound themselves repeatedly, unless great care is taken to keep this from happening.

If the planets in square are active, the person usually overreacts in the areas concerned, and if the planets are passive or restrictive, he or she will be excessively inhibited. The effects of this aspect are not steady, however, which makes it even more difficult to handle. It seems to take effect only at the most inappropriate times and wreak havoc with one's timing, sexual and otherwise. With a Jupiter square, for instance, the individual may approach a partner with immense ardor when gentle tact would be more appropriate. Or with a Saturn square, the person might be afraid to make a move when the time is right and thus miss a golden opportunity.

There is no way around this except through experience and self-observation. By noting the effects of the square in various situations, the individual can learn to anticipate and control them.

People who have several squares or other hard aspects in their charts tend to improve as they get older, whereas those who are blessed with easy aspects at birth may decline in growth and productivity unless they work on using their good aspects.

The Trine

The trine is the most supportive aspect and has a very stabilizing effect on the planets involved. It can absorb much of the difficulty brought on by any hard aspects to the planets in trine and can resolve other conflicts in the chart as well.

It can also be a very lazy aspect, so that the individual takes his or her easiness and talent for granted. If this is done for a long period of time, the talents and the support of the trine will wither away, requiring great effort to make them workable again.

However, the effects of the trine are generally helpful to sexual expression, creating difficulties only if there are nothing but easy aspects in the chart. A certain tension is required to make sex exciting, and if that is lacking, the individual will not be an active, exciting lover. This does not mean that there will be no sex drive, but the lack of motivation in this area may lead to frustration and lack of development. Hard aspects cause a person to strive to learn more about sexuality, and without them the person may fall behind in real understanding of sex.

The Inconjunct

The effect of the inconjunct on sexuality is very visible, because it tends to make the individual overdo things in the area governed by the planets involved. It is a restless, ambitious aspect that never quits, and as a result, it leads to much experience. But its effects need to be channeled so that the extra energy is not wasted or used redundantly. If used well, the inconjunct can lead to sexual achievement, but if used in the wrong way, it will wear out the individual's welcome in love and be a source of irritation.

The Opposition

The opposition upsets or unbalances planets in such a way that when one planet is strong, the other is weak. Thus the individual swings from one extreme to the other, which can create problems.

It is not easy to control the effects of the opposition, although continual self-monitoring and conscious modification can help significantly. But it is just as important to adjust one's lifestyle so that the extremes can be tolerated and enjoyed as much as possible, instead of trying to repress them altogether. Much of the enjoyment in sexuality is in the extremes that it may go to, so the opposition can be very stimulating.

Aspect Balance

If one or more aspects seem to be linked with sexual difficulties, it is important to look to the strong points in the chart for balance and for possible cures. As in other situations, the individual should be sensitive to areas of weakness and concentrate on those areas that will make good use of the more supportive aspects. If possible, someone with many hard aspects should stay away from sexual situations that demand a relaxed, mellow style. And someone with few natal hard aspects will be happier in an affair that is not characterized by a high degree of tension or excitement.

I do not advise people to simply avoid problems and to not try to overcome them. But those problems will crop up often enough no matter what, so it is not necessary to seek them out. When they do occur, one should look to the supporting aspects in the chart for ways to deal with them. For example, an individual with the Moon in difficult aspect and a strong Mercury may be able to get out of emotional difficulties by intellectual efforts. But someone with Mercury in hard aspect should abandon an intellectual approach to love and rely on intuition.

Sex is a matter of tension and release, and without aspects, both natal and mundane, that supply that tension, the release will not be satisfactory. Instead of looking at hard aspects in a chart as obstacles to overcome or get around, one can see them as fueling and directing the sexual impulse so that there can be real satisfaction. The issue is to first determine what areas of the chart the hard aspects are touching and to then make sure that they do not block the path to pleasure that is made possible by the tension. In the long run, in sexuality as in every other area of life, it's not what you're born with that makes for success, it's what you do with what you have.

Chapter Four
Case Studies

Up to this point we have looked mainly at all of the separate astrological factors that are important in analyzing a chart from a sexual point of view. The task now before us is to synthesize those factors and create a whole picture that makes sense intellectually and that checks against the reality of the client's experience.

How can the natal horoscope be used to understand an individual's sexuality and the styles in which it is expressed? Although both experience and conditioning determine the details of a person's sexual expression at any given time, the natal chart does provide an overview, which can suggest new directions for the individual to pursue or reveal paths that may take the person out of sexual difficulties.

When examining a chart in a sexual light, the astrologer should step softly, because it is all too easy to make incorrect interpretations. A chart can only outline the possibilities of a person's sexual style; the actual outcome is not predictable, for it depends on the person's upbringing and opportunities for sexual experience.

Although a chart may indicate strong or unusual sexual desires, there is a good chance that the individual has not had the opportunity to express them and would be insulted or upset if told about those indications. Age, of course, is also a factor. Sexual energy can be sublimated into many other areas and remain below the surface in sexual expression. On the other hand, even if a chart does not show a lot of active potential, through the right circumstances the person may find quite adequate sexual expression.

We shall approach our case studies by giving some life information about each person and by using the delineations from the second portion of this book. In this way we can piece together a complete picture of three women whose sexual needs and inclinations in love are known to the author. To insure their privacy, we have changed the names of the three women. By combining background biographical data with the astrological indicators, we shall see how accurate the chart analysis can be. In addition, we will discuss a very critical component of practicing astrology—the astrologer's own attitude toward the subject at hand. Between synthesizing the chart and presenting that information to the client, there is an important process of self-examination that the astrologer must undergo. This is the humanizing process that translates the astrological symbols of the chart into compassion and understanding.

Adrienne

Our first case is of a person whose need for love is as great as anyone's, and of the obstacles she encountered in her path toward finding satisfactory expression for that love. Adrienne is now thirty-two years old, and her life to this point has been very stormy. Her chart quite clearly reveals the problems she encountered in relationships throughout her growing and young adult years. She was born on October 22, 1945 at 11:49 AM A.S.T. to well-educated parents. Her father held an important government position, and her mother was a teacher. The type of man her father was can easily be seen by the hard aspect of her natal Sun to Mars and Saturn in the seventh house. He was sophisticated and restrained on the surface, but underneath, his temperament was radically violent. Adrienne's parents' marriage was a violent relationship and ended in divorce when she was six years old. The mother was awarded custody of our subject and her older brother and younger sister. Adrienne's difficult relationship with her mother is shown by the tight T-square in the chart involving the Moon, Mercury and Pluto in fixed signs and houses. Her mother was very possessive and became overly involved in all of her social acitivities, which of course only served to alienate Adrienne. The T-square implies a tremendous amount of conflict in sexuality, and her mother was a perfect reflection of that. Her mother never remarried but eventually became deeply involved in a lesbian relationship with a much younger woman. Obviously the mother's ambivalent feelings about her own sexuality did not help Adrienne establish her own sexual identity.

At eighteen years of age, Adrienne met the man she was to later marry. This was at the height of the drug culture movement of the sixties, which these two exemplified. They traveled all around the United States together, taking psychedelic drugs and having no particular goals or purpose. Their relationship led to an accidental pregnancy, which led to their marriage in October of 1964. The child, a daughter, was born six months later.

This marriage was destined to end in a painful way for Adrienne. In a clairvoyant session she learned that they had been married in a previous lifetime and that she had run out on him, leaving him with the full responsibilities of their life together. She knew instinctively that in this lifetime it was her turn to take on the burdens of raising their child, and for that reason she never asked for child support or alimony after their separation in 1966. But she was by no means content after her marriage broke up. At that point, she had taken so many drugs and had lived in such an unbalanced way that her whole personality structure was very unstable. She turned to psychotherapy and to the comfort of relationships with men who were quite a bit younger than herself, who were by no means old enough to handle her problems. She treated each new affair like a game of conquest in a very sadistic sense. By 1969 Adrienne was no longer capable of sustaining a relationship and had tired of her string of unsatisfactory affairs. She had outgrown drugs but did not have anything meaningful to replace them with.

That lifestyle came to an abrupt end when an unfriendly ex-lover slipped some LSD to Adrienne's daughter, who was then four years old. Panicked, she took her daughter to a physician who immediately had Adrienne arrested. He also set in motion court proceedings to have her daughter taken out of her custody. In 1970, after a year of ugly legal struggles, Adrienne regained custody of her daughter. They spent the next year moving from place to place, Adrienne still without any sense of purpose or direction. Compulsive and changing sexuality was Adrienne's lifestyle until continual disappointment and a feeling of worthlessness led to a manic state that was an important factor in a near-fatal accident, which radically changed her life.

This event occurred the following year, while Adrienne and her daughter were living in a rural commune. It was December 24, 1971 at 3 PM E.S.T., a clear, bright afternoon. Without the slightest hesitation, Adrienne walked right out into the middle of the street into an oncoming car that was traveling at forty miles per hour. The accident sent her into a coma for two weeks, during which time it was uncertain whether she would survive. The point of impact was to her hip and leg, perforating her uterus and causing later speech and motor balance impairment. Her transits at the time of the accident tell the whole story, but that is somewhat beyond the scope of our discussion. Suffice it to say that the timing for this accident was no accident, but was perhaps destined to occur in order to transform her outlook on life. When she regained consciousness after being in the coma, she described in fairly vivid detail her out-of-the-body experience. Adrienne recalled visiting other solar systems and meeting with great beings who guided her and pointed out the direction she should take in life.

Her recovery was steady during the next year. While undergoing a lengthy program of physical therapy, Adrienne became very interested in studying medicine as a serious career. In 1972 she managed to get her life together sufficiently to be accepted at a well-known university where she is currently finishing her medical education and soon will become an MD. For a lost young woman whose life had seemed like such a waste only a few years earlier, this was a long way to come. At this writing, her plans are to complete her degree program and to practice medicine in an underdeveloped country.

Unfortunately, Adrienne does not get along well with her daughter, who is now twelve years old. At last, however, she is leading a productive, useful life and working out some of the hard aspects in her chart through a vital career that challenges her active intellect and drive for security.

Turning now to her natal chart, we shall see that much of Adrienne's life is described by the astrological indicators. We will focus mainly on how her chart shows her romantic involvements in love and the problems she must overcome in order to have a satisfying relationship.

The aspects of this chart could be those of a person who throws herself into one affair after another without success because of her feelings of inadequacy and her inaccurate images of her partners. But it could also be the chart of a person who simply puts sex aside altogether as something that is impossible to deal with. Which analysis is correct? In reality, as we have seen, both analyses have applied at different times in her life.

The wide fixed T-square involving Pluto, Mercury and the Moon at the cusp of the fifth house might mean some hidden sexual compulsiveness, alternating in expression between the need to rule and the need to be ruled by using words or intellectual concepts. Adrienne's Moon in Taurus in the fifth house shows she believes that a long-lasting relationship must be based on honesty; she would want to stick to her commitments in love. She has certain leadership qualities and enjoys sex as a form of personal and aesthetic expression. The opposition of the Moon to Mercury indicates swinging back and forth from rational thinking to emotionalism. With Mercury in Scorpio in the ninth house, Adrienne is most intrigued with sex when it is rather secretive and mysterious, and she looks upon a partner as an emotional traveling companion in an adventure of love. The square of Mercury to Pluto requires her to

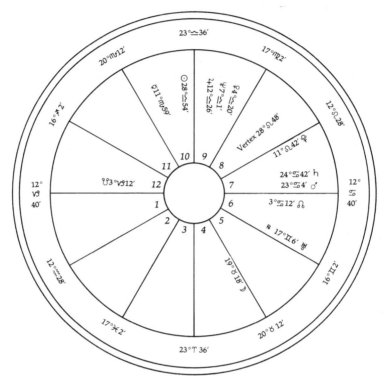

Adrienne's natal chart

make a conscious effort to avoid arguing with a lover, no matter how convinced she is that her opinion is right. Although Adrienne now realizes that this is true, she got to this realization only after many years of negative attitudes.

Learning to forgive her partner's errors is also a major challenge for her. The additional square of the Moon to Pluto indicates a deep-rooted need to be in control of emotional situations. This makes it difficult for Adrienne to succeed in love and be willing to relinquish some of her control and to trust her partner to be responsible for his share of the commitment. This pattern of behavior is deeply rooted in her insecurity and may well take her an entire lifetime to undo. With Pluto in its own house, a lot of what happens in a relationship is below the surface and takes a long time to become apparent.

Fortunately, the Moon-Mercury opposition also sextiles and trines Adrienne's Ascendant at 10° Capricorn. This helps her to express her feelings to others quite easily by combining words with subtle nonverbal body language that is usually very effective. However, because Pluto is also in inconjunct aspect to the Ascendant, she must be on guard against using sexual conquest and achievement as a gauge of her personal power over others, because that is counterproductive to real love. With the empty end of that T-square being Aquarius, Adrienne needs the balance of objectivity and detachment. This will come as she focuses more on her own values and needs, clarifying what is true for her and allowing that it may not be true for others. Her Capricorn Ascendant is anything but frivolous in love, with Saturn as her personal ruler.

Saturn, which is a strong and significant influence in Adrienne's chart, is angular, in the seventh house and conjunct Mars in Cancer, giving her slow but steady energy potential. This is a placement of great intensity for Saturn, which causes her to put a good deal of pressure on a partner. The conjunction with Mars gives a very uneven rhythm in the timing of sexual expression, which can be overwhelming for her mate, who may feel engulfed by Adrienne's compulsive energies. Clearly, relationships for Adrienne are stormy, passionate involvements, and she is often wracked by anxiety and feelings of inadequacy, especially considering the square of this conjunction to natal Sun. This detracts seriously from her feelings of self-worth and causes her to act out rashly. Because she is a Libra, we know that she thrives on growth and development through relationships, and she is not easily scared off by a difficult involvement.

Since Adrienne has the Sun in the tenth house, her real identity is tied up with her ability to express herself in a profession. Because this consumes so much of her energy, relationships may have to take a back seat to her career. Ideally, Adrienne needs a partner who supports her need to fulfill herself professionally.

The Venus-Neptune-Jupiter stellium in Libra in the ninth house indicates that in love, Adrienne is an intellectual optimist and idealist, but it also implies certain built-in disappointments in that area. All three planets are quite strong here, since Venus is in its own sign, and Jupiter and Neptune are dignified by house and aspect. The Libra influence again emphasizes the desire for continual change within a love relationship, with beauty being a cherished value. Adrienne wants romance to be a creative adventure and is very attracted to men of foreign origin or of unusual interests and backgrounds. The trine from Uranus in the sixth to Jupiter brings much brilliance and originality. This trine allows Adrienne to guide a partner to fuller enjoyment of sex through easy experimentation, and this is reinforced by the close sextile of Pluto to Jupiter. As we know, Jupiter tends to overdo itself, and with her Jupiter and Neptune square to her Ascendant, she can get very carried away when making a point and not see herself clearly at all. This square makes for overstatement, perhaps shown in a tendency to form hasty, unrealistic images of partners.

In addition to Adrienne's other very close aspects, she has a tight square between Venus and the nodes. This configuration tells us that the fulfillment of her love desires on the personal level is not compatible with her main path in this lifetime. Because Venus is conjunct Neptune, Adrienne's love consciousness must grow to encompass more than an intimate one-to-one relationship. Both that conjunction and the square to the nodes, which are in the sixth and twelfth houses, tell us that love must be given in service in this lifetime, and that Adrienne's evolution lies in caring for the needs of others through her work, which she at last has understood.

Thea

The woman who is the subject of our second case study departs considerably from the average. Thea is a person who is now experiencing love and life to her full capacity. Born on June 13, 1944 at 12:10 PM C.S.T., she is now thirty-three years old. Thea has been working for the past six years as a therapist, counseling individuals, groups, families and children. She committed herself to a career in the field of human growth services at the age of thirteen. This early sense of purpose resulted in part from the fact

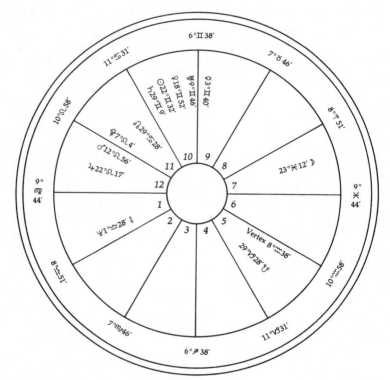

Thea's natal chart

that she felt somehow responsible for her mother's postpartum depression, which continued off and on throughout Thea's childhood. So Thea decided to take the position of someone who would make others happy, who could fill the voids in others' lives. This service, she felt, would earn her her parents' love and make her accepted by her older brother and sister.

Thea's father and mother were hard workers in their respective fields who had been hard hit by the Depression of the 1930s. He was a labor-union organizer and spokesperson, and she was a social worker. Both parents held high humanitarian values and instilled in Thea a strong awareness of social justice and equal rights.

At present, Thea has been married for nearly eleven years and has a six-year-old daughter. Her husband is active in the fields of education and art. Thea sees him as a man whose strength lies in his ability to realize his visions in the world, a quality that Thea says she lacked. She acknowledges that she has profited by his encouragement to assert herself actively in the world. In turn, Thea feels that her husband benefits from her insight into the world of feelings and human nature. Others who know Thea say that her family life appears to be extremely satisfying and that it is characterized by unusually open communication and sharing. Put simply, her life is really working, which is rare in this society. It is for that reason that Thea's chart is used here as an example in our investigation of people and love.

What comes as a surprise to many people is that Thea and her husband engage in extramarital sex by mutual agreement and that this arrangement is also working, which again is very rare. They made this agreement after careful consideration of each partner's needs and of what both felt was reasonable and appropriate for their relationship. As would be true for any couple in our society, in creating an open marriage, Thea and her husband had to work through all the internal and external obstacles that one would expect. Interestingly enough, it was Thea who initially proposed their conventional monogamous marriage to her husband; four years later he proposed that their marriage be opened.

Let us see how well Thea's natal chart reflects her experiences in life, especially her concept of love and the way she shares herself with others in love.

One is immediately struck by the powerful stellium of five planets—Mercury, Uranus, Venus, Sun and Saturn—elevated in Gemini. With this stellium, she is extremely effective in expressing herself, and she is not likely to be forgotten by anyone who comes to know her. Since the planets involved in the stellium are both personal and generational, she is an agent of communication to the world, her message being that what is, is and that everything in life is interconnected. She communicates clearly and makes a great effort to create the rules of communication with others. This is a result of her early struggles with communication, which made her keenly aware of the need for effective communication; thus she has worked at becoming an expert at the process of coordinating words with nonverbal signals.

Her tenth-house Sun in Gemini broadens her potential for variety and her responsiveness to mental stimulation. She chooses to be with others who, like herself, are energetically striving to achieve their professional goals and for whom there is little separation between work and love. Venus in this position represents her love of her profession and her ability to integrate love within her profession. This placement also indicates the delicacy and finesse she experiences in lovemaking and her enjoyment of gentle stroking and talking. Sun conjunct Venus is her high self-esteem and tolerance of others, who are naturally attracted to her.

Thea's serious nature is reflected by the Sun's conjunction with Saturn in the tenth; she considers her commitments carefully and remains loyal to them. This conjunction also brings sadness and painful separations into her life. Saturn in Gemini represents her ability to verbalize her needs and shows her serious attitude toward relationships, in which she seeks to clarify critical areas. With Pluto sextile Uranus, she digs deep into her subconscious to confront her own taboos in sexuality. Saturn in the tenth conjunct Venus is her seriousness and devotion in love once she is secure in the ground rules. Sun sextile Jupiter gives her stability in relationships, which are long-lasting and rewarding. With Jupiter in the twelfth, she sheds light on all the hidden problems in relationships.

Her Sun square Moon indicates inner dissatisfaction, motivating her to ever higher levels of achievement. She gives herself little or no credit for her accomplishments and thus needs her partner's constant reassurance that she satisfies him. Her Moon in Pisces in the seventh house is her concern with her partner's and other people's values and her ability to know another's heart. Thus Thea acts as a guide and nurturing force in relationships. With the Moon square Venus, there is a struggle between her emotions and her desires, which is working itself out within her open marriage, a relationship in which she lives with the man she loves and is free to bring other lovers into her life.

The Moon inconjunct Jupiter shows her tendency to give compulsively to others, and the Moon square Saturn is her hesitancy in giving to herself. Moon opposition Neptune describes her vivid imagination and her need for a balanced relationship with a partner who is realistic and objective.

Mercury in her ninth trines Neptune, again representing her ability to verbalize her desires and needs and her enjoyment of talking, reading and writing about love. Mercury is also conjunct Uranus and the Midheaven and sextile Pluto, which indicate Thea's originality and her ability to stimulate change.

In addition to the Gemini stellium, Thea's chart includes one other outstanding feature—the conjunction of Mars, Jupiter and Pluto in Leo. Mars conjunct Jupiter in the twelfth gives her great energy and willingness to go out of the way to assist others in realizing their potential. With Mars also sextile Uranus, Thea is inventive and able to make experimental styles of sexuality work for her. Uranus in Gemini is experimentation and intellectualization and, in the tenth, she has a reputation for originality and inventiveness. She is demanding and settles only for the best.

Thea acknowledges that over the years she has learned that she is both lovable and loving. She says that her marriage continues to offer opportunities for growth to herself and her husband through all of the various stages of their relationship. She says that it takes time, willingness, honesty and trust to make it work.

Life for Thea has its ups and downs, of course, and she makes no pretense of having all the answers. Her current goals are to continue working as a therapist and growing with her own family. She says she is learning how people love and don't love each other, and she now knows that self-sacrifice does not equate with love. This knowledge is transmitted through her to everyone whom she knows and counsels, who find her to be an inspiration to their own growth and development.

Mona

Our third case is much more sketchy in detail, yet no less interesting in light of her sexual inclinations. It is the chart of Mona who was born November 2, 1944 at 11:05 PM E.W.T. in Philadelphia, Pennsylvania.

One of the many close aspect configurations in Mona's chart is the fifth-to-eleventh house opposition of Venus in Sagittarius to the conjunction of the Moon and Uranus in Gemini. This configuration alone indicates the possibility of rather unusual tastes in sex, especially with Venus the only personal fire planet in the chart. This mutable opposition shows that she has a very adaptable style in lovemaking and is happy to participate in any kind of loving that pleases her partner. In addition she would be inclined to talk quite openly about sex, blending humor into the seriousness of love.

The independent nature of the conjunction of the Moon and Uranus, along with the fact that these planets are in the eleventh house, shows that she is definitely her own person

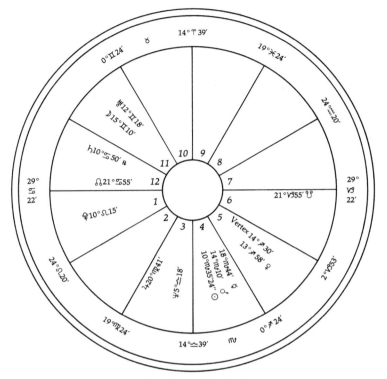

14° ♈ 39'

19° ♓ 24'

0° ♊ 24'

♂

24° ♒ 20'

♅ 12° ♊ 18'
☽ 15° ♊ 10'

♄ 10° ♋ 50' ℞

10 9

11   8

29°
♋
22'

☊ 21° ♋ 55'   12

1   7

21° ♑ 55' ☋

29°
♑
22'

♀ 10° ♌ 15'

2   6

3 4 5

Vertex 14° ♐ 30'

13° ♐ 58' ♀

24° ♌ 20'

♃ 20° ♍ 41'

♆ 5° ♎ 18'

18° ♏ 44'
14° ♏ 10'
10° ♏ 35' 24"

♂
☿
☉

2° ♑ 53'

19° ♍ 24'

0° ♐ 24'

14° ♎ 39'   ♍

Mona's natal chart

and is capable of switching her interests in romance at the drop of a hat. Friends would be extremely important to Mona, especially those who could appreciate her flair for the unusual.

Her Venus indicates that she is fairly choosy about the kind of lover she accepts; a lover must be as adventurous and unusual as she is, someone who can share her attitude toward sex as a source of limitless entertainment. The opposition to Uranus leads to many ups and downs in relationships that are anything but conservative.

This Venus-Uranus opposition is close to a mutual square with Jupiter, the only planet in earth in the chart, suggesting that there is little restraint on this individual and that she would tend to go overboard in sexual gratification. This could be a case of too much of a good thing, which turns out to be less than pleasurable in the end. In Virgo, Jupiter is capable of designing and arranging an infinite variety of detailed settings for love, carrying out the most intricate fantasies. Jupiter's third-house placement only increases her sexual imagination and ability to express herself, both physically and in words.

Mona's Sun, Mars and Mercury form a stellium in Scorpio in the fourth house, giving her a strong potential for intense sex. This angular stellium in a fixed sign shows that she pursues what she wants relentlessly, even though her motivations remain beneath the surface of her own consciousness, since these planets are in the fourth house of the midnight side of the chart. These three personal planets in Scorpio mean that she is very much in the dark—a mystery to others as well as herself. This stellium seems to contradict the mutable planets in her chart, because her fourth-house planets indicate great insecurity and a need for intimacy in relationships. In addition, Mona's parents probably had a profound effect on her image of herself, to such an extent that she might feel most comfortable in relationships involving some parental role-playing. Overall, this stellium gives her a great deal of energy, both physical and mental, which she may express intensely, but it is quite likely that this energy will be directed inward, against herself, in a destructive way.

As if these factors didn't provide enough intensity, Pluto sharply enters the picture in an angular, first house position in square to Mona's Scorpio planets in the fourth. The mutual reception of Pluto and the Sun emphasizes her drive for personal power in this life, which is closely tied to a deep-seated fear of death. With Mars also involved in this square, along with Mercury, both her words and actions can sting her mate without mercy if she is provoked or threatened by a challenge to her authority.

Saturn is weakly placed in Cancer in the twelfth house, indicating that Mona may keep her sexual inhibitions hidden from her own as well as others' sight. But out of sight, of course, does not mean resolved, so she would have periods of emotional withdrawal in which she would hold herself back almost involuntarily for fear of what would happen if she let go. Saturn, fortunately, trines her Scorpio stellium. This is a very supportive aspect, which, considering the indications of instability in her chart, gives her a desperately needed measure of practicality and common sense. Saturn also widely squares Neptune in the third house, which makes it very difficult for Mona to accurately assess what is real and what is fantasy. With this square, she is likely to change the rules of the game without warning, because she has not clearly defined in the beginning the given assumptions in her relationships with others, making Mona both untrustworthy and untrusting of others.

The lack of personal planets in cardinal signs indicates that Mona is not very aggressive. But of course, that is offset by her fixed square in angular houses, which includes three of Mona's personal planets. The Mars inconjunct the MC is a little puzzling, but it might mean that she actively tries to publicize her activities.

The picture that emerges is of a woman who goes to extremes and may be involved in unusual or bizarre sexual practices that she tries to publicize. That seems like a rather audacious conclusion just from looking at the horoscope, and it would not be wise to make such a statement without other information about the person. The same indications could mean that Mona is a rather intense, career-oriented musician with a lot of unusual friends. Such a person might be quite withdrawn and would be outraged by the first diagnosis, even if it were latently correct.

In fact, the first conclusion is correct. Mona is a bisexual nymphomaniac who lives as a sex slave of her lesbian partner and advertises in the classifieds of underground newspapers for other sex partners. Once this is known, the rest of the chart confirms the details. The fact that Mona's lover supports and dominates her is shown by the Saturn trine and Pluto square, with Saturn ruling the seventh. The grand trine with Pluto, Venus and the MC tells us that she thrives on sexual experience, which she obtains in large measure with little effort. The trine also explains her habit of advertising in the paper for sex, and with the Mars-MC inconjunct, there is always more on tap than can be used. As depicted by Jupiter in Virgo at the cusp of the third ruling the fifth, with Venus in the fifth conjunct the Vertex, Mona spends her time and mental energies dreaming up new forms of sexual expression.

The heavy tension of the fourth house, both by aspect and ruler, indicates a troubled and perhaps violent or very repressive upbringing, which may be the source of Mona's behavior pattern. Any attempts to alter Mona's lifestyle are not likely to work, because it is supported by the grand trine, and while she is motivated by fear and hostility, the pattern is satisfying enough to be hard to give up. Only when this lifestyle becomes nonsupportive or impossible because of age is Mona likely to change.

The three cases that have been presented here are indicative of the many different inclinations in love that an astrologer may come across in counseling clients. No matter how unusual, each client must be treated as a unique individual and given the respect that she or he deserves. In the remaining portion of this chapter we will look at some of the issues that may arise when the astrologer looks at the love relationships and emotional needs of clients. It is my intention to pose questions that I hope will stimulate each of you to consider these issues and examine your own attitudes about love, thus becoming a wiser person and a better astrologer.

When you, the astrologer, discuss love in a client's life, you are "hitting below the belt." A wise astrologer will beware of judging the rightness or wrongness of any love relationship that a client asks about. *There is no such thing as a wrong or bad love*, there is only need and desire. As is the case for any professional counselor, the main task of the astrologer is to assist the client in discovering what his needs and drives are and how his values, choices and actions affect his life.

Before discussing the factors in a client's chart, the astrologer requires one quality: love for the client, which can be communicated only from the heart. Intellectual platitudes do not heal the emotional wounds that a client may bring to the astrologer. Only genuinely caring for the client will give you a true vision of his needs and potentials. This is what Carl Rogers refers to as "unconditional acceptance." We are all human, and if you haven't already walked the same path as our client, you very well may in the future.

Love is one of the most common reasons why a client seeks out astrological counseling in the first place. Either the person has been unsuccessful in love, or he is deeply in love with another person and wants a better understanding of the relationship. Many times a client begins by talking about a completely nonemotional subject, yet he is searching all the while for a way to drop the facade and talk about the problem that is really bothering him. It is then that you need to be alert to nonverbal body messages as well as to words.

It is as important for the astrologer to build trust with a client as it is for the client to build trust in a relationship with another person. If the client senses that you are interested only in the fee, he will go away worse off emotionally than when he arrived. You have to be there with the client, emotionally as well as physically and intellectually, to guide the person along the way in love and life. In the realm of love the astrologer is playing with fire, and you can spread it out of control or extinguish it thoughtlessly through inappropriate attitudes and remarks. The client does not need your judgment, for he most assuredly carries too much guilt and fear already. What he does need is the psychological space to explore himself and the freedom to be who he really is.

Many questions of ethics arise in the course of astrological counseling. Often a married couple prefer to come to an astrologer separately to discuss their relationship. In this case the astrologer is obligated to maintain strict confidence. A good rule of thumb is to be truthful, for the chances are, your words will be repeated to others, and usually the client's feelings will color his interpretation of what you say.

What do you do if you feel that your client is involved in a potentially destructive relationship? First, in your own mind, you must establish the way in which this relationship could be destructive to the client: emotionally, physically or intellectually. This is often shown by hard aspects to the client's inner planets from the partner's outer planets, including Saturn. The relationship may involve emotional or physical abuse or repression if the client's Sun, Moon, Venus, Mars or Ascendant is involved. If the client's Mercury is involved, then the client may not be able to communicate easily with the partner. Also look at what aspects the partner's outer planets are making to the rulers of the signs on the Ascendant and the other angles.

Before one attempts to offer any advice about how to handle this type of relationship, it is crucial for the astrologer to reach an understanding with the client of why he or she got involved in the relationship in the first place. The natal aspects to planets in the client's chart that are being influenced by the partner's planets often tell the whole story.

Relationships are the proving ground for growth. We need to test our strengths and weaknesses through others before we can know if we have learned the lessons we are on this planet to learn. This doesn't mean that the astrologer should stand by idly and watch the client suffer needlessly in a tormenting relationship. The astrologer's aim should be to help the client find the hidden inner resources that will help resolve the problems that brought him or her into that relationship. Then the client can more consciously choose what direction to take. Often a single session with the client is not enough to arrive at this point. You may need to counsel the client on these problems several times before he or she feels strong enough to attack them independently with success.

How about the client who is seeking advice from you on a relationship that is not sanctioned by law? This can include adultery, bigamy, sodomy or incest. Do you know how you stand on these issues? It is a good idea to take some time to explore your own internal code of ethics and values before attempting to read a chart for anyone with these types of concerns.

What are your attitudes toward people who seek relationships out of their social or economic class or their religious, ethnic or racial group? Examine carefully your own belief systems and your own early conditioning on these matters, because they will influence your ability to help someone else handle these same concerns.

How do you feel about couples living together before marriage or living together with no intention of marrying? What do you think about homosexuality, bisexuality and transsexuality? In the past, many people did not consider these proper topics for discussion, let alone practice, but we can no longer afford to ignore these aspects of human behavior. Are you prepared to be there when your client needs you to listen and be open and offer understanding?

More and more people in their mid-teens to early twenties are seeking answers to questions through astrology. Many of these young people have had little or no experience in love and in sexual relations. The astrologer should be exceptionally cautious about stating what the young client's chart indicates about sexuality. The best rule for the astrologer to follow is to let the client reveal what's on his or her mind. Given the chance, the client will open up and ask for exactly the kind of help he or she needs. It's a good idea to have the names and addresses of some good resource places and people who can give your client sound guidance in such areas as birth control, abortion and pregnancy counseling.

Do you know how you feel about people who marry more than once? About a man being involved with a woman who is much older or younger? Or about parents who expose their children to some of the more intimate aspects of their love lives? While these are not astrological issues, they are human issues, and it is the human being who comes to the astrologer for help with these problems.

One of the realities of life is that one must be willing to give something of value in order to receive something of value, whether in relationships or in buying and selling goods or services. This fact of life means that a couple may have to give up a certain amount of freedom, time or space in order to make their relationship work. It's strange how few people are willing to acknowledge this fact. The astrologer can be of great help to the client by pointing out just what he or she must let go of or give up in order to achieve success in a relationship. The client, of course, is free to make choices, but hopefully the astrologer can help the client be more realistically informed when making those choices. Similarly, it is vital that the client not feel guilty about expecting something from the partner in return. Love doesn't occur in a vacuum. It takes two.

An astrologer can be very helpful to a client who is making a decision about a relationship by studying the transits and progressions relative to the birth chart. Transits can give valuable perspective on how temporary or permanent a relationship is likely to be, based on the influences at the time of the first meeting or acquaintance. Generally, relationships that begin under benefic aspects from transiting outer planets, including Jupiter and Saturn, to natal personal planets are of the greatest benefit in the long run and may indeed be quite long-lasting and secure. Under these transits the individual is likely to attract a partner with whom there is a strong sense of karmic destiny or fate.

Circumstances under which the individual is likely to find romance are often indicated by the houses that the transiting planets are passing through. For example, planets passing through or aspecting the ruler of the ninth house may indicate relationships opening up through travel or through being in an environment of higher learning. Similarly, influences transiting through the first house or aspecting its ruler may open up opportunities for the individual to strike up a relationship with the friend of a relative (eleventh from the third) or to discover a new romance with the relative of a friend (third from the eleventh).

One way that the astrologer can help a client who is distressed because of lack of love is by looking into the possibilities of a more favorable geographical location, where Venus would be in an angular house or where a discordant planet would be removed from the individual's seventh or fifth house. Moving to such a location might have a tremendously freeing effect upon the individual. This does not mean that the client should be encouraged to leave town or to think that moving away will solve any problems, but being in another locale may be just the change that the client needs to stimulate more open expression in love and therefore attract a satisfying relationship.

Chapter Five
Sun

The Sun in the Chart

The Sun represents your basic inner ego energies, and its position in the chart denotes your overall inner direction. Its influence is quite general, referring more to your orientation and style of life than to particular physical or mental attributes in love.

Any difficult aspects to the Sun mean that you are under a certain compulsive pressure, the effects of which depend on the nature of the planet aspected. Easy aspects, on the other hand, lend self-confidence and a feeling that you know where you are going.

Where the emphasis of the Sun by sign and house is different from that of other planets in the chart, there may be a dichotomy of inner direction and mental or social influences. For the most pleasure and reward from sexual expression, you must take into account all these factors, but in the long run the position of the Sun is likely to have a stronger effect.

Thus your eventual path of development will be fundamentally shaped by the position and aspects of the Sun, especially concerning your inner feelings about sex. However, at first your sexual attitudes will probably be determined by the accepted social norms.

Sun in Aries

Your fiery inner drive makes you the motivating force in any relationship. You tend to have so much physical and sexual energy that you can awaken all sorts of feelings in your partner, even feelings that have long been dormant.

It would be a good idea, however, to bank your fires a bit. Even though you may be overflowing with energy, your partner may tire more quickly, both physically and emotionally, which you must take into consideration. A calmer approach would be good for you personally as well, because your appetite for experience is voracious; overindulgence prevents you from savoring each valuable moment of a love affair.

It is wise to read about sexual technique or learn the ins and outs of lovemaking with a highly skilled lover, because in your eager enthusiasm, you often brush past many of the finer points of sex. You will find a wealth of pleasure in lovemaking if you slow down and linger over each step, even though your high energies are pushing you to go faster. That inner high-intensity flame can heighten the details of love if you govern it. Few people have your ability to etch every experience into your mind and body.

Sun in Taurus

You are a meat-and-potatoes person when it comes to loving, possessing both consistency and endurance. For you, love is something to be taken in good-sized portions, with enough left over for a second helping.

You are very good-hearted and generous with your lover and will go to any length to lavish favors on your partner. In return, you expect great loyalty and consistency more than physical generosity, although you do prefer a physically demonstrative partner.

You would do well to choose a lover who is emotionally adaptable, for you are not one to give in very much; when you make up your mind, it stays made up. Two stubborn people make for a contentious relationship.

The ideal partner for you would be someone who enjoys sexual variety, someone who can introduce you to new and exciting forms of lovemaking. You have a great capacity for sexual enjoyment, but it is not your usual style to initiate experiments. You'll be happier if the initiative comes from your partner.

Unlike some others, you seldom fall into the trap of jealousy, for you value your lover's feelings about you more than technical chastity or faithfulness. For this reason, you are one of the most easy-going partners a person could have.

Sun in Gemini

You have the potential for a broad variety of sexual experiences; indeed, you will not be truly satisfied if you repeat the same kind of lovemaking over and over again. This does not mean that you require a number of lovers to achieve happiness, but within one relationship you need the stimulation of change to avoid sexual boredom. It would be wise to choose a partner who enjoys experimentation or is willing to learn and to try whatever you dream up.

However, sex is not your most important form of expression. You should avoid lovers who feel, as many people do, that personal intensity in lovemaking is the indicator of success in a relationship. For you, sex is recreation more than a personal statement, and you need a partner with an equally lighthearted approach who will become involved with you in other ways as well.

It is unusually important to you that your lover be your friend, because no matter how good it is, sex alone is simply not enough. It is only one of many expressions of personal togetherness and communion that you need for a rewarding relationship. Your most fulfilling moments come when you are deeply in touch with your lover, and this does not happen in the bedroom alone.

Sun in Cancer

You tend to be self-protective in your relationships or, if you are highly motivated, you may look for just the opposite—selfless, sometimes too self-denying, emotional entanglements.

Probably you will keep your really meaningful relationships quite private, so that the outside world is unlikely to know what is really going on in your emotional life. The advantage of this is that no one can interfere in your personal affairs, but also there may be no help when you need emotional assistance or sympathy.

The physical care and well-being of your lover are very important to you, and you may be generous to the point of lavishness, although you try not to let your generosity appear too ostentatious. What you want is to have a good effect on your lover, not to put on a show for other people's recognition.

With the Sun in Cancer, you want to surround and envelop a lover, so you should find someone who is not too independent, someone who won't be annoyed by your constant small tokens of affection, which some might consider too clinging or possessive. Indeed, the physical tokens or souvenirs of a loved one may become symbolically important to you, which can spill over into a certain emotional (not physical) fetishism.

It is very important for you to balance your emotional life carefully, so that you are neither too closed off from others nor too open. You don't want your highly sensitive inner workings visible to just anyone. Your personality can be compared to the animal symbol of this sign, the crab—hard-shelled, but exceedingly tender underneath.

Sun in Leo

Leo is the sign of the lover, and the Sun here gives your personality grace, generosity and charm. You give and receive love freely, and you surround your partner with tenderness and affection.

You must be especially aware of the kinds of attentions your lover likes and dislikes. Your innate tendency is to lavish affection on your partner, which may startle or overwhelm someone who isn't used to it. You *can* give out too much of a good thing.

Do not expect your lover to return your affections in the same style. Even the deepest love can be expressed in many different ways, which you may have to search for. Few people are as open and direct as you are, so you will probably have to spend some time finding out about your partner's channels of communication.

Although you may not be the dominant partner in every relationship, your partner should give you plenty of room and not try to confine or restrict you in any way. You are a very loyal partner, as long as you are given freedom to be. You must also grant that same right to your lover and avoid possessiveness or jealousy. Loyalty comes from the heart, and you will know through feelings rather than actions if a partner is right.

Whenever you have problems in a relationship, analyze them with your feelings, not your mind. Then your inner radiance can dispel the darkest emotional clouds.

Sun in Virgo

Of all the Sun signs, Virgo is the most adept at the care and feeding of a lover. You will go to great lengths to find out and provide whatever pleases your partner.

You also put a high value on a lover who is aware of what pleases you. You must, however, make a particular attempt to let your lover know just what makes you happy, because other people are not likely to be as observant as you. What you consider neglect may just be an oversight. Don't wait for your lover to stumble accidentally on your favorite turn-on; let your tastes be known from the beginning.

You will do well to find a lover who is very meticulous about being physically loyal to you. Carrying on more than one affair at a time would be difficult for you, because you want to give each one such detailed attention. Therefore you are more comfortable with a long-term affair that gives you plenty of time to structure the relationship. For you, a partnership is like a house—the more careful the craftsmanship that goes into building it, the more enjoyable and rewarding it is to live in.

Giving and receiving gifts, particularly hand-made presents, may be a very potent expression of love for you. But do not be disappointed if your lover does not appreciate your gifts as much as you do, for not everyone is the same. Instead, find out what kind of communication your partner prefers and direct your love energies there.

Sun in Libra

What you most desire in a relationship is continual growth and development. If the modes of communication and expression between you and your lover do not change and evolve fairly continuously, you are likely to become bored with the relationship. Or you may decide to take steps to alter it yourself.

Therefore you should avoid a lover who wants to settle into a warm, comfy, secure relationship. Your desire for change will just upset such a person, and he or she will seem like a stick-in-the mud to you. Seek a more adventurous person who is always looking for new ways to make your affair more spicy and keep it in motion.

Do not be disappointed if a few relationships break up because of this urge for change—that's just part of the game. The true test of a happy relationship is whether each of you can steer the right course between evolution and stability.

If you can steer that course, you will indeed be an explorer in the realm of emotions and interpersonal communication, and you will learn a lot more than most people about what makes a relationship good or bad. Because of this knowledge, you may be able to guide your partner through the areas you understand so well. In that case you must take particular care to be subtle in your approach, especially if your lover is not one who responds easily to direction.

If you and your lover are creative and mutually responsive within your relationship, your love will be a continuously exciting adventure.

Sun in Scorpio

Of all the Sun signs, Scorpio is most closely identified with sexuality. You feel life intensely and need to express your passions in all that you do. In a love relationship you want all or nothing, and you are quick to let a partner know there is no middle ground.

Your basic drive for power is most clearly seen through your ability to manipulate others in less than obvious ways. You will be very tempted to use your sexual magnetism to gain material or psychological advantage over your lover. For this reason you may attract less sophisticated partners whose naiveté allows you to be in command. But you will soon tire of that game and look for something that is more meaningful on a long-term basis.

You usually are very clear about what you desire, and you know it is worth waiting a long time to get what will satisfy you. This can make you seem quite cold to those who want to get to know you but don't understand your secretive nature. You might explain to those people that you simply need to be alone. This small courtesy will win you much support from others, who may be able to help you.

As you mature, your interests will become more fervent in any area that you focus on. You tend to immerse yourself in an activity or an affair, then you are changed by it and finally become completely detached from it.

Sun in Sagittarius

It is very important for you to become personally involved with a lover. In the long run, casual sex will not have much interest or reward because, for you, physical sex is an expression of closeness and communication, not just the satisfaction of a physical appetite, no matter how strong that is. Therefore you are happiest if you can share intellectual interests with your partner in a lasting relationship.

Indeed, growth and continuing communication take precedence over physical relations in a partnership. You can't derive full enjoyment from sex when you are not really in touch with your lover. But when you feel personally very close to your partner, sexual desire is likely to be considerably heightened.

You should look for a partner who does not take sex too seriously, someone who thinks of it as friendly rather than a goal in itself. You don't like to be pressured into sex when your mind is on something else. You would enjoy a lover with whom you can spend a lot of time, working as well as playing together, perhaps.

The key word about your attitude toward love is *sharing*—the closer, dearer and more intimately friendly your love relationship, the happier you will be.

Sun in Capricorn

You are a very steady and reliable partner in a love relationship. When you make a commitment, you intend to stick by it. But you don't commit yourself hastily; in fact a potential lover has to persuade you that you're ready to be involved.

When you are, you want your lover to live up to all of your expectations, just as you are willing to give completely of yourself. You are not a very easygoing partner, for you are quite demanding of others as well as of yourself. Not everyone is as consistent or strong as you are, however, so try to take human foibles and weaknesses into account before judging your partner.

In fact, for long-term happiness, it would be good to seek a lover whose style and personality are quite different from yours, who will continually inject freshness and originality into the relationship. You may serve as a stabilizing factor and emotional home base for such a partner. And while you are the steadying influence, your lover may be able to draw you out and allow you greater emotional expression within the relationship.

You tend to hold in feelings that you would like to communicate, so you need a fluid and sensitive companion who can explore the depths of your personality without treading on sensitive areas that you are not yet ready to share. Despite your inner vulnerability, you must remain master of your feelings in order to artfully sculpt the relationship.

Sun in Aquarius

You are a very understanding lover, with a special ability to be helpful when a partner is having emotional difficulties. Your sympathy and tolerance of others' foibles may even appear excessive to some people. But you do draw the line in what you will put up with, and when a partner goes past that point, he or she will find it very difficult to get back into your good graces.

You can enjoy a wide variety of sexual experiences, and if you limit yourself to one partner, that person should enjoy lovemaking as a continuously changing adventure, not just as a series of repetitions, however affectionate.

You are not the type to be tied down intellectually or emotionally, so you must have a partner who respects your freedom, and that respect will bring you closer to your lover. True freedom and equality bring a closeness, a mingling of mind and body that can't be attained in any other way.

Achieving the kind of communication you want requires contact on many levels with your partner, so a close relationship will develop slowly. Once established, it will last a long time and be strong enough to withstand the heaviest assaults.

Although you find sex by itself naturally satisfying, you are quite capable of carrying on a love affair without any sexual contact at all. You can transmit the same deep and loving communion through other channels of expression, and that is the essence of an affair for you.

Sun in Pisces

Of all the Sun signs, Pisces is the most empathic and psychically attuned to a lover. For love of a dear friend or partner, you will make any sacrifice.

But you must be careful to set limits on how far you will go in helping or cooperating with your lover, for you may find that you are being used as a doormat. Make a special effort to determine the limits of your partner's personality as well as your own, for with your naturally psychic and empathic talents, you may blend with your partner so much that you lose your grasp on yourself.

You tend to idealize love and your lover, and the importance of unity with him or her may outweigh sexual or intellectual communication. You should look for a partner whose feet are really on the ground, who will provide a firm base from which to launch your love. Sexually, you usually find that your partner's style of loving suits you fine. For you, sex is a vehicle to your lover's soul rather than an end in itself. You are quite capable of carrying on an extended platonic relationship.

In a well-balanced relationship you can be quite consumed by love, and the totality of loving is an experience that transforms and uplifts your personality.

Sun in the First House

This position indicates that you are a person who stands out in a crowd. At any social gathering, you have the first choice of potential partners. Because of this outstanding quality, you don't need to strive to make a stronger impression when you encounter someone who is attractive to you. In fact, that might work against you, because you would probably seem rather overwhelming. Better to relax and let your naturally magnetic presence do the work for you.

You tend to be quite direct and honest in your approach to people, and you don't bother to beat about the bush with a potential lover. Elaborate courting is not your game. Because of your honesty, your love affairs begin and end quite abruptly, as you have no desire to continue a relationship that is no longer working well.

You tend to dominate your partner, simply because you're the first one to make a move in most situations. Here you must be particularly careful of your lover's feelings, for you may cause emotional harm without intending to; you must make an extra effort to see that you both have equal expression within the relationship.

The main advantage of this position is that it indicates a strong, forceful personality. But you must use that power carefully in your love relationships.

Sun in the Second House

Your style of loving is very concrete, and you go out of your way to give your lover tangible evidence of your affections. A few words of love are not enough without a gift to back them up. You also particularly treasure any tokens of love that your partner gives you, for they represent an assurance that the relationship is thriving.

Similarly, the highest values you seek in a lover are faithfulness and loyalty, qualities you are most willing to demonstrate once you have chosen the person you feel is just right for you.

But you don't take a lover hastily; in fact, it takes you quite a while to really settle into a relationship. Once that is done, you are a model of steadfastness and often are the main source of stability in the union. Remember, however, that your partner may not be quite so settled and may require more freedom while still remaining true to you. Therefore, you should try to be more tolerant with your love than you would be with yourself and avoid letting feelings of jealousy hurt your relationship.

83

Whatever the twists and turns of fate, your perseverance can pull a relationship through its most difficult hours to achieve the goal that you consider most important—a solid, enduring union of souls.

Sun in the Third House

Most people need the physical presence of their partner in order to carry on a love affair, but you are quite capable of conducting an affair at a distance—over the phone, by mail or tape correspondence. You are able to do this because of your enhanced ability to transmit love through images and ideas.

You have a more vivid imagination and greater potential for sexual fantasy than most, which in this very verbal age is a great advantage. You can put into words the usually vague but powerful feelings in love, which if unexpressed often disrupt a relationship.

For this reason, you would do well to choose a partner who is fairly open and not afraid to talk about sex. By frankly discussing your likes, dislikes and fantasies, you will be able to achieve a much fuller sex life. Only the attitudes and feelings that are left unexpressed will get in your way.

It would be a good idea to read extensively about sex, for the more information you gather, the better lover you will become. To many, reading books about sex puts the subject in a cold, intellectual light, but to you it just paints in the colorful details so you can understand it better. Because of this, sex is a subject that will never become boring, as long as you have a partner to communicate with.

Sun in the Fourth House

You express your love as much through the surroundings you create as through physical sexuality. Thus your actual lovemaking at the end of a long evening is no more important than the carefully prepared food, entertainment and good company that lead up to it.

For this reason you will generally take a lover only after the two of you have become fast friends. A sudden, mad affair with a stranger is too unsettling and leaves you quite unfulfilled, even though it might be the height of excitement for someone else. You require a fuller relationship to get true satisfaction from the sexual experience.

You are much more at ease when you can make love in familiar surroundings that you can control. This may be partly because of some natural insecurity, but it is just as much because giving love includes much more than the physical act for you. You can express yourself more fully when you have a full range of familiar means at your disposal.

Therefore, you would be wise to look for a lover whose idea of a good time is an intimate evening at home rather than someone who likes to paint the town red. Indeed, by following a pre-established ritual leading to physical love, you both can reach the limits of the sexual experience. Such a technique is outlined specifically in Tantric yoga, which would be well worth your while to investigate.

Sun in the Fifth House

This position indicates that you have a healthy, open attitude toward sex, that you are able to integrate the sexual experience in a creative fashion. For you, lovemaking is a positive and enjoyable form of recreation.

You should feel quite free to engage in almost any kind of sexual exploration or experimentation, as your naturally joyful attitude will turn each encounter into fun and surprises, even where others have to be more wary.

You do not sharply separate your love life from the rest of your pursuits, and much of the same pleasure you derive from sex you also get from other forms of recreation and social contact. Any creative activity in which you have developed talent, such as music, dancing, painting or photography, can provide the same kind of happy satisfaction that sex does. Because of this attitude, you are generally free of the sexual hangups and fixations that others are often afflicted with.

Because of your sunny nature, you should choose an outgoing partner who will accompany you without hesitation wherever the urge leads you. Your lover should be as much a free spirit as you, if you are to make the best use of your personal and sexual creativity. As long as you give yourself plenty of room, sex will always be a source of, happiness and joy.

Sun in the Sixth House

For your most successful sexual development, a love affair should have a definite framework—a set of reference points that tells you where you stand at all times. Thus you are better off with one steady partner than trying to play the field. Your strength in personal affairs is your ability to build a solid, enduring relationship.

Friendship with a lover is very important to you, and without it the most passionate night will seem somehow empty. Loyalty and comradeship are more important to you than skilled bedroom technique; they are the irreplaceable qualities that you require for a fully satisfying relationship.

For this reason, it would not be wise to seek a partner who is the outgoing, constantly-in-motion life of the party, even though you may be attracted to such a person. You would be better off to look for a more subdued person whose personality will mature along with yours, whose development will be intimately linked with yours.

If there is any problem with this position, it is that you may occasionally get into a rut in terms of sex, so that you become bored with the whole subject. In that case it is a good idea to try something unusual as a sort of vacation from the daily routine. Then, when you return to your everyday habits, you'll feel renewed and closer to your lover.

Sun in the Seventh House

With this position, it is most important to choose a partner who can be your equal in all ways, because you are inclined to be quite dependent on him or her.

This position is ideal for becoming involved with another person at all levels. Unless a lover evolves into a friend, business partner or close companion in some way, you are likely to lose interest. Anything less than a full relationship tends to become wearisome or to fall apart from inattention.

Marriage in and of itself may or may not be important to you, but a strong personal partnership is essential and means more than any legal contract. You should choose your partner very carefully, for you are likely to be very dependent on him or her, particularly when the chips are down. Similarly, your lover must be able to rely on you fully; the relationship must be entirely mutual if it is to sustain itself.

This should come quite naturally, because relationships are generally the primary focus of your life. Indeed, much of your reputation is based on your ability to get along well with others and your desirability in a relationship.

Sun in the Eighth House

This position gives sexuality a very physical form and makes tangible intimacy very important to you. Words are no substitute for a touch, you feel, and you learn more about your partner in a brief embrace than in a lengthy conversation. Every breath and movement has a connotation, and you should rely on your gut-level feelings about a relationship rather than on intellectual observations.

Because of your talent for intuition, you may have considerable subliminal power over others, so that you can control them without their knowledge. You must always be careful to use this "animal magnetism," which may be more or less psychic, in ways that do not take undue advantage of your partner or that get you into needless power games. If you feel inclined to control your partner too much, bring it into the open and express it perhaps in more unusual bedroom play. In that way it can bring joy and benefit to both of you. Control should be exercised in a relationship only if both partners are aware of what's happening and willing.

You may be attracted to a lover who is considerably older or younger than yourself, a situation in which one partner is a good deal more experienced and teaches the other. Such an affair can be particularly rewarding and often more intense than any other kind, as long as each person retains individual integrity and equality. But no matter who you are involved with, intensity is your key word.

Sun in the Ninth House

Your sexual energies are vigorous and enthusiastic, and in a love affair you are likely to put the highest value on spiritedness. You tend to be bored by considerations of intricate sexual technique, but you can get quite involved in thinking up new general approaches to lovemaking. The setting for love affects your mood, but you don't like pretentiousness. The more naturally it happens, the better.

You would do well to choose an energetic partner who can also take care of the details you may overlook, such as contraceptives or locking the bedroom door. In your enthusiasm, you tend to forget such details, so it helps to have a practical partner.

You have an innately loving and gentle, almost parental approach to sex. You may be most happy with a younger partner, someone who will respond to tenderness as much as passion and who can also match your abundant energies.

When you and your lover encounter problems, usually you can reach the heart of the matter and come up with a solution. Your vision encompasses the essentials of any relationship, and you always have your finger on the pulse of what's happening.

Sun in the Tenth House

Probably you will find people to become personally involved with at your place of work rather than at a social gathering. You prefer the company of others like yourself who are striving to achieve professional goals.

Whether or not you deserve it, you probably have quite a reputation as a good lover, because others tend to believe only the best that they hear about you. This is obviously an advantage, and it will help you in your business life as well as in your personal dealings by enhancing your ability to influence people in all situations. The only problem is that it may be difficult to live up to others' fantasy image of you when you are put to the test.

Your career or daily routine may use up all of your energies, leaving you drained by the end of the day. Therefore it would be wise to keep weeknights for yourself, reserving weekends and holidays for entertaining a lover; then you can put your full self into it. Otherwise you may find that your business life is always in conflict with your love life, and both areas suffer. As far as timing goes, it is best to separate them as much as possible.

With that problem solved, you will be able to follow your natural urge to throw yourself totally into whatever you're doing, without having to reserve any energy for other activities.

Sun in the Eleventh House

You have a natural desire and ability to turn yourself into an eminently desirable partner for almost anyone you meet. As a result, you will have to carefully weed out many casual acquaintances from among the friends who truly love you.

Socially, you tend to be quite upwardly mobile and quite successful in finding others who live up to your high social standards. This ability can bring you great success and even wealth, but you must be careful not to leave old and faithful friends by the wayside. In the end, it is they who will stand by you and mean the most in your life.

In general you are a good influence on your lovers, causing them to dress better and take better care of themselves than before you became involved with them. This is true also of your environment, which you tend to rearrange and improve.

Since your social life is quite important to you, try to avoid the lone wolf or wallflower type of lover. You're much better off with a partner who likes to be right in the middle of the crowd with you. The more involved you are externally, the more fertile and happy your personal involvements will be, each one stimulating the others and propelling you along an upward spiral.

Sun in the Twelfth House

The Sun is the most important astrological factor as far as the personality is concerned. In this position it indicates that you have a strong sense of privacy and individualty. It is, indeed, the antithesis of the popular philosophy of letting all your problems hang out in public.

You disclose your inner feelings only in the most intimate circumstances and only to those whom you feel are your closest friends. Such openness is, in fact, the highest honor and token of love that you can bestow upon a friend or lover, although they will not always recognize that fact.

Because of your natural reticence, you don't actively seek new relationships, but rather tend to wait for others to seek you out, waiting for signs of true interest and worthy intent. This does not preclude an active and enjoyable social life, but for a truly intimate affair, you feel that "all things come to him who waits," which they do.

Others may see your personal life as quite mysterious, attracting speculation about behind-closed-doors affairs. They will seldom be able to accurately assess your private life, but the very mystery will make you seem more attractive and desirable. This effect is seldom intended, because all you want is privacy, but the results can be quite beneficial.

Sun Conjunct Moon

This position indicates that you can throw yourself wholeheartedly into an affair with no reservations or second thoughts. Once you have made up your mind, you will stick with your decision for better or worse. Naturally, this makes you the truest and most loyal of lovers in a solid and creative relationship, without any suspicion or jealousy of your partner.

But if you get involved in a less than satisfactory affair, you are likely to prolong it unduly, even after all real feeling is gone. Finally you will drop it as suddenly and decisively as you began it.

This position makes you intensely emotional, to the point that you may be somewhat manic depressive. When you are happy and in love, the world is paradise, but when you are rejected by a lover or breaking up an affair, it is as bleak as hell.

Therefore you would do well to seek out an even-tempered partner who can have a stabilizing and supportive influence on you. This position gives the emotional qualities of genius, but you tend to lack everyday common sense when swept away by your intensity. You would find a partner of similar intensity exhilarating, but that kind of relationship would very likely burn itself out. The key to this position is to use its high energy without being overcome by it.

Sun Sextile Moon

You are likely to have a relatively even temperament, so that you take everything in stride in a relationship without becoming upset over minor problems. For this reason, you are able to get along with a more volatile or unpredictable lover without getting into arguments or difficulties.

Indeed, you may be happiest with such a partner, someone who can be a continually stimulating influence and provide experiences that you might not otherwise have, through lack of interest or opportunity. A fairly active partner can be a source of sexual and emotional growth who gets you moving when your pace slows down.

Although you may be the main source of stability or patience within a relationship, do not let your lover use you as a doormat because of your easygoing tolerance. You must assert your own rights within a relationship even when the subject does not seem worth the effort. Otherwise your personal boundaries will gradually erode, leading to an imbalance within the relationship that may be difficult to correct.

In general, however, you prefer a relatively peaceful relationship in which growth comes in easy stages and tensions do not run high. If there is stress or tumult, you are likely to go around it rather than make changes through confrontation.

Sun Square Moon

Your inner dissatisfaction continually motivates you to higher levels of achievement; each accomplishment must be better than the last to be worthwhile in your own eyes.

The fact is, you probably do not give yourself as much credit as you deserve. You find it difficult to relax and really enjoy the benefits of your work. For this reason, you may doubt that you can really please your lover and give him or her sexual and emotional satisfaction.

In this area you must simply rely on your lover to tell you honestly whether or not he or she desires more than you are giving, for you are not a very accurate judge yourself. But when you are reassured that all is well, try to set aside your self-doubts, for they will only lessen your own and your lover's enjoyment.

Because of your continual efforts to do better and provide more, you will probably be one of the best and most experienced of lovers. Although you may always strive for improvement and imagine a better future, do not let that prevent you from enjoying the fruits of your loving in the present.

Sun Trine Moon

Your resilient personality is basically in tune, which gives you a flair for both luck and timing in love relationships.

Although you have an innate ability to take things in stride and make your projects come out right, try not to take your success for granted. If you do, you may miss some golden opportunities that would have been worth the extra time and emotion in order to develop a long-term relationship.

Since you have more internal stability than many people, you can deal more easily with a partner who needs a lot of emotional support. In fact, you may find such a relationship unusually rewarding. Your even style can be very soothing to a lover whose mood swings are more pronounced, and such a partner can bring you to emotional peaks that you might not normally experience.

In general, your love relationships grow steadily and are not so subject to sudden ups and downs as those of other people. This good fortune will be considerably extended if you become actively involved in the lives of others. The growth that can be provided by less even-tempered people will broaden your experience and deepen your emotional qualities.

Sun Inconjunct Moon

You are highly motivated in your personal involvements. Emotionally, you are not inclined to keep still, and you tend to create a lot of motion and instigate change in people to whom you become close. Each new situation suggests new steps along the path of love experience.

Because of this quality, you will develop a wide range of talents in love. But at the same time, you may also move from one involvement to the next without getting as much as possible from each one. Or, you may not tarry long enough with each aspect of a relationship to bring it completely to blossom.

For this reason, you will be most happy with a less energetic lover who can slow you down and stabilize you, so that you won't miss out on the lingering long-term benefits of love. To a certain extent such a partner can complete the emotional directions that you begin, filling in your originality with substance and loyalty.

If your partner does not have that ability, you may have to make an extra effort to be patient and slow down somewhat. By going back over already covered ground and repeating previous experiences, you may find there is much pleasure still to be developed before moving on to something new.

Sun Opposition Moon

As a person born under a full Moon, you partake of some of the qualities that the full Moon is supposed to represent. You are inclined to have wide mood swings and to get involved in something either with total enthusiasm or not at all. Your reactions are not usually in between.

Thus, in a love affair you tend to go to emotional extremes, to be alternately in heaven and in hell, depending upon the circumstances of the moment. You may find that your moods are particularly changeable during the full Moon and sometimes the new Moon, for that is a time when everyone's emotions run high.

Ideally, you should find a more even-tempered partner who can absorb some of your emotional peaks and derive energy and pleasure from doing so. This kind of balance will make your love affair much more enjoyable, and your partner will give you support when you need it.

When you are not involved in a relationship, you can handle your emotions better by making a graph of when your ups and downs occur. In that way you can anticipate your moods better. This will also help in an ongoing relationship that is under stress and needs to be calmed down so that you can make more emotional progress.

Sun Conjunct Mercury

You have a good ability to make plans and to take the direction in which you want to go. Thus, in a love affair you usually can explain and clarify your goals and desires to your lover quite accurately, so that he or she really understands.

However, your understanding of your lover's needs may be colored by your own desires, so that you misinterpret some rather clear cues about how your lover wants to be treated.

It is a good idea to tell your partner that you tend to misinterpret signals, so that he or she will make things extra clear when there seems to be a misunderstanding. You can profit greatly from seeing yourself from your lover's point of view and making adjustments accordingly.

Your own style of expression is to speak from the heart. It may be difficult and certainly counterproductive to pretend, for you have little talent for that art. You will be most comfortable with a partner who appreciates your directness, someone with whom you do not have to be roundabout or diplomatic in order not to hurt his or her feelings. Expressing your thoughts directly and quite thoroughly to your lover is important in your relationship.

Sun Conjunct Venus

You probably have a high degree of self-esteem and can provide much of what is desired in a relationship. Because you are less demanding than many, you may be much in demand as a lover.

With your effortless, natural charm, you stand out in contrast to those who must struggle to make themselves attractive. Because of this quality, people may be jealous of you, so you would do well to be especially modest and offer to take a back seat now and then.

You are capable of expansive desire and can receive generous amounts of loving without tiring or finding that it cloys. For this reason you may be able to entertain several love relationships at the same time without being physically or emotionally exhausted. You can handle your lovers so diplomatically and gracefully that each one feels that he or she is getting enough attention, and jealousy does not arise. If there is a problem in this situation, it is usually caused by someone who would like to be involved with you but cannot be.

It would be a good idea to rest occasionally from sexual activity. If your sexual expression is too constant and regular, you may take it for granted or become desensitized.

Sun Conjunct Mars

You have great energy, and when you launch yourself into an activity, you do so with a great deal of physical energy. So when you are involved in a love relationship, you make a large commitment of effort, at least as others see it.

However it may be a good idea to bank your fires a bit for several reasons: first, to avoid running out of energy in an affair by using it all at the beginning and, second, to avoid imbalancing the relationship if your lover cannot match your physical intensity.

At the same time, your lover will be able to lean on you for support; when both of you are under stress, you can endure and go the extra mile. This ability will be improved if you attempt to regulate your flow of energy and avoid the temptation to use all your energy at once.

Along this same line, you may be rather impulsive in love as well as in other areas. Although this trait may work against you at times, particularly in financial affairs, in love it will give you an unusual and special enthusiasm and spontaneity, which your partner will surely cherish, because you can throw yourself wholeheartedly into love at a moment's notice.

Sun Sextile Mars

You probably have a rather even flow of energy, and once you begin an activity, you work at it more steadily and consistently than many others. Because of this, you are an especially dependable lover, particularly in physical stamina, and you are capable of fairly lengthy sessions of lovemaking.

However, you are not likely to be too demanding in lovemaking but will abide by your lover's physical limits, for you are quite adaptable. For this reason, you should let your lover know that he or she should signal you when to begin or end your lovemaking. By clearly defining the situation, you will not let it trail on meaninglessly for lack of communication.

You have plenty of energy in reserve, but you are not likely to use it except when motivated by an active partner who draws out your capabilities. Therefore, you would be happiest with a fairly demanding lover who can bring you up to your highest level of ability; otherwise, you might not make the effort.

Once activated, you are capable of expending strong physical and emotional energies that are even and dependable. Your lover may rely upon you in love as well as in other areas of life.

Sun Square Mars

You may have some difficulty in properly expressing your energies. As a result, they may build up to an uncomfortable level or find release at times or in areas that you have not deliberately chosen.

Pent-up energies can also add fuel to repressed anger and frustration, which may then overflow at inappropriate times or in situations that are not really that important. You will be most comfortable with a lover who understands this problem and can absorb or defuse these energies.

However, you have a unique kind of spontaneity, and you may initiate and enjoy love at unexpected times and places. This can add a great deal of fun to your love life if your partner is willing to make love into an adventure and if you temper your spontaneity with a modicum of wisdom.

As you grow, your abilities and, particularly, your endurance in love will probably increase significantly. You may find that the areas in which you felt insecure in early youth will become strong points with increasing age and experience. This will happen, in part, because of your ability to amass a great amount of energy in order to solve a problem. Also, practice brings perfection, and experience brings confidence in personal relationships and sexuality.

Sun Trine Mars

You have a strong, easy flow of energy and a low-key approach to life. Your lover can rely on you, for you are not subject to many ups and downs in the physical side of a relationship. For this reason, you can handle a partner who is much more irregular. Indeed, such a lover would be quite stimulating, arousing dormant energies in you that would not normally be explored. You can be especially supportive to a person whose moods are less steady by helping to even out his or her personality style.

Although you are most content with regular sexual expression, periods of abstinence are less difficult for you than for most people, because you can quite easily transfer your sexual energies into other areas.

However, you may get into a habit of expressing your energies in other ways; then, when it comes to actively seeking a partner or finding expression with your current lover, you tend to be lazy or indolent. To this extent, you need a lover who can motivate you and not wait for you to make the first move.

Once motivated, you have considerable stamina in love and are more than willing to go along with your lover's plans or with whatever develops.

Sun Inconjunct Mars

Your sexual nature is highly active and restless, seeking expression consistently and sometimes without letup. It isn't that you have such a powerful sex drive, but that you have an inner urge to develop your style and experience in loving.

Because of this drive, you will probably become an expert lover. You may have a number of important relationships in your life that differ greatly in style and content. It may be that you are always dissatisfied with the status quo, so that you are always looking for newer, more and better forms of sexual expression.

In your search for excellence in loving you will achieve the best, although lovers who do not live up to your standards may be disappointed. But avoid seeking new experiences merely for the sake of novelty or because you are unable to sit still emotionally.

In this respect you may be most content with a lover who is willing to explore with you but who also has a calming effect, someone who can absorb the energies you emit that might lead to unnecessary or harmful changes. When these energies are channeled creatively within the relationship, they will bring you continuing sexual achievement. On the other hand, if you turn them toward outside encounters, you are likely to damage the mutual affection and trust between you and your partner.

Sun Opposition Mars

You release your sexual energy intermittently in rather unpredictable cycles that may swing from frantic activity to total inactivity. This will enable you to reach special peaks of enjoyment, but there will also be times when you don't feel up to any expression at all.

For this reason, you may be happiest with an even more energetic partner who can moderate your own energy swings, someone with patience and understanding, who will not be disappointed or demanding when your energies are at a low point.

When you are riding high, your partner should be able to equal your level of emotion, drawing on your energies if necessary.

You may tend to rush into an affair without much forethought and then have grave misgivings afterward. In most cases, both your actions and your subsequent harsh judgment of them may be rather extreme. You would do well to be less disapproving of yourself, as well as more cautious. A more conservative partner will be helpful in this regard and will help you bear up in times of emotional difficulty or self-doubt. Also, these problems will tend to diminish as you get older.

Sun Conjunct Jupiter

You have an expansive nature, and you tend to get involved in any activity, including love, in a big way. Generally you are quite generous, and in a love affair you enjoy showering your lover with gifts.

Naturally, this can become quite expensive if you are not careful. However, you don't need to express your generosity through material gifts that may be beyond your means. It is enough to be generous with your attentions to your lover.

In the mundane financial aspects of an affair you need a more thrifty partner who can keep you from occasional inappropriate extravagances. Also if you can find someone who will take care of the details of your life together, you will be saved lots of trouble, for your talents are not likely to lie in that direction.

Similarly, you are less fascinated by the details of love than by its overall feeling. Be sure that you do not neglect your lover's specific needs, for you may tend to overlook them. If there is any question about this, simply ask, and then take whatever steps are necessary to correct the oversight. Tell your lover to ask or remind you, if you do overlook some special need.

Sun Sextile Jupiter

You probably have a good sense of judgment about entering new relationships or expending time and energy on a love commitment. You are not likely to overcommit yourself or spend too much money or effort on a relationship that will not pay off emotionally.

In a successful ongoing affair, you tend to be quite even in your approach to new developments. You avoid making too many changes too quickly, which will generally result in stable, long-lasting involvements, particularly if your partner is similarly inclined.

However, because you are so steady, you may find that as time goes on, love is not as exciting as it once was. You may need to force yourself to break out of the mold and be a bit more daring in order to stimulate new emotional growth within an affair. This is a healthy step in your emotional development, although it may make waves within a relationship at first. However, the end result will be real progress in your mutual emotional evolution. Also it will revive the sexual side of the relationship as well. Either you or your partner may initiate these moves, but the result in either case will be an enlivened relationship.

Sun Square Jupiter

In a love relationship you tend to do either too much or not enough. In the long run, you would do well to find a partner with a steadying hand who can let you know when you seem to be going over the edge.

At the same time, you have the ability to take huge risks and make great leaps in a love affair, which can be most enjoyable and exciting. But if you keep this practice up too long or apply it too often, you may accidentally get into trouble with your partner as well as with others around you.

Much of your difficulty in this respect results from crossed communication rather than from lack of judgment. Therefore you should check with your lover about his or her needs, desires and dislikes before making a major move. This extra care will help make your movements more effective and keep you from overstepping boundaries that you are not really aware of.

You should let your partner know about your impetuous tendencies, so that he or she can pay extra attention to making needs clear. In that way you won't be drawn into situations that would be counterproductive to your mutual enjoyment. Mutual communication will enable you both to enter new areas of love together, rather than one partner being swept along, perhaps unwillingly, by the other.

Sun Trine Jupiter

You have a very solid sense of judgment about how an affair is progressing, particularly if you are the one who initiates the changes. You make your moves at the right time, and in most instances, you will be rewarded for doing so.

Because of this talent, you may enjoy guiding a partner who lacks your keen judgment or at least needs direction about when to make changes in the relationship. In that case, however, you should make sure that your partner wants your advice and doesn't consider it an infringement on his or her private rights of decision.

However, you may let your steadiness and stability inhibit you from trying something stimulating and experimental from time to time. Therefore you may be happiest with a partner who can occasionally inspire you to action and instigate emotional or sexual investigation. Even if that goes against your better judgment at first, in the long run it will provide a special stimulus to growth within the relationship.

You must trust your lover and occasionally be willing to make a leap into space. Then be careful to reserve judgment and not blame your partner if it doesn't work out. If it is successful, you both will be happier.

Sun Inconjunct Jupiter

You may be rather restless in a relationship, needing continual innovations or wanting new involvements all the time. This may be expressed as a desire for change and improvement, or it may manifest as a general dissatisfaction with each relationship.

The only problem to watch for is that you may needlessly change your partner or your style in love before you have gotten the most benefit from what you already have. This sort of compulsive erotic shopping around can waste your emotional and physical potential as well as that of your partners.

Of course, continual improvement in the quality and variety of a relationship is both desirable and beneficial, but it should be done with careful forethought, not simply because of a desire for change.

You tend to be a rather demanding lover, and you need a partner who is willing to go the limit with you. As long as you are motivated by a desire for the finest and most rewarding love experiences, you both will be able to reach unique heights of emotional and sexual enjoyment, which will be a focus of others' admiration.

Sun Opposition Jupiter

Although you may be a most inventive and enthusiastic lover at times, probably your sexual inspiration comes in fits and starts rather than in an even flow.

When your feelings are particularly strong, you may go to emotional extremes in a relationship; but when you are not filled with emotion, you may neglect to put sufficient energy into changing and developing as needed.

Thus you need a partner who understands your swings of creativity, who can keep you from overexerting yourself or existing in a creative vacuum.

At the same time, your lover should be willing to try out some of your more extreme or far-out ideas. You both may reach new heights of enjoyment or understanding in this way, and to deny or censor your wildest ideas would destroy your native creativity and expression in the future.

Although balance is important in sustaining a long-term relationship, one of your special talents is the very topsy-turvy creativity of imbalance. You should not neglect this or fail to mine its possibilities so that you and your partner will derive the most potential excitement from your relationship.

Sun Conjunct Saturn

Because you take life fairly seriously, you have a special capacity for intensity in love. You are not likely to enter into a love relationship frivolously, and once committed to a partner, you hold fast with considerable loyalty and tenacity.

However, you may consider an affair very important and special, while your partner is looking only for enjoyment and amusement. Thus you must be very sure that your lover is at the same level of involvement, so that you can avoid unintentional emotional injury.

You may be happiest with a lover who is a little less serious than you, who can shine a light of cheerfulness and merriment when you are feeling down. At the same time, you can be a stabilizing influence on a more lighthearted partner, so that each of you can help the other.

If a love affair does not work out, you should take care to avoid bitterness or harsh words. Such feelings will only prevent you from becoming involved with another lover and will hurt both you and your former partner. Better to part ways with a sad smile and move on to something new.

Sun Sextile Saturn

You are likely to be fairly stable in your approach to love, and you don't usually get in over your head emotionally. Because of your stability, you may enjoy a partner who is much more volatile and less sure-footed. At the same time you can serve as a stabilizing influence on such a lover and on the relationship itself. In return your lover can spark your interest when you have intervals of emotional laziness.

You could also be quite happy in a relaxed, low-keyed relationship, but you must resist the temptation to let the situation drift. You tend to avoid changes that may be stimulating, simply because they are too much trouble. In a quiet relationship you should make a special effort to introduce new elements from time to time for the sake of variety. Otherwise the affair may become unalterably sluggish and peter out from lack of regenerative change and growth.

You have a healthy self-image, which will help you handle yourself in approaching an affair or making advances to a prospective partner. Be sure to tone down your self-confidence with modesty, however, for others may not be so secure, and you do not wish to seem superior in this respect.

Sun Square Saturn

You may have a problem with your self-image, not giving yourself enough credit where it is due. This is likely to deprive you of self-confidence, which most people are attracted to in a partner.

You should meticulously list your strong points and accomplishments for yourself so that you will understand your abilities and achievements and not needlessly downgrade yourself. This will allow you to enter an affair in a more positive frame of mind about yourself as well as your partner. Often, a negative attitude is transferred to your lover, making you overdemanding or critical of the progress of the affair.

If there is any question of quality in an issue between you and your lover, always take a bright and optimistic attitude, even if it is forced. Such a positive posture can actually move the relationship in a better direction by opening up all the possible options, which might otherwise be subconsciously closed off.

Whereas others tend to rush into some aspects of love rashly and unwisely, you are more cautious. You should probably try to be as free as possible. Follow your whims and fancies about styles of sexual expression, and give yourself plenty of room to explore without inhibition or worry.

Sun Trine Saturn

You understand yourself well and have a very stable self-image. This allows you to keep both feet on the ground even in times of stress, with which you can deal firmly and unexcitedly. You are a very reliable partner, and you will be happiest in a long-term relationship.

Since you are quite down to earth and dependable, you can help stabilize a more flighty or unpredictable lover, even providing a shoulder to lean or cry on in times of need. At the same time, such a partner can be a major motivating factor for you and keep you from getting into an emotional rut, which may otherwise happen at times.

Although you are not likely to be sexually experimental, it is a good idea to introduce new ideas into any relationship. After you've tried something new, it will become more and more enjoyable as you get used to it. Even if it isn't spectacular the first time, it may be worth repeating the experiment. With your personality, experiences grow on you slowly rather than developing suddenly. If you pursue your pleasures with patience and tenacity, they will flower. Let your partner take the lead, with you following along until you see how it develops. Techniques that seem like a bother at first can bring the most pleasure once you get the hang of it.

Sun Inconjunct Saturn

You must make every effort to keep from being overly critical of your own or your lover's efforts, even though you are working strictly to improve and refine the relationship. You have a sharp eye for perfection, and what is a simple improvement to you may seem to your partner like strong criticism.

When you do make changes in a love affair, it is best to do it by actions rather than by words. This will demonstrate the benefits of making a change without having to be negative about your earlier situation. This is also a good tactic if you believe that a change should not be made; simply make your case by showing how good the present situation is, without verbalizing your disagreement.

Indeed, you should make a special effort to appreciate and enjoy the achievements that have already been made in your relationship. Try not to shift around too much from a belief that you must continually make improvements. Love will not go sour merely because of lack of innovation. If you can learn to relax and enjoy love without self-criticism, the needed changes will probably occur spontaneously without any extra push from either you or your partner. A love relationship tends to have a life of its own that goes beyond what the two of you contribute.

Sun Opposition Saturn

You may be subject to wide swings of feeling about your progress in love, so that sometimes you feel very confident, and other times you are overly self-critical. Neither peak of feeling is realistic, though there may be some truth in your reaction. You should try to pursue a middle course in your judgment in love.

An understanding and supportive partner can help even out your moods and stabilize your self-image. He or she can provide a mirror of your feelings that you can rely on.

In this respect it may be useful to discuss your opinions and verbally analyze your situation, for unexpressed thoughts more easily run to extremes than do ideas that are set down in words. When you have feelings of self-doubt, talk them out with your lover. Don't make hasty negative assumptions about the quality of your affair, until you both have thoroughly examined whether your criticisms are really true.

In this way you will avoid getting into a superficial affair too deeply or taking too lightly a potentially deep and long-lasting relationship. A carefully thought-out, even approach to love will spare you unnecessary emotional pitfalls.

Sun Conjunct Uranus

You may find that you particularly enjoy sudden and spontaneous affairs that tend to be extreme. In fact, you seek them out. In general, your style is unique and rather demanding of any partner who tries to keep up with you.

To a certain extent, you should temper your desire, so that your approach is more in line with that of your lover. Otherwise your relationship may burn itself out before it has had a chance to develop.

You may have a special taste for anything new and unusual in love. With proper precautions, that approach can result in a very intense love life, but you should be sure to take into account your lover's needs and possible inhibitions. Your partner may not be quite so eager to experiment and try out the new, so you may have to introduce innovations more gradually, in order to make your lover comfortable. In that way you both will enjoy what happens.

You may prefer a lover who tempers your sometimes rash decisions, someone who serves as a steady focus to which you can always return. From that perspective you can judge the quality and extent of your own accomplishments. Such a partner will be able to handle the on-and-off, all-or-nothing quality of your love and make your affections flow more evenly.

Sun Sextile Uranus

Probably you require a continual succession of new thoughts and inspirations to make a love affair interesting and enjoyable. Your ability to come up with new ideas makes you a very creative lover who always has something special to please your partner.

You are probably happiest with a partner who can match your flow of sexual inspiration, moving in step with you to develop the direction of your relationship. However, you are quite capable of pleasing and getting along with a less inspired partner to whom you are a spark of originality and creativity. A lover like that would learn a great deal from you, but depending on other factors in your personality, being the only one who adds new material to the relationship may be too much of a burden.

On the other hand, you can enjoy a lover who is even more active and original than you, but only in fits and starts. You have the ability to fill in the gaps as well as enjoy the peaks of love when they occur. This kind of symbiotic relationship may be tumultuous at times, but it can provide deeper insights into love than a more even and predictable affair.

Sun Square Uranus

Your patterns of desire may be somewhat erratic, and your sexual interests and style may fluctuate considerably. Because of this characteristic, you may have timing problems with a partner who isn't on the same wavelength at the same time.

It is a good idea to be as adaptable as possible and to follow your lover's lead if there is any confusion, for it will not be as easy for him or her to follow you. In any case, you should have a rather flexible lover who can match your style and intensity at any level.

Although you may tend to rush headlong into an affair that looks good, make a point of stepping back and investigating where you're going before making a final commitment. Decisions made in haste are more likely to work against you than those that are well-thought-out, so you should be very cautious.

Inspiration and original ideas in sexuality come to most people in flashes beyond their control. You, on the other hand, can take control of this function through work and exploration and devise new directions that will be quite successful when you try them out. This will require considerable effort and study of sexuality, however. You must know the subject thoroughly before you can exercise your creativity and express your energies with evenness and control.

Sun Trine Uranus

Inventiveness and originality in love come naturally to you without great effort. You tend to move easily from one step to another in the growth of a relationship, accepting changes effortlessly and comfortably.

Take care to remember, however, that your lover may not be able to do this. Some physical or emotional changes in a relationship may be much easier for you than for your partner, so at those times you must be particularly supportive and understanding.

In general, you may have a better sense of timing than your lover, but try not to emphasize that, for your partner may resent it. It is better to help your lover improve by demonstrating rather than by talking about it, which may have the opposite effect of what was intended.

Thus you may have to delay some innovations in lovemaking until your lover is really ready for them, so that you don't rush into things that aren't yet appropriate. You respond best by using your inner vision to temper and refine the relationship and to regulate your partner's energies.

Sun Inconjunct Uranus

You may be highly motivated to make self-discoveries through developing and changing your sexual expression. However, you often run the gamut of emotions rather quickly. Thus, in your search for new discovery, you may not fully develop some forms of physical and emotional expression that you could pursue further. It is important to remember that your partner may not be quite as swift as you and may want to linger and enjoy the fruits of affection when you are ready to move on.

You should try to rein yourself in from time to time and give your partner time to catch up. In that way also you will have time to develop your recent discoveries. Making an effort to relax and enjoy the fruits of your labors will surely pay off in understanding.

Because of these tendencies, however, you can become very well versed in many unusual aspects of love, both physically and emotionally. Since you are a compulsive explorer and innovator, you will be happiest with a lover who is ready for anything you suggest, although perhaps at a different pace. Indeed, it may be best if your lover can fill in for your lack of interest in developing the ideas that you originate.

Sun Opposition Uranus

You may find that your energies come in rather sudden spurts and that you are either very insightful in matters of love or don't understand it at all. But that is quite natural, and if you channel this trait properly, you can reach unusual heights of sexual experience and discovery.

This on-and-off quality can be a problem if your lover has the same style and if the two of you aren't quite coordinated. However, when you both are on the same wavelength, you can go to extremes of originality and intensity in sexual and emotional expression. Of course, at other times, nothing at all will happen.

In the long run, you may be most content with a more regular lover who can inspire you when you are low and ride your energies when you are at a peak.

You should be careful, however, to commit yourself only to what you are capable of carrying out and not jump in and out of a relationship once you have begun. It is all right to honestly change your mind about an affair, but don't make a final commitment until you have given it a lot of thought. You may change your mind several times before you really know whether you want to stay with it.

Sun Conjunct Neptune

You tend to be very idealistic and to have many high expectations about love and sex, which may not be totally realistic. Because your standards are so high, you are likely to experience some unhappiness when circumstances prove that you or your lover cannot live up to them.

Therefore, it is a good idea to emphasize your forgiving nature and let reality be a large factor in determining what is enjoyable. You can still work on being a perfectionist in love, for that will lead you to refine a relationship. But at the same time you should continually take stock of whether your goals are actually attainable or whether they are simply fantasies.

You do have a special talent for fantasy, and you will enjoy a partner who also likes to develop and fulfill sexual fantasies. Many roles that are too demanding for real life can be acted out in the bedroom in an exciting and fulfilling manner. This can be an important technique for refining your idealism and using it practically in everyday life, while achieving even better sexual expression.

Sun Sextile Neptune

You are probably quite realistic about what you can and cannot expect from a relationship. In judging an affair, you don't let imaginary standards outweigh reality.

Of course, your expectations in love may be quite demanding, but you will not walk into a relationship in which you know they cannot be met. Although this is a sensible approach up to a point, you may turn down an interesting affair by judging the possibilities ahead of time. Grappling with difficult human situations may challenge or alter your view of life. Therefore, try to be supple in your views and reconsider your assumptions from time to time, or place yourself in a situation that will test and refine your ideals. Ideals are rewarding only to the extent that they enlarge your experience.

You tend to be quite a gentle and thoughtful lover, and you can easily attune yourself to your partner emotionally. This will allow you to achieve greater closeness with your lover, even if he or she has difficulty in verbalizing sexual or emotional needs. You can understand them intuitively, when words would just get in the way.

Sun Square Neptune

At times you may be uncertain and confused about how you should assert yourself in love. Sometimes, what seems to you to be an accepted procedure either doesn't work or is counterproductive to your actual wishes or goals.

In many cases it may be better to let your partner make the first move, enabling you to make a stronger and surer response. Also this will allow you to see more clearly where each of you stands.

Be meticulous and realistic about your expectations in a love affair, for you may often ask the impossible, either of your partner or of the situation itself, which is a sure road to disappointment. If you work to clarify what you can reasonably expect, you are more likely to attain your goals. Your partner can be of great service in helping shape the direction of the affair and in resolving what is possible, impossible and desirable.

As time goes on, you will develop a special ability to outline the specifics of a relationship and define its reasonable limits. That will come only with knowledge and experience; you can't achieve it in a hurry, but should gradually develop your skills until you have reached maturity.

Sun Trine Neptune

You probably have a good sense of proportion about what can and cannot be achieved in a relationship. Your expectations are usually quite realistic, so that you are not disappointed because of lack of judgment.

You are not usually a very demanding partner and can freely forgive your lover when a situation does not work out as you wanted it to. Also your partner can depend on you, for you are the leader in establishing your mutual goals. The standards and expectations you set are ones that can be reasonably met by both of you, thus leading to success rather than disappointment.

Your partner should be able to provide an extra challenge within the relationship, so that you both can feel that you are really accomplishing something together and that your love is moving in an upward spiral, not merely marking time.

But when difficulties arise or when the affair faces reversals, you are the one who takes it in stride and moves evenly forward. You can put the relationship back into gear for new and more successful efforts together, so at such times you should take charge.

Sun Inconjunct Neptune

You tend to set increasingly demanding standards in a love relationship, and if used wisely, this characteristic can lead to a remarkably rewarding love. Each time you succeed, you set a higher goal, which you then act upon to keep the relationship alive and growing more refined.

But you should avoid being overly critical of yourself or your partner if you are unable to fulfill mutual promises or goals. Instead, decide what you both can achieve enjoyably and forget about past failures; if you let them haunt you, they will detract from your future efforts to build and meet your expectations.

You may tend to think too far into the future concerning how much to pursue an affair and how much it will bring. Sometimes you should simply relax and enjoy what you already have, which you may miss by setting your sights so far ahead. Although it is a good idea to keep an eye on tomorrow, love can best be enjoyed by living for the moment, savoring the pleasures of the here and now.

If you keep these factors in balance, you will be motivated toward rapid continuous growth in a relationship. You can achieve a great deal in love as long as you avoid pushing the affair too far too fast, so that you or your partner becomes wearied.

Sun Opposition Neptune

You tend to have rather high goals and expectations in love, and if you have any problem, it is in living up to them. From time to time you should relax your standards a bit and enjoy the pleasures of the moment, even if they are not all you might want.

However, if you maintain high expectations for too long, you are likely to give in and settle for far less than you can achieve. Instead, you should scrutinize your goals and ideals in love, measuring them against what is practical and available. This will help you avoid swinging from one end of an emotional arc to the other, being too demanding at one time and totally uncritical at another.

Oddly enough, when you are not actively involved in a love relationship, you are likely to transfer your affections to a pet, upon whom you may lavish the love and care you would otherwise give to your partner. At any rate, you are probably quite fond of small animals, kind and affectionate to any pets that you own. Although this is only one method of evening out your flow of love expression, it can be a creative outlet for your innate and usually active kindness.

Sun Conjunct Pluto

The intensity of your personality means that any affair you get into is also quite intense. You throw yourself wholeheartedly into a relationship, holding nothing back.

Because of this attitude, you can virtually dissolve in an affair that is going well, blending with your lover in such a way that the union is more than the sum of your personalities.

When everything is going well, this can bring you to the very height of sexual fulfill-ment. But do not insist that sex at that high level must be the only expression of your love or that it must necessarily happen. While pursuing that desirable but elusive goal, you may overlook the thousands of smaller joys that a love relationship can bring.

Therefore, you would be happy with a lover who has a good sense of humor and can help you enjoy the lighter and more amusing aspects of your affair. Also, such a partner can lead you to styles of loving with which you may not be familiar. You, on the other hand, can provide the basic motivation for the more serious and intensely fulfilling moments of the relationship. With this combination, you can keep from becoming overly serious in love, and your partner can achieve heights of intensity that would not otherwise be possible.

Sun Sextile Pluto

You may have a special talent for continual and creative growth within a relationship, and you are able to achieve this without putting either yourself or your partner under pressure to produce or change unwillingly.

Because major developments in an affair may occur quite easily and almost unnoticeably, you may not be completely aware of them. For that reason you may not have total control over them. Generally that is not too important, because these changes will take care of themselves without much attention from you. However, from time to time you should stand back and reevaluate your relationship to see what changes and transformations it has gone through.

You may be able to sustain a long-range relationship that seems to go underground for a long time, perhaps with a partner whom you do not see very often. Despite the lack of contact, there will still be significant developments, and the bond of affection between you will be strengthened. Thus, even if you are happily married, an old flame may remain dear to you, or your affection may develop as time goes on. Such a relationship should be as open and understanding as possible, so that your full-time partner will not feel threatened by an older, more intermittent relationship.

Sun Square Pluto

You may feel that you have to be in charge of a relationship and in control of your partner. This need to have control may also apply to other areas of your life quite apart from your love life. It is important to handle this carefully so that it won't wreck a potentially good relationship or draw you into a one-sided and less than fulfilling affair.

Essentially, this need for control or dominance results from the fear of being subject to hostile or harmful forces that you cannot govern; ultimately, it is the fear of death. Such anxieties usually begin at a very early age and infuse many aspects of later life, particularly relationships.

Therefore it is important to be able to trust your love completely, knowing that he or she will never willfully harm you emotionally. If your trust is rewarded over a period of time, it should be possible for the two of you to develop a balanced and fulfilling relationship. Try to sustain your trust through sheer will power, if necessary, of which you should have plenty. Then, in spite of occasional emotional problems, you will be able to build a well-balanced affair that gives both of you maximum expression.

When the temptation arises to dominate or be dominated, which may also happen, you can express it enjoyably and safely in various bedroom games. In this way you can act out your needs through sexual role-playing rather than in everyday life, where there is more potential for harm.

Sun Trine Pluto

You have a basically resilient character that can make a long-term effort without too much strain or worry about its eventual success. You are likely to have less insecurity than other people about most things, including sex and love.

For this reason, you can be a particularly helpful and supportive lover, seeing your partner through any emotional difficulties or hard times. When your lover falters or hesitates for lack of strength or will power, your strength will allow you both to pull through. You must be very understanding and perceptive, for you may be unaware of your lover's fears and inhibitions. Otherwise you may unknowingly offend simply because you cannot imagine anyone having such worries or concerns.

You yourself should also be cautious, for you may charge ahead fearlessly when there is real physical or emotional danger. Although confidence will generally see you through, your luck cannot hold forever unless it is tempered with wisdom and a keen sense of observation. With those qualities, you can be expert, not only in handling yourself but also in emotionally supporting those you love.

Sun Inconjunct Pluto

You may feel an urgent need for continual love expression, so that you are never left wanting or intermittently fulfilled. This means that you are a very affectionate partner but also rather demanding, for you expect your attentions to be returned in kind, which may be difficult for your partner. He or she may be unable to keep up with you or may feel too heavily obligated within the relationship.

To a certain extent, you may manipulate your partner, just to make sure that you will have the attention you need. Gaining such control over your lover may guarantee a continuing relationship, but it will take away much of the freedom on which love depends.

If you and your partner agree, you can act out your need for control in fantasy role-playing. In that way you both may be able to reach great heights of pleasure and fulfillment. That is a creative use of dominance and control for sexual enjoyment and growth. At the same time, these energies will not contaminate other areas of the relationship, where you should be more equal in order to get the most out of your love. You may derive more from sexual experimentation than most, which may be a very satisfying and creative outlet for your energies, which would otherwise be frustrated or bottled up.

Sun Opposition Pluto

Your confidence in love may fluctuate greatly. At times you feel quite sure of yourself—even overestimating your luck or ability—and at other times you don't give yourself the credit you deserve, thus crippling your own actions or initiative.

Since you do not always have a clear or accurate view of yourself in such matters, you should rely on a trusted partner's view of what is happening. That will help to even you out and allow you to function on a middle ground instead of at emotional extremes.

Because of this kind of fluctuation, you may feel very strongly about a lover at one time and totally indifferent at other times, with not much in between. You may experience times of exceedingly heightened sexuality, but also you may abandon an affair that has much potential or attribute great depth to a relationship to which your partner is not really committed.

To balance this, your lover should have a fairly even and reliable temperament. He or she should have enough influence over you to keep you from making hasty or rash moves. At the same time your partner can be inspired and uplifted by the heights to which your intense love energy can take you.

Sun Conjunct Ascendant

Your personality stands out, and you have the ability to be psychologically forceful when necessary. Since you were born at sunrise, you are indeed the early bird and usually have your choice of desirable partners when there is competition.

You tend to dominate a relationship, not from a need or desire to have control, but simply through the strength of your presence. To this extent, you should make an effort to be modest or even retiring at times, so that people will not find your natural style overbearing.

Your talent for selling yourself will allow you to get your way, but you should use this talent with respect, not abuse it. You should try to convince someone else only about matters that are really important, not about anything that comes up, just to exercise your abilities. You have the potential to be either a vibrant, glowing personality or a crashing bore, depending on how wisely you use this gift.

Thus, in seeking a partner, do not make conquests gratuitously; instead, pursue only someone who has special appeal, who presents real potential for a creative relationship. This will mean the difference between having a reputation as a desirable partner who has successful affairs and a person who simply collects lovers.

Sun Sextile Ascendant

You are probably a fairly communicative person who enjoys company and has a good command of the social graces. Naturally this makes you a desirable partner, at least on first meeting, so you have an advantage over many others in choosing a partner or being chosen.

Although you have a certain natural charm, don't become lazy and depend on charm to get what you want; otherwise you may be left behind by less talented rivals, just like the hare in the fable of the tortoise and the hare. Follow up your initial advantage and put an extra effort into a relationship that promises to bear fine fruit.

You may have to make a special attempt to be sure that your lover understands the sincerity and depth of your commitment. Be sure that your love extends beyond the pleasure of the moment, however enjoyable that may be. This is important in overcoming the effects of your relatively smooth style, which some people may see as too glib or not very intense. You should fill out your natural grace with substance, so that your lover can feel the impact of your affection and know that your love is more than skin deep.

Sun Square Ascendant

You may tend to overstate your case in a love affair; although you mean to be sincere, your partner may find your words too good to believe. On the other hand, you may express yourself incompletely or convey the wrong kind of intensity.

Because of this tendency, it may be a good idea, when in doubt, to express yourself as clearly and concisely as possible, so there can be no misinterpretation. Of course, your partner can provide valuable feedback about your actions, and you should listen with special care in order to get a more objective view of yourself.

Probably you have a good deal of energy, which you may use either in your career or in building and developing your home life. In either case you should be careful not to overdo it, for that would deplete your energies and endanger your health. Let your partner share your efforts and shoulder some of the burden instead of taking it on alone. Doing that will save some of your energies for loving and other pleasant pastimes, and it will also draw you closer to your partner. If your accomplishments are shared, you both can take pride in them. As a result, a relationship that begins unevenly will become increasingly unified as time goes on.

Sun Trine Ascendant

Generally you have a good, easy flow of energy, and you don't have difficulty transmitting your emotions physically. Your expressive brand of body language will enable you to achieve instant communication with a potential partner and allow you to judge immediately, simply by the way a person moves, whether he or she is really interested in you.

You can transmit desire and interest to a potential lover without words, simply with movements and expressions. Needless to say, this gives you a natural advantage in love, particularly when first choosing a lover, for you will be spared much of the time-consuming rituals of courting.

But you should not take your easy ability in such matters for granted or assume that love will always arrive unbidden on your doorstep, even though it has happened before. Instead, use your native talent to meet the challenge of a lover who is not at ease, who needs extra attention and even training in the arts of love.

This kind of affair will keep your talents well-honed and in good repair so that as you get older you will retain the advantages of your youth; also you will experience a sense of achievement in helping a lover gain the abilities that you were given at birth.

Sun Inconjunct Ascendant

You probably have a more restless and motivating kind of energy than many other people. Depending upon how you use this energy, it may result in constant productive activity or in a nervous undirected frittering away of your efforts.

For this reason, you should always have some project to spend your energies on and a partner who is willing to participate in your projects. It would be ideal to find a lover who can finish the projects that you have begun, for you are likely to commit yourself to new activities before completing the old.

With the right partner, this potential problem can be handled easily and quite advantageously, with you initiating ideas and your lover completing them. However, that should not be the case in your lovemaking, for starting something without finishing it can be exceedingly frustrating to a lover. You should make sure that your partner has gotten complete satisfaction from one sexual technique before moving on to another, even though you may be impatient to move along. But this same tendency will lead you into many areas of sexual exploration in search of something new. With some discipline, this will greatly enhance your potential for sexual enjoyment.

Sun Opposition Ascendant

Your partner's welfare and state of mind are of critical importance to you and will be a major factor in decisions about your own life. When you do not have a current love involvement, seeking out a partnership will be of paramount importance to you.

In an active relationship you will expend a great deal of energy on whatever your partner is involved in, which can be interpreted as concern or as meddling, depending on how you handle it.

Be careful not to let concern for your lover outweigh your own needs or cause you to neglect yourself or repress your own energies. If there is conflict between your needs and those of your partner, try to benefit the relationship by using both energies.

Whatever your situation, you will be happier and more creative when you are involved in an active partnership, although it need not be a sexual relationship. Having a partner who participates in your creative affairs will make you much more productive and satisfied. Also you may be the motivating power force behind your lover's creativity.

Chapter Six

The Moon in the Chart

The Moon represents, in part, how you react to situations, sexual or otherwise. If this reactive style is consistent with other planetary indications, your behavior will be quite reliable and predictable. If this is not the case, your behavior will be characterized by more variety and sometimes inconsistency.

The Moon has to do with your response to love, which depends on your situation. When you are the one who is initiating activity, this factor is operating less than when you are responding to circumstances. How you feel about a certain sexual experience may depend on whether you or your partner suggested it. Being aware of this can help you structure your relationships to take advantage of each partner's type of response to suggestions.

Some people consider that the influence of the Moon is more important than the Sun in the charts of women, but that is true only if you consider that a woman should always take the passive or receptive role, which is a somewhat dated notion now. I believe that it is better for both men and women to use both the initiative (Sun) and reactive (Moon) centers of their personalities in patterns that will provide the most enjoyment and the best communication.

Moon in Aries

You are a highly responsive person who tends to make lightning decisions in matters of the heart. You aren't likely to lose a lover through making up your mind too slowly, but you may on occasion rush into an affair that you should have avoided. It doesn't hurt to look before you leap.

With you, an affair does not usually build up gradually; it begins full force and continues with high-keyed intensity. You enjoy nonstop emotional involvement, but you may do well to learn to pace yourself. Your lover may not have as much energy and may find your pace wearing after a time. Also, a relationship that is too intense may become obsessive or burn out prematurely. Remember, you have the rest of your life to enjoy it.

You have a strong appetite for anything new and exciting in a relationship, and you have a special talent for keeping the spirit of an affair fresh. You try anything for the fun of it, not necessarily because it is far-out, but simply because it's new, and why not give it a try? This can lead to endless adventures, but take care not to leave your lover behind, still trying to catch up with your last experiment.

A natural leader in love, you always have fresh and interesting ways to express yourself and your affections. Just be sure that your partner can keep up with your stride.

Moon in Taurus

You are a person of great emotional substance, and you provide an excellent shoulder for an upset lover to cry on. You are not easily or quickly angered, but once your ire is aroused, you are a formidable antagonist with a long memory for grievances. Therefore it is a good idea to air any differences with your lover right away, because otherwise they may mount up and damage the relationship later.

You do not rush into a love affair, preferring to build it in careful stages. Then, even after the affair is over, a warm and lasting friendship will continue.

Your preference is for straightforward simplicity in a relationship. Elaborate courting rituals are not your style, for they just seem to confuse the situation. You may not insist on total fidelity, but you want your partner to tell you the truth at all times so you know right where you stand. In return, you are scrupulously honest with your lover, even when it hurts, for you believe that a long-lasting relationship must be based on honesty and must live up to that ideal.

In a relationship you are the salt of the earth, a friend and lover your partner can always depend on, even in difficult times. You don't commit yourself lightly, and when you give your word, you stand by it, particularly a commitment given in love.

Moon in Gemini

Your style of lovemaking is very supple and adaptable; you happily participate in any kind of loving that pleases your partner. Indeed, you could become a true expert in sexual technique.

Do not let the physical elements of sex interfere with or overcome the emotional side of loving. Sometimes deeper communication gets lost in the complexities of a pyrotechnical sexual performance, and for that reason it may be better to keep it simple and sincere.

Many people find it hard to talk about sex, but you should have little trouble in discussing it openly, finding out just what your lover's tastes are and how you can best please each other. Your partner should have a good sense of humor, because someone who takes sex very seriously is seldom willing to talk much about it, oddly enough.

You should choose a partner who is not too possessive, for you need to know that you have freedom, even if you don't choose to exercise it. Be careful about making a personal commitment, for a lover may take it more seriously than it is meant, which could cause harm inadvertently. A few words spelling out your expectations from time to time will make the relationship go more easily.

Moon in Cancer

You have a very sympathetic nature, and you are always willing to listen to someone's problems and sorrows. While you are young, you may be very involved with people who are in emotional difficulties, which can be a great drain on your personal strength. As you get older, you learn to avoid such people even when you are attracted to them.

The best way to handle this problem is to take a middle road, if possible. You will derive great satisfaction from helping and comforting a troubled lover, which is fine as long as you can avoid letting your partner's problems take over the affair. In a balanced relationship, you can be a refuge for your partner without being a doormat.

You may find that you are often involved in several relationships at once, not because you want variety but because you are so unwilling to let go of a relationship that is finished. Old lovers tend to linger in your imagination, which can get in the way of current involvements. Once you have established a relationship, although the quality and nature of your love may fluctuate considerably, it will never die.

Moon in Leo

You are very open and mellow toward your lover, and you are a very enthusiastic and outgoing love partner. Indeed, you should sometimes temper the force of your naturally wholehearted reactions, for they may be more vehement than you intend or your lover expects.

Your partner should enjoy social gatherings, because you blossom in company and feel unfulfilled if you are alone for a long time. You need stimulation and attention from others in order to keep going at a fully creative pace.

Generally you are an optimist, which helps the physical side of a relationship. But your optimism may cause you to prolong an affair that can't possibly work out, on the premise that something will come along and resolve the whole situation happily.

Physically and emotionally, you enjoy the presence and love of many different people, but you will probably entrust your truly heartfelt loyalty and love to one person only. For this sort of relationship to flourish, your special partner must understand how you feel and cast aside all feelings of petty jealousy. In that case you will be assured of a long and deep relationship.

Moon in Virgo

You have very specific standards about what you want in a lover, and you tend to be cautious in selecting one. Once you find the right person, the affair will probably go much as you want it to.

Also you are particular about the surroundings when you make love, for you are not comfortable just anywhere or at any time. In order to really let go and enjoy sex to the utmost, you should be fairly well acquainted with your surroundings, particularly if they are at all unusual.

115

Try not to be too possessive of your partner or, if you must be, find someone who will be absolutely faithful to you. In any case, you should be very specific about your demands and expectations early in the relationship, so that your partner doesn't inadvertently do something that particularly upsets you.

You are very good at helping your partner and others straighten out personal problems, and you give down-to-earth advice on how they can better fulfill themselves, in relation both to you and to others. But don't give your partner unsolicited advice, because it will fall on deaf ears.

You are happiest with a lover who lets you handle all the arrangements, particularly for lovemaking. You handle them better, and you will be happier yourself.

Moon in Libra

You have a special talent for solving others' problems, because you see both sides of a situation clearly. Your frequent involvement in the emotional lives of others also gives you a greater range of experience for dealing with your own problems.

In a relationship, you may be on a continual clean-up and improvement campaign, which is beneficial only to a point. Every affair can be improved, but in the interests of harmony, it's just as well to sweep the smaller problems under the rug. Concentrate on the difficulties that are actively troubling the relationship.

You improve the general environment by rearranging things—both physical objects and social situations—creating beauty and a better balance, for which others will be grateful. Be careful to respect other people's boundaries, however, because some people would rather not change their situation, even if it isn't perfect.

The world will be a continually interesting challenge to you, particularly if you find a partner who is as willing as you are to confront truth and deal with it directly and clearly.

Moon in Scorpio

You are especially sharp at focusing on what is important in a situation, particularly in a long-term affair, and acting upon it accordingly. You have probably learned that what is obvious to you is not always obvious to others; therefore you should be fairly discreet in expressing your opinions until you are quite sure of your partner's views.

This ability may be helpful in the long run, but it may cause you to miss some opportunities if you wait too long for a potential lover to open up to you. At the same time, however, it will save you the annoyance of inadvertently becoming involved with a prying or overdemanding lover.

Very likely you will choose a partner who takes life less seriously than you do, someone who will provide daily enjoyment and happiness and let you handle the larger problems.

Sexuality is likely to be a very intense and deep means of expression and communication, through which you show your greatest affection for your partner. In an ideal relationship, you may totally transcend your personality in sexual consummation, making it an almost religious experience. If this doesn't work out, however, don't hold it against your lover, who probably cannot participate at your level of intensity. When the time and circumstances are right, the experience will be all the more satisfying.

Moon in Sagittarius

Your most distinctive trait may well be your sense of humor. Even in scenes that would cause others to be downhearted or discouraged, you can find a spark of laughter and mirth that brightens the situation and makes it more enjoyable.

This can be a problem only if it is overdone. People who take life too seriously may not appreciate having their homemade tragedies belittled with humor, so you should find a lover who shares your easygoing and broad approach to life.

Probably you have a very rich fantasy life, which some people might consider overabundant. But you create fantasies for their own sake basically, and you enjoy creating them as much as fulfilling them. Acting out sex fantasies is always desired, but it can be more troublesome than just cooking them up, because the acting-out process tends to get in the way of enjoyment.

In the long run, your style of loving is more in the spirit of a warm, friendly fireplace on a late fall night: merry, comforting, the essence of happy comradeship. Like good wine, your love relationship will grow mellower and fuller with age. The more you partake of it, the more you will treasure it.

Moon in Capricorn

You are not one to rush into a relationship, but you don't usually back off from one, either. You prefer an even, measured style of emotional response. People will depend upon you and respect you as. a lover and friend.

You will be happiest with someone who sincerely tries to be loyal and true and does not play the field. This does not mean that you want a dull lover—quite the opposite, you will thrive on the challenge presented by a lover with a more volatile style. What you do want is a partner who is basically committed to you, so you know you are working with something real and lasting.

For you, the most important aspect of sexual expression is sincerity, not great heights of physical prowess or technical achievement. Forced attempts at sexual variety may simply get in the way of meaningful personal communication.

You have a significant ability to sublimate sexuality into other realms of affection. You may find much emotional satisfaction in caring for your partner in ways that are not physically sexual: gifts, favors, meals and financial support, for example.

However you express it, your affection is basically unswerving. The best relationship for you is one that is long-lasting, so that you have ample opportunities to express your love over a long period of time.

Moon in Aquarius

Although your temperament is fairly even, there is potential for unlimited variety in your responses to a lover, depending on your partner and the location. You do not simply go along with whatever your partner asks, however. In every situation you are truly creative and responsive, an equal partner in the emotional and sexual inventiveness of the relationship.

You prefer a partner who provides a challenge rather than one who presents a ready-made framework for an affair. If all the shots are predetermined, you feel too cramped. You will be happier if you can work out the problems together and come up with the specific sexual style that best suits your personalities. In a way, you are a role-player who creates the roles instead of trying to fit into those created by society or by other people.

A lover who is verbally clever would be ideal for you. If the two of you can analyze your affair in some detail, you will understand it and enjoy it more. Much of your sexual response is filtered through your mind, and if you're in the dark about what's happening, you won't be up to par sexually.

You will be happiest in a relationship that has plenty of time to develop. In affairs of the heart, time is on your side.

Moon in Pisces

Your emotions are very intense and finely tuned, and you can usually see into the heart of an affair more quickly than your partner. But your flashes of insight are not steady. You are likely to have considerable mood swings and changes of heart within a relationship until it has settled for a long period. Only time can give your affairs more concrete definition.

For that reason, you should find a lover who is more stable than you. Such a partner will see through to the real you underneath and won't be thrown off by your seeming inconsistencies.

Because you are more concerned with a lover's internal values than with their external expression, others may think that your friends and lovers don't match your style. But you are hardly aware of any inconsistency, because you see directly to a person's heart, ignoring external trappings, which few others can do.

Concerning physical matters, you are likely to be rather impractical. It would be good to have a partner who can handle the bothersome petty details of existence so that you can then attend to the more meaningful issues in life without being distracted. Under such circumstances, you can transform love into a clear, pure vehicle for personal understanding and revelation, both for you and for your lover.

Moon in the First House

Your emotional state plays a prominent role in your decisions, and you respond strongly and quickly to the moods of those around you. Others see this quality not as aggressiveness but as sensitivity, for you are always the first to sense what someone else is feeling.

You are usually on top of any social situation and probably have the first choice of interesting or important partners in any group. This is a valuable attribute, but try to restrain yourself a bit, because others may think of you as too forward if you are always the first one in line.

It is important to move within a social framework, for that offers the best opportunities for your voluble style of self-expression. Being stuck with one or two people for a long time may dull your sensitivity and cramp your style.

You have the ability to make up your mind very quickly in emotional affairs, and you choose the partner you prefer without hesitation. But it is wise to learn as much in advance as possible about your potential partners in order to avoid a too-hasty decision. If you can occasionally stand back and look at yourself as others see you, you will be able to make emotional decisions on a surer footing, which will lead to longer-lasting, more trouble-free relationships.

For you, a personal involvement is always very high-keyed, even if brief. If it can't be intense, you don't want it. Although this is physically very enjoyable, it may mislead a lover into believing that your relationship is permanent when you consider it transitory. You should make your attitude clear from the outset so that your partner knows where he or she stands.

Moon in the Second House

Good physical health and financial well-being are necessary to your emotional security, and you are not likely to be happy in a money-starved love affair, no matter how romantic it is. In order to really feel free to express your feelings, you need to be relatively comfortable, so that financial worries aren't continually nagging at the back of your mind.

At times you may seek solutions to your emotional difficulties in a relationship by searching for financially higher ground. You may demand expensive presents or love tokens from a partner to assuage problems between you. Although it is perfectly legitimate to treasure gifts of love for their emotional value, this can be dangerous, because you are dodging problems whose roots lie elsewhere. Such a situation can be expensive for your lover and emotionally costly for both of you.

Your basic desire for honesty and integrity in a relationship should lead you around this obstacle, for you are guided by a strong set of fundamental values. You will probably seek out a partner whose basic beliefs about life are equally sure. You will be most content with someone who is no swinger but who will treasure you loyally and give your relationship a firm sense of direction.

Moon in the Third House

You usually express your loving feelings verbally, and you should not hesitate to let your lover know just how you feel. The more you can discuss your feelings, the deeper they will be, and the more understanding and contact you can have with your emotions.

It is also a good idea to talk out personal problems extensively with your lover, because for you, that is the best way to deal successfully with them.

Indeed, words may be your primary method of transmitting love and understanding at all levels. Even telephone calls and letters are important channels for keeping a love relationship alive, even when there is no physical contact. In any intimate situation, your words of love and encouragement will heighten the sexual experience, so don't hold back; let them flow freely. In most cases they serve as an ever-increasing stimulant to love.

Your best relationship with a lover is one that is chummy and casual, with much of the intimate informality of a brother-sister, "old pals" relationship. Too much formality creates a block between you and your partner; you are much more comfortable when you can enjoy an easy, offhand communication of your love for each other.

Moon in the Fourth House

For you, the ideal relationship is one that provides an emotional bulwark for times of trouble or distress. You are happiest with a partner who is absolutely true to you, who is always there when needed. There should be no conflict of interest because of emotional ties to another person.

Partly for that reason, you will probably fall into a live-in relationship, because it provides the greatest opportunities for warmth and expression of your love. You are not able to give all you have in a single night, and both you and your lover will find it far more satisfying to live together twenty-four hours a day. That will draw you closer in countless ways.

Living together allows you to pamper your lover, surrounding him or her with attention and affection. Indeed, your style of loving turns the place you share into a home. No matter how simple or unassuming it is, you warm it up and decorate it, giving it the sacredness and security of your own cozy castle.

You should look for a lover who will truly appreciate all this attention, neither ignoring it nor feeling suffocated. Ideally your partner should cherish the wealth of care and thoughtfulness that you can provide.

Moon in the Fifth House

You have a certain infectious quality that enables you to lead others in good times. You are usually up for any occasion that promises fun and enjoyment, even if others are reluctant to jump right in.

Thus it is easy for you to become involved in a love relationship just for the joy and entertainment it provides. But you may be unwilling to confront the more serious or problematical aspects of a relationship, because you don't intend to get involved in such complications. Nevertheless, any long-term relationship runs up against difficulties, which you must face squarely and seriously. It may be easier to follow your partner's lead in this respect.

Normally you take the lead in turning lovemaking into a smiling art form, in which you relish every joyful movement and lead the dance to greater heights. For you, sex is an important form of personal and even aesthetic expression. It revitalizes you and feeds your creative inspiration in other areas of self-expression, including art, music, poetry or any other creative work.

Moon in the Sixth House

You are good at creating fantasy structures of love, which an affair must fulfill if it is to come out right for you or be really satisfying. When an affair doesn't proceed according to your expectations, you may be unsure how to respond. Probably the best way to handle this is to prepare a number of scenarios ahead of time and simply switch from one to another as the affair goes on. For this reason, it is not a bad idea to read more about sex in a good modern manual so that you will be prepared for any situation that comes up.

There may be a problem of equality between you and your lover, for you have a certain inclination to either serve or be served by your partner. This can be worked out in carefully arranged bedroom games of dominance, which can be very exciting if you both are up for them. Outside of the bedroom, however, you should strive for equality with your lover as much as possible, for in the long run that will sustain the relationship better.

Once you have gained experience in love, you can be a very considerate and thoughtful lover, who as both teacher and lover can gently initiate a younger person in the ways of love. In that case, it may be difficult for your lover to make the transition from student to equal, but that must happen if you intend to have a long-term relationship. Well played, a Pygmalion affair like this is much to be envied.

Moon in the Seventh House

You give of yourself easily and are always ready to be a friend to someone who shares your interests. You are a very natural partner who brings more experience to a personal relationship than most.

You may often find that you are the guiding hand in an affair, as your partner may not be as surefooted and may need the support of your wisdom to get along in the relationship. You should look for a lover who is sensitive enough to know when to take your advice and follow your suggestions.

Since you value true equality in a relationship very highly, you must take care not to become the more "equal" partner. You must know when not to give advice as well as when to give it. Your lesson is to learn patience and perseverance. Many problems that arise between you will disappear on their own and do not require a full frontal attack. If you hold a steady course, the affair will go more smoothly than if you throw all your emotional energy into combating minor difficulties.

If you make an effort to see yourself as others see you, it will be much easier to sort out the important from the unimportant. Then you can create an easy balance between yourself and your lover.

Moon in the Eighth House

You are drawn to deep, internalized, somewhat mysterious relationships on a very high level of emotional intensity. Such an affair churns with powerful feelings, which may be extremely exciting. However, you must make an extra effort to stay in control of the situation so you aren't swept away by the emotional storms you create.

When a relationship does get out of hand for some reason, the best solution is to demystify it by simply talking out the problems. Although that takes away from the excitement, it also relieves the pressure. You may find that the large, shadowy problems that loom so large in your mind shrink to almost nothing when you face them in the light of day.

You probably prefer an older and more experienced lover whose knowledge and abilities in lovemaking you can explore. Or you may find similar qualities in someone who is very different from you in nationality, class background, marital status or some other way, someone who brings a wealth of new and interesting experience to your partnership.

The more skilled your lover is, the better, because physical gratification is highly rewarding to you. The more you can develop it, the more the relationship will flourish.

Moon in the Ninth House

You gravitate toward people with whom you have a lot in common philosophically and spiritually. In a new relationship, that is likely to be the first area of contact, with physical intimacy following later.

In the philosophical realm you are an explorer, and you thrive on a love relationship that allows you to broaden your horizons. You will be most drawn to a lover who can open your mind as well as gratify your body.

With the right lover, you are willing to make changes in yourself and your lifestyle, if that will further the growth of your personality and enrich your life. Really creative loving is a challenge of adaptability, and the more new experiences you can encompass, the more satisfaction you will derive.

For that reason, you are best off with an adventurous partner who will respond to your initiative and be ready to explore new areas. And your explorations together need not be just on the physical level; you both can reap much satisfaction from sharing all sorts of fantasies, mentally exploring concepts of loving and gratification that may not be wise or even possible on the physical level. However far your fantasies travel, in reality you will be most happy in an active, growth-oriented relationship.

Moon in the Tenth House

Maintaining status in your social affairs is central to your lifestyle, and your reputation as a lover is important to you. At times this may keep you away from a relationship that would be very rewarding, but you fear that it would interfere with your social or professional progress.

On the other hand, you are often able to turn a love relationship to your advantage in other areas, so that you enjoy and profit from the connection. Just make sure that love is always the primary goal of the relationship; if that goes down the drain, so does everything else. A union of convenience seldom lasts and is usually emotionally damaging to both partners.

External events may play a large role in shaping your love life, in the form of unavoidable separations from a desired partner or a new relationship springing up suddenly and unexpectedly. There is little you can do to prevent this, so just relax and enjoy what fate provides.

In general you prefer a dynamic and future-oriented partner whose energies kindle your own. Such a partner will spark you to greater efforts, both in your personal relationship and in your professional life. You need plenty of action and achievement for full satisfaction in a relationship.

Moon in the Eleventh House

You will be most attracted to a lover who has a good deal of class and breeding, and you do all you can to help the person you love become more successful in the world. Indeed, your own presence and style have this effect.

You must do this carefully and thoughtfully, however, for otherwise your lover may mistake your attempts at betterment for a sneaky form of social climbing. It is simply that you want the best for your lover, and you do everything you can to achieve it.

You have a certain ability to create social harmony among disparate people and can turn a lackluster gathering into a good party. You are at your best in an active social setting, which you try to create wherever you go.

It's fine that you enjoy such social occasions, but don't neglect those intimate moments alone with your lover. If you do, your partner may feel left out or upstaged by others around you.

You may renew relationships with old flames periodically throughout your life. This is natural and should be no threat to any current relationship, as long as you make sure that your present partner understands what you are doing. If your lover respects the fact that you belong to no one but yourself, you won't have any problems with envy.

Moon in the Twelfth House

You must be careful not to be too hasty in responding to a lover, and always think twice before committing yourself outright about any matter. This will save you a good deal of backtracking and unintentional emotional injuries because of hasty or badly worded remarks. There are many times when it is better to spare your lover's feelings by not rushing in and telling the whole truth, even though you feel you should.

This is particularly true in the rather touchy area of clandestine love affairs. Some couples are able to enjoy outside affairs without too much jealousy or resentment, but if you decide to have an affair, you should keep it to yourself.

No matter what kind of affair you are in, it will take a good deal of soul searching to discover your lover's and your own true emotional motives. Hidden actions and attitudes have to be uncovered and sorted out, but the reward is a deep level of mutual self-understanding that few others achieve.

For you, a truly successful love relationship is one that is intensely uplifting, even cathartic. You get little satisfaction from more casual affairs, even though at first they seem attractive. In the long run you feel truly satisfied only by an in-depth relationship, that requires great effort.

Moon Conjunct Mercury

You probably have a ready wit and a lively imagination, and you respond to the world with diverse but definite concepts. In a relationship, you are able to reduce vague emotions to specifics in order to solve a problem or overcome an obstacle with your partner so that you both can work out the problems that you unearth.

However, at times you may become too intellectual and detached from your feelings, so that they have less impact than emotions that are less well thought out. Thus, even though you are open about your feelings and can communicate them easily, they may not be as intense as your partner's or as strong as you would like them to be.

You can remedy this problem simply by throwing yourself into lovemaking, which is intense and which gives you little time to ponder your feelings. Also a drink may deemphasize the mental and stimulate the physical.

Moon Sextile Mercury

It should be fairly easy for you to communicate your feelings to your lover, for you are seldom at a loss for the right words to express your emotions. This is a very valuable asset in love and can minimize the problems in a relationship because there will be fewer misunderstandings or misinterpretations between you.

Remember, however, that your partner may find it more difficult to express his or her feelings to you, so do not assume that everything is clear and out in the open, just because that is how you work. Your partner may have many emotions hidden beneath the surface that are not easily expressed. You should use your own expressive talent to investigate and bring these emotions to light.

You may find that your lover's feelings are more intense than yours, just because they are somewhat repressed; the emotions that do get across have more pressure behind them. You can be of great help by assisting your lover in discussing emotional problems so that the two of you can work them out. Problems that remain inaccessible will only cause friction for reasons that you won't understand, but when brought to light, these difficulties can be disposed of quickly.

Moon Square Mercury

You may find that your intellect sometimes is at cross purposes with your emotions, so that you either express your emotions incorrectly or they interfere with your clear communication of ideas. Similarly, emotional problems may inhibit your reasoning ability and prevent you from expressing yourself clearly in other areas.

You would be most comfortable with a partner who does not share this problem, someone who can reflect your feelings reliably and accurately when you cannot see yourself clearly. Such a lover can be an anchor for your emotions.

When you make an emotional commitment in a relationship, you should make sure that both you and your partner understand the agreement. Double check that the two of you are not making opposite interpretations of the same statement. It is a good idea to phrase your beliefs in several different ways to ensure clarity of interpretation.

As time goes on, it will become easier for you to express your emotions, and you will be more insightful about them after you overcome the initial difficulties. Only by knowing in detail all the possible areas for emotional misunderstanding can you learn how to express yourself clearly and meaningfully in a love affair.

Moon Trine Mercury

You should be able to express your feelings to your lover quite clearly and to let your emotions have free and easy play. While your partner may have to struggle to tell you about his or her underlying motives, you can air yours with ease.

This is a decided advantage in a relationship, for in most cases it spares you and your partner the pain of bottled-up feelings or misconstrued emotions, at least through internal misunderstanding. This gives you room to explore your partner's feelings and look for any problem areas that your lover is unaware of or can't uncover.

You should be particularly aware of your partner's problems, not only for the sake of helpfulness, but also for your own protection. Since you do not have trouble expressing yourself, you may assume that your lover is the same as you. Here you may be quite in error, and your partner may resent you or simply feel distant, thinking that you lack understanding. The best way to show you care is to get in there and help, even though that may be more trouble; a worthwhile relationship is worth all the effort.

Moon Inconjunct Mercury

You may feel a strong and driving need to bring your emotions to the surface and express them clearly so that they can be thoroughly understood. To accomplish this, you will make a great effort and be quite demanding of yourself and possibly of your partner as well.

Certainly, in time this approach will result in penetrating self-understanding, but with your lover you should take a more gentle approach. Most meaningful self-knowledge comes from within and cannot be externally motivated, so you should encourage and support your partner rather than insist on emotional expression.

You have a restless mind that is constantly on the move, which encourages rapid changes of emotion, sometimes just for the sake of self-exploration. This habit may be rather wearying to a lover who can't keep up with your changing feelings. From time to time you should consciously relax and explore one emotional situation in depth before moving on to the next. Otherwise, in your hunger for knowledge you may consume more than you can thoroughly digest.

Moon Opposition Mercury

You may find it difficult to combine your rational expression and your emotions. As a result, you may be so deeply involved in an affair that you can't see what is really going on, or you may be so removed that you can't be fully and enjoyably involved.

You may be most comfortable with a more evenly balanced lover whose judgment you can rely on. Then you won't need to be so critical of the situation; you can throw yourself into it wholeheartedly and depend on your partner's interpretations when problems occur.

However, if you are not directly involved emotionally in a situation, you often have a clearer view than other people, particularly concerning others' emotional difficulties in which you have no part. Similarly, concerning a past affair of your own, you can understand exactly what happened and why. With time and experience you will have a clearer and more balanced view of your current dealings.

In the end, you will be very discerning about your emotions, not through direct intuitive insight but through your ability to compare your current situation with what has gone before.

Moon Conjunct Venus

This position usually indicates a desire to look and dress well, maintaining a well-put-together physical apearance. You may not dress elaborately, but you always look fresh and shining, avoiding the deliberately unkempt look.

You are very sensitive and sympathetic to others, seeing their best characteristics first and their lesser qualities later. That attitude has hazards, of course, and you should be aware of others' faults, so that they don't cause damage before you notice them.

Also you are reluctant to make firm decisions quickly, so you may lose a lover through indecision. In the long run, that is just as well, for when you do make up your mind at last, your emotional commitment is that much stronger. You don't waste time in brief, shallow affairs, even though you are attracted to them rather strongly.

Physically, your style of loving is soft and gentle, sensitive even in the throes of passion. You are always aware of your lover's needs and desires, and thus you are able to push upward to the highest levels of mutual pleasure.

Moon Sextile Venus

It is easier for you than for many others to fulfill your emotional desires, partly because you are lucky and partly because you don't try to seek the impossible, which could bring you disappointment. You are more likely to get into a warm, quietly affectionate affair than one that is tempestuous and demanding.

This is a fortunate characteristic that will spare you many of the heartaches that others plunge into compulsively. It also makes you a particularly desirable partner, for you offer your lover a mellow and gentle style of loving that always seeks to please without being contentious.

Because of this style of response, you can tame and calm a more fractious lover and act as a general peacemaker in a relationship. In general, this is an excellent trait, but do not let your partner take advantage of your desire for harmony and keep you from reaching your goals. Be helpful and giving up to a point, but practice saying no to unreasonable demands, even though it goes against your nature. No worthwhile partner will ask for more than you can easily give.

Moon Square Venus

At times you may have conflicting styles in love, so that you are physically attracted to a partner who does not suit you emotionally, but you are not sexually excited by someone whom you get along easily with.

To resolve this dilemma, you can take one of two approaches: either learn to get along with someone you desire, or learn to desire someone you get along with. Although your immediate response may be the former, it will probably be more profitable to find a lover whom you get along with well, unless you can enjoy a relationship that presents lasting difficulties.

Another possibility, if you and your partner can work it out, is to have an open-marriage arrangement, allowing you to live with someone you get along with and take more desirable lovers now and then. Even without such an arrangement, you will find it easier to develop desire through mutual exploration than to confront the emotional problems that arise with someone who is sexually exciting but is otherwise not in tune with you.

In time, you will learn to even out your tastes and find a lover who is satisfactory in all respects.

Moon Trine Venus

You have a talent for finding relationships that are emotionally and physically satisfying and that tend to go smoothly without too many mishaps or emotional obstacles. At the same time, you know how to avoid explosive or tumultuous relationships, the kind that romantic novels are made of. At times you may wish for a more exciting affair, but you are really much better off as you are.

To add some action and excitement, you may become involved with a lover who is less stable than you. You can be a stabilizing influence on such a person if your lover is willing to accept it. Also, this is a good exercise for you, because your sense of judgment will lose its edge if not used regularly.

You should make an effort to be understanding of people who are not so well balanced and who experience more frustration and disappointment than you. When they are envious of your stability or angry, treat them with forgiveness. Because you are better off emotionally, you bear the responsibility of absorbing some of that energy in a gracious manner.

Moon Inconjunct Venus

You may be subject to rapidly and sometimes continually changing emotions and desires in love. Thus you may find it difficult to stay put with a quieter partner. Because of this characteristic, you may be interested in all kinds of sexual experimentation. As a result, you may become quite an accomplished lover and adaptable to a variety of styles, depending upon your partner.

However, continual changes may sometimes be a mechanism for not facing emotional needs that need extra work and attention. If you always look for something new, your relationship is bound to be shallow; your experiences will be varied, but they will lack depth.

It may be difficult for you to slow down, however, for emotional or sexual repetition can become quite tedious. You are likely to chafe at the bit if your partner can't maintain your pace. One way around this is to backtrack rather than stand still, reliving moods and techniques that you have experienced before. This will enable you to explore love in more depth without wearing out any aspect of it. You may find that you have missed a lot by moving on too quickly the first time and that each facet of love contains a wealth of enjoyment.

Moon Opposition Venus

You may not be inclined to blend emotional and physical love, so that you get involved with a partner who provides one or the other but not both. This can mean that you keep your close friends separate from your lovers, and if a partner must be both, as in a marriage, you may have some long-range difficulties.

This problem may stem in part from social attitudes that you learned as a child, in which sex was separate from "real" love. That sort of belief is a holdover from our

Puritan past, when sex was considered a necessary evil, not to be confused with pure love and affection. A good way to get over the problems that result from such attitudes is to give yourself a good education in modern sexual mores. The many available sex manuals and therapy programs can go a long way to alleviate the problems that may come up.

In the bedroom you can indulge in some role-playing in which your partner is cloaked as a stranger, which can heighten lovemaking. Various scenarios of this type may provide some exciting experiences in loving, bringing you and your partner closer, both emotionally and sexually.

By looking at sex as an exciting journey of exploration with a friend, you both will derive maximum enjoyment from the experience.

Moon Conjunct Mars

Your emotions are very strong, and you react to a potential partner's advances quickly and forcefully. Similarly, an ongoing relationship tends to be quite volatile, with great energy put into love.

However, you should resist the temptation to move too hastily, particularly in making a commitment or expressing anger toward a loved one. Always give yourself some leeway to reconsider, for you may become cool to an idea as quickly as you became interested. Or if you flare up at your lover, you may realize afterward that you didn't really mean to be so intense.

Your partner can always depend on you for strength and support, particularly when a lot is needed right away. On the other hand, for long-range endurance, you may have to depend on your partner.

As a lover you are quite intense; you may learn to make love last and savor the more delicate qualities that may be lost in the heat of the moment. A lover who can bank your fires a bit will help you achieve the full range of enjoyment that lovemaking offers.

Moon Sextile Mars

More than most people, you can maintain an even flow of emotional energy. Because of this, you will not burn yourself out in the initial excitement of an affair, but will make it last and explore its possibilities more fully. This is just one outcome of your basic ability to react to life with strength but moderation.

In lovemaking you can pace yourself in response to your partner's energies without getting out of sync or pushing your partner faster than pleasure dictates. Instead, you can hit a perfect stride, so that both of you get the most out of the experience.

However, you are probably happiest with a fairly active lover who encourages you to use up all your available energy without any left over at the end of an experience, for that could be frustrating for you. The more you exercise, the better you will become, and without practice, your abilities and enjoyment of lovemaking will diminish.

As long as you have enough outlets for your energies, you will have an active and rewarding love life. If you feel that your partner is cramping your style, you both should make some adjustments; and if that does not work, you should find a new and more compatible partner.

Moon Square Mars

You may tend to fly off the handle when you encounter an obstacle or when you cannot make things work out just as you want. Of course, this tendency will have a negative influence upon your love life, since love does not usually flourish in an atmosphere of temper tantrums. Sometimes, however, lovemaking is at its most intense right after a fierce argument, when your passion is still running high.

But in most cases you should try to curb this tendency. When you feel the flush of anger coming on, try to calm down and restrain yourself. It is better to sublimate that energy into determination to overcome the obstacle you face; that is a more creative and productive outlet for your anger.

Some of your problems may result from trouble with initiation and timing of lovemaking. When you have the energy, you may not be in the mood, and vice versa. You can get around this problem somewhat by agreeing in advance on a specific time for lovemaking when you know you will have the energy. The expectation will provide the mood. For this arrangement to be fully effective, you should change the time and place now and again so that loving remains a treat rather than a fixed obligation.

Moon Trine Mars

You should be able to respond to your partner with measured endurance, thus meeting the needs of the most demanding lover. You tend not to notice demands that others would consider too great, because you see them as a challenge to your abilities that can keep you fit and trim.

Remember, however, that your lover may not be up to your level of energy, and be prepared to slow down if the situation so demands. But if this happens very often, you may decide that you would be happier with another partner. Holding in your natural energy too much will result in an explosion of pent-up need or in atrophy of your abilities.

In general, your partner can call on you for strength in times of need, for you happily go an extra mile without considering it a sacrifice or putting your lover in your debt. You should not be overly generous with your strength, however, for your partner may lean on you too heavily. After a while, that will unbalance the relationship and also sap your strength, for it is not inexhaustible.

Moon Inconjunct Mars

You may find that your energy level depends upon your emotional state: at times you may push yourself to the point of exhaustion, and at other times you may be totally unable to move because of emotional problems.

You are much more likely to be overactive than to be immobilized. Therefore you may be too responsive to your lover, losing sight of the appropriate time to stop and rest. That problem can be solved by asking your lover to tell you when to slow down.

However, once you have tackled a problem, you are almost tireless. You assault the obstacle from every direction until it is removed or until you are totally drained of energy. This may be both physically and emotionally stressful for you and your partner, so you should learn to slow down and concentrate your energy in one place. In the long run that should be more effective and much more restful.

As you get older, this energetic approach to life will mellow and turn to your advantage. The eagerness of early youth is sometimes undirected, but as time goes by, this is replaced by motivation and effective achievement.

Moon Opposition Mars

You may find that changes in your emotional state cause great variations in your energy level, so that at one moment you are full of get up and go, and the next moment you are drained of energy.

To a certain extent, this is a natural state for you and should not present any problems if you are aware of it and structure your life accordingly. In fact, at times you can commit extraordinary energy to an affair; when you are in high gear, you can reach the highest peaks of fulfillment.

If your swings of energy are too extreme or if you happen to be in a situation in which that style is inappropriate, you may have to forcibly calm yourself down and feed that energy back inside yourself. The result of this process usually is that the next low point is not as deep or as draining.

To a certain extent, a partner whose emotions are more even will help regulate your energy flow and take up the slack for you when needed. Sexually, this balance will make your performance and enjoyment more consistent. You will be less likely to overwhelm your lover with intensity or leave him or her wanting. You will have the right amount of energy to make loving what it should be so that it fulfills your own and your lover's needs.

Moon Conjunct Jupiter

You probably respond to life with great gusto and flair. In an active love affair, you are inclined to be emotional. You are quite open and candid about your feelings, seldom holding back your opinions about your lover. You will be happiest with a partner whose style and feelings are similar; if that is the case, a very creative and honest relationship will result.

If there is a problem with this placement, it may be that you tend to overreact to unimportant events and spend more energy on an affair than it is worth. This style may be too intense for a more retiring lover and may scare off potential partners who feel that they aren't up to your level of energy.

Once involved with a partner, however, your happy, positive energies will sweep the two of you into an affair that bubbles with enthusiasm and joy. Because opposites attract, you may be involved with a more moody or melancholy person. Although you can teach such a person a great deal about loving life, the relationship could be a drain on your resources. It might be better to share your creativity with someone who will augment rather than sap your energies.

Moon Sextile Jupiter

Your flow of creativity is fairly well balanced and your view of life is optimistic but not unrealistic. In other words, you are positive in your approach, but you do not see the world through rose-colored glasses.

For this reason, you are not likely to rush into a relationship but will grow into it step by step. An affair unfolds more and more with each successive commitment. With this style, you aren't likely to have many whirlwind affairs, but your relationships are likely to be successful and rewarding in the long run, without much risk of heartbreak.

Logically, you should find a lover with similar inclinations who will not try to rush you into something that neither of you is ready for. With time and gentle effort, the relationship will blossom, as long as you are not rushed by compulsive emotional urgency.

If you handle your affairs in this way, you will be admired and idealized by your friends, because you manage to avoid the pitfalls that they continually stumble into. Be modest about your abilities, however, for admiration can easily turn to envy, if it is not correctly handled.

Moon Square Jupiter

You should take care to restrain your emotions somewhat, for reactions that you feel are appropriate to the occasion may appear overstated to those around you. Your view of the world tends to be quite positive and optimistic, but not always entirely realistic. Because of your too-bright outlook, you may get into situations over your head.

This applies especially to commitments in a love relationship, which you are likely to walk into without really watching where you are going. This habit can get you into affairs that weigh you down with responsibilities, thus spoiling your innocent pleasure in loving, which was your initial inspiration.

You will be most compatible with a lover who has both feet on the ground, a trustworthy person whose advice you can listen and adhere to. As you gain experience, it will become less necessary to depend on your lover. In any case, it is valuable to see yourself as others see you.

You are usually cheery and jovial, no matter what the circumstances, which is a real asset for attracting potential lovers. As you get older, your optimism will give you a special kind of magnetism because of the vibrant inner tension of controlled emotional extravagance.

Moon Trine Jupiter

Your style is marked by an easygoing warmth that is neither extravagant nor retiring, which indicates that you have ample love and affection to give to the world. Naturally, that makes you attractive to others, and it will be quite easy for you to become involved both wisely and enjoyably with partners of your choice.

Do not let the easy flow of your emotions lead you to become lazy in love or to take your positive situation for granted, however. Building a meaningful love relationship always requires active effort and some stress and difficulty. Even though you can avoid problems more easily than most, you should be willing to work on developing an important affair.

In general, you are favored in love, and you can transfer this ability to your partner if he or she is less fortunate in this respect. You should not neglect this talent, for it will keep your creative energies in tune and enable you to be a helpful and creative force in your lover's life. If you are careful not to make your lover feel indebted to you, you will have a sparkling relationship and a partner who will be steadfast in times of need.

Moon Inconjunct Jupiter

Your dynamic, restless creativity will allow you to experience a wide range of emotions within your love relationships. This means that you will have a very active love life, but it may also keep you under pressure to produce emotionally. You may have a difficult time slowing down your creative energies to keep pace with your partner.

Along with this, you may have a sort of compulsive generosity. As a result, you may heap too much affection upon your lover, which may be confusing or smothering instead of having the intended effect of simple love expression.

Thus, you will be happiest with a lover who has the energy and stamina to keep up with you or with one who can calm your emotions effectively. Without such a partner, you will simply have to force yourself to slow down. Simplify your emotional commitments and thoroughly explore what you already have before going on to something else.

If you learn to pace yourself, you will become an accomplished and emotionally aware person, who can draw upon a deep well of experience to enhance a relationship.

Moon Opposition Jupiter

You will find that you tend to swing to emotional extremes; either you are head-over-heels in love, or you are not at all interested in a potential partner. Actually, this attitude can make love even more enjoyable. It is a problem only if you close your eyes to your lover's major faults, which might bring you harm later.

To avoid such problems, even though you feel very sure about your feelings for a new lover, don't make a binding commitment right away. Give yourself plenty of time to reconsider your decision or uncover aspects of the relationship that you have passed by or intentionally overlooked in your initial enthusiasm.

This is not to say that you will necessarily revise your opinions negatively; probably you will not. But it is better to give the relationship some time, so you can be safe instead of sorry.

In general, your personality is quite excitable and exciting; you want to be actively creative and on the move at all times, meeting people and living a fairly volatile emotional life with little boredom. You should look for a partner who can keep up with you or who will be content to stay home while you pursue a more active life.

Moon Conjunct Saturn

You tend to have a rather cautious view of love and will not rush into a relationship without giving it a good deal of thought beforehand. This approach will certainly help you avoid some unwise affairs, but it may also cause you to drag your feet and lose an impatient lover who cannot wait for you to make up your mind.

Once you make a decision, however, you usually stick to it to the end, so you are the most loyal of partners once you have committed yourself to a relationship. However, you demand equal commitment and loyalty from your lover, insisting that your partner conform to the letter of the law in this respect.

In lovemaking, you tend to be conservative, valuing tenderness and communication over technique. You will be most compatible with a lover whose views are similar rather than someone who always wants to experiment. However, a lover with a lively imagination could help you by instigating change and variety when things slow down.

Before passing judgment on yourself or your lover, wait to see how the situation develops—very often it will come out better than you expect. Try not to be so critical, but at the same time maintain your high standards.

Moon Sextile Saturn

You are an emotionally stable person and cautious about committing your feelings to another. This attitude will spare you the emotional upheavals of a rash or unwise relationship. You are more likely, after much thought, to enter into a long-range affair that builds slowly but surely.

At times you may be too serious, so you would benefit from finding a lover with a good sense of humor who can show you the lighter side and cheer you up when you are down. Indeed, you can afford to have a less stable partner, for whom you provide a steadying influence; such a relationship would benefit both of you.

You insist on meaningful affection in an affair and will not find real satisfaction in sex unaccompanied by sincere and lasting love. You are also sincere in lovemaking, and thus you can be a particularly considerate and thoughtful lover. Your lover can surely make up for your lack of frivolity.

In the long run, your relationships should be rich and long-lasting; others will consider you lucky in love, but it is talent, not luck, and the credit belongs to you.

Moon Square Saturn

You may find it rather difficult to be spontaneous in your emotional responses, and you may leap to unwarranted negative conclusions. You can avoid this by simply reserving judgment in emotional matters as much as possible. This will allow you to glide into affairs that you might have shied away from through inhibition or distrust.

A profitable way to improve your judgment and your ability to enter positive emotional situations is by reflecting on your past experiences. By going over them in detail, analyzing your good moves and your mistakes, you will learn to let your mind guide you when your emotional evaluation of a situation fails. This approach may make you a bit intellectual in love at first, but in the long run it will provide a solid emotional framework that will give you even and positive response within your relationships.

It is particularly important to give yourself credit for your abilities, so that you will have the confidence to use them with assurance. You may be unnecessarily hesitant, and the best way to prevent that is to know yourself well. Hesitancy comes from lack of self-knowledge rather than insufficient self-confidence.

Moon Trine Saturn

You have a very even, well-balanced style, which will give you considerable emotional security; you can weather most of the difficulties that arise within a relationship. Indeed, you may be a shelter for your lover, a stalwart helpmate in time of distress.

Your relationships are usually serious, but you have a good sense of proportion and are not likely to become too somber or unhumorous regarding your affairs. In lovemaking you have a measured pace and are not as immediately intense as some people. In time, as the relationship grows, your intensity will build until it becomes very strong.

Because of your native stability, you can cope with an insecure lover, for you can provide the stability that your partner lacks. Such a relationship would help you combat your tendency to be emotionally lazy and to avoid change. Do not let your partner lean on you too much, however, for the relationship may be based on dependency rather than love, which will not serve either of you well.

In the end, you will probably have one highly developed and satisfying love relationship, and as you get older, the years will smile on you.

Moon Inconjunct Saturn

Your emotional standards are highly developed, which may keep you away from some affairs that could be quite enjoyable. You should be a bit more relaxed and easier on yourself and your lover. Then the situation will evolve by itself with a minimum of control or enforced direction.

Make an extra effort to be generous toward your partner and forgiving if your lover hurts you inadvertently. Similarly, if you have acted selfishly or thoughtlessly toward your partner, don't be too harsh in your judgment of yourself. You are as human as everybody else, and we all make mistakes.

However, when you let yourself go, you have a talent for very highly refined lovemaking. You are satisfied only with the very best, and you will go to considerable trouble to locate perfection.

You may tend to be quite impatient with your lover or with your emotional situation in general; as a result you may give up on an affair before it has had a chance to develop. In your case, relationships do not usually bloom right away, so don't give up in haste unless the affair has proved unsuccessful over a long period or has simply stopped growing. The kind of excellence you seek is not built in a day, but takes time and effort.

Moon Opposition Saturn

You may become discouraged rather quickly when there are problems in a relationship, and as a result you may become quite distant from your partner. This, of course, is quite the opposite of what you should do to solve a problem; instead, you should make every effort to get closer to your lover so that communication can be restored and your love renewed.

Naturally, this will not be easy if your lover is like you in this respect. If you both withdraw at the same time, it will be very difficult to repair the situation. Therefore you should choose a lover whose outlook is optimistic, someone who can help you bounce back when you are blue or if you lose touch with the relationship.

No matter what kind of partner you have, you should try to endure periods of difficulty or alienation. They probably will not last too long, and afterward the affair will pick up where it left off, if you give it a chance. This is especially likely if you tell your lover about the difficult periods in advance so that there will be no blame to interfere with your good feelings later.

Oddly enough, you are able to effectively pursue several affairs at once. When things are at a standstill in one affair, you can turn your attention to another until the first renews itself.

Moon Conjunct Uranus

Probably your friends consider you a bundle of surprises, for you have a way of doing the unexpected in most situations. You have a unique style of thought, especially in your emotional response to others and in your way of modifying the suggestions of those around you.

You will be most compatible with someone who has a similar flair for the unusual or who appreciates this talent in you. If that is the case, you can feel free to explore all the nooks and crannies of your imagination without fear of offending your lover.

You tend to change your mind rather suddenly and completely. When that seems appropriate to others, they admire your decisiveness, but when it does not, you may be considered inconsistent or flighty. For handling everyday affairs, you need a steady, reliable partner who is not so changeable, so that the duller necessities of life can get done without interruption.

You have a real talent for inventive experimentation in love, and you should feel free to follow your imagination as far as your body will allow. This can make sexuality very creative, but keep an eye on your lover to make sure that you aren't going too far or too fast for mutual enjoyment. Your partner has the extra responsibility of following your lead and learning from your example.

Moon Sextile Uranus

You have an easy ability to express sexual and emotional freedom. You can range wide in your creativity without losing touch with the essence of loving affection. This makes you a particularly satisfying partner who will enrich the life of any lover you choose.

Changes in your relationships will occur with a certain regularity, which contributes to healthy growth, for you are not likely to get into bottleneck situations in which changes are made only after intense pressure. In this respect, you may be able to ease your lover through difficult situations by using your own insights to clarify and resolve problems in the relationship.

However, you should make changes only when they are warranted, for it is easy to get into the habit of switching things around just for the sake of variety. If you are in doubt, let the situation be for a while before attempting to introduce innovations.

After a long period of time, you may find that you have covered a lot of territory and have radically rearranged your relationship, but in small steps rather than in one traumatic leap.

Moon Square Uranus

Your attitudes toward love and your partner may be rather erratic and subject to frequent changes over time. Make very sure that there are real reasons for making any major turnaround in an affair, for unnecessary changes are likely to wreck it.

You should outline your needs and desires quite carefully to your lover, perhaps even in writing at times. That will give you a better intellectual grip on your changing tastes, so that you will be less likely to confuse or disorient your partner. Your lover should be a person who expects the unexpected and can tolerate your sometimes arbitrary shifts in attitude.

You can use this aspect of your personality most creatively by being the initiator in sexual situations, rather than altering your partner's directions. In that way your innovative spirit will be free to create, and your lover can suggest refinements.

Pay attention to what you are doing so that you can avoid going to extremes. If you take control of your emotional self, your emotions will not take control of you, at least not without your knowledge and intention.

Moon Trine Uranus

You treasure freedom of self-expression very much, and you are able to use it positively without abusing the privilege. Thus, you can be very creative and guiltlessly innovative in love and sexual expression without going beyond the limits of enjoyment.

To this extent, you will get along well with a partner who depends on you for change and variety in your relationship. You have enough creativity for two in this area. However, it is important that your lover give you a free hand and not try to edit your ideas without adding anything new.

You have the ability to handle unusual affairs with ease and few upsets. In fact, such a relationship can stimulate your creativity. While others might feel insecure in a situation that is out of the ordinary, you are only encouraged to extend and develop it.

Dealing with such situations is made easier by your ability to communicate clearly. Matters seldom get out of hand because of confusion, for you always make very clear just how you feel about your partner and the relationship.

Moon Inconjunct Uranus

Although you are very creative and inventive, at times you may exercise these talents too hastily, so that you do not take time to explore each idea fully before going on to the next. This is likely to be a problem for your lover, who may find it difficult to keep up with you or to be satisfied when you move on.

This is especially important in lovemaking if new techniques are involved. It takes time to develop them so that you both can derive full pleasure and achieve true communication as well. If you move on too hastily without completing what you have started, frustration will result, particularly for your lover, and what is intended to bring you closer together will have just the opposite effect.

Thus it is a good idea to pace yourself and, with your partner's help, to get all possible enjoyment from one activity before moving on to another. At times this may seem difficult, because for you, half the pleasure is in the invention. Here your lover may have to step in and show you how much can be done with what you have dreamed up.

In any case, you will have a wide range of love experiences that will continue indefinitely, which in time can make you quite an expert on the subject.

Moon Opposition Uranus

You may find that your emotions change dramatically and rather suddenly, sometimes without any warning. This makes your love affairs rather tumultuous, but with the potential for great excitement.

For you, making changes in an existing relationship or heading toward a new one does not happen gradually but all at once, sometimes with considerable force. This kind of extremism can be toned down by a trusted, stable lover whose advice you will take if you are overreacting to a situation. By having a clear, objective view of yourself, you can better govern your mood changes and separate the need for real alterations in a relationship from irrational dissatisfaction.

You may have several on-again off-again relationships going at one time in which nothing much happens for a long time. Then suddenly your encounters will be quite intense. This approach makes it difficult to maintain a regular relationship on an even keel for a long time, unless you develop considerable discipline and control over your changeable moods. But this problem is partly balanced by your great intensity in love expression, which can give you very memorable emotional and sexual experiences.

Moon Conjunct Neptune

You are a rather idealistic person, and you require a lover to live up to very special standards. However, you must be sure to outline exactly what you do want, so that your partner won't unknowingly fail to fulfill your desires. This may be difficult for you at times, for your ideals tend to be rather vague and hard to express in words. But remember that it will be much harder to get what you want from love if you do not define for your lover exactly what that is.

However, your vagueness will make you something of a mystery to your lover, which can be quite nice, especially at the beginning of a relationship, giving you the upper hand quite often. But in the long run, it is a good idea to let your partner know where you stand, in order to balance the affair.

You may be capable of carrying on quite a lofty platonic relationship. Physical expression does not always have to accompany love, even in a very close relationship. In some affairs, spiritual qualities may take the lead and force sexuality into the back seat. In any case, spiritual communication will always be important to you in a relationship, and sex for its own sake is not so appealing, although you may do it on that level to please a friend.

Moon Sextile Neptune

You have a fairly realistic idea of what you can expect from a relationship, and you respond accordingly. In general, you don't make impossible demands of your lover.

In line with this, you are quite understanding, and you readily forgive a lover who cannot live up to your ideals or to his or her own standards. You recognize that it may be better to tailor your demands to your partner's personality instead of the other way around. This is desirable up to a point, but don't let a partner fail you continually without putting your foot down.

Probably you can achieve a very intuitive kind of communication with your partner. This ability can make loving an easy, flowing experience, eliminating, in part, the need for verbal expression, which can be quite clumsy. Your style of sexual expression is delicate and gentle, and works best when it is on a rather ethereal, spiritual plane. With this approach, you may become involved in a relationship that is basically platonic. However, you are too well-balanced to entirely give up the pleasures of the flesh.

Instead, you will enlarge your horizon to encompass all aspects of love, not insisting upon having those that are difficult or inaccessible.

Moon Square Neptune

You must be particularly careful to make your responses clear to your partner, for you may often be misinterpreted because of phrasing your thoughts inaccurately or not saying exactly what you mean. This is very important, but by making sure that you and your partner agree on what you mean, each of you will be saved much backtracking and emotional entanglement.

In general, you should make an extra effort to be strictly honest in a relationship, because it may be very easy for you to get what you want through dissembling. You may not mean to harm others, but this habit will tend to snowball, and even a little white lie may backfire or evolve into a big black one that may seriously damage a relationship.

By making the extra effort to be honest, you will become very knowledgeable about the meanings of truth and honesty. You will learn more than most people learn about language and how shades of meanings can be either informative or confusing.

A well-educated partner with a sharp mind will be an asset to you in this respect. Together you can make precise verbal communication into an art and a special way of transmitting love within your relationship.

Moon Trine Neptune

You have a great capacity for empathy and can be the kindest of lovers when you choose. Your nature is very forgiving, and you value your lover's intentions more than the results, which cannot express the love behind them so well.

You may communicate with your lover quite wordlessly, in a continuing flow of love and affection that needs little physical expression. You can anticipate your partner's needs and conduct the relationship on a lofty, ethereal plane.

However, be sure to check now and again that your lover is receiving your wordless messages. You should touch ground occasionally so that you won't get lost in the mists of spirituality that sometimes surround a love affair. This may be particularly important in the area of sex, so that you know you are still meeting your lover's needs. Otherwise, physical frustration will interrupt your more spiritual communication.

In the end, your view of love will include balanced proportions of the mental and physical, without neglecting one for the other. Also, you can act as a balance for a lover who is not quite so even and who must struggle to keep from swinging to extremes.

Moon Inconjunct Neptune

You may tend to be entirely too idealistic about love, setting standards for yourself and your lover that cannot realistically be fulfilled. This attitude is likely to doom the relationship from the beginning. Therefore, make a special effort to be less demanding. Differentiate between what you can really achieve in a relationship and what can happen only in fantasy.

One way to channel this kind of energy is to express your fantasies through sex. In your bedroom you can play out many delightful ways of relating that are not possible in everyday life. This can be a source of considerable enjoyment, for you probably have a fertile imagination and can provide many enjoyable scenarios for you and your lover to play out.

Just take care to plot out the action in advance, for otherwise your lover won't know in detail what you really want. By outlining what will happen beforehand, you will avoid any awkward situations.

If you take this direction, you will be able to create opportunities to act out situations that others only dream about, while still keeping a good grip on reality in your everyday interaction.

Moon Opposition Neptune

You should select a rather pragmatic partner who can keep fact and fiction separate, for you tend to have problems in that area. You tend to swing between being extremely lucid and clear in your emotional response to being totally unable to express yourself or get across how you feel.

Thus you will be most happy with someone who can confirm your feelings and provide an objective view of how you react and interact with others.

You have flashes of intuition that are sometimes quite accurate, but at other times way off base. A partner who is more down to earth can help you separate what is real from what is not. But such a person will help you only if you trust him or her and act on the advice given you. At times you must be willing to go against your own judgment in order to benefit from your partner's help and to understand where you may have strayed from reality.

You probably have a very vivid imagination, which can add greatly to your love life by providing a wealth of fantasies that you and your partner can enjoy.

Moon Conjunct Pluto

Your emotions have an intensity that can lead you into very strong love affairs. You aren't likely to take love lightly; instead you throw yourself into it with total commitment.

Although this approach makes for very powerful and penetrating experiences, you may find that your emotions somehow run away with you, and you lose all control over them. If you are not careful to stay in control, you may have relationships that are destructive and one-sided although very intense and all-consuming, particularly on the physical side.

Often your love attachments have a feeling of fatedness, such that you and your partner seem to have been brought together by destiny. Losing yourself in such a relationship seems inevitable. If you feel this way, take care to stop and think before going on with the affair. No relationship is so fated that you cannot avoid it if necessary, and to give up your right to choice in love invites disaster. Such a relationship may be either tremendously uplifting or quite enslaving, and it is not likely to be anything in between those two extremes. So keep your eyes open; the choice is yours.

In any case, if you strive for balance between you and your partner, your very powerful love energies will take the right direction.

Moon Sextile Pluto

Your emotional responses have a fundamental security that will see you through the most difficult times. You know that in the end everything will turn out all right. It is not so much that you are sure your current affair will work out well, for indeed it may not, but that you have a kind of universal faith. Your long-range emotional security comes from within yourself and is not dependent upon your partner or the relationship, so difficulties in that area may trouble you but will not cause irreparable damage.

At times you may seem somewhat detached from a relationship, because you are not so dependent upon your partner as others often are. Your detachment does not indicate a lack of love or commitment in any way, and you should assure your partner of that, so that he or she will not worry. You are fortunate to be emotionally self-sufficient so that you can enter into a relationship as an equal partner. If there is any dependency, it is more likely that your lover will lean on you. This may be flattering, but you should help your lover outgrow this dependency, for without it you will have a much easier and richer relationship.

In any situation, your inner strength will buoy you up, so despite any difficulties that arise, you are assured of a relatively happy ending.

Moon Square Pluto

You have a deeply rooted need to be in control of emotional situations, but you must learn to handle this desire with care. It is quite difficult to succeed in love and at the same time to have total control over your partner, especially in today's world, so some adaptation is necessary.

It is possible to satisfy this need in part by making clear assignments of responsibility within a relationship so that each of you knows who is in charge of what. Your need to control your partner stems less from lust for power than from fear of losing control in general. Knowing that everything is under control in your relationship will help relieve that fear.

Naturally, the only sure way of knowing that everything is secure is to be in charge of the entire affair, but this cannot be accomplished in a balanced relationship. Instead, make your relinquishment of power in certain areas a special gift of love to your partner; your trust will help cement the relationship and enrich your mutual commitment. Any control you have lost will be balanced by the achievement of a more powerful and secure relationship that transcends both of you.

Moon Trine Pluto

You have a basic inner security that enables you to handle difficult situations with strength and assurance when others are falling to pieces. When your emotional life is in shambles, you are able to take effective steps to restore it.

Naturally, this means that you can be supportive of your partner, particularly in times of stress. You don't require a lover who is extremely emotionally stable, for you will not often need to lean on your partner. In fact, it is more likely to be the other way around. However, do not let your lover lean on you too much, for that will sap your strength.

You can risk emotional adventures that might prove harmful to others, because you have a reservoir of emotional strength. You can deal with extreme situations and, in fact, you may even feed on them. Certainly strength does not increase without exercise, but before launching into a new adventure, consider the possible damage to your partner from a forced emotional or sexual adventure.

In the end you are likely to be the stronger partner emotionally. You should try to help others who are less fortunate in this respect, not only because you can afford it, but because it is the right thing to do.

Moon Inconjunct Pluto

You tend to be emotionally intense at all times. Although this may be very enjoyable, it can also be quite exhausting for both you and your lover. It would be a good idea to lighten your mood occasionally and give yourself and your partner a rest; that will improve your mental as well as your physical health.

If this is hard to do while you are together, simply take a vacation from each other now and then. When you are reunited, you can pick up the affair with more pleasure.

Certainly you will seek very intense sexual expression and will want a lover of similar temperament. There may be a theme of control or dominance in your bedroom pleasures, which can be quite healthy and enjoyable. Just be sure to restrict its expression to the bedroom, avoiding control in the everyday aspects of your life.

You may find that you have a wide range of emotions within a single relationship and that the more you and your partner push each other to your limits, the more accomplishment and pleasure you feel. However, that approach may prove to be too much for your love at times. You should be sure about your partner's limits ahead of time so that you will not cause any emotional injury or damage the relationship.

Moon Opposition Pluto

You may experience emotional blockages at times, finding it difficult to express your feelings. This is often followed by a rush of previously pent-up emotions. Because of this habit, you may either underreact or overreact to your lover. You should make every effort to be more even in your responses and to make your lover aware of this problem so that you can communicate more easily without being misinterpreted.

You will be especially compatible with an intuitive lover who divines your feelings when you cannot express them. Knowing that your partner understands will reduce some of your internal emotional pressure.

Also, a partner who is fairly even and stable emotionally will put you in better emotional balance.

In such a relationship, you may contribute by intensifying your lover's emotional experience, thus lending added depth and meaning to the affair. Your ability to go to extremes of emotion will draw your partner along, and at the same time you will be slowed down enough that you won't go over the edge.

You may have the most intense emotional and sexual experiences with a partner who is similar in temperament, but you must be careful about such an affair. Unbalanced situations and power games are likely to be a part of the relationship, which could be quite damaging, in spite of the potential for enjoyment.

Moon Conjunct Ascendant

Your strong personal presence makes you very noticeable and also causes you to have very quick, direct emotional responses. This gives you a certain advantage in choosing a lover, because you are quicker on the draw than your competitors.

At times, you should slow down and think twice before responding to your lover, however. Your emotional honesty may be somewhat threatening to a partner who finds it difficult to believe. This problem may be compounded by your tendency to change your mind on a whim, making you seem flighty when you are simply being straightforward about your feelings. For these reasons, you should use extra caution and forethought, so that you will know how your responses are being interpreted by others.

At the same time, you should not pretend, for you are not likely to be very good at that. Your real feelings usually show in your face, and any attempt to hide them may be all too obvious to others.

You may find that your mental and physical health are closely linked, that emotional problems lower your resistance to disease or that physical illness is a source of distaste or depression. In either case, you will be happiest with a lover who is sensitive to this problem and will help counteract it.

Moon Sextile Ascendant

You probably find it relatively easy to communicate your emotions when you choose to, and you are never at a loss for words. In general, you are quite communicative, with a rather easy and open approach to people.

Just because you express yourself well, however, do not assume that everyone understands you perfectly. People may tend to listen selectively and interpret your words according to their own assumptions and desires.

You may have to reevaluate your friends or partner in this light and attempt to find out how they see you so you can take this into account when dealing with them. That should defuse any jealousies or misinterpretations that have arisen from your honesty, which can sometimes work against you.

You do not need to rely on words alone to get your messages across, for you have a natural command of body language. Even when words fail, you can make your responses clear just by the way you move. The emotional ambiance you create subconsciously gives a clear picture of how you feel.

Moon Square Ascendant

At times you may overreact to emotional situations and expend too much psychic energy in coping with a relationship. This approach is not necessarily bad or counterproductive, but your partner may be a bit puzzled when you get so wrought up about a situation that doesn't warrant it.

The basic detriment of this attitude is the drain on your energy, leaving you unable to deal with a really demanding situation. Since your emotional overreactions tend to run in set patterns, you can get around this difficulty by relying on your partner to let you know when you are going too far. If you take note of when and where that happens, in future situations you can consciously hold back a bit and save a good deal of stress.

Part of the reason for this overexpenditure of energy may be that you feel you can't communicate effectively, that nobody understands your message unless you really assault them with it. This may be true in part, but you can solve that problem by being very verbally precise and not relying on subtler clues of expression or body language to get the message across. In your case such tactics may actually belie your words.

Moon Trine Ascendant

You probably can express your feelings to others quite easily and naturally, and your body and emotions are usually fairly well in tune. This is a particularly happy combination because it means that you usually have pleasant relationships.

As a result, you will be able to communicate with others on an emotional level without the necessity for precise verbalization. Why elaborate in words, when a meaningful look will do? With most partners, this means ease of communication and lack of tension, but you may run across someone who simply doesn't understand that kind of language, who requires elaborate explanations in order to transmit the message of love.

That sort of person is not usually your type, but you may lose a real jewel of a person if you neglect the intellectual side of communication. Because you have much natural talent in one area, you may become lazy and neglect other areas, which could inhibit your ability to relate to others.

Therefore, enjoy and use your natural abilities for emotional expression, but also investigate methods that are not so familiar, that can expand your emotional horizons.

Moon Inconjunct Ascendant

You are capable of a high degree of emotional response, and your emotions are almost constantly flowing, your feelings always in action. This means that you will have a rather volatile love life, subject to many changes.

You may find that the physical and sexual side of a relationship is a major motivation for emotional changes and that your emotional development leads to further physical progress, and so on.

However, this principle also works in reverse: if your sex life becomes stagnant, so does your emotional life, and it may be very difficult to get things going again. If you want to sustain a major, ongoing relationship, however, you should learn to slow down, for continual change can be physically and emotionally exhausting. Both you and your partner need an occasional breather.

Perhaps the best way to accomplish this is to spend some time away from each other now and then. That will give you the rest you need, and the internal growth you have experienced in that time will rekindle the relationship, thus avoiding the stagnation that might have occurred if you were together.

Moon Opposition Ascendant

For you, having a lover or close friend at all times is critical to your emotional expression, and without one you may feel emotionally sterile. When you are alone, you may find it difficult to really put your heart into doing anything, whereas with a partner your energies really begin to flow. You become excited and committed, not only to the relationship but to outside activities as well.

As a result, you will become quite an expert on your lover's emotional ins and outs, simply because you exert so much energy in that direction. Your lover will be a mirror of your emotions, which will help you to become more well-rounded and self-aware.

Your partner will also help you communicate your emotions to others, aiding you in getting across messages that you find difficult or impossible to express. As your lover comes to know you better, he or she will know when you are saying one thing and meaning another. With people who do not know you so well, that trait may present problems.

The longer you pursue a relationship, the more self-aware you will become. Your partner will teach you about aspects of yourself that you did not understand and bring you to a high level of emotional self-understanding.

Chapter Seven

Mercury

Mercury in the Chart

The position of Mercury in your chart describes your mental style and inclinations. Since the stimulation for sexual expression is related to your attitudes and fantasies, Mercury is quite important in the discussion of sexuality. Depending on how you use imagination in the service of love, you may create a rich set of experiences or, on the other hand, you may inhibit your expression of love.

It is important to remember that the body cannot always go where the mind suggests. Some forms of sexual expression that seem exciting or enjoyable beforehand may be less interesting or even impossible in actual practice. But it is quite possible to enjoy those experiences in imagination, leaving the more practical forms of expression for real life. Your ability to do this successfully depends on how consistent the position of Mercury is with that of the other planets in your chart.

Mercury is basically an asexual planet and thus it is not a major indicator of your actual sexual expression or desires. Instead, it describes what you think about and the embellishments you dream up to add subtlety and variety to your sexual experience. To that extent, Mercury can have a powerful enriching effect, even though it is not a strong internal motivating factor, except through curiosity.

Mercury in Aries

Your mind is so quick that it often races ahead of the situation you are in, anticipating what is yet to come. Although this means that you are usually in firm control of the situation, you may leave your lover behind in moments of affection, because without realizing it, you skimp on some of the meaningful details of love.

Therefore it is a good idea to consciously slow down and adjust your pace to your partner's, so that loving is a truly shared experience, not just separate self-gratification.

You are happiest when you act out your fantasies immediately, rather than lingering over and refining them. You should make this clear to your partner, however, for many people are content to let their fantasies remain in their imagintion. If that is you partner's expectation, you could be disappointed.

Even if your sexual imagination is forceful or even violent at times, do not attempt to repress or censor it, for that would work against you. Such fantasies, when worked out with a loving partner, can be most enjoyable and are tamed considerably in the realization.

For a full relationship, you need a lover who is as direct and clear about sex as you are, someone who can absorb your high energy and give the affair a regular pace. Then you won't overlook the many delicacies of love.

Mercury in Taurus

For you, love is not a highly technical affair, as it is for some others, but a direct encounter of feelings between two people. Rather than choreographing a sexual encounter ahead of time, you prefer to let it happen spontaneously.

On the other hand, you really enjoy making love in rich and sensuous surroundings, either natural or man-made, and the lusher the better. Indeed, making love in a steaming tropical jungle could be most pleasing, but be sure the vegetation is not poison ivy. A velvet and brocade bower is a more readily available setting that can satisfy the same sensuous taste. The richer the setting, the more intense are your feelings.

You shouldn't spend too much time preparing the mood or setting for love, however. Too long a delay without actual sexual expression tends to bottle up your feelings, making it difficult to express them naturally when the time comes. Like food, sex needs to be partaken of regularly, even if it is simple fare. Too great a hunger can spoil an elegantly prepared meal. Whereas some people can sublimate their sexuality in other areas, you are at your best if you express it directly and often enough to avoid frustration or tension. A lover who has similar tastes and needs will keep you happiest and on a sexually even keel.

Mercury in Gemini

You have a distinct ability to express your sexual needs and desires verbally, and you are happiest with a lover who can express love on a mental as well as a physical plane. You can learn to use words with great erotic impact, and the better your love vocabulary, the more expressive your lovemaking will be.

This ability can be useful in simple courting as well as in making love, for your verbal expressiveness greatly enhances the experience. Indeed, you and your partner will derive much pleasure from erotic conversations or discussions. Even a phone call at the appropriate time can be turned into a love affair.

You may also enjoy discussing lovemaking with your lover both before and afterward, affectionately going over every detail and exchanging ideas about what each of you enjoys most. Fantasies are also a fertile topic, and your prolific imagination can dream up many scenarios that are impractical in reality but that are great fun to talk about.

Reading about sex will further enrich your fantasy life and give you new paths to explore. By developing and trying out a variety of sexual techniques, you can have a fuller love life and greater communication with your lover.

Mercury in Cancer

Although you have a fertile imagination, you share your fantasies only with your dearest and most trusted friends. This part of your life is very private, and those few who share it are privileged indeed.

Don't be too cautious about sharing your feelings, however, because even a casual lover should know something of what is going on inside you. Otherwise you will not reach a satisfactory level of love and communication in an affair.

Once you are truly involved with someone, however, your lover becomes everything to you. For you, the ideal affair is one in which both partners are truly lost in each other, needing no outside contact or stimulation for happiness. Unlike more sociable types, you would enjoy being stranded with your love on a remote tropical isle with only each other for company and affection.

This may be the truest and most total form of devotion, but you should avoid being overprotective of your lover. That tends to have the opposite of the desired effect, making your partner feel cramped and in need of elbow room. As long as you both know that you are each other's firm refuge, that is enough for security and happiness.

Mercury in Leo

This position is ideal for an easygoing relationship. You don't bother with the kind of highly detailed self-analysis that can get in the way of a natural love affair. Too much thinking spoils the spontaneity for you.

On the other hand, in a more involved or complex relationship, you may overlook or ignore the real problems that have to be dealt with in detail to keep the affair on an even keel. It is wise for you to avoid tangled relationships in which you have to unravel many problems. If you do get into a complicated affair, rely on your partner or a close friend to help straighten it out.

Your idea of a good time with your lover is simple and direct—you prefer spontaneous pleasures to complex plans and arrangements, which tend to get in the way of a happy outing or celebration. The only caution here is that your mind may outdistance your body in capacity for enjoyment, which can lead to exhaustion.

Mercury in Virgo

You have the power to develop very elaborate and detailed fantasies. The more specific and varied each love scenario is, the richer your sexual expression becomes.

The only word of caution is that few real situations can fulfill your fantasies in every respect, and therefore you should not be too demanding of your lover. But at the same time, let your partner know exactly what you like and how you like it. Together you can derive great pleasure from acting out a shared fantasy, with every move discussed and choreographed ahead of time, as if it were a play performance.

You may enjoy using love objects and articles associated with sex. Many different garments and bodily adornments can have powerful sexual connotations and can be used to enrich both foreplay and lovemaking.

Considerable pleasure may be obtained from elaborate kissing and other forms of oral gratification, because you have a very strong desire to devour and be devoured by your lover. Indeed, when lovemaking is inconvenient because of circumstances, a prolonged and sensuous kiss can be a sufficiently deep expression that satisfies the appetite temporarily while promising more for the future.

Mercury in Libra

With your lively imagination, you prefer a love affair that is constantly in motion. You don't want your role in a relationship to be static; you like to continually change your position in relation to your partner, rather like a game. This can be a fine way to enliven a relationship, but do not let it devolve into a competition or a series of rounds of one-upmanship, which can happen if your partner takes the game too seriously.

You envision love as an intrinsically beautiful structure that requires continual upkeep, both physical and emotional, to keep it as close as possible to perfection. You enjoy physical lovemaking, but only if you are personally involved with your partner. A one-night stand does not allow that and is likely to be a disappointment.

Because of your appreciation of the art and technique of love, you may keep careful mental notes on your lovers, comparing them to each other in various ways. This helps you understand the variety of factors that make up an enjoyable relationship.

Probably no partnership can live up to all of your ideal criteria, but don't let that get you down. Much of your pleasure in an affair comes from constant change and improvement, always reaching new levels of beauty and enjoyment.

Mercury in Scorpio

You are probably very intrigued with the physical basis of sexual expression—the relationships between the different parts of the body in lovemaking, the advantages and disadvantages of various sizes and shapes in any sexual situation. There is much artistry in this, which you should develop. This area is often ignored but it can be a great help in getting the most out of sex.

The dark and powerful aspects of sexuality have great appeal for you, and you really enjoy sex most when it is rather secret and mysterious. Too much bright light on the workings of a relationship tends to take away the excitement, making it too mundane. Thus, a clandestine affair has a special appeal for you, and you may act secretive about an affair even when there is no reason to do so, except for the excitement it provides.

Don't let dated social taboos prevent you from trying every kind of physical sexual expression that appeals to you, even if it's labelled perverse or bizarre by the sexually fearful. Repressing such desires will only frustrate you, and expressing them with a willing partner will greatly enhance your sexual experience and understanding.

But you should avoid using sex or sexual attraction as a tool to gain power or influence over others. Sexuality can flourish only when it is free of other motivations.

Mercury in Sagittarius

You look upon sex as a very natural function, so it is not likely to be a source of great worry or anxiety to you. At the same time, it may not be a highly motivating force, either. To you, sex is just one of many areas of enjoyment and communication between partners, neither more nor less important than other forms of personal interchange.

But when you get down to making love, you do it with gusto and abandon. Even though you aren't considered a swinger, you approach the sexual experience in a much more open fashion than most people, for you see no reason to be self-conscious.

Thus sex outdoors or in other natural settings, which is too challenging or inhibiting to some, is easy and enjoyable for you. And even if you haven't the opportunity to actually do this, it is something to contemplate pleasurably.

Your open attitude can make loving much easier by helping to break down the inhibitions of a lover who is willing but not quite ready to stray from the sexual straight-and-narrow. You may sometimes be a sexual teacher, not verbally, but by example and by understanding.

In your actual lovemaking, do not suppress the impulse to express yourself vigorously and vocally. It's bound to add to the excitement and should be toned down only in too-close quarters with easily upset neighbors.

Mercury in Capricorn

When it comes to sex, you are not overly verbal, but you are fairly clear and firm in your opinions about it. That is an advantage, in that one can suffer from too much uncertainty about sex. But don't let your set ideas cause you to become too conservative or unwilling to try something new. You could miss out on a lot that way.

It is a good idea to ask your partner about what pleases him or her most in bed, because with your direct approach to lovemaking, you could easily pass over something that is very important to your lover. Once you know your lover's tastes, you will take care to fulfill them in a thoughtful fashion. Be sure to ask again from time to time, for your lover's needs may change, and the more aware of them you are, the better.

Very likely you agree with the common views of what is normal and abnormal in a sexual relationship. But you can enjoy unusual sexual expression precisely because it is unusual and therefore exciting. If you avoid different experiences without question, your sex life will be less interesting.

Because of your self-assurance, it may seem natural to dominate your partner sexually. But you should try not to do this, even though it seems easiest and best for both of you at first. Instead, seek out your lover's thoughts and fantasies and give them equal weight with yours. That kind of true interplay will always enrich your relationship.

Mercury in Aquarius

Contemplating sexual experimentation may be quite stimulating to you, but the experience itself may be less exciting than thinking about it. But don't hold back because of that fact—all your experiments will be pleasurable and enlightening, and you will treasure the knowledge and understanding that you gain thereby.

You may be quite curious, particularly about the more unusual forms of sexual expression, but you are also cautious, and you won't jump into a situation without first doing some background research.

This may entail reading about the subject beforehand or even watching others so that you know what you're getting into. Puritan mores to the contrary, this can be a particularly pleasant way of enjoying sexuality, for it leaves your mind free to savor each detail without having to think about every move. This is particularly true with unusual forms of sex, which may indeed be difficult to accomplish and are better enjoyed visually, perhaps followed by easier and more natural lovemaking.

You can be quite varied in your approach to loving, because you understand so many different aspects of sexuality. Thus you can be an excellent lover for any partner you choose, whatever the style or preference.

Mercury in Pisces

You don't talk about sex very much, not because you are inhibited or uninterested, but because words don't seem necessary and can't really express your feelings on the subject. Your style of loving is very tender, and in expressing it you give yourself totally to your lover. All you really need for fulfillment is a quiet understanding of the love you share.

Although giving of yourself is your clearest expression of love for your partner, do not give, particularly sexually, unless you really feel like it. If you do, sex will become a task and an obligation rather than a free and open expression of loving. If you want to be heavily self-sacrificing sexually, express it in bedroom games for that purpose rather than in emotional servitude, which will only hurt your relationship.

You don't necessarily need to be in a relationship all the time, because you are able to sublimate your sexual energies through a variety of other channels when the right lover isn't around.

It may take time and care to find just the right person, but when you do make up your mind, it will probably happen in a flash. Ideally, in such a partnership you both will use sexuality to uplift and transcend your personalities, making your oneness greater than the sum of its parts.

Mercury in the First House

Sexually, this position might be characterized as making love with the lights on. You want to explore and understand all the techniques of lovemaking and all the mutations of a personal relationship, never leaving any possibility untried. This does not mean that you are addicted to strange and new sensual experiences just for their own sake, but you insist on checking out each one so you won't miss out on any potential enjoyment.

With this position, the key phrase might be, "That looks like fun—let's try it." Why pass up something that could be enjoyable? This does not mean that you are indiscriminate in choosing your partners, but once you become intimate with a lover, you don't hesitate to explore your new territory. You are wholly committed to turning every aspect of the relationship into a good time for both.

Naturally, you should seek a lover who is similarly inclined, so that your creativity and variety in loving won't be stifled. Be sure to keep open the lines of communication between you about your sexuality and desires in order to avoid misinterpretation and physical frustration. This is a very healthy position, which allows you to try a wide variety of sexual experiments without falling into destructive relationship patterns.

Mercury in the Second House

It may be that to derive the greatest benefits in love, you will have to set aside, at least for a time, your rather strong opinions about sexual practices. At least you should try to see things from another point of view—you may be pleasantly surprised.

If you have definite do's and don'ts about sex, make sure your partner understands them ahead of time so that they don't cause problems or conflicts at the last minute. But it is wise to be flexible, so you won't miss out on experiences that can broaden your potential for pleasure in love.

In most large cities there are boutiques that specialize in delightful bedroom accessories. These can add scope and variety to the sex experience by expanding your sexual horizons and add immensely to your pleasure and your lover's enjoyment in lovemaking.

You place a high value on honesty and consistency in a relationship. This does not necessarily mean that you are overly possessive or that you demand total faithfulness of your lover. But you insist on knowing precisely what is going on so that you won't build up any false illusions or expectations. If you feel secure in the openness of a relationship, you can relax and happily explore new dimensions of love and sexuality.

Mercury in the Third House

You may find that for you, sex is not a necessary component of a close love relationship and that intimacy of the mind is as important as physical intimacy. In any case, you value verbal communication with your lover very highly, and you will not be happy with someone who is mute about his or her affection or who does not appreciate it when you detail your loving feelings.

Your pleasure in verbal expression may extend even to the delightfully humorous experience of making love while carrying on a conversation. This can be particularly amusing if your lovemaking is interrupted by a phone call. You see no reason not to answer it and carry on at the same time. The caller might wonder why you are out of breath, but you can handle that and even delight in your divided attentions. Only make sure that your lover is as amused as you and does not think you are taking lovemaking too lightly.

You may have some problems with a partner who wants to delve heavily into the inner emotional motivations of your relationship, because you are not likely to be interested in such probing. If an affair is going well, you see no need to ask questions, and if it isn't, why continue? If carried too far, this attitude may lead to rather shallow, short-lived relationships. Every partnership benefits from some in-depth probing during rough times, and you would do well to get help from your partner in this area.

Mercury in the Fourth House

In matters of the heart, you are not likely to waste words, and when you speak, you address the essentials of the situation. Although you can often discern the root of a problem immediately, you should approach critical matters very carefully with your partner and unravel the solutions gradually. In that way you won't overwhelm or offend your lover if he or she is oversensitive about an issue, and your remarks won't be overlooked because of their brevity.

Your style of loving may be strongly influenced by that of your parents, and you may find it enjoyable and reassuring to repeat many aspects of their relationship. On a less introspective level, making love in old-fashioned surroundings or in your childhood home may be particularly erotic to you. If the opportunity comes up, your old bed or that of your parents may be a highly charged spot for lovemaking.

You will profit by investing your energy in a long-range relationship, even if it offers no immediate return. Such a relationship pays off in depth of emotion, which you will seek when short-lived affairs have had their day. Despite your enjoyment of a variety of sexual experiments, in the long run you will derive the greatest satisfaction from the simpler joys of tenderness and sincere devotion.

Mercury in the Fifth House

You express your sexuality more playfully than most people. Where others seek a heavy, unsmiling affair in order to feel the intensity of passion, you enjoy a bantering, laughing relationship that leaves both of you feeling warm and friendly inside. For you, sex is a source of fun and merriment more than an expression of inner drives or conflicts, as it often is for others.

Partly for this reason, you may feel most at home with a younger lover or someone who is as young at heart as you are. You don't usually get hung up on details of technique or sexual expertise, except to freshen and revivify a relationship. It is the quality of eternal newness that you are concerned with, rather than sexual accomplishments.

Surrounding yourself with pleasant and entertaining details—beautiful surroundings, lovely music—during lovemaking will surely enhance the joyousness of the occasion.

Erotic art or photography may add to your enjoyment, and if your partner is not self-conscious, an automatic polaroid can capture your happiest moments to be treasured and enjoyed again later. As long as it adds to the experience for both of you, any happy bedroom game will be a joy, with no regrets afterward.

Mercury in the Sixth House

Depending on how flexible you are, your carefully considered approach to sex can be either a help or a hindrance to you and your lover. In terms of sexual technique, you cannot become too skilled—every new idea that might enhance lovemaking is worth learning for future enjoyment. On the other hand, do not become too technical about lovemaking and lose sight of the open communication that is at the heart of every successful love affair.

You find it quite natural to analyze your feelings and emotions about a relationship, which is necessary up to a point; it can help you understand what you are doing and thus avoid many pitfalls. But do not let your analysis get in the way of spontaneity or keep you from expressing your natural feelings for fear of upsetting the situation. Better to follow your true emotions and let the relationship restructure itself accordingly.

This is important, because you have a natural inclination to go out of your way to please your partner, even bending over backward to make everything come out right. This is very laudable and gives you a real sense of accomplishment, but don't neglect your own pleasures and desires. Repressing your own needs will only backfire later, but if you express them to your lover, it will warm and further develop your intimacy.

Mercury in the Seventh House

You will be happiest with an active lover who not only participates in but initiates the action in your relationship. Such a partner serves as an energy source and a mirror for your own personality, lightening and refreshing your self-image and your feelings about love.

At the same time you go out of your way to help and understand your lover by immersing yourself in his or her joys and problems. However, even in the most intimate relationship, you must be especially careful to respect your partner's right to privacy. Your genuine concern for your lover's welfare may seem to your loved one more like prying than helping.

You will be most happy if you can share much more than just a physical love relationship with your partner, although that is an essential and important part of most love affairs. The more areas of interaction between you, the more satisfying the relationship will be to you, although not necessarily to your partner. You may have to tread lightly in some areas.

To learn more about your lover's personality and bring the two of you closer, you are willing to try almost anything your partner suggests to enhance the relationship. But remember what your limits are and that for a truly fulfilling affair you *both* must find enjoyment in what you do.

Mercury in the Eighth House

In a love relationship, your innate inclination is to dig deep. In fact, you are not likely to have a shallow or lightweight affair, because you turn even a casual encounter into a deep and meaningful relationship. Take care, however, that you both want to make that commitment, for you may be hurt inadvertently by a well-meaning partner who simply doesn't want to become so involved. Intensity in a relationship is wasted unless it comes from both sides.

It is a good idea to study and understand the very physical and organic aspects of love, from which you can learn many pleasurable and useful sexual techniques. Also, this will provide a wealth of personal and universal symbolism that can enhance your understanding of relationships and of life in general. Much of the duality in sexual symbolism applies to other areas of life and can be of great use to you.

As an offshoot of your studies you may discover views of love that are nearly forgotten in this so-called "liberated" age. These older beliefs are full of insight and value and will richly fill out your own love experiences. Do not believe only the current dogma of sex; instead, dig deep into the wellsprings of the past to discover a greater range of human experience, not from a scientific point of view, but from the point of view of the participants.

Mercury in the Ninth House

You may find great personal satisfaction and fulfillment in sexual role-playing, acting out little dramas in which you and your partner adopt certain attitudes and then play them out to see the results. This should not be done in a static way; the roles should shift from time to time so that each player gets to play the game of love from every angle.

Essentially, you are able to look upon love as an adventure, an exploration in the endless realm of pleasurable possibilities, given the right motivation and opportunity. Whether your inclination is to have one partner or many, you thrive best in an active situation with a great variety of sexual experience, both physical and emotional.

You are not likely to get bogged down in repeating the same experience over and over, so you should find a partner who prefers variety also. For you it is enough to taste and sample and then move on to other delights; you feel no need to make a pig of yourself.

Thus your lover does not serve as a source of security for you, but as an emotional traveling companion with whom to share the good times and weather the storms. As time goes on, you will savor remembrances of past adventures with your lover while sitting cozily, and more safely, in front of a glowing fire.

Mercury in the Tenth House

At times you may find it difficult to enjoy sex simply as sex, because it seems to get entangled in other areas of your life. Or you may use it to reinforce personal ties, even in a nonsexual relationship. You must try your best to rid your sexual life of other motives and avoid using sex, even unintentionally, to bribe or reward your partner's behavior.

You should look for a partner who stimulates you and helps you improve, both physically and emotionally. At its peak, love can be an energizing challenge that transforms and revitalizes you and your partner. Do not let this aspect of it devolve into sexual competition, however, because that would be self-defeating. You should respect your lover's feelings and be sensitive to the times when it is better to be still.

Through circumstance you may have quite a reputation as a sexual achiever, but you shouldn't let it go to your head. The essence of love is thoughtfulness and consideration of your partner, without which your good fortune in love will be lost. In the long run, honesty and reliability are your mainstays in a relationship.

Sometimes your head may be too full of other ideas for involved lovemaking, or your mind may drift. It is best, therefore, to reserve moments of intimacy for times when your mind is free, and you can concentrate on what is happening.

Mercury in the Eleventh House

You are probably an optimist in matters of love, and as a result, your love life improves continually, or so it seems. This makes for generally happy feelings, but from time to time you must summarize your situation as realistically as possible and make whatever adjustments are necessary. This process can tell you when to end a relationship that has been dragging on, to make room for a more profitable new one.

This does not mean that you simply abandon your old lovers; quite the opposite, in fact. Anyone with whom you have been intimately related will always remain a friend, even if you no longer have much in common.

Your sex life now may be changing and adjusting to the current awareness of sexual technique and variety of expression. It is good that there is greater freedom of expression in sex than there ever has been, but remember, it is freedom to do what you want. You are not obliged to try something new just because it's there or because others are doing it. Choose the pleasures that you enjoy rather than everything that is novel. With that attitude, sex will uplift and transform your relationships, and for you, that is its highest function; techniques are only tools to help you gain that end.

Mercury in the Twelfth House

You may find it somewhat difficult to clearly express your emotions or intentions to your lover in words; the right phrase often occurs to you only when the appropriate time has passed. Therefore, you do better if you communicate in more physical ways—using body language, touch, facial expressions, even gifts. For that reason, you need a partner who does not need to have everything spelled out to understand what you are trying to get across. To a sensitive lover, a meaningful glance is worth a paragraph.

You tend to be fairly closemouthed about exactly what goes on in your relationships, and you consider inquiries into your love life as an invasion of privacy. Not everyone will respect your privacy, but rather than offend an innocently prying friend, you should tell a few white lies. Usually that will end the questioning, leaving you even more an object of mystery.

Even though you aren't particularly verbal, you are drawn toward probing the deepest and most mysterious aspects of your own relationships and of human relationships in general. In this area, you need to explore various experiences at first hand; advice from other explorers of the subconscious can serve only as a guide. Experience, both good and bad, is your best teacher.

Mercury Conjunct Venus

You are very good at letting your partner know about your needs and desires, so you seldom suffer frustration because of inability to communicate what you want.

You also have a good eye for aesthetic proportions, both in your surroundings and in your lover. You may express yourself artistically, most likely in the visual arts, and will gravitate toward other artistic people. You are not attracted to those who lack grace and finesse, even though they are sincere.

You may be a gifted speaker, or at least you express yourself in a gracious and charming manner. Because of this talent, you may find much satisfaction in conversation with a lover who appreciates or shares your ability.

You are quite open about discussing sex, and you use all your learning and conceptual abilities to improve your sexual expression. Similarly, conversational lovemaking may be a special pleasure. You should ignore any outmoded social convention about being silent during lovemaking, for verbal expression can greatly enhance your enjoyment.

Mercury Sextile Venus

You have an easy talent for expressing your desires, but you may not have explored it thoroughly or derived the greatest pleasure from this ability. Perhaps you take verbal expression for granted, because you have always been good at it, but you have not tried to find out just how much enjoyment it can bring.

On the most obvious level, you are able to successfully fulfill your fantasies because you can outline them in detail to your lover. Then, instead of just trying them once and forgetting them, take the trouble to perfect the scenarios you devise and get the maximum pleasure from them. Each time you return to them, they will improve.

On another level, you can use your verbal and conceptual abilities to heighten the anticipation of love by discussing what will happen, savoring it mentally before accomplishing it physically. The mind has a wealth of pleasures to add to lovemaking, but it takes a little effort. The effort is not in doing them well, which comes naturally to you, but in motivating yourself to get past the awkward beginning stages. When you've really got things rolling, you will know that it was worth every ounce of effort.

Mercury Conjunct Mars

You express yourself directly and forcefully, and you put a lot of energy into what you say to your lover. Words are an important tool for making an impact and, whether or not you use words well, you do talk a lot and with a will.

Take care to avoid overstating your views, letting your words speak louder than your deeds. Speak forcefully only when you plan to carry through on your words, or you will find that no one takes you seriously.

You may derive a certain stimulation from debating and arguing with your partner. In fact, you are more likely to argue with your lover than with a stranger, for that is a form of affectionate expression for you. This kind of mental exercise may not be especially pleasing to your lover, however, and he or she may take you more seriously than you intend. Step carefully in this area, therefore, and argue only when you know your partner will not be annoyed.

You are able to express your love with great conviction, which can be most valuable to a verbally orientated lover who has difficulty relating to more intuitive or bodily forms of expression. Where others might confuse such a person, you are able to hit home with strength and love.

Mercury Sextile Mars

You have a good understanding of your style of verbal expression, and you can make your ideas clear to your partner without excessive debate or argument. You say just enough to get the message across in even, well-thought-out words, and that is all.

However, you may not feel motivated to think in depth about what you really mean or question the validity of your statements. To this extent, you would be compatible with a lover who is an intellectual gadfly who can stimulate your mental development. It is valuable to have a sometimes skeptical partner test your ideas, particularly your assumptions about sex. You may have some mistaken ideas that you have taken for granted, which have kept you, unknowingly, from pleasure and greater development in that area.

Once you accept the necessity of revising your ideas, you approach the problem with sensitivity, working on it until the idea meets the real needs of your relationship. Even if you yourself do not discover the need for changing your view, you won't balk, but will rationally make the necessary change.

Mercury Square Mars

For you, unclear communication can be a real source of irritation, and you may be overdemanding of your partner when he or she doesn't say exactly what is meant or what you want to hear.

You should resist the temptation to argue just to make your feelings known and exercise as much restraint as possible. In the short run this may mean considerable frustration from resisting the urge to contradict your partner when you believe he or she is wrong. However, in the long run you will have a much clearer view of the truth, and you will see where you and your partner have strayed from it.

Practicing restraint will also teach you the inadvisability of haste, and you will learn to be far more patient, controlled, and accurate in your speech. One way to work toward this goal is by employing self-awareness techniques, such as leaving a tape recorder on when you and your lover are together and later reviewing what was recorded. This will show when to check your tongue and wait patiently for the problem to resolve itself. Basically, these problems will fade gradually as you continue to mature emotionally.

Mercury Trine Mars

You should be able to express yourself clearly and strongly, communicating your meaning without expending too much energy. Indeed, you can be forceful and persuasive in the most suave and quiet manner, while others have to raise their voices to make the same point.

With this talent, conversations with your lover can be both effective and peaceful. You can settle arguments by moderately proposing the obviously correct solution in such a way that neither of you is dissatisfied with the outcome. Also, you can use your strengths to help a less articulate partner communicate, which is necessary in order to keep an affair active and growing. When your partner is at a loss for words, you can step in gracefully and provide them, and if an argument seems about to break out, you can resolve it by stabilizing the interaction.

Do not take these talents for granted, however. Unless you work to realize and develop them, they will decay with time, and you will lose the ability to speak and know you will hit the mark. In this respect, a challenging partner who can use your help will stimulate and enlarge your abilities.

Mercury Inconjunct Mars

You may feel compelled to express your ideas verbally; you get carried away by the need to develop and express your concepts. This compulsion can make you tremendously creative verbally, or it can turn you into a motormouth who never stops talking. It all depends on how you use your talents.

Clearly, your need for verbal expression is a result of your very active and restless mind. One way to express that need is to use your partner as a sounding board for your ideas. For that, you need a receptive lover who is as verbal as you are. Otherwise, your ideas may fall on deaf ears, and your partner might think you a bore as well, which would not profit either of you.

Another way to tap some of this energy is to express your ideas in writing. Then you will not be tempted to inundate your lover with your latest brainstorms; he or she can peruse them at will, and you can refer to and revise them later. By writing down your ideas, you will make them concrete enough to judge their value and their possible commercial potential.

You may particularly enjoy writing down your love fantasies and submitting them to your lover for revision before playing them out, thus providing the chance for maximum fulfillment for you both.

Mercury Opposition Mars

You may tend to communicate in fits and starts, finding it easy to speak clearly and intensely to your partner at one time and quite impossible at another time. Or you may feel strongly about expressing your love at one time and undermotivated at another.

Because of this trait, you will be happiest with an intuitive lover who can glean your meaning from the slightest indication when necessary, who will not demand that you spell out exactly what you mean all the time. At times you may not really know what you mean, at least not enough to put it into words.

At other times, however, you may talk too much, drowning your feelings in the words that would not come at all before. You will be fortunate to find a partner who can tell you when to shut up, especially if you are willing to listen. Oddly enough, as a result your style of expression will become more even, and you will be less subject to moods in which you cannot say what you mean.

On occasion, you may have sudden inspirations, and you should have a pad and pencil by your bedside so you can set down your ideas before they slip away.

Mercury Conjunct Jupiter

You are a person who finds great creativity in the realm of ideas. In love, therefore, you are quite inventive, overflowing with thoughts about how to make loving better and more interesting.

Many of these ideas may be best expressed verbally, so you would be happy with a lover who appreciates not only the physical side of sexuality but its more imaginative mental side as well. Together, you can dream up and carry out expansive fantasy scenarios. It would be good to have a lover who can fill in the details, because your abundant ideas are likely to need refining if they are to work out well.

Try not to go overboard in verbal expression, however, because it would be better to be considered a creative thinker than to be a windbag. Therefore, wait till your inspirations are full-blown before you discuss them; otherwise you may find that people have lost interest by the time the creation is complete. Also you have quite a flair for the dramatic, so your brainstorms appear to be born fully formed, and your erotic fantasies, in particular, have great impact because they are presented whole and fully developed.

Mercury Sextile Jupiter

You tend to be quite creative and imaginative in love, with a regular flow of ideas rather than fits and starts of inspiration. Thus, you are likely to develop sexual scenarios in stages, making continual improvements as new ideas come to you.

Instead of contradicting your lover concerning the direction of your relationship, you attempt to blend and compromise if the two of you are at odds about which way to go. This approach will avoid many standstills and blocks to your progress, so you can go far in creating new experiences, even though you are not the only factor determining your direction.

From time to time you may get locked into too much of a routine in lovemaking, and then a break toward the adventurous might be in order—something different enough to be challenging, that neither of you has done before. Because of your relative stability in handling new ideas, you can cope with and enjoy such experimentation. Instead of being a threat, it is a stimulus to mind and body. Working in a new direction has the effect of heightening both your pleasure and your closeness to your partner.

Mercury Square Jupiter

Although you are likely to be quite creative in the realm of sexual fantasy, your creations may go somewhat beyond what is practicable. It may be that many of your fantasies can be played out only in the imagination, because they would stretch your own and your lover's abilities far beyond what you could do in fact.

Before attempting to carry out any sexual fantasy, you must carefully weigh how realistic it is. Many ideas that are stimulating to the imagination are not really pleasurable in realization. To determine what can be enjoyably done, trust your lover's advice about the practicality of your ideas. By having an outside opinion always available, you can avoid scenes that would be less than fulfilling and also achieve some that you had not thought possible, with the help of an imaginative partner.

With practice, you will become very experienced in love and knowledgeable about what will and won't work out in a love relationship. In many cases, you will learn through making errors, but even love scenes that don't succeed have humor and warmth, particularly when you look back on them affectionately with an old lover.

Mercury Trine Jupiter

You have much imagination in love, but you may not have tapped it fully. Creativity comes quite naturally to you, at least in the realm of ideas, and therefore you may tend to take it for granted.

For this reason, you may require a somewhat demanding partner who can goad you into action when things get dull, so that your abilities stay in trim. You have a much more creative sexual imagination than you give yourself credit for.

This is particularly helpful in judging which sexual scenarios will actually work out to enhance the pleasure of both you and your partner. In fantasy it is easy to devise very stimulating ideas, but if carried out, some could be quite disappointing or even unpleasant. You have a good sense of just how successful a fantasy will be when acted upon and can help your partner avoid directions that would be sexually disappointing or harmful, steering toward those that will actively enhance the relationship.

As a general rule, you should be extra cautious, but at the same time you should be willing to drop your inhibitions now and then and follow your partner into something you have some doubts about. Not only will that be exciting, it will test and improve your judgment in such matters.

Mercury Inconjunct Jupiter

You have a very fertile imagination that tends to keep going nonstop. This can lead to the most creative and interesting forms of love expression if you are willing to take the time and energy to put your ideas into practice.

You may have to slow down a bit and pick and choose the ideas that you will fulfill, for the products of your imagination are likely to be more than you can cope with or realize physically. In addition, you may have to spend some time polishing your ideas before you can put them into practice effectively.

To a certain extent you can be helped in this pursuit by a fairly practical lover who can put your fantasies into working order. Still, you will have to slow down a bit in order to accomplish the goals of pleasure and satisfaction that you seek.

You may do well with a partner who has a strong capacity for verbal expressions of love. Much of the excitement in your fantasies may be in the ideas themselves, with physical fulfillment strictly secondary. This is often true when your imagination runs wild in scenarios that you and your lover could not possibly achieve or afford, but which can be great fun to contemplate together.

Mercury Opposition Jupiter

Your imagination may work in fits and starts, so that sometimes you are brimming over with good ideas and sometimes you can't think of any way to improve or add to your love life.

This is really quite natural for you, so don't bother to beat your head against a wall because inspiration hasn't struck. But on the other hand, don't compliment yourself too much when you seem to be a storehouse of genius. Each phase will come and go, and it will all balance out in the end.

There are some ways to make your mind work more evenly, which you might try. The easiest way is to find a lover who can fill in when you are uninspired and come up with mutually enjoyable pleasures. That is not always possible, of course, or you may be emotionally attached to a person who does not have that talent. In that case you may enjoy writing down your ideas when they are flowing freely. You usually have more ideas than you can implement at that time, anyway. In this way, you will build up a storehouse of fantasy and potential pleasures that you and your lover can draw upon when you are feeling less creative.

In fact, you might find it stimulating and enjoyable to keep a bank of love ideas together so that you can choose which fantasy to fulfill when the mood moves you.

Mercury Conjunct Saturn

Your imagination may tend to be very intense, and you may get much pleasure from fulfilling the same sexual fantasy over and over again. Once you have settled on what you enjoy, you will enjoy it for a long time.

However, your partner may not share this attitude, so you should make an effort to see that he or she gets enough variety, even though you may be happy with an unvarying diet in love. And if you follow your lover's lead into new territories, you may discover some new experiences that will provide lots of mileage in the future.

You may tend to take your lover's words very seriously or be too grave in your thinking about love. Love and sexuality can provide much mirth and merriment as well as the more intense and serious kinds of pleasure that appeal to you. If you can learn to be a well-rounded lover, you will get great enjoyment from your relationship, and your lover will be able to derive much pleasure from your attentions.

Although sex is certainly a fit subject for deep thought and commitment, it can also be a source of frivolity, a light and pleasant pastime for you and your lover that does not require emotional pressure.

Mercury Sextile Saturn

You have a generally stable mind and imagination, and your judgment about affairs of the heart is quite solid, at least insofar as such affairs can be mentally analyzed. You definitely know the difference between a fantasy that is strictly for the imagination and one that can reasonably be fulfilled in the bedroom.

In this area, you should draw upon your lover's ideas about sexual possibilities, for you may not be able to fulfill the actively creative role all on your own. Rather, you should tap your partner's mind for possibly pleasing ideas and then use your own stable judgment to determine which ones can be effectively carried out.

You should make an effort to convince your lover and yourself that you possess this skill in judgment, for you may have overlooked it yourself. Your ability to analyze the practicality of an affair is considerable, and the more you practice, the better you will get. This will make the relationship much more stable, because you will avoid situations that cannot work out, that would cause injury or disappointment if you tried them. This will benefit both you and your lover, even though you occasionally have to put your foot down and say no.

Mercury Square Saturn

You may have some difficulty in communicating your needs in love to your lover. This may be because you lack verbal talents, but more likely it is because you feel inhibited about your desires or worried that your lover may not approve.

Usually, if you say what you mean in spite of your doubts, you will be rewarded rather than scorned, and the more often you do this, the fewer communication problems you will have. Your ideas may sometimes be rather heavy, but love has room for a wide range of emotions and needs, not just hearts and flowers.

However, you should resist the temptation to criticize your partner repeatedly in love matters. If your lover won't deal with a problem after you have mentioned it several times, it may go deeper than you realized. To keep on attacking it from the same point of view will be counterproductive and seem like nagging.

When you do have an important criticism, say it and be done with it, but let the details iron themselves out without harping on them.

Mercury Trine Saturn

You are rather pragmatic about love and are not likely to be too demanding of yourself or your partner about dreaming up changes in your relationship. Instead, you put great value on your mutual accomplishments, savoring the styles and techniques of lovemaking that you have developed together.

This kind of steady patience is particularly valuable when your relationship is going through a fallow period when nothing seems to be happening, even though exciting changes are bubbling under the surface. To apply too much pressure for movement at this time can be harmful, but you have the good sense at such times to do nothing but wait for creative developments.

At times, however, you may have to lean on your partner to make the major changes in your affair. Your fairly steady hand can deal with a partner who is very creative, if somewhat unsteady. Such a lover would be very good for you, supplying the ideas that you then regulate and polish.

With that combination, your relationship can have maximum stability and growth while effectively avoiding both extremism and stagnation.

Mercury Inconjunct Saturn

You should resist the temptation to criticize your partner in matters of love, particularly sex. Your lover may indeed deserve the criticism and need to make improvements, which you could suggest, but negative criticism in love almost never has its intended effect. Instead, it tends to kill the affection that brought the two of you together in the first place.

Thus, if you see room for improvement in your relationship, approach the subject positively, making creative suggestions for new experiments in order to improve what you have already achieved in the affair. In this way you can gradually work your lover out of bad habits and into good ones without risking hurt feelings or alienation, which criticism sometimes causes.

You should take a similar approach to yourself, for you tend to be too self-critical. If you feel you have done something wrong or have mishandled a situation, relax and start all over again without self-recrimination. With more self-confidence, you will do better, and you can take advantage of your mistakes instead of letting them weigh you down and inhibit your future performance.

Mercury Opposition Saturn

At times you may be very hard on yourself or your lover for mistakes or misunderstandings that were not really anyone's fault. Fortunately, when you look back on the incident, you realize that you have overreacted, and you take steps to correct the situation.

You will learn that it is better not to criticize until you have had time to think over the situation and judge whether your harsh response is warranted. This is not to say that you should be entirely uncritical of your lover, for any affair requires examination and change in order to grow creatively. But this examination should be done as objectively as possible. With time and practice, you can certainly develop the ability to stand back and see your relationship clearly. While you are learning, however, caution is in order.

From time to time you may take the details of an affair too much to heart, or you may overlook something that doesn't mean much to you but is very important to your lover. Do not let such incidents scar your relationship or cause you to hold a grudge against your partner. Make a special effort to explain what has happened so that it won't recur, and then simply forgive and forget.

Mercury Conjunct Uranus

You have an original and unusual imagination in all matters, including love. In a relationship, you are likely to be the one who introduces new directions. You tend to be the source of stimulation and change in an affair, so you can work well with a less imaginative lover because you have more than enough ideas for you both.

Certainly you will not let a relationship become stagnant; in fact at times you may try to introduce innovations too suddenly, which may be hard for your lover to cope with. It would be wise to slow down and implement your ideas more gradually, so that your partner can enjoy the fruits of your imagination. This approach would help you as well, for sometimes, in your continual quest for originality, you abandon a technique or approach to love before you have mined all its pleasurable possibilities. In part this can be corrected by a lover who effectively slows you down. But you can compensate for it by periodically returning to older styles of affection and exploring their previously undiscovered possibilities.

At any rate, you will never be hard up for new and stimulating ideas. Properly handled, these can bring you and your lover endless enjoyment and excitement.

Mercury Sextile Uranus

You probably have a relatively even flow of inspiration, so that lovemaking never becomes dull from repetitiveness or lack of imagination. Along with being an originator in love, you also have the talent to develop an idea or a fantasy fully instead of leaving it half-formed or unfulfilled.

In this respect, you may be happiest with a lover who has a great imagination but who tends to leap from one thing to another. You can richly fulfill your own and your lover's fantasies in such a way that you can play them out again and again, each time with new and different pleasure.

There may be a drawback to this talent, however, an inclination to dream up fascinating ideas without bothering to implement them. Most fantasies can be realized with a willing partner, and they will surely enhance your enjoyment of a relationship, even though it may be an effort to make the right preparations. You just need internal motivation and the energy to start things going; the rest will take care of itself.

Mercury Square Uranus

You may find it hard to decide exactly what is most pleasing to yourself and your lover, always thinking that the grass is greener on the other side of the fence. Once you get there, of course, you find that it isn't. This may apply to the partners you choose as well as to your methods of lovemaking.

The reason for this attitude may be a certain intellectual impatience; when you fail to achieve total satisfaction right at the outset of a relationship, you are disappointed. However, it takes time to develop enjoyment in love. You should turn your restless energy to devising ways to improve and heighten your love experiences, bringing them to the peak of pleasure and communication.

This lesson will come from experience. You will find that when you spend real time and energy on a relationship, it brings much more long-term satisfaction than a newer, perhaps more original, affair, which may also be rather shallow. The net result is that you will develop considerable judgment and discrimination concerning which relationships and lovemaking techniques have real potential and which offer only temporary surface stimulation. Knowing this will save you much wasted time and effort in love.

Mercury Trine Uranus

You have a natural ability to discern which directions in love will be profitable and which will not. You find pleasure in the most original styles of lovemaking, because you pick only those that will truly give you enjoyment, bypassing intuitively those that might involve problems.

In this area, your lover should be willing to trust your judgment, for that will help you both avoid trouble and wasted time in your relationship.

On the other hand, you can rely on your lover for energy and impetus to lead you in new directions, for you may not feel motivated to enact even your own good ideas without a little boost from your partner. You can then develop and refine your lover's imaginative suggestions in stable but interesting directions.

With the right partner, you can explore a wide range of love experiences without running into snags, unlike many couples, who pursue fantasies or techniques that sound interesting but turn out to be unsatisfactory for both parties. You may miss some areas of possible enjoyment, but at best you will enjoy an extraordinary breadth of sexual experience.

Mercury Inconjunct Uranus

Your imagination in love, as well as in many other areas, is almost limitless, but it may be hampered by your disinclination to refine the ideas and fantasies you dream up. Your desire to come up with original and innovative ideas may cause you to miss the substance of those that you have already devised.

Because of this trait, you will be happiest with a lover who is less original but who enjoys working out the details of your ideas with you. Such a lover will enrich your love experience immeasurably and allow you to truly enjoy the fruits of your own imagination.

If there is any lesson to be learned, it is that newness in love is not necessarily good in itself, but it is valuable if it furthers communication and growth of affection between you. Indeed, too much innovation can be so distracting that it slows down the growth of a relationship. It may be wise to slow down and go back over your past innovations, savoring them in depth before moving on. In this way you will bring depth and meaning to your undoubtedly wide variety of love experience.

Mercury Opposition Uranus

In love you are sometimes quite inspired and full of ideas for improving your relationships, and sometimes your mind is entirely blank in these respects; you are not likely to be in between. This is natural for you, and if you handle it properly, you can still achieve regular growth and development in an affair.

The key is to spend your uninspired moments developing the ideas and approaches that you have dreamed up in more creative moments. And when you are overflowing with ideas and fantasies, you should not rush into fulfilling them. Although they don't seem extreme in your imagination, they may be difficult to fulfill enjoyably, and if the fulfillment of your fantasy backfires, it will result only in disappointment.

This can be done in several ways. First, you can simply file your ideas for more careful development later, which will allow you to consider them more carefully and weed out what cannot be accomplished pleasurably. Also you can rely on your lover to judge your ideas from outside and decide how practical they really are. With the right lover, this is an ideal approach, because it doesn't put a damper on spontaneous realization of your love fantasies.

Mercury Conjunct Neptune

You are likely to have a very rich fantasy life, and fulfillment of these fantasies can be the deepest and most rewarding experience for you. In love, your horizons are unlimited; you will never run out of ways to make love continually interesting.

However, you may have some trouble in finding ways to carry out your love fantasies in reality. If you have run into problems in playing out your desires, you may have given up, letting your fantasies live only in your imagination. If that is the case, your affections are likely to be too internalized.

Probably the best way to get around this is to go over your fantasies in detail with your lover, perhaps even writing them down. Together you can decide which ones to realize and how to go about it.

In this fashion you can effectively live your dreams without the disappointment of killing an unrealistic fantasy in trying to realize it. At first it may be difficult to express your desires, for they may lie on the emotional plane as much as on the physical, having more to do with how your lover relates to you than with what is actually done. Learning to discuss these desires will help you relate as you want to.

Mercury Sextile Neptune

You have a good imagination in love and a fairly rich fantasy life. You also have the talent to discern which fantasies can realistically be played out and which are better left in the imagination.

It will be helpful if your lover is willing to take your advice on such matters and won't try to force you into something that can't work or be pleasurable for both of you. However, you may need your lover to give you a little extra push to work out those desires that are realistic and can bring you both pleasure.

In part you are unwilling to go into the elaborate details required by some fantasies, and in part you enjoy simply contemplating them, which gives enough mental pleasure so that you are not really motivated to put them into effect. Probably you will find that actually living out your love dreams when possible will provide much more pleasure and enjoyment than simply savoring them in your imagination. Save your more impossible fantasies for that.

In general, you should have a fairly fruitful imagination in love, and you need never be bored for lack of stimulating ideas that will please both you and your partner.

Mercury Square Neptune

You may have some difficulty communicating to your lover just what pleases you and what desires you would like to fulfill. Therefore, you should try very hard to make your desires perfectly clear, even writing them down so there won't be any mistakes. If you provide your lover with a written scenario of your fantasies, there's far less chance of disappointment than if you just assume that you have been understood. At any rate, it is good to go over the details together, to weed out the ideas that are exciting to imagine but not so pleasant in reality.

It is most important that you try hard to be strictly truthful with your partner, because quite unconsciously, you may get wrapped up in unnecessary white lies, which can become big black ones without your realizing it. Deceit, even if unintentional, is deadly to any relationship, so be forewarned.

If you take extra care to hold to the truth, even when it is painful, you will develop a high degree of discernment and an unusual ability to ferret out the real meaning of a situation. This will result in better affairs.

Mercury Trine Neptune

You probably have a good ability to realize your fantasies and to help your partner fulfill his or her hidden needs and desires. You can discern what is practicable and what is not, and you know what methods are most effective in making a fantasy come true. In part this ability stems from your characteristic patience, taking the time to make sure all the details are right before playing out your ideas. Fantasy is fragile stuff, and small errors in judgment can bring a whole imaginative construct tumbling down. You are very good at preventing this, and also you can salvage experiences that start to go awry by using your flexible imagination to adjust to unanticipated needs.

However, you may not be aggressive enough in asserting your own desires. Although you are a most thoughtful partner who will not impose unwanted ideas on a lover, you may be frustrated if you don't step forward and ask for what you want. In this respect, it would be good to have an encouraging partner who actively motivates you to fulfill your needs, so that they don't just gather dust in your imagination.

Mercury Inconjunct Neptune

Your fantasy life may be quite demanding, and you may find it somewhat difficult to satisfactorily act out your desires in reality. Unless the scenario is just right, it's not likely to be pleasurable for you.

This happens for two reasons: first, the dream you are trying to realize may be too fixed and detailed to be practicable. In that case, you should either simplify your fantasy or leave it in your imagination. On the other hand, your fantasy may be so vague that it can't be worked out without more details. Then, all that's needed is a little imaginative work to fill in and integrate all the necessary details.

In any case, you will be happiest with a lover who is willing to go to some effort in playing roles and structuring scenarios, so that you both can get the greatest benefit from your sexual creativity. And you should be extra thoughtful toward your partner and avoid setting extremely high standards for sexual success. Unfortunately, reality seldom lives up to your dreams; when it does, rejoice, but when it does not, don't waste time in disappointments. Better to take love as it comes and enjoy whatever surprises it offers that you may not have imagined.

Mercury Opposition Neptune

You may be subject to wide swings of judgment concerning what you can and cannot achieve in a relationship, both emotionally and sexually. At times you have a really firm grip on reality, and at other times it slips away entirely.

You will be happiest with a lover whose judgment you can rely on when in doubt, someone who will take the responsibility for such judgment from time to time. Although you may have richly inspired fantasies, many of which can be realized, you should accept it when your lover says you have gone overboard in your imagining.

You may be the major source of imaginative ideas in the relationship, with your lover serving as a check on your runaway creativity.

Having a partner who balances you in this respect will help you to have better judgment as time goes on. Instead of learning only from your mistakes, you can chart an even and rewarding course between reality and fantasy.

Mercury Conjunct Pluto

You are likely to place considerable importance on intellectual communication in a relationship. Probably your deepest experiences are in the realms of the mind rather than of the body. You prefer to have the upper hand intellectually in an affair, but you should avoid personal power struggles to bring this about.

If your partner does not agree with you on some matter, do not make it a matter of pride to force your opinion on him or her. Instead, respect your lover's thoughts, and if they don't match yours, reconsider your own views. Handled in this way, disagreements can transform both of you, expanding your knowledge and views, rather than devolving into blind battles of personal control.

You value deep, penetrating thought, and you don't usually approach a subject lightly. However, you should take time to enjoy the more frivolous side of love, where pleasure is its own reward and no probing questions are asked. This may not be the most rewarding or exhilarating aspect of affection for you, but it will balance your tendency to become too one-sided or fixed in your views.

By learning to be more lighthearted, you can direct your intellectual and emotional energies better. And with your lover's help, you can see when you are getting too deep and involved before it's too late, which can save you a great deal of energy.

Mercury Sextile Pluto

Your ideas are quite stable and unwavering, which means that you can be of great help to a lover who has lost his or her sense of direction. This talent comes not so much from an ability to debate issues brilliantly but from a sure inner knowledge of your beliefs, which you demonstrate in actions as well as words.

You can deal with people whose personalities or beliefs are very different from yours without being influenced to become like them in any way. This allows you to have a wide range of experiences that might be harmful to others but that are educational and broadening to you.

You should make an extra effort not to take your beliefs for granted, assuming that anyone who disagrees with you, particularly a lover, is wrong. This is an easy trap to fall into, and it will do you no good in your lover's eyes. Beliefs are of value only if they can stand up to questioning and criticism, and unquestioned self-assurance will only make you appear smug.

If given healthy exercise, however, your resilient personal faith will see you through the vicissitudes of opinion and morality in love. You will emerge in good shape, and your innately honorable thinking will make you respected and desired as a partner.

Mercury Square Pluto

You must avoid the temptation to argue with your lover, no matter how convinced you are that you are right and your partner is wrong. Instead, make a great effort to allow each other the right to your own opinions. In that way you will avoid many potential pitfalls in your relationship.

There are many ways to do this and still maintain a functional relationship. One way is to divide the responsibilities, so that you each know who is responsible for what. Otherwise, there will be confusion about who is to blame when things go wrong. This approach will clarify the facts at issue, so that they are not subject to debate. Then, just be sure to avoid saying, "I told you so," a statement that asks for retaliation. You'll find that your affair will go much more smoothly.

In time you will overcome the temptation to argue. That will enable you to know when you are wrong and to forgive your partner's errors. Most important, you will have an increasingly clear perspective on reality and more effective control over your ideas.

Experience will teach you to use demonstrable reality as your most effective argument, which will eliminate the need for wasted words and emotions and will enhance your partner's respect for you.

Mercury Trine Pluto

Although you cannot always put it into words, you always know right from wrong in a relationship, and the principles you apply to your personal affairs are sound, effective and reliable. This is the result of your upbringing and your innate knowledge rather than of the beliefs you've evolved on your own. Even though you may rely on your sound judgment, you can't take all the credit for it, and you should be modest about your abilities.

You will get along best with a lover whose principles agree with yours or one who will take your word in this area. A lover whose convictions are too different from yours would cause sorrow, and the relationship would become increasingly distant.

Take particular note of this point, because you can bear endless contradiction without complaining or feeling put off. You may tolerate a partner who differs radically from you when you would be better off ending the relationship and seeking out someone whose outlook is closer to yours. However, if your lover is unsure of his or her convictions, you can serve as a support upon which your lover can rebuild inner convictions and faith.

Mercury Inconjunct Pluto

You are probably a compulsive truth-seeker, either in a concrete physical sense or in a more lofty, though less specific, spiritual sense. This is an admirable trait, but if you pursue this theme too diligently, your partner will go crazy. Although you believe that you are striving to get to the heart of a matter, your lover may feel that you are prying, relentless or simply boring. Stand back and listen to yourself now and then to find out whether you are taking things too seriously, seeing significance in every trivial detail.

The lesson for you to learn is to relax and be willing to go by appearances instead of feeling obligated to uncover all the deeper truths. Many situations are nothing more than they seem on the surface and can be enjoyed without any further knowledge. Quiet moments of companionship with your lover can be as important as soul-searching conversations or ego-searing flights of personal self–discovery.

If you can "turn off your mind, relax and float downstream" now and then, love will come more easily, and inner knowledge will be revealed in time.

Mercury Opposition Pluto

You may have a wide range of basic beliefs about love that encompass seemingly opposite views. Or you may have gone through a series of radically different stages of belief, each of which has transformed you.

You may fear that you can't keep a firm grip on what is right and wrong in your beliefs, but you do understand that everyone's needs are different, and that's that.

Because of this attitude, you are a very understanding and tolerant lover who can get along with someone who feels very differently about life than you do. But resist the youthful temptation to entirely grasp whatever belief system you have at the moment, rejecting all others, particularly those you held previously. Going to such extremes does you no credit and can be instrumental in breaking up a perfectly good relationship.

By going through such phases, however, you will eventually broaden your view of the world and stablilize your concepts of love. You will be able to embrace and enjoy myriad contradictory views.

Mercury Conjunct Ascendant

You have a quick mind and can usually make a remark while others are still gathering their wits about them. This does not necessarily mean that you say the right thing, only that you say it first.

Taking this into account, you should take care not to seem too forward, so that you offend a potential lover or your current partner. Be assertive, but avoid hastiness, for you might have to backtrack to correct your errors.

Probably you can use body language to good advantage and to express yourself. This ability allows you to dispense with words and speak with often more meaningful gestures. You should be sure to take advantage of this gift, which may be more hidden than your urge to communicate verbally. In matters of love, body language is more effective than the best-turned phrase, so it is worth developing.

An additional benefit is that it deepens the effect of your verbal communication. Words are cheap, and at times you may say a lot without communicating your real emotions. When punctuated with the right body language, however, even a shallow or trivial remark carries great emotional and erotic impact.

Mercury Sextile Ascendant

You coordinate your flow of words with body language quite easily, and you should have little difficulty getting your message across to a potential friend or lover. With a minimum of words or bodily expressions, you can have a quiet but effective style that wastes no words unless you choose to.

However, you may sometimes assume that your partner understands your message and thus fail to pursue it aggressively enough. This can be a problem in developing a new relationship if your partner is not used to your subtle methods of communication. You may have to use more explicit verbal cues to make your intentions known. In a long-standing affair, the smallest gesture can connote a paragraph of meaning, but to a new lover, the same gesture can be meaningless or even baffling. Thus, with a new partner you should make an extra attempt to express yourself clearly until the two of you have developed an expressive personal language.

You are likely to be more comfortable in an already developed affair in which your talents of subtle expression can be brought into play. A new relationship tends to be more of a burden and less immediately rewarding, although it will probably become more rewarding as time goes on.

Mercury Square Ascendant

You should make a special effort to decide with your lover about the best modes of expression and communication between you. This will be very helpful, because your verbal messages often contradict what you are saying in body language, at least from your partner's point of view.

Thus you may find that you have been misinterpreted when you thought you were being very clear. It is usually best to tell your partner to listen to your words and ignore your nonverbal signals. Once that is established, be scrupulously honest and accurate in your expression; then, communication between you and your lover should flow rather easily.

Because of this tendency, you tend to stay with an ongoing relationship in which communication is already established rather than venture into a new affair where the rules must be created anew. This is a positive factor in that you will stick to an affair when the going is rough and pitch in to make things better. However, you may hang onto a relationship that is finished simply because communication is easier than it is in a new affair.

In the long run, your experiences—particularly your difficulties—in communication will cause you to become more keenly aware of and expert at coordinating your words and your nonverbal signals.

Mercury Trine Ascendant

Your well-developed ability to communicate your needs and desires to a partner is a natural talent rather than a learned skill. You know intuitively what gesture will add extra meaning to your words, producing maximum effect with minimum effort.

You can share this talent with a lover who has difficulties in expressing his or her feelings; indeed, with such a partner you can analyze and develop your abilities further. When your lover is having trouble finding the right word to express an emotion, you can put your finger on it. This helps release many inner tensions and joys in your partner that might otherwise be sources of difficulty or frustration for both of you.

In doing this, you can become more analytically self-aware as you learn that what is easy for you is not necessarily easy for others. This will make you more patient with others' problems as well, as you begin to understand the complexity of effective communication, even though it seems easy at first. As you come to understand yourself better and find new areas that you wish to pursue, you will further develop your talents of self-expression.

Mercury Inconjunct Ascendant

You might make a special effort to condense your messages to your lover and refrain from going on at length on any one subject. This may be hard at times, for you continually see new details that you want to talk about. However, a subject that seems to you to need elaboration may be an oft-heard tale to your partner.

One way of getting around this problem without losing the quality of communication is to refrain from talking about a subject at all until you have thoroughly thought out all the details of what you are going to say. This will save you from either repeating or contradicting yourself. Also you will seem even more ingenious or insightful than you are, for you will be expressing a series of developing thoughts all distilled into one.

In general, you have an active mind that works twenty-four hours a day. You will be most compatible with a partner with a similar style or one who is tolerant of your flights of thought whenever they occur. At times you drive yourself too hard intellectually, and sometimes the best answer to a difficult problem of communication is to simply abandon it and do something that is relaxing for both of you.

Mercury Opposition Ascendant

You may find that your ability to tell your partner what you mean varies considerably. At times you hit the nail on the head unerringly and at other times you seem to miss by a mile. This applies not only to your ability to communicate but also to your desire to do so. Sometimes it seems urgent to communicate exactly what you mean, and at other times it doesn't seem worth the bother.

Naturally, this can lead to serious gaps of communication between you and your lover. You need a partner who understands your needs and desires intuitively when you are feeling uncommunicative.

In any case, you will be happiest if you have a fairly close partner at all times, for you derive a great deal of intellectual stimulus and inspiration from any kind of relationship. A partner somehow gets your ideas flowing and serves as a sounding board for ideas that would not come so easily if you were alone.

This does not mean that you need a particularly intellectual or verbal partner, although that would enhance the quality of your inventiveness. You just need someone who can provide a mirror for you and your ideas, so that you will have the additional knowledge you need to continue to create.

Chapter Eight

Venus

Venus in the Chart

The position and aspects of Venus have a direct effect on your physical and emotional desires in a receptive or passive sense. If the position of Venus is not consistent with other planets in the chart, your physical or emotional desires may be quite unrelated to your long-term inner goals or direction. For example, close friendship with a lover may be important to you as a goal, but it may not figure at all in your concern with immediate physical gratification, and vice versa.

Venus represents the basic nature of your love desires, and it is quite important to satisfy them if you are to gain consistent reward from sexual expression. You should make a place for these desires even if they do not fit neatly into the pattern of an established relationship or your inherited code of moral ethics. A relationship that does not fulfill the partners' basic physical needs will almost certainly flounder, no matter how much effort is spent on keeping it going. And while it does last, such a situation will cause only frustration and resentment, perhaps unspoken.

Venus in Aries

Your appetite for love is quickly whetted, and you wish to possess the object of your affections without delay. If there is too much dallying about with a potential lover, you are likely to lose interest and move on to a new partner.

Your style of loving may be very intense, even violent upon occasion. On the other hand, your desires are usually satiated rather quickly, particularly if the experience is a very intense one. This enables you to thoroughly enjoy a brief but fiery affair that would leave another person unfulfilled. In a longer-range affair, however, you may feel that your partner lacks the intensity of passion you desire or that you wear yourself out while your lover is still getting into stride.

You may have to make an effort to pace your desires and be more consistent in your tastes to match your partner's. At the same time, your lover must understand that an apparently inconsistent or fickle desire is actually one in a series of sudden but sincere enthusiasms that must be seized and enjoyed on the spot before the impulse takes another direction. Although such an affair may take some time to develop, you would be happiest with a patient and understanding lover who can adjust to your timing rather than someone whose rhythms are similar but out of sync with yours.

Venus in Taurus

Your appetite for love is fairly consistent, and ideally you should have a lover whose attentions are unflagging and whose style is consistent from day to day. For this same reason, it is a good idea to always have a partner, even if the relationship is not permanent. Prolonged abstinence is very hard for you to endure, and you may compensate by overindulging in some other area, such as eating.

You take great delight in surrounding your lovemaking with a varied array of sensory pleasures; heavy velvet fabrics or musty perfumes enrich the experience and prolong the atmosphere well after physical loving is over, allowing both of you to savor and review your intimacy. Physical surroundings can be a gold mine of sensory potential for enhancing sexuality, and you can delight in and take advantage of that fact.

You admire strength in a lover, not necessarily physical power but inner stamina, a heart of oak. You need to admire your partner and feel sure that he or she is durable and independent, someone who can love you without leaning on you. It would take a larger-than-life personality to fulfill your ideal, so try to be understanding when your partner doesn't live up to your highest expectations—nobody's perfect.

Venus in Gemini

You enjoy delicacy and finesse in love, and you treasure the touch of an experienced and thoughtful lover. Your greatest pleasure may come from gentle, sensuous tickling and stroking, which may even become a satisfactory substitute for sex now and then. The softer and more ethereal the physical quality of love, the more you respond to it.

However, you also appreciate being told how much you are loved, and the more verbal your partner is, the better, both in everyday interchange and in lovemaking. Not everyone can express loving feelings so fluently, however, so do not feel rejected if your lover is not verbally affectionate. Instead, look for other ways in which he or she transmits affection and learn to reply in kind. Similarly, do not take too seriously an ill-chosen word from your lover, for you are likely to read too much into it.

You feel that a good relationship is based on sincerity and good will, but your lover's physical skill is also a very important factor. You respond most to considerable variety in love, and you need a partner who can deliver it. Love at its best is a happy, sometimes complicated game of constantly changing stimuli, but underlying it is a much simpler emotional base of mutual friendship and companionship.

Venus in Cancer

Your appetite for love is very strong, but you do not usually satisfy it in a regular, even way. Rather, it builds up for a long period of time and when it does find release, it is often quite explosive. This happens partly because you are unwilling or unable to let your partner know your desires until the internal pressure has become very great. It is better to work out a clear system of communication so you will not suffer frustration because your partner is unaware of your needs.

For you, love at its best is an all-encompassing experience in which you completely possess and dissolve into your lover in such a way that the barriers between your personalities are washed away. In everyday life as well, you look for total devotion from your lover, and you give it as well.

Although your style of loving is very intense and exhilarating, it can also devolve into a mawkish dependency that is not healthy for either personality. True devotion must rest on mutual strength and trust between equals, so you should avoid the sometimes natural desire to totally own or be owned by your lover. Such roles can be healthily played out in bedroom games, but should be scrupulously avoided in everyday life if you want to maintain a lasting, loving relationship.

Venus in Leo

This position indicates that you have a generous helping of desire and a healthy sexual appetite. You take love by the mouthful, rather than sipping it slowly, and an affair once started tends to go all the way.

Your taste runs to all-over-the-body sensuality rather than to localized, more fetishistic tastes, although you may indulge in them on special occasions. Sensual body massaging and tickling are favorite pastimes, as is foot massage, which can stimulate the whole body.

Your pleasure in lovemaking is greatest in well-appointed surroundings, not necessarily lavish but with everything to satisfy your whim—a loaf of bread, a jug of wine, and so on. You aren't concerned with impressive trappings; you just want pleasure to be readily available. A lush meadow suffices as well as a king's palace as long as there is potential for rich enjoyment.

If there is any drawback to this position, it is that you demand high standards and will not stand for niggardliness or boredom. If a love affair becomes stale, you decide it's time to move on, even if other loyalties have built up between you in the relationship. Your active, creative desire may occasionally cross swords with necessity.

Venus in Virgo

You are likely to be most comfortable with a familiar lover who knows your habits and desires very well. You are aroused by very specific things and equally turned off by others, so your partner should be completely aware of your likes and dislikes.

Indeed, you should spend some time sorting out your desires, for you may be missing out on some fairly unusual ways of gaining pleasure simply for lack of investigation. Do not let antiquated moral taboos keep you from living up to your love potential, as you may find stimulation in many things besides your lover.

Cleanliness is quite important in loving, and showering with a lover can be a delightful erotic treat in itself. Also it eliminates a host of problems that might arise in lovemaking, leaving both of you free for pleasant experimentation.

183

You and your lover can find pleasure in writing down your fantasies in detail and exchanging them. In this fashion you can get and give exactly what you both want in a way that is unlikely to happen in more spontaneous love play; this will make your lovemaking, in its own way, a dream come true.

Venus in Libra

You may be quite attracted to somewhat unsettled relationships, which is natural with this position. A quiet, uneventful affair is boring to you, for it is continual change and growth that keep you interested and creative in a love relationship.

You insist that you and your lover be equal, not in a static equilibrium, but rather in continuing readjustment that keeps both partners on an even basis. Reversing sex-typed roles from time to time can be very helpful by giving each of you a view from the other side. This tends to break down ingrained and often subconscious sex barriers that can get in the way of a creative, flowing relationship.

You particularly admire physical beauty in a lover, but do not let a person's appearance blind you to the beauty, or lack of it, in his or her soul. Let your judgment of beautiful form be more than skin deep.

In the long run, you will be most satisfied with an all-around lover whose accomplishments and qualities are not just physical but extend in many directions. This partner's experience in love can be the foundation for a very broad-based love relationship. Thus, although youth and beauty may appeal to you most at first, you are more likely to be fulfilled by an experienced and mature partner your age or older.

Venus in Scorpio

You have a very deep, gut-level style in love, and when you set your sights on someone, you don't give up until you get what you want. When you finally do achieve your goals, your pleasure extends to the very foundations of your personality.

Indeed, it is extremity of enjoyment rather than moderation that is the key to your pleasure. You are not too demanding of a lover in terms of skill or technique as long as the experience is sufficiently intense. You are more interested in the end than the means, and for your personality, that is just right.

Do not let this view of lovemaking cause you to overlook the many methods of heightening sexual intensity, particularly when a relationship is becoming too low-key. Bedroom games in which one or both partners are sexually restrained for a time helps build the requisite intensity for an all-consuming experience.

Whatever your method, your enjoyment will be greatest if sexuality takes on the aspect of tremendous power, an uncontrollable flood in which both of you are caught up. This is ideal for the actual sexual experience, but in everyday life you should take great care to let control return to both of you individually, so that the basic equality between you is not lost.

Venus in Sagittarius

You have a natural and healthy appetite for sex, but sex for its own sake is not likely to be enough. You are more interested in the feelings and principles behind it than in the act itself, and sex without personal involvement is surely less than satisfying.

You are not strongly motivated to learn complex or unusual sexual techniques, except perhaps to please a lover who has a special taste for them. For you, sexual pyrotechnics tend to get in the way of necessary love communication, distracting you from the warmth and friendship that truly fulfilling sexuality means to you.

Your kind of experimentation is in the lover you choose rather than in the way you go about lovemaking. You are uninterested in one whose personality is modest or commonplace, preferring a more adventurous and unusual type. You feel that such a lover will greatly enhance your own experience and that the relationship will be a continuing exploration of new territory.

For this reason, your lovers are in general more outgoing and volatile but less cautious than you. Therefore you have to play the role of stabilizer from time to time. In that way you can enjoy the adventures you get yourself into and at the same time keep them from getting out of hand.

Venus in Capricorn

Your tastes in sexuality tend to be simple, even austere, for you feel that too many complications get in the way of and distract from the course of events. You do not require a great deal of physical attention, for you can glean plenty of substance from what seems little to others and find meaning where many would overlook it.

You may find satisfaction in a relationship in which one partner dominates the other or in which each person's realm of authority is very clearly delineated within an overall balance. At any rate, clarity is essential, for a muddied relationship will not allow you to fully enjoy your sexuality.

A partner who is quite a bit older or younger, probably older, best suits your sexual style. This is not so much for the sake of knowledge and experience but for the quality of distance mixed with intimacy that often characterizes such a relationship.

Although you want sure and certain affection from your lover, you prefer someone who is fairly discreet and treats your relationship not frivolously but with respect and decorum.

Venus in Aquarius

You seek special styles and unusual varieties of love, and you look for partners with similar interests. This may be a mental exercise as much as a physical one; that is, the appearance of the unusual may be sufficient without having to explore it in depth physically.

You need a lot of action in order to be mentally stimulated in a relationship, so your affairs may become quite complicated and multifaceted. This may be very interesting and exciting, but try to avoid too much complexity, because that can lead to shallowness in some other area of the relationship.

Similarly, you may be tempted to get involved in several relationships at once. This can be a stimulating, even head-spinning experience, but it could prevent you from becoming involved with any one partner in a truly deep and lasting relationship. In any case, you should avoid jealous lovers who cramp your style or try to impose limits.

If you can overcome and rise above the problems of cross-conflicts and jealousies, however, you have the capability of openly and honestly sharing your love among several partners, which will enrich and enlarge the experience for all.

Venus in Pisces

You most enjoy the attentions of a lover who gives the utmost in love and devotion and holds nothing back from you. Under such conditions, you can achieve a total communion in love that is matched by nothing else. Sex in itself is not so alluring to you, but with the right lover, it can be a powerful vehicle for deep communication.

Because you prefer not to be too verbal about your needs, you appreciate a lover who can intuitively plumb your feelings and discern your most intimate desires without asking. But that is a lot to expect of anyone all the time, so try to meet your partner halfway and help him or her get to know you well.

Your sexuality may become mixed with religious feelings and to that extent may elude physical manifestation entirely for periods of time. There is some advantage to being able to attach the power of sexuality to higher spiritual goals, but unless you are careful, this tendency can degenerate into sexual confusion or religiosity without transcendence. Doing this successfully requires considerable self-awareness, and you should think very carefully before turning your sexual energies in this direction; it takes great strength of mind to make abstinence pay off spiritually and not simply end up as frustration.

Venus in the First House

This position lends a good deal of social charm and grace as well as physical attractiveness. Your attractiveness makes it easy to have a creative and fluid sex life, because it eliminates many obstacles to becoming involved with others. If there is any problem with this position, it is the opposite, that of too many potential partners.

You are naturally responsive to other people's needs, and many will look to you for sympathy and understanding. You should use this natural talent carefully to avoid becoming a shoulder for everyone to cry on. And don't let anyone mistake your empathy and diplomacy for weakness, or people will try to manipulate you and take advantage of your willingness to listen.

The main key to sexual success for men and women with this position is to be attractive and receptive rather than aggressive. Wait for the other person to make the first move, because asserting yourself strongly often seems inappropriate or awkward. Anyone with such a great natural advantage should use it to seduce and enfold a desired lover rather than take him or her by storm.

Venus in the Second House

You like being surrounded by fine objects of great value, and a sumptuous setting adds immensely to your enjoyment of lovemaking. Rich, well-tailored clothing, a beautifully appointed bedroom with sensuous linens, soft lights, stereo—these and other pleasurable trappings are the order of the day.

Indeed, you are fortunate enough to be able to enjoy many of the erotic devices and love toys that add extra spice to a romantic adventure. A well-stocked cupboard will increase your enjoyment and enrich the experience for you and your partner.

However, you are most comfortable in a relatively secure setting where you know you will not be disturbed. You like to be able to call the shots, or at least know what to expect. Too much spontaneity, particularly concerning location, makes you somewhat uneasy and detracts from your enjoyment. If this is the case, you should be sure to tell your lover, so that you can arrange your lovemaking at the time and place where you both will get the most pleasure from it.

Although you may put particular value on a partner with a fine appearance and high social standing, do not forget that diamonds in the rough may be worth far more than polished gems, if you take the time to refine them.

Venus in the Third House

Love talk and a verbally affectionate lover may be particularly important to you. Compliments and sweet nothings whispered in the ear, as well as dialogue during lovemaking, constitute a significant area of sexual enjoyment. You enjoy knowing what is coming and being told about it, perhaps in detail. Similarly, you derive considerable pleasure from discussing lovemaking with your lover and devising ways to improve and enhance it in the future.

Along the same lines, you may enjoy reading erotic fiction—not gross pornography, but literary erotica designed to reach the libido through the intellect. This will be a source of enjoyment and information, which you can revise to suit your own love life.

You should find a lover who is equally knowledgeable about sex and willing to put that knowledge to good use. Your partner should be quite communicative and willing to discuss lovemaking with you, someone who won't simply spring surprises that you aren't prepared for. You need to understand most aspects of love mentally before you can fully respond physically.

Venus in the Fourth House

You should look for a lover who can be very close to you, someone with whom you can share your most intimate secrets. You will not be happy with a partner who treats you casually, as if love were an offhand entertainment rather than a close personal commitment. On the other hand, do not force closeness where that is not appropriate, and avoid smothering your partner with love or infringing on his or her individual freedom.

You need a relaxed lover who makes you feel at home wherever you are. The better you know your partner, the more at home you feel, so you are happiest in a long-term relationship in which you have time to become very close to your partner. A brief love affair has a certain spark of mystery and excitement, but it leaves you feeling less than satisfied, as if you didn't have the time to get to know each other.

You aren't particularly interested in fancy sexual technique; in fact, you feel that it clouds a sex experience rather than enhances it. Effectively transmitting warmth and affection is the most important element for you, and sexual pyrotechnics can often be counterproductive to that. However, you should try to learn enough to please your lover, who may not feel the same. For you, a little variety goes a long way.

Venus in the Fifth House

Sex can be a source of limitless entertainment for you, if you have a lover who is active and energetic enough to provide the variety and delight you desire. For you, love is a happy, joyful experience, and your partner should share your optimistic approach.

You also prefer to get right down to business, so you would be impatient with a lover who insists on elaborate social courting rituals and the like. Whatever you want, you want it then and there. You will be happiest with someone who doesn't beat around the bush.

Although you value close personal communication with a partner, you feel that it is better achieved on a mental plane rather than through sex. Lovemaking is pure joy and recreation and need not be burdened with extraneous meanings or motives other than the simple pleasure of physical contact.

You enjoy an artful lover, but one who retains a sense of youthful innocence, for whom experience and technique are not ends in themselves. Love must always have the purity and beauty of a flower. Therefore, many of the more compulsive and unusual forms of loving in which others find pleasure are of little interest to you. Anything that taints the sunny radiance of love is to be avoided, and anything that furthers it is a joy.

Venus in the Sixth House

You appreciate well-crafted lovemaking, and you admire a lover who works at improving your relationship and refining the gentle art of love. Although sudden surprises tend to overwhelm you, a regularly changing and advancing relationship is essential to you for maximum personal and sexual fulfillment.

Thus, over a period of time, you may become quite an expert on subtle sexual techniques. Sex is a constant learning experience, but do not let that aspect of it take precedence over the purer joys of personal communion and emotional enjoyment.

Although you and your partner should be equal within the relationship, equality is not necessarily your ideal in lovemaking itself. You may be particularly pleased by a lover who serves you or, on the other hand, one whom you serve and obey sexually. Such bedroom games can be very enjoyable and provide an outlet for inequalities in other areas of the relationship. However, to accomplish this successfully requires a good deal of self-awareness, and the two of you should reevaluate the affair from time to time to see if you both are getting the satisfaction you desire. Sex must not become a chore for either partner, and no matter how you stand in relation to each other, both partners should get an equal amount of pleasure from it.

Venus in the Seventh House

Your enjoyment of love is very dependent upon your partner's enjoyment. You don't get very much pleasure from sex if your lover is uncomfortable or physically dissatisfied with what is going on. As a result, you are a particularly considerate lover, because one of your primary concerns is to see that your partner has a good time in order that you can too—what you might call a policy of enlightened self-interest.

For the same reason, you usually adapt your sexual style and technique to your lover's preferences. That is fine up to a point, but don't neglect to let your partner know quite clearly the special techniques that please you.

You are most stimulated by a lover who is really quite different from you in many respects, at least in personality. You aren't looking for someone who reinforces you so much as someone who fills out and complements your personality, thus broadening the scope of the relationship and making it more complex. A partner who is similar to you in style or experience may fail to hold your interest.

However, be sure that you are an equal partner in any relationship and do not let anyone exploit your need for a lover by giving you less than you deserve.

Venus in the Eighth House

You strive for relationships that are very intense and therefore quite involved. You may be drawn toward people who seem mysterious or challenging in some way, which can have both good and bad results. You may find a partner who is a gold mine of unexplored love territory, or you may wind up with someone whom you cannot reach or who is balky and problematical. But in love as in other areas of life, the chance for high gains is equal to the chance for great losses.

You find little satisfaction in the intellectual trappings of love, and you require plenty of physical attention within a relationship. A platonic affair will leave you unfulfilled, and to separate the physical from the emotional and carry on two affairs simultaneously may be too difficult to sustain. Therefore, you are happiest with a demonstrative lover who pays attention to your physical as well as your emotional needs.

For this reason, you might as well dive into love headlong. The more you can lose yourself in a love affair, particularly in its sexual aspects, the more satisfying it will be. Just try not to let your life outside of the relationship become unbalanced by it.

You may have the feeling that even a new relationship is as old as the hills and that you are somehow linked to your partner beyond time. This may or may not be the case, but in the best relationships it will seem that way.

Venus in the Ninth House

You have an innate appreciation of anything new and special in a relationship, and sex at its best is a constant adventure for you. This does not mean that you feel compelled to explore unusual or bizarre ideas in a physical or technical sense. In fact, such underdeveloped physical approaches may leave you cold. What you want is a continually fresh emotional attitude to love that does not get into a rut.

You may find that quality in a relationship that is an adventure and a learning experience in itself. A foreign lover or one who is culturally different from you might be very exciting, symbolically offering a highly fulfilling emotional travelogue.

You may not have to travel so far to find this quality, however. A lover whose approach to life and sex is certain and unhesitating can fulfill the same needs while speaking your language. All that is required is high spirits and a joyful enthusiasm for life, which can make each experience fresh and new for both of you. Enjoyment is more a matter of appetite than opportunity, and armchair travelers can have more, and safer, adventures than the most reckless explorers in the physical world.

Venus in the Tenth House

You may be particularly drawn to individuals who are well-known or outstanding in their professional field. Indeed, excellence is a major factor in your feelings of love and admiration for someone. You also have high standards for yourself.

However, you must be careful to make a distinction between your partner's personal needs and emotions and his or her achievements or reputation. One frequently belies the other, and it is the inner person to whom you must relate if the affair is to be long-lasting and satisfying for both of you.

You are anxious to be well thought of also, and you may be quite successful in building a professional reputation. But you could run into the same problem in reverse—your partner will expect you to live up to your external image rather than just being yourself. In either case, the problem is one of impossible expectations or of inner goals confused with external ones. If your lover is also involved in your professional life, the affair can become a real tangle of crossed wires and ulterior motives.

Therefore it is best to insulate your private life from your own and your partner's public endeavors. In this way, both areas will have a clearer sense of direction, and you won't waste energy and emotion through confusion or misinterpretation.

Venus in the Eleventh House

You prefer a lover who is well coordinated physically, emotionally and socially, someone whom you can show off proudly to your friends so that they will have a higher opinion of you. For this reason you tend to associate with very fine people, who will improve your social standing if you can keep the right perspective.

In this area your judgment must be very acute so that you can separate true substance from the showy or trendy. Try not to harry your partner unnecessarily about details of dress, image and social acceptance. Although externals are important, a long-range relationship must be based on internal excellence, and that is the standard you should emphasize. It is better to do what you can to improve appearances than to force an unwanted responsibility on your lover.

This is particularly important, because you want your partner to be more than a helpmate or a showcase; you want a close and dear friend whose love will endure beyond the convenience or necessity of the moment. Therefore, by being patient about small matters, you can cement a lasting relationship that will elevate you both. That would go far beyond momentary considerations of social importance, heightening your own self-esteem as well as drawing respect and admiration from those around you.

Venus in the Twelfth House

At times you may find it difficult to decide exactly what you want out of a relationship, or you may find out what you would really have enjoyed only after the affair is over. This can be the result of choosing a lover too hastily, so the more consideration you give to this, the better.

For this reason, it is a good idea to prolong your courtship in order to find out what each partner wants and expects before making a commitment. Although you take longer to make a final definition of a relationship, this gradual, in-depth approach can result in an affair that is deeper, firmer and better founded than most, with more self-understanding.

You appreciate a lover who doesn't discuss your personal life with others; in fact, you are quite attracted to the idea of carrying on an affair in secret. This can be an enjoyable amusement, but avoid becoming involved with a lover with whom you can't have a lasting open relationship. Taking a secret tryst too seriously is a sure road to heartbreak.

If you desire the sweetness of suffering that love can produce, you should play out this scenario actively in the bedroom. If you express this need through unwitting self-denial, neither of you will grow and learn from the experience.

Venus Conjunct Mars

You are likely to be sexually attractive to others, not because your physical appearance is so striking, necessarily, but because you emit a kind of animal magnetism that suggests sexual experience.

As a result you probably won't have any difficulty in finding a lover, for potential partners usually come to you. However, you may have problems in choosing the right partner and eliminating the others.

You may be quite interested in sexual experimentation, for several reasons. First, the simpler, more straightforward ways of loving come naturally to you, so trying out new methods of enjoyment is easier than it is for people who feel less at ease with their sexuality. Second, you probably have more opportunities for varied styles of loving because of your many potential lovers.

In addition, opportunities for new experiences tend to occur at just the right time for you, when you are in the mood for change, rather than when you are settling into a style you enjoy. In any case, your sexual expression tends to be intense, and it will always be important to you.

Venus Sextile Mars

Because of your good sense of timing and taste, you are usually able to get what you want physically in a love affair. But you don't demand styles or techniques of loving that your partner does not enjoy or is hesitant to try.

This does not mean that you are sexually conservative or overly thoughtful, necessarily, but that your desires are quite in tune with your lover's. Therefore your demands follow suit.

Similarly, your partner's ideas usually fall in line with your current desires; you do not often find yourself in need when there is no one to satisfy it, or find your desire flagging when your lover is in the mood. Of course, you may go for some time without a lover, but the effects will not be deleterious, because it tends to happen at convenient or even helpful times.

In general your sexual expression is quite regular, making it a warm and natural part of your relationship. If there is any problem, it is that sex on a regular schedule can lose much of its excitement; the rhythm and style should be broken up and changed a bit to keep it lively. You can learn to do this, or the impetus may come from a more irregular and volatile partner.

Venus Square Mars

You may find it difficult, particularly while you are young, to be in the right place at the right time sexually. Opportunities for sexual encounters may arise when you aren't in the mood, or circumstances may hinder you when you're ready to go ahead.

The result of this difficulty can be a tendency to associate sex with anger or frustration. If properly channelled, this association can make sexuality very intense when you do find expression. It can also lead to arguments or recrimination within a relationship, which you would do well to avoid.

You should spend a good deal of time exploring your desires and understanding them in order to have a really fulfilling sex life. The more subconscious work you do in this area, the more control you can exercise over your needs, regulating them to coincide with opportunities for fulfilling them.

Essentially, this could be called the art of sexual self-discipline, which in the long run will make you a steady and accomplished lover. Mistakes are part of any learning process, so instead of mourning your errors in love, analyze and learn from them. The information you derive will improve you sexually and emotionally. Such opportunities for learning should never be wasted.

Venus Trine Mars

Probably sex comes quite naturally to you and in general causes fewer problems than it does for others, who are often less comfortable with the subject. As a result, your experiences with sex are favorable, which reinforces your healthy attitude.

You are not inclined to be experimental in sex, not because of inhibitions about what should and should not be done, but because you derive sufficient pleasure from the simplest styles of loving. The farther-out variations either lack appeal or seem too bothersome.

Remember, however, that your lover may not feel the same way. Doing the same thing every time can be quite boring, even though you find it endlessly enjoyable. Take a moment to learn about your lover's fantasies and do your best to fulfill them from time to time. Once launched into them, you may have a fabulous time, so do not let a certain sexual laziness prevent you from fulfilling your considerable sexual potential.

Because of your inherent sexual stability, you may be able to handle and enjoy a lover who is far less secure sexually. Helping such a partner will stimulate you to explore your own sexuality more. Very often the most exciting sexual experiences have their roots in fear or insecurity.

Venus Inconjunct Mars

Your sexual style is somewhat restless, which makes it difficult to get the fullest possible enjoyment from a sexual experience. You may move in and out of love affairs quite quickly, or you may constantly search for the most satisfying style or technique within a single relationship.

As a result, you will probably try many different kinds of sexual experimentation, from the simplest to the farthest out. This can be quite gratifying, but you cannot derive real fulfillment in love just from physical techniques. As long as you are aware of that, you will derive nothing but pleasure from a continuing sexual dilettantism. If you are not aware of the limitations of this approach, you could feel quite frustrated, as if you were on a sexual treadmill going nowhere.

In any case, you should spend some time going over older methods of sexual pleasure, which you may have abandoned too hastily. Continually pursuing the new too often results in shallow communication between you and your lover, simply because of the extra attention needed for new and unfamiliar ways of relating. A more secure lover may be quite good for you, and you may learn that combining the old with the new leads to a much more deeply fulfilling relationship.

Venus Opposition Mars

You probably prefer a relationship characterized by a strong active-passive sexual polarity. This does not necessarily mean that you and your lover are not on equal terms, but that you have opposite roles in lovemaking. In such a case, each of you might play each role on different occasions, but you are likely to be most comfortable when one partner is definitely in charge and takes responsibility for the other's pleasure in lovemaking.

In the passive role, you can totally abandon yourself to pleasure, while in the active role you are fully able to command sexual achievement. The chances are, you can reach much greater heights of pleasure and fulfillment in this way than in a situation of greater sexual equality in which you may experience a certain frustration from holding back. In addition, learning to play both roles will add enormously to your self-understanding and to your intimate knowledge of your lover.

Also, you probably have wide swings of sexual desire, which you can take advantage of to heighten the intensity of fulfillment. Here, a lover who is emotionally in tune with you is a great advantage. Otherwise such swings may bring you into conflict instead of intensifying your love, which can often be accomplished by clear verbal monitoring of each other's feelings.

Venus Conjunct Jupiter

You probably have considerable sexual capacity, and you do not appreciate a lover who is stingy with affection. You regard sex in a very positive light; in a love affair, you feel, the more the better.

You are a very giving person and will go out of your way to please a lover who gives you the kind of love you appreciate. You may find, however, that when you are without a lover for an extended period, sexual desire may be sublimated into compulsive eating. Then, if you gain too much weight, it will be more difficult to attract a lover, so watch it.

In general, sexuality is a source of real happiness and delight for you, and you are likely to be luckier in love than most. Your positive attitude toward your desires enables you to engage in sexual experimentation with good results, even in areas where others might be emotionally hurt. In most cases your good will brings you through when things go awry.

Remember, however, that your lover may not be as stable or optimistic as you are, and you may push your partner further than he or she is ready to go. Make a special effort to be sensitive to your partner's insecurities and sexual inhibitions, even though they seem foolish or puzzling to you.

Venus Sextile Jupiter

You have a fairly even flow of sexual desire that renews itself regularly; it does not get bottled up or go to extremes. Your style of loving is particularly friendly, and sex for physical gratification alone has little appeal for you; you want your lover to be a special friend as well.

This tends to keep you out of stormy or difficult relationships in which there is dormant hostility or enmity. Love-hate relationships are definitely not for you. If an affair gets too rough, you will be happier if you bail out than if you try to ride out the unpleasantness.

In general, your natural optimism, mixed with luck, will lead you into happy and satisfying relationships. Although you are willing to develop a relationship sexually by adopting new attitudes and techniques, you usually have excellent judgment concerning what will add to an affair and what will simply confuse or complicate it. If your lover learns to trust your judgment, you both will avoid many difficulties. However, you may be happier with a partner who has considerable imagination and initiative in this area, because you are less likely to initiate change than to pick the right direction and go along with it.

Venus Square Jupiter

You may tend to go overboard in sexual gratification, which can actually lead to frustration rather than fulfillment. This may manifest as a very strong physical sex drive, but very often it is also a mental tendency to misjudge your sexual desire or capacity.

Thus, in sexual experimentation, always take a second look to make sure that you're not taking on something that you can't handle. Too much of a good thing ceases to be pleasurable. Similarly, you may commit yourself too readily to a situation or technique that you cannot excuse yourself from, even if it turns out to be less than pleasurable.

Therefore, it may be wise to rely on your partner's judgment of your desires, even though you may feel quite sure of them at the time. That approach can spare you much exhaustion and embarrassment.

Time and self-understanding will help you become more skillful in judging your desires. As you gain more sexual experience, you will learn when to stop and when to dive in. As you develop sexually, you will learn how to bring yourself to the very limits of sexual enjoyment without going over the edge or getting into situations that you can't handle or do not really enjoy.

Venus Trine Jupiter

Your relationships are usually easy and quite peaceful, developing evenly with a minimum of strife or difficulty. You are not likely to get into sexual situations that you don't enjoy or can't handle. You make progress gradually instead of flinging yourself into the new simply to add to your sexual repertoire.

In this respect you can be a stabilizing influence upon your lover. Your affections do not flicker but grow steadily with the relationship, which is both a love affair and a friendship. You may prefer a lover who needs your stability and whose less even nature will add variety to the relationship. An affair that is too even can lead to sexual and emotional boredom, and a partner with a lively imagination can provide you both with fun and enjoyment.

You probably have a healthy sexual appetite, and full, regular loving is a natural part of any relationship. But you do not overdo love, so you always have a reserve of untapped sexual energy for the next time. Because of this, your stamina is less likely to flag as you get older. By properly pacing yourself, you can stay trim sexually and emotionally until a ripe old age, and the not-infrequent sexual problems of middle and old age will not trouble you.

Venus Inconjunct Jupiter

You should resist the tendency to experiment for its own sake, rushing into new sexual styles and techniques before you have thoroughly mastered the old. You are inclined to concentrate on sexual experimentation, and there is nothing wrong with that, but it is better not to continually change direction. You may be tempted to do so, but you will find that each new direction becomes less satisfying, unless you have first built a thorough foundation.

This is particularly important for your partner who may not be so well prepared to leap into new experiences. To do so without sufficient preparation will merely result in less communication between you. Also, you will derive more pleasure from an experience that you are both familiar with, so that you can give each other your full loving attention, undistracted by new and perhaps confusing details.

Essentially, patience in love is a virtue, for you can always look forward to new experiences ahead. Just be sure to take one step at a time in getting there. Love will continue to improve in the future only if the foundations have been solidly laid in the past; that applies to sexual technique as well as to emotional substance.

Venus Opposition Jupiter

You may have rather wide swings of sexual desire, both in quantity and in style. At times you may be highly motivated to try out new and unusual forms of sexual expression. At other times you prefer a more conservative approach, or even prefer to do without sex entirely.

A steady and patient lover who controls these extremes by holding you back from rash moves and providing extra motivation when needed would be most helpful. Even without such a steadying influence, however, this tendency to go to extremes will even out with age and experience. Problems will arise only if you have an especially demanding partner who insists on trying to change your style.

However, you should consider your lover's rhythms of desire, particularly if they do not match yours. Otherwise you may deny your partner pleasure simply because you're not in the mood, or you may force your lover into sexual experiences that are pleasing to you alone. In such cases, discuss your needs and come to some agreement so that neither of you is neglected, and you both can take advantage of your ups and downs.

Venus Conjunct Saturn

The intensity of your desire may border on the painful if you cannot find satisfactory expression. As a result, you take your sexual needs quite seriously. This does not mean you are humorless about love; in fact, you may have a very good sense of humor in this area. However, the intensity of your needs gives you a rather grave quality, which if not properly handled, may seem rather overwhelming to your lover.

You may be attracted to partners who are older or who seem older. Similarly, you may want a lover who restricts you and ties you down emotionally. A dominant/dependent relationship can be fulfilling to a certain extent, but it is better to express this need in the bedroom rather than in your daily life, where this can be quite destructive to the growth of an affair. Your role—dominant or dependent—may vary with your mood, or it may be more or less fixed, depending on your partner. Such role-playing can be quite stimulating and rewarding if kept within limited bounds.

You are quite tenacious in your desires, and once you have set your heart on something or someone, you don't usually give up until you get it, even if you have to wait for years to achieve your goal.

Venus Sextile Saturn

You may have a rather conservative attitude toward sexual experimentation. You find considerable satisfaction in traditional forms of lovemaking, and you view the potential of other techniques with some skepticism. At times this attitude may cause you to miss out on something good, but in most cases it won't. Your natural prudence helps you avoid unnecessary emotional difficulties and wasted time.

You are quite consistent in your demands of your partner, and an erratic or unpredictable lover would not satisfy your needs. You are not the type who lavishes affection and desire on your lover; instead you express your love with a quiet dignity and grace that in no way cheapens or debases the strength of your feeling.

As a result, you are more comfortable in a well-developed and lasting relationship than in a whirlwind affair. The love you desire grows in stately fashion over the years and is not subject to changes through whim or fancy. Thus you are a very loyal partner who knows what you want and what you must give in return to a partner who matches the more enduring qualities of your loving.

Venus Square Saturn

You must do everything possible to avoid being pulled into destructive relationships of your own making. However, it is sometimes difficult for you, both physically and emotionally, to avoid them. You tend to identify love with pain, and thus you may pull a relationship into an unpleasant downward spiral, which nevertheless has certain erotic overtones.

This difficulty can be avoided in part by approaching a relationship more realistically. Your expectations of an affair tend to be so high that you can't possibly live up to them, and therefore you automatically experience failure and disappointment. Then you decide that you can never get what you want from an affair, which usually turns out to be a self-fulfilling prediction.

Instead, take love as it comes and enjoy it for what it is at the moment, without making any judgments, if possible. By taking this approach, you may be happily surprised to find that the affair turns out better than you expected.

Not expecting anything from an affair is not the same as expecting nothing from it, however. Expecting nothing means that you probably will get nothing, while not expecting anything means that your hopes are nonspecific. By taking this view, you can gain fulfillment from a variety of results without limiting your enjoyment.

Venus Trine Saturn

Your views about what you want from a relationship are quite clear. Your style is not flamboyant and you may lean toward the conservative, but you are sure of your pleasures and derive much long-term satisfaction from them. You are not usually taken in by passing fads or trends in love. In general, you get the greatest enjoyment from tried and true methods.

This approach makes love a very easy and mellow experience, from which you derive a great deal of security. However, you should make a special point of observing whether your partner is getting the same satisfaction. It's quite possible that your lover will want some variety now and then to liven things up. Although you may not be that interested in experimentation, you will certainly not find it harmful in moderation, and both your lover and your relationship will benefit. In this area, you have the ability to help your lover choose successful directions, avoiding any that might be frustrating.

It is a good idea to plan your experiments together ahead of time, rather than trying them out without warning. The more thought that goes into developing them, the more successful they will be in providing you both with a maximum of new pleasure.

Venus Inconjunct Saturn

You should do your best to avoid the sometimes irresistible temptation to be highly critical of your own or your lover's sexual performance. Although rigorous standards are important in many areas of life, in sex they tend to kill spontaneity and to make both partners concentrate on performance rather than pleasure.

Much of this comes from having great expectations of a love affair. When your expectations are not all fulfilled, it is much easier to blame yourself or your partner instead of chalking it up to experience. In love, so much depends on natural compatibility and uncontrollable circumstances that it is seldom all the fault of the participants when things go wrong.

If an affair is not working out, instead of subjecting yourself or your lover to a barrage of criticism, simply give it up and look for greener pastures. And if an affair is going well, do not analyze it too closely, for you may inadvertently spoil it.

Probably you will always be somewhat discontented about your relationships, but if you voice your criticisms very quietly, the affair will have a better chance to develop and improve.

Venus Opposition Saturn

You may often encounter obstacles to getting satisfaction in love. It may be that there are no available partners, or it may be that your partner will not go along with what you want in bed.

The result is that when you finally succeed in achieving satisfaction, the intensity of your desire is like a river in flood that washes over you with uncontrollable power. Sometimes the blockage is internal, perhaps manifesting as a total lack of desire followed by intense sexual need.

Needless to say, you need a fairly tolerant lover who can put up with your sometimes frustrating behavior and can also ease you out of your down periods and help put you on a steadier track. You also need a lover who does not frustrate your needs. If that does happen, it may be better to call off the affair for a while rather than continually run into obstacles. Eventually, frustration turns into resentment and anger, which will probably break up the affair anyway, but with a lot more time and trouble. Similarly, you should go out of your way to see that you do not frustrate your partner, even if it means inconveniencing yourself emotionally or sexually from time to time.

Venus Conjunct Uranus

You have a kind of physical desire that is aroused and turned off quite abruptly and strongly, so that you may be completely uninterested one moment and very turned on the next. This can lead to some exciting whirlwind trysts, but there may be problems in a long-term relationship unless your lover is very closely in tune with you. In general you do better in a loosely structured partnership in which you and your lover have maximum freedom.

Your tastes in love may run to the out-of-the-ordinary, and you can get a great deal of pleasure and reward from unusual kinds of sexual experimentation. You are not likely to become fixated on an out-of-the-way variation, so you should feel free to try almost anything that is physically safe. You should find an uninhibited partner who is eager to participate in anything that turns up, for nothing turns pleasure into displeasure faster than a lover who gets cold feet.

At the same time, you would benefit from having a lover who has good judgment about what will and will not work sexually, because often your fantasies turn out to be quite impracticable in reality.

Venus Sextile Uranus

You have the ability to be inventive in pleasing yourself and your lover. Your easy and regular flow of originality will keep your love life fresh, but you don't get carried away with compulsive sexual experimentation or variety for its own sake.

For this reason, you may be best suited to be the initiator of sexual change and growth within a relationship, for you often have a clear and effective view of which directions can be profitably pursued and which cannot. Even if you are not the initiator, you should have some control over where you and your partner are going, because your inclinations are sound and can be followed with beneficial results.

There is a good chance that you will find real enjoyment and reward in a relationship that is different from the so-called norm, a freer, more open kind of affair than most, based on individual security rather than the security of a relationship.

Whereas others may prefer to stay with older, established styles, your greatest creativity is in continually introducing new material into your emotional and sexual life. In that way you avoid repetition, and you can savor each experience just long enough to use all of its pleasure potential. You will look back on the experience fondly, but you won't need to repeat it, seeking new and fresher grounds of love instead.

Venus Square Uranus

You should make an attempt to regulate your desires, for they may lead you to places that you will not really enjoy. This does not mean that you cannot benefit greatly from sexual experimentation, but you must take the utmost precautions not to leap into it recklessly. When sexual fantasies are realized, they often turn out to be quite different from what they seemed. If they are not carefully thought out ahead of time and regulated when you carry them out, such fantasies can be rather unpleasant.

Since your desires come fairly suddenly and strongly, you will find it hard to regulate them at times. Your inclination is to strike when the iron is hot, which can lead to rash or hasty judgments. Better to think it over and wait until the next time; you'll be able to structure an enjoyable fantasy with enough detail to make it truly satisfying.

In time, you will become quite adept at this, fabricating unusual yet rewarding forms of sexual expression that will be sources of great enjoyment for both you and your lover. It will help if your lover can serve as a check and balance on your fantasies, helping you develop and enact them realistically.

Venus Trine Uranus

Your mind probably plays a very creative and productive role in bringing about fulfillment of your desires. Distinctive and inventive forms of expression may be the touchstone of your sexual satisfaction.

However, you must take into account that what you consider normal and average may be quite unusual or even far-out to your contemporaries. You may feel that your tastes are quite run-of-the-mill, but others probably think of you as having a unique, even odd or eccentric, style.

To each his own, however, and you will do well to stick to what you enjoy, for that is surely best for you, no matter what others think. You would feel quite stifled if you tried to force yourself into someone else's mold, which would result in repression and anger. You are a person who needs freedom and space to move in, and you can use it more enjoyably and effectively than most.

Indeed, you can handle great freedom in a relationship, including some form of open marriage, better and more happily than most people. You and your lover can have the space to create and to love each other from the stable platform of individual security.

Venus Inconjunct Uranus

You may spend so much time devising new and interesting approaches to love that you lose some of the personal communication that should exist in a relationship. Certainly you have a strong desire for change, especially as a means to improvement and exploration.

You can be an achiever in this area, and probably your approaches to sexuality are distinctly original. However, you should realize that you can have too much of a good thing. You tend to rush in and out of new experiences, which can leave you glutted without being really satisfied, stimulated without being realized. Therefore you should attempt to structure your love life somewhat. Spending more time on each area and developing it more fully will result in much more satisfaction.

You should listen to your partner's comments about your methods of achieving gratification, lest you impinge on others' rights to achieve the same happiness. Some ideas that are intriguing or exciting to you may be too much for your lover to handle, so take that into consideration and modify your behavior accordingly. If you cannot experience everything immediately, remember that tomorrow is another day, and there are many more days to indulge in a wide range of new and inventive pleasure.

Venus Opposition Uranus

Your desire, although strong, may be an off-and-on phenomenon, so that you are quite attracted to a given partner, then utterly cold in swift succession. This can lead to a relationship with many ups and downs, or it can result in a series of quick but intense affairs.

In the first case, the more latitude and space there is in the relationship the better, so that both you and your lover can be free and unfettered by jealousy when the flame is not burning hot.

In the second case, you may choose partners who are radically different from you in age, appearance or culture, which adds to the excitement of the affair. Your personal life can be very educational, providing you with contacts and connections that will serve you well in many other areas of your life.

In either case, you will doubtless be known as a person of unusual and distinctive tastes, and you will be happier in less conservative circles, where such attributes are admired and not feared. It is quite important not to hold down your fancy or try to make it conform to any other standards than your own. Your inclinations are unique to you, and you should not hesitate to exercise the freedom of creativity that can be yours.

Venus Conjunct Neptune

You probably started life as a starry-eyed idealist and, depending upon your age, you may be one still. Usually, your idealism is dampenend by the setbacks of harsh reality during your twenties; it takes a number of years to sort out your priorities and effectively integrate your ideals into real life. In the interim, a certain worldly cynicism sets in, which serves as protection against further injury by the world to your hopes and dreams.

Your idealism affects your sexual and emotional life quite strongly, because few affairs can ever live up to your standards, and thus you set yourself up for disappointment. But because you make such high demands of yourself as well as of your partner, you may be sought after as a partner or lover. However, when you do choose a lover, he or she may be disappointed, for physical sexuality probably takes second place to spiritual communication; unless your lover shares this attitude, you both will feel disappointed and frustrated, particularly in youth when sexuality runs strong and spirituality is not yet developed.

To avoid these problems, you should state your intentions clearly before becoming involved with a lover, although you may not feel inclined to do so. A bald, delineated description of what you want and expect, even if that seems impractical, will save you endless grief. Most of these problems will be resolved by maturity.

Venus Sextile Neptune

Although you are fairly idealistic about love, you do not expect your dreams to come true of their own accord. Therefore, you take practical steps to realize them as much as possible. Although you romanticize sex, you do not place it upon a pedestal where it loses its physical earthiness; instead, you idealize the physical pleasure of sex, enjoying it as an art form separate from the spiritual communication and nonmaterial aspects of love.

The effect of this attitude is to help you remain psychologically independent of your partner. You can choose how you want to communicate without suffering sexual frustration or feeling that you must throw yourself into a relationship just because you are sharing a bed. If you and your partner are sexually compatible, that may be quite enough for you, until the relationship develops further or another potential partner arrives on the scene.

In the long run, you will want a soul mate as well as a bed mate, but they do not have to be the same person necessarily. That arrangement might not be very easy for your partners to cope with, but it has proved viable for some. Just take enough time and be choosy about your partners.

In any case, you are most likely to achieve your dreams of love by combining romanticism and practicality which, in your case, can be wed.

Venus Square Neptune

You should make a particular effort to examine your motives in your sexual and emotional desires before pursuing them actively. This is not a question of honesty or morality but of making sure that you really want what you think you want and that you will be satisfied if you get it.

It is really important to stand back and take a second look at relationships or partners that seem, at first glance, to promise everything you want. You would be wise to look every gift horse in the mouth. By examining an affair realistically, you can avoid wrapping your lover and the affair in your own dreams and wishes, bestowing on them much that is not really there, which will subsequently prove disappointing to you.

This does not mean that every seemingly golden situation is rotten underneath, but that you should be aware of that possibility. More than most people, you would be likely to miss it until too late, unless you are careful. By being scrupulously honest with yourself and by asking the opinions of trusted friends, you may gain a much more realistic viewpoint and avoid becoming enmeshed in affairs that will surely go awry. This is especially important, because once into an unsatisfactory situation, you find it quite difficult to extricate yourself, and your efforts to rectify the situation frequently make it worse.

Venus Trine Neptune

Instead of being earthy, your approach to physical sexuality is somewhat detached, almost intellectualized. You view sexuality more as an enjoyable form of behavior rather than as a force that takes possession of you in a more blunt, bodily fashion.

This can be a healthy attitude, because it prevents you from being controlled by sex, which drags some people into relationships that are otherwise unsuitable. For you, sexuality is one of many facets in a life relationship. Because of this attitude, you can construct a relationship that approaches the ideal and yet is still workable: in other words, it can be an all-around success.

Such a relationship cannot develop quickly, but that is all right because you are not subject to the feeling of uncontrollable urgency that might cause you to stray from the path too soon. You can afford to wait until the time is right to make major partnership decisions. Until that time, you can enjoy sexual expression as an art form or pastime that heads off frustration without being forced into a long-term commitment before you are totally ready.

Throughout life, your goals and ideals are realistic enough that you can fulfill them rewardingly, unlike those who set foggy or unrealistic goals that inevitably lead to disappointment.

Venus Inconjunct Neptune

You are determined to live up to the high ideals and standards that you have set for yourself and your partner. In fact, your standards may be impossibly strict, so that they are simply a highway to frustration and disappointment. On the other hand, they may be difficult to fulfill but richly rewarding when you and your lover have made them come true.

The difficulty, therefore, is in discerning which standards are possible to reach and which are not. You can simplify this problem by being aware that you are aiming above the mark, so that coming up a bit short will not be such a surprise or disappointment. When you do score a bullseye, however, your elation will be doubled, thus using your own tendencies to double advantage.

It is also important to give yourself and your lover the fullest credit when you do achieve a goal and to rest on your laurels briefly before renewing the pressure for further accomplishments.

At all costs, avoid punishing yourself and your lover for failures; that will only undercut your ability to strive and succeed in the future.

Another way to relieve this pressure is by shifting your ideal of perfection in a love affair from accomplishment to striving for it; if the love and effort are there, that is what counts the most.

Venus Opposition Neptune

You may find that your goals and standards get in the way of achieving happiness or sexual satisfaction. From time to time you may rebel and cast away your standards, simply enjoying the available pleasures of the moment. Indeed, those moments probably give you the most enjoyment and satisfaction.

But later you may feel guilty, believing that you have lowered your standards and settled for less than you should have. These moods can be modified by reevaluating and perhaps lowering your standards in love, which are probably unrealistically high. When it comes to judging your own actions, go easy, because nobody's perfect.

When you consider your lover's qualities, remember that what is real and meaningful is the warmth and sincerity of feelings, even if they are only of the moment, not the package they come in. By reshaping your short-term goals, you will save yourself endless frustration and guilt. Your desires will become more even, which will increase the likelihood of success in your long-term affairs as well.

Coming to terms with the rules by which you play the game of love will allow you to set them up so that you do not have to choose between suffering and breaking them. Instead of being frustrated, you can use your goal-orientation to enhance achievement by continual reinforcement.

Venus Conjunct Pluto

This position indicates deep-seated and sometimes uncontrollably powerful desire. When a would-be partner strikes your fancy, it is seldom as a casual pleasure but as a tremendous physical and emotonal need that aches to be satisfied at almost any cost.

This makes you an arduous and astute suitor against whom other suitors have little chance. Your problem, however, may be that you are too intense, and unless your desired lover shares that intensity, it may be too overwhelming or frightening.

If you and your partner are willing to plumb the depths of desire, however, you can attain the ultimate in sexual stimulation; the more your desire is fed, the more it wants. The only limits are those of physical stamina.

You look upon sex as an almost religious opportunity for self-dissolution and union with the universal whole. You never consider it simply as entertainment, but as something to be taken very seriously. For you, sex contains the seeds of enlightenment through immolation of the ego in the fires of physical passion. You might do well to investigate Tantric yoga, which is the best-marked path for those with the inner urge for cosmic sexual exploration.

Venus Sextile Pluto

You are sure enough of the nature and extent of your desires that they don't usually control you against your will. This is not to say that you handle your sexual needs in a very controlled way, but that they do not get in your way or pull you into affairs that are unsatisfactory on other levels. In general, your physical sexuality fits in to your relationships rather easily and will not be a basic source of conflict, unless your partner brings sexual problems to the relationship.

In an affair, you can be firm about what your needs are so that they will not go unsatisfied, but at the same time, you don't make excessive demands. In fact, you are able to absorb and relieve tension, sexual and otherwise, in a relationship, and you can often serve as a release for your partner's pent-up emotions. Because you are secure in your own needs, you can assist those who are less secure with their problems.

However, when you help your partner, make sure that you do not neglect your own desires. Normally this will not happen, but since your needs are not so urgent or insistent, you may forget them when more pressing matters are in the spotlight.

Venus Square Pluto

You probably have rather strong desires, but you may sometimes have trouble getting them properly satisfied. However, you should be especially careful in the psychological methods you use to obtain gratification.

This is particularly true if satisfying your needs might upset the quality of your relationship. You have a certain ability to manipulate others with your desires, thus gaining dominance over them. You should use this ability carefully and only at the right time and place. A certain insecurity or fear of not getting what you want can motivate you to force your partner, in ways that may be to subtle for you to notice, into fulfilling your desires. But this use of power within a love relationship is usually quite destructive in the long run, and you should do your best to avoid it. If you make your needs known, either your lover will take care of them or you can move on to a new relationship.

Another way to channel these tendencies is to act out your power fantasies, of dominance and the like, in the bedroom. This can release much built-up tension in a mutually enjoyable way and prevent it from spilling over into your daily life and interfering with equality in the relationship. Just be sure to keep the two worlds separate and agree on everything with your partner before acting out your fantasies.

Venus Trine Pluto

You have a firm grip on what you want, both sexually and in your general life goals, and you will pursue these goals quietly but firmly until you reach them. You are not particularly aggressive in this, but you will not be thwarted for long by circumstances or an obstinate partner.

Sexual pleasure, which is quite important to you, has an enlivening effect on your whole life style. A sexually rewarding relationship makes you blossom in all other respects. You do not seek sexual pleasure compulsively, however; you fall into it through circumstance, and when times are lean, you are confident that the situation will improve. This belief keeps you going and prevents you from settling for second best just for temporary gratification.

This same inner trust will carry you through difficult times when you are not getting the satisfaction you need in a relationship that is sound and shouldn't be abandoned. Again, this is a manifestation of your determination to make sure things come out right for you, which in the end they will.

You can be quite supportive of a less secure partner who needs emotional support to pull through or who needs help in finding more satisfying outlets for sexuality. A sexually creative and satisfying relationship is necessary to the successful attainment of your own desire.

Venus Inconjunct Pluto

You should do all you can to bring your sexual needs and drives to the surface and grasp them intellectually. They are quite powerful, but in ways that you may not recognize, which means that they can control you without your knowledge.

Similarly, you sometimes use your needs and desires to manipulate and control others, often without knowing it. By being more self-aware, you will have more control over the way you relate to others sexually.

Sex is always a motivating force for you, whether it is expressed physically or sublimated into other areas, and it will make you tenacious and determined to get what you want, no matter what the cost. You should avoid the temptation to use others in harmful ways to attain your goals, sexual or otherwise, although that would be easy for you to do.

You may find it difficult to completely exhaust your sexual energies in an encounter, which can leave you with a certain feeling of dissatisfaction. But if you look at the left-over energy as merely the starting point for future enjoyment, you will have a positive outlook rather than feeling that you haven't had enough. If you practice patience in bed, things will go much more easily.

Venus Opposition Pluto

Your desires are quite strong but rather irregular, appearing and disappearing without your having much control over the time and place. You may experience intense need for a time and then be completely uninterested, so that the most intensely arousing situations leave you cold. Similarly, desires that you wish to inhibit can be kept buried for a time, but then they may flare up beyond your ability to repress them.

Perhaps the easiest way to control this problem is to educate yourself about the exact nature of your needs so that they are closer to the surface, where you can observe them. Upon closer inspection, you may find that many buried desires can be brought to light and enjoyed under the right circumstances. Most sexual needs, except those that would cause bodily harm, can find healthy expression with an understanding partner.

By living out even your darkest fantasies, you can keep the pendulum of your desires from swinging so widely, and you can even out your personality in general. Releasing your unconscious fantasy life will probably transform your sex life and also your life in general, giving you a much richer sense of freedom and self-control.

Venus Conjunct Ascendant

You have a magnetic personality, and your personal appearance has a sort of natural glow. You can get into relationships quite easily, at times even too easily. In fact people are so anxious to become personally involved with you that you have little privacy left.

Because relationships are so easy for you to start, you should be careful to become involved only in those that are meaningful and worthwhile. Otherwise you may dissipate your energies among many relationships without developing any one enough to be truly special. Your gift of charm must be treated with respect and developed into an admirable grace rather than devolving into shallow glibness.

Because of your magnetism, you attract others who are outgoing and electric. As a result, your social environment will be sparked by active and relatively aggressive leaders in what they do. Your lovers, also, tend to be active types who are attracted by your magnetism.

Your disposition is rather gentle and tender, and you will be most compatible with lovers who appreciate subtlety rather than a primitive, physical approach. This does not preclude a more rigid personality underneath (the iron fist in the velvet glove), but your outward approach is usually delicate and genteel, marked by a distinct sensitivity to the needs and feelings of others.

Venus Sextile Ascendant

You express your desires quite effectively through your movements and appearance, so that you do not have to use many words to let your lover know your needs. In general your bodily appearance helps you get what you want; you seldom have to overcome physical difficulties in expressing your desires.

This does not mean that you are necessarily the picture of ideal beauty, but rather that you are at ease with your body and can readily and naturally express your desires through it, which makes you more attractive to others. You have a certain easy charm that makes people feel at home with you, knowing that they don't have to puzzle out your intentions in any area.

Do not assume, however, that others are as easy and clear about their feelings as you are. Very frequently, potential partners may transmit exactly the opposite of what they mean and assume that you will do the same. Therefore they will misinterpret your intentions. If this seems to be happening, you should fall back on clearly spoken words to express your needs and desires, even if that is not so natural or comfortable for you. In the long run, it may save you a lot of trouble from crossed wires.

Venus Square Ascendant

You are probably less concerned with your physical appearance than with the status and beauty of your home or general surroundings, by which others will judge you. Thus, a beautifully designed and well-kept home is a more potent expression of your love and your desires than a fancy suit of clothes.

Your reputation and what others think of you may seem quite important. You may structure your life to show the world that you have a particularly beautiful and loving relationship.

Both these tendencies impel you toward very rewarding and satisfying relationships that offer you and your lover a great deal. However, you are inclined to express your desires symbolically rather than physically and directly, which may get in the way of communication with your partner.

When such difficulties arise, do not hesitate to be quite verbal and specific about what you need and desire from your lover, even though you feel that your actions have made this clear. For many people, words speak louder than deeds, and your lover would happily take care of them if you spoke up.

Venus Trine Ascendant

You probably have a natural talent for making your desires known with few words. People find it easy to get to know you, for you don't put up barriers to communication with others, and you are open, frank and fun-loving.

Probably you get along most easily with lovers who don't beat around the bush too much and get lost in the technicalities of expressing themselves. A simple smile or gesture should be enough; more than that simply obscures the message.

However, you should be patient with those who are not so fortunate in their expression. They may be excellent partners, even if they have problems in coordinating their bodies with their inner needs. You are more than capable of helping such a partner overcome internal communication problems, so that together you can develop a very rewarding relationship.

You have a talent for looking very attractive with little preparation; you don't need to be dressed to the teeth to look striking. Your physical attractiveness is derived less from decoration than from your easy coordination and an aura of naturalness and sincerity. You have an advantage over people who have to make an effort to put themselves together, but you should be very modest about it, because you may inspire undue jealousy or resentment in your peers. Use your talent to help others, not to compete with them.

Venus Inconjunct Ascendant

You may spend a lot of time improving your appearance and making yourself attractive to a potential lover. Indeed, you may have become quite an artist at making yourself look irresistible.

This is a valuable attribute, but do not let it get in the way of natural, unpremeditated communication about your own and your partner's needs. Beauty is in the eye of the beholder, and all your cosmetic efforts are for nothing if you're not the right person. If you are the right person, you need no extra frills. Indeed, too much preparation can put a certain distance between you and your partner, making it hard to get at the real you beneath the window dressing.

Except for this difficulty, you are probably very good at making your needs known to your lover without words. Indeed, you may unknowingly overstate the urgency of your desires, so give some thought to being more subtle, particularly on the verbal level, because nonverbally you may be saying enough. Don't say more than you need to, for your lover might expect more than you can deliver, which would be unfair. Save your energies for the deeds you are anticipating rather than using them up in the anticipation itself.

Venus Opposition Ascendant

Having a partner and a close love relationship is of the utmost importance to you because it allows you to satisfy most of your personal needs, both sexual and emotional. Your personality blooms when you are united with someone else, and you do not feel really whole alone.

You are an excellent and very loving partner, who lavishes affection on a lover because he or she is the source of much that is important in your life. Just be careful not to let a partner take advantage of your good nature and generosity, making sure that he or she returns similar amounts of generosity. If there is abuse of your good nature, your tendency may be to ignore it, deciding that a bird in the hand is worth two in the bush. You should not do that, however, because if you drop an unsatisfactory affair, your natural inclination toward partnership will draw another, perhaps better, partner to you quite quickly.

Be selective in your generosity, and your love affairs will blossom more fully and be longer lasting. If you are tolerant of faults in the short run but demand that they be corrected in time, you both will come out better in the end. In any case, you are more likely than most to have a solid, loving partnership which will be one of your life's major rewards.

Chapter Nine

Mars

Mars in the Chart

The position and aspects of Mars have to do with the style of your sexual drives in an assertive, active sense. It is important to take these drives into account, especially if they are not always consistent with your intellectual estimate of them. If Mars is in easy aspect and well positioned, your energies may be quite consistent and even overabundant. But if its position is more difficult, you may have to readjust your expectations to be more in line with the type and rhythm of your sexual energy.

Almost everyone has plenty of sexual energy for a full and rewarding sex life, but this energy should not be used casually or wasted. Like any other source of energy, it should be conserved and used intelligently to avoid unnecessary shortages and to produce the most pleasure.

If you can learn to be aware of the style and timing of your internal sexual energy, you can more easily attune yourself to your partner's style and assert yourself effectively when you choose to.

Mars in Aries

Although you may not be particularly forward in your social manner, when it comes to physical affection you are usually the initiator and in some ways the aggressor. Therefore you are happiest with a partner who lets you play that role most of the time and who will not conflict or compete with you.

You are spontaneous and eager, and you like to participate actively in lovemaking. But in your eagerness, take care not to get carried away and leave your lover emotionally behind in an earlier stage of lovemaking. The lessons you must learn are those of restraint and staying power. You will get more sustained pleasure out of love if you bank your fires a bit, even letting your lover carry the load so you can relax.

Because you become physically intense within a rather short period, you can gain more satisfaction from a brief affair than most people. You can pack a full relationship into a lightning affair that would leave others unfulfilled.

Do not let your impulsiveness lead you to make premature commitments or act rashly from either love or anger. You may take the opposite view just as intensely a short time later, so always leave yourself plenty of room to maneuver.

Mars in Taurus

You take a while to warm up to lovemaking, but once in gear, you sustain a steady and unfaltering pace that allows plenty of time for full sexual expression. You should give careful consideration to your lover's rhythms and timing so that you do not either wear out or exasperate your partner. At times, even though you are still enjoying yourself, you should move on to something different, just to provide sufficient variety for your partner's swifter tastes. If you find a lover who can lingeringly savor each development, as you do, you will be in luck.

Your regular sexual drive needs consistent outlets to keep in balance, so you are best off with a regular partner, not depending on the vagaries of changing social contacts to find a lover.

You may enjoy expressing your love by making things by hand for your lover. This physical love-labor can be especially meaningful, lending the gift far more impact than store-bought merchandise. This is particularly true with love toys and bedroom accouterments when you want a personal touch rather than more sterile machine-made products.

You are quite frank in your expression of affection, and you need a partner who does not intellectualize love too much but encourages you to manifest it directly in a manner that you both understand without words.

Mars in Gemini

You are quite sensitive, and you learn the delicate art of lovemaking very quickly. For that reason, you need a lover who responds to a rather gentle touch, who is ready to search for every possible means of sexual expression. You easily translate thought into action, and therefore you can become quite expert with a minimum of physical experience as long as it is backed up with a maximum of knowledge.

However, you can be too knowledgeable, trying to pack too many different techniques into one night of love so that each individual expression is less meaningful. Better to savor each technique and reserve some for later enjoyment—there's a lot of life and love ahead of you.

On the opposite side, however, although you value the emotional communion of love, you grow bored if the physical expression is always the same. Your lover should be willing to experiment or at least go along with whatever you devise for variety's sake.

You may enjoy using props and mechanical embellishments in lovemaking, particularly in acting out sexual fantasies. Such expression can be quite fulfilling, as long as it is not a substitute for emotional communication.

Mars in Cancer

Your sexuality may have a very uneven rhythm, building up without expression for a time and then bursting out with considerable intensity. If your lover is forewarned, this

214

can lead to a very rich physical experience, but take care not to overwhelm your partner with unexpected amorousness. You are much more likely to get a satisfactory response if you let your lover know your intentions ahead of time so that he or she is fully ready for you.

Similarly, try not to be overprotective of your lover. Almost unconsciously, you may spin a web of protection around your partner, and even though it stems strictly from love, it may be too confining if he or she is an independent type. Take care not to interfere even obliquely with your partner's social contacts unless specifically requested, lest your good intentions get you labeled a busybody.

As a lover, you are particularly sensitive to your partner's needs in a very intuitive and nonverbal fashion. At first, you may be hesitant to rush into expression that might in some way offend, but once the general boundaries of a relationship are established, you sense your lover's physical needs and satisfy them faultlessly.

Mars in Leo

Your approach to lovemaking is rather direct and friendly, and you may be somewhat frustrated by a lover who requires extensive courting or who insists on innumerable verbal games before approaching the physical side of love.

However, once lovemaking is assured, you make elaborate preparations, particularly in lavish surroundings and sumptuous fittings. But remember to consider your partner's ideas, because some people respond to such elaborateness by becoming self-conscious and unable to fully let go.

You are the warmest and most open of lovers, but you may tend to go through one or two basic scenarios over and over without being entirely aware of it. This may become wearing, but if you consult your partner for suggestions and new directions, this needn't become a problem.

You are generous to a fault with your lover, particularly in supplying aids for lovemaking and tokens of affection. This can be most meaningful to you, but don't be surprised if your lover requires less or does not fully appreciate all your efforts. Where the hand fails in such matters, the heart will provide.

Mars in Virgo

You are a very careful, sensitive lover who gives much thoughtful preparation to making sure that the atmosphere and setting for love are just right. You like to make sufficiently varied plans so that the experience is spontaneous but always with accessories at hand to enhance it.

Thus you check out the setting of even a seemingly off-the-cuff seduction such as making love outdoors—making sure the grass is soft and without brambles, poison ivy or distractions that might put a damper on events. In general, however, you prefer a well-appointed room with all the accouterments so that you are in control of the overall situation and can concentrate on the more delicate details of intimacy.

Your most outstanding characteristic is attentiveness to the myriad particulars of sex—all the tiny nuances that make it an endlessly varied pursuit. But take care to keep spontaneity alive and not become locked into a complex but static series of maneuvers. There is a wealth of delight in the intricate rituals of sex, but they must be enlivened by inner emotion and sensitivity to your lover's needs.

Mars in Libra

You are likely to be the one who instigates change within a relationship, and your affairs are seldom static. You usually take the initiative in beginning a new relationship as well as in breaking off an old one that is no longer satisfying.

Although you may be consciously trying to bring about change in a spirit of honest adjustment and possibly conciliation, you may slip into a pattern of shifting and change for its own sake, which can be destructive to the positive aspects of a relationship. Be very sure that something needs to be changed before stepping in and rearranging.

On the other hand, you are so interested in fairness within a relationship that you will take a back seat if you feel it will serve the interests of equality. Just take care that you are a promoter of equality rather than an enforcer, for that is self-defeating.

In physical affection, you are very considerate and anxious to please, making a point of knowing what your partner enjoys. You go out of your way to provide your lover with special and unique attentions. Your style is quite active and volatile, and you are at your best with someone who is similarly responsive.

Mars in Scorpio

Your energies tend to be rather muffled and smoldering, in that you harbor a desire for a long time before allowing it to break out, and then it is very intense. For this reason, your lover may not be truly aware of the nature or extent of your needs, which when revealed may surprise or overwhelm him or her. It is wise to express yourself verbally beforehand so that your partner is prepared.

Because of this rather dominating high energy, you often rule a relationship, directly or indirectly, particularly in its physical aspects. To you, sex is a kind of mutual self-immolation, which you sometimes lead your lover into without warning. You need a partner who is open to sexual adventure and self-abandonment, someone who can experience your kind of sexuality.

You may rely particularly on the physical and organic aspects of sex for relaying cues of affection to a lover, and therefore you should avoid sexually conservative types unless you relish continually shocking your partner. True communication takes a while for you to develop, but once established, the ties are very deep and not easily broken.

Mars in Sagittarius

You tend to approach any involvement, sexual or otherwise, with gusto, jumping right into what's happening without much ado or extensive preparation. For this reason, you should give some special attention to developing foreplay technique so that you do not rush your lover into the action without an adequate buildup.

On the other hand, you have a particular talent for bringing an overly thoughtful or melancholy lover out of the dumps and into a gleeful love session by your own open and positive approach.

Your sexual style borders on the athletic, providing a very energetic and healthful way of keeping yourself in trim. Your partner should be equally enthusiastic about such sport. But take care not to wear out your lover or neglect the more tender forms of love communication through these robust expressions of sexual energy.

Probably you are not the one to initiate fantasy role-playing except in the most general terms, but you should be receptive to more specific suggestions from your lover. Be sure that your partner's fantasies and your own do not remain unfulfilled and that the details don't get lost in too-hasty actualization. In fact, a lover who fills in the details of your sexual expression would be ideal.

Mars in Capricorn

You may make quite specific demands of yourself about your sexual role, which means that you can be a very astute lover when you are in tune with your partner. But that can't always happen, and you must learn to adapt to other styles of loving at times in order to truly please your lover. Insisting too much on your own patterns can lead to a real communication gap between you and your partner.

You tend to be sexually faithful to your lover, not because you are conservative, which may not be true at all, but because you don't want to keep changing your style for various partners. That would lessen your own enjoyment. You will be much happier if you develop and refine one love relationship to the point of true artistry instead of diffusing your energies without real accomplishment.

You probably prefer having fairly specific boundaries of sexual expression rather than an emotional or physical free-for-all. You like to have the situation under control so that you know you can deliver all that is expected of you.

Take care that you and your partner agree about the boundaries, lest it appear that you are trying to take control of the relationship. When your shared goals are clearly outlined, you will find the greatest mutual fulfillment.

Mars in Aquarius

Your style of expression is multifaceted and you focus on exploring a number of forms of fulfillment rather than developing one particular area.

You may be tempted to play the field to find maximum opportunities to extend your range of expression. This can be rewarding, but it can result in a lack of communication and a certain sexual dilettantism. Ideally, you should find a partner who wants to be as wide-ranging as you are, combining variety with truly satisfying intimacy. This should not preclude the possibility of having others share your mutual enjoyment, but one steady partner will provide the fairly regular expression you need and the real closeness that only a long-range relationship can provide.

You go out of your way to discover and fulfill all your lover's fantasies, which makes you a particularly desirable partner. But be sure to avoid jealous lovers, for you must remain free to express your personality, even if you do not choose to exercise that freedom.

When you try out new varieties of sexual expression, however, you should define each sexual vignette quite carefully, so that it can be carried out fully without confusion.

Mars in Pisces

You have a particularly subtle form of active sexual expression that requires a rather sensitive lover in order to bring it out most fully. You tend not to be overtly aggressive, and often your sexuality becomes sublimated into seemingly nonsexual gestures of affection toward your partner. Since properly interpreting these gestures may require acute perception on the part of your lover, you should trace them yourself as well as tell your partner of your needs.

You are capable of great self-sacrifice as an enjoyable outlet for tendencies that might be extreme in everyday life. Just remember where the bedroom ends, so that in other areas of the relationship you can be equals.

True satisfaction comes from the fine and often ethereal intertwining of your own and your lover's actions. Your relationship will be most enjoyable when there is a high degree of unspoken understanding between you. Too-explicit words and deeds cannot really express the more delicate and refined quality of your sexuality.

Mars in the First House

Your sexual energies are quite direct and are not likely to become confused or sublimated into other areas. This is a very honest approach to an area that is seldom treated that way, and you may have to hold back for a partner who prefers to be more circumspect about sex. However, you are happiest with someone who has a similarly open style with whom you do not have to continually repress your natural drives.

You probably have a good deal of stamina in sexuality as well as in other physical pursuits, and you don't tire easily. Indeed, you are likely to get the most pleasure from fairly lengthy lovemaking and may be somewhat frustrated by a hasty conclusion. Be sure to take your lover's energies into account, however, because what seems to you like a short run around the block may be more like a marathon for your partner. For that reason, you would do well to match yourself to a lover of similar energy.

You may be impatient in matters of love, wanting to get on with the affair with a minimum of talk or banter. That is an honest reflection of your feelings, but you should avoid being too hasty; often the delays before a relationship is consummated give you time to think twice about whether you really want to commit yourself to that particular lover. By slowing down, you can avoid relationships that are too crowded with undesirable complexities.

Mars in the Second House

You express your love in very physical ways—not bodily but by surrounding your loved one with a variety of physical comforts, gifts and tangible tokens of love.

Also you like to use physical props and special surroundings to enhance lovemaking, everything from soft lights and satin sheets to the farther-out accouterments of loving when experimentation is the order of the evening.

This is an excellent position in that you can achieve an endless variety of sexual stimulation simply by altering your physical surroundings to make them more sensual and pleasing, even without changing the position or basic bodily approach to lovemaking. A fur rug, a velvet coverlet, a bare wooden floor—all lend a new excitement and tension that transforms and elevates sex when boredom threatens.

On the negative side, you tend to be physically possessive of your lover, with all the problems that incipient jealousy brings. This is because you consider your sex partner in too physical a light. In sex play, this can be highly exciting and lead to the most intricate physical enjoyment for both of you, but out of the bedroom, avoid that attitude. It's fantastic to be a sex object in bed, but not in everyday life.

Mars in the Third House

You are likely to be a rather conversational lover, and your gracious or stimulating phrases add a great deal to lovemaking. From sweet nothings whispered in courting to more graphic phrases motivated by the passion of the moment, words can serve as an erotic embellishment that stimulates the body and fires the imagination.

You may express this talent by writing love poetry or just by knowing how to talk a lover into bed, which can be a valuable gift in itself. Also you are a rather inventive lover who continually devises new delights for your partner, making boredom unlikely.

On the contrary, if there is any problem here, it may be that you concentrate too much on variety and neglect to develop deeper personal communion within a relationship. This can be a particular problem if your lover is not verbally expressive.

You are a very congenial person, and you aren't likely to be overly emotional or pompous about an affair, although you may be voluble about it. Your style in lovemaking is gentle and delicate, and you are happiest with someone who appreciates tenderness in love rather than violently intense sexual expression.

Mars in the Fourth House

You tend to be a careful and thoughtful lover who creates an all-encompassing sexual experience for your partner. You are able to transmit a certain intimacy and security through lovemaking that few others can achieve.

To enhance this quality, you should express your love in somewhat protected, familiar circumstances that complement your style. You are not one to spring surprises on your lover, nor do you particularly appreciate unexpected twists or turns yourself, for they tend to throw you off your stride. For that reason, an affair may sometimes get bogged down for lack of variety. This is easily remedied by discussing with your lover the exact style and nature of experimentation beforehand, so that instead of being strange or alien, it is a refreshing change.

Although your sexual technique is pretty fundamental, your manner of loving has considerable strength, and your partner can always depend on you in a pinch. Indeed, the feeling behind your love may be quite parental, which can be very comforting and reassuring to your partner. You should, however, be aware of how you are using this, because an attitude that seems warm and reassuring to one partner may seem condescending to another. You will be happiest with a lover who considers you a sort of parent figure, although to be just that would be unwise.

Mars in the Fifth House

Your great zest for life is reflected in your sexual style. Because you approach sex in a very open, almost playful way, it does not have the pitfalls it has for so many people in our rather repressed culture.

Indeed, you may be completely puzzled by someone with a more tangled or out-of-balance view of sexuality; when you are involved in a sexual experience, it all seems so simple. Don't let this prevent you from trying to understand friends or acquaintances who have sexual problems, although it is just as well not to get too deeply involved in their problems, for that will only dampen your own enjoyment.

Your open and nonserious approach to sex will be either shocking or refreshing to your lover, depending on how open he or she is. You are most comfortable with someone who is as sunny and pleasant as yourself, although you may find a certain attraction in cheering up a morose soul. That can be a creative use of your energies up to a point and can bring you down to earth when you need it. However, in the long run, tangled personalities get on best with their own kind. You will be happier with someone who treats sex as a joyful, healthy physical and emotional recreation.

Mars in the Sixth House

Your style of lovemaking is quite specific, with content and technique rather closely tied together. For that reason, in order to achieve the fullest sexual expression, you should become familiar with a variety of sexual styles and scenarios.

You may at times lack spontaneity and, indeed, you are best off when you can draw that from your partner. But you more than make up for this lack in your physical achievements as a lover, from which your partner may draw both pleasure and enlightenment.

Indeed, you may go to great lengths to learn techniques that especially please your lover, sometimes neglecting your own pleasure in the process. Going to such extremes may be counterproductive, however, unless both of you recognize and enjoy it as an unequal but mutually pleasurable bedroom pastime.

You probably enjoy quite specific and detailed fantasy scenarios and are most fulfilled by a lover who joins you in such games with creativity and gusto. Don't worry if your fantasies are out of line with so-called normal (often a password for dull) expression. Only when your full sexuality comes totally alive will you find the fulfillment and self-understanding that you seek.

Mars in the Seventh House

You may gravitate toward rather intense, strenuous relationships in which both you and your partner emit and demand a great deal of energy. At times this can be wearing, unless you learn to draw freely on your lover as your primary source of energy and motivation. This will eliminate the occasional friction of competition between you and save you a good deal of effort, which your partner will be happy to expend.

You should be particularly careful that your respective roles within the relationship are clear, to avoid disputes over what territory is whose. Secretly, however, you may enjoy such disputes because they add to the emotional intensity of the relationship. You like to venture out on the shaky bridge between anger and passion, but this can spell trouble for your relationship unless you both are very strong. Few people can sustain a really stormy relationship without breaking down into real hostilities.

However, you are best off with a regular partner who is around much of the time, for you derive a great deal of your energy and drive from your partner, if only through inspiration.

Mars in the Eighth House

You like to maintain a certain air of mystery concerning your style and motivations in sexuality, which can add both power and attraction to your image as others see it. But don't get so lazy that you let those same motivations remain a mystery to yourself. In order to stay in control of your sometimes complex and subterranean inner forces, you must make a particular effort to explore them and reach an effective level of self-understanding.

Sexual activity has a very invigorating effect on your constitution. You should avoid lengthy periods of abstinence, for that tends to tie up your mental and physical energies so that they work against each other, leaving you at less than peak capacity physically. This need is quite physical, and although you have considerable ability to sublimate sexuality into other areas, too much sublimation will physically drain you and emotionally tie you in knots.

Because of your own makeup, you are rather good at unraveling the tangled skeins of others' personal lives. In a love affair you can pursue seemingly well-hidden motives that reveal your lover's special needs, and then satisfy them. Indeed, you may have a certain mystic or psychic flair for sexual technique, which you use as a tool for delving deep into your lover's buried sexual and emotional desires.

Mars in the Ninth House

You may have developed a rather externalized approach to sexuality in which you decide on your moves and expectations ahead of time; then physical fulfillment depends upon each partner properly playing a predetermined role. This is one of the surest roads to sexual satisfaction if both you and your partner understand each other's expectations beforehand. If you share the same general concept of how sexuality should be externally expressed, then there is much ready-made enjoyment in store for you and your partner.

However, you may find that much-played roles become less interesting after a while, and then you both should decide upon a new direction before launching into it. In this way you can find endless adventures in the realm of sexuality, limited only by the creativity and imagination you put into it.

You may become a connoisseur of special sexual roles, developing a number of fairly well-defined relationships through which to express myriad forms of sexual communication. It is a kind of sexual adventurism in which you retain control of what is going on so that you have both variety and the security to express yourself freely.

Mars in the Tenth House

You will find that whether or not you seek it, your activities, both in and out of the bedroom, attract attention from others. You must be especially careful to keep your private affairs private, for they tend to spill out into the open unless you are attentive and make an effort to keep them to yourself.

Your love affairs may have a strong effect on how you handle your career, and you may stand to benefit greatly from your love associations. Although this can be desirable, it can also stir up much jealousy among associates who think you are trading sexual favors for professional ones.

In fact, this situation may be unavoidable at times, particularly if you share more than just the bedroom with your lover, so that your private and external affairs become inextricably intertwined, as in a husband-wife business enterprise.

If your love life does become involved with your professional life, make sure the relationship promises to be lasting and enjoyable, because a breakup for emotional or sexual reasons could mean catastrophe for both of you in several areas.

On the other hand, you may be so preoccupied with your career or other interests that you have little or not time for personal intimacy. In that case it is best to schedule regular "breaks" to give yourself the chance for needed personal expression, even if it means cost or delay in more mundane matters.

Mars in the Eleventh House

You expend extra energy in any close personal relationship even if it is not sexual, for you place a high value on loyalty and friendship, both in yourself and in others.

For this reason you prefer a long-lasting affair that has time to develop, rather than newer and less firm attachments.

On a more mundane level, because of your desire for excellence in a relationship you gravitate toward partners who have a good reputation in such matters. In that way you move among the very best, just as you strive to be the best yourself. As long as you remember that internal qualities are paramount, this path will be continually rewarding, but if you concentrate on external qualities, you may be just a social climber or trend follower, which could be less than satisfying.

Similarly, don't let your weakness for a lover's flattery and admiration blind you to your faults. A lover's compliments are best taken with affection and a grain of salt, whereas compliments from an adversary cannot be too highly prized.

In lovemaking itself, you strive for excellence and make every effort to create a graceful aesthetic experience that has substance as well as form. Accomplishing this will be the deepest expression of love and friendship between you and your lover.

Mars in the Twelfth House

You have a needling desire to realize your deepest and most out-of-the-way motivations, both sexual and otherwise. For this reason you are willing to give up much in a relationship in order to explore the unknown and stake your claim in unfamiliar territory. Naturally such a course is always tenuous and can be treacherous, but the satisfaction of creating a special and unique relationship is reward enough for you.

A partner who will go along with you on such voyages of exploration may be hard to find. You may have to go far afield to secure one, perhaps enduring periods of unfulfillment in the search. That's the price of being special, so just acccept the bad with the good.

Do not wander into strange territory without carefully finding out about it first, for your tendency to act rashly could lead you into trouble. Here experience is the best teacher, and in time your judgment will improve concerning new experience that will be safe and rewarding for both your partner and yourself.

If you are careful, the rewards will be well worth the risks, and the fulfillment you experience will be special and unique to you.

Mars Conjunct Jupiter

You put a great deal of energy into anything you do, including love. Once you get started, the sky's the limit, and this approach can provide the most exciting and potent kind of pleasure in loving.

However, it can also overwhelm your lover, so be sure that he or she can scale the heights with you, or else modify your own energies a bit. You should be very careful in this respect, because after you are under way, it is easy to overlook your lover's needs and capacities. Take them into account ahead of time so that you won't have to be inhibited later.

Once you have established the boundaries, however, you are capable of bringing forth unusual intensity in yourself and in your lover, so that lovemaking is an exhilarating, even rejuvenating, experience. Probably you will be the initiator, in word if not in deed. You and your partner can profitably explore many new styles without danger of losing your love in physical sexuality. Quite the contrary, the more excitement you stir up, the more love and communication will result. Boredom will never enter your relationship.

Mars Sextile Jupiter

You have a good sense of proportion in initiating new styles and techniques of loving. Rather than go overboard in this respect, you introduce new ideas into a relationship at just the right intervals to keep things interesting. Also you are a pretty good judge of which ideas will work out well, so most of your experiments meet with success.

Because of this talent, you can balance a lover who tends to go off the deep end now and then. You have the physical ability to turn an apparent error of sexual judgment into an experience that is pleasant for both of you. You do this by physically taking charge of the situation when it becomes shaky and returning it to an enjoyable state of balance and pleasure.

This may simply be the result of your good coordination and flow, since sexual situations most often go awry because of bad timing or unexpected obstacles. These problems must be handled gracefully in order not to lose the spirit of the occasion. You can pull a situation out of the fire before it stops being loving, thus saving many a scene that would otherwise have turned into a bust.

Mars Square Jupiter

Before engaging in sexual experimentation, you should make sure that what you are planning is both enjoyable and physically possible. At times you may overestimate your capabilities or appetite and get into situations that are not as pleasurable as you had anticipated.

Sometimes you simply misjudge your abilities, but also you may overdo some new aspect of sex until its pleasure value is worn out. It is a good idea to rely on your lover for cues about when to stop and start, for variety and stimulation.

Naturally, if you pay attention to your lover's rhythms and needs, this will not be a problem at all. For this reason, you tend to have better and deeper sexual experiences with a partner you know and love than in a new affair, when you must rely on instant judgment. The more you develop the physical aspects of a relationship, the more satisfying it will become and the more newness and variety it will pleasurably sustain.

When you are in doubt about trying something new, you should rely on your lover's judgment. In that way you can avoid much unprofitable experimentation, and your experience in loving will have the most positive reinforcement.

Mars Trine Jupiter

You have an easy, healthy kind of sexual energy that does not impose itself on a lover. Instead, it is a bountiful reserve of desire, a willingness to participate to the fullest in order to please.

Your timing in making moves is particularly good, and as a result you have unusual success in love initially. You have a good sense of when to initiate something new so that it is exciting without making your partner feel insecure. In this fashion you can move on to new areas regularly and keep the relationship continually fresh.

Because you do not usually go to extremes, you can profit considerably from a partner who tends to go too far in sexual experimentation. That kind of lover will give you an added sexual pickup, and you will be a stabilizing factor for him or her. In that way, the extremes will not bring danger or difficulty but will be occasional focal points of high excitement.

Indeed, this kind of love life can be quite valuable, preventing you from running along at the same speed sexually. That can lead to boredom, even though you are careful to introduce a little newness now and again. Sometimes it is best to take the big leap.

Mars Inconjunct Jupiter

You may continually search for new exciting ways to express your sexuality. Certainly you are highly motivated and inventive in a physical sense and probably quite tireless.

You should remember, however, that most people need a certain amount of familiar repetition in order to establish the feeling of security that is essential to really pleasurable loving. If you introduce too many changes, your lover, in trying to keep up with you physically, may simply lose track of you emotionally.

Thus, you should temper your enthusiasm and set limits of energy and experimentation for each sexual experience. If you share these guidelines with your partner, both of you will know what to expect and what demands will be made.

In general, it is helpful to listen to your partner's opinions about what's going on and adjust your own actions to maximize your mutual pleasure. This may mean toning down your style a bit and perhaps reining in your eagerness for the new and exciting. However, in any fruitful relationship you can look forward to going further in the future, which should make it easier to restrain yourself from doing everything at once.

Mars Opposition Jupiter

Your energies, sexual and otherwise, often seem to come in uneven spurts, rather than in a steady flow. This is also true of your desire to experiment with new styles and techniques of loving.

The result is that you often burst into several new areas all at once, and then you have to retreat a bit and spend some time exploring and developing each one. This is a healthy approach, as long as you do not take on more than you can handle pleasurably. Also you should avoid repeating the same experience until it turns into boredom or inactivity.

At certain times you may be sexually creative on a mental level, cooking up tempting fantasies that have great possibilities, even though you are not in the mood to fulfill them on the physical level. When that happens, try to jot down your fantasies so that you can act them out later when you have the energy to do so.

This is particularly valuable for you because you need to have a variety of possibilities to choose from during times of high energy. Otherwise you may find yourself in a situation of energetic repetition, which is not a satisfactory release of your energies.

Mars Conjunct Saturn

You may be slow to make the first move in love, but once you have committed yourself to action you will not give up until you have achieved your goals.

To this extent it is good to have an encouraging partner who lights a fire under you, actively drawing you into sexual expression. Once lit, you burn more steadily and continuously than most people.

Try to avoid feeling obligated to please yourself or your partner. Sex should not be a duty but rather a spontaneous occurrence that gives pleasure to both partners. Total spontaneity may be difficult at times, but in that case it can be just as stimulating to plan ahead and, in a manner of speaking, make an appointment for sex. Stepping up the anticipation has a heightening effect on your pleasure and also gives you a sense of security, which may be desirable at certain times. But if this approach leads to anxiety about performance, it should be discontinued.

In general, however, it may be best for you to plan ahead for sex without letting your lover in on the plans, which will allow you both to have your cake and eat it, too.

Mars Sextile Saturn

You tend to have a certain laziness in sex, a wait-and-see attitude that can cause you to miss out on much that is enjoyable. Of course, with this approach, you are not likely to get into sexual difficulties because of rash or unthinking conduct, which is an advantage in certain situations.

Ideally, you should find a partner who is more sexually precocious, who can bring some excitement, even risky excitement, into your life. Your role would be to provide the discretion necessary to contain the excitement, so that the experience is effective and enjoyable for you both. If your partner provides the initiative energy, you can pace a relationship, giving it a regular timing that assures continuous sexual expression and satisfaction. Such a combination of personalities would be particularly energizing and successful, because it would keep you from becoming too ensconced in your sexual habits, while giving your partner enough stability to build increasing enjoyment within the relationship.

226

If you do not have this kind of partner, you should make an effort to inject variety into the affair periodically, even if it does not seem all that necessary to you. That will stimulate your lover and encourage progress that you may not see or appreciate until later, when the relationship shows new growth and revitalization.

Mars Square Saturn

You should make a special effort to free yourself from sexual inhibitions, for you tend to hold back unnecessarily and thus miss much enjoyment in love. It isn't so much that you have a narrow view of what is right and wrong in sex but that you are sometimes unable to let go and implement your ideas of what is permissible or enjoyable.

The only advice is to throw caution to the winds now and then, and enjoy love without restrictions. It is particularly important to allow yourself some mistakes and refrain from self-recrimination when they occur. An optimistic attitude of try, try again will certainly enhance your record of success. By anticipating failure, you hamstring your efforts to enjoy sexuality, whereas a positive attitude will keep you going, even when things don't work out just right.

As you learn more about your abilities and potential, you will find that you can produce just the sexual result that you want and have an extraordinary control over your expression in that area. However, this will come only with plenty of practice, using your mistakes as guideposts, not as stumbling blocks to further sexual expression.

Mars Trine Saturn

Probably you are quite secure in your patterns of sexual expression, which you approach with the confidence that comes of success. Your sexual stability is enviable, but without other stimulating influences, you may tend to fall into a rut sexually. You should be particularly aware of this problem, which can happen without your noticing it until your lover falls asleep from boredom at an embarrassing moment. That certainly takes the wind out of the sails of a relationship.

One way to prevent this is to alter the pattern of your sexual expression now and then. But it might be easier to let your lover lead the way into new sexual territory, while you provide the stability to help you both over the rough spots. By so doing you can turn the unexpected twists into enjoyable aspects of the sexual experience.

Once your direction is established, you can fulfill yourself and your lover in such a way that love is never overdone. There is always enough desire left to continue later with a steady flame. While your lover may fan the flame now and again, you can make sure that your mutual expression is always creative and does not burn itself out.

Mars Inconjunct Saturn

You should make every attempt to be gentle with yourself and avoid self-criticism or blame concerning sex. You may be inclined to inhibit your expression, feeling that you can't come up to your own or your lover's expectations, but probably you are in error about that.

It may be that your sexual standards are very high to begin with, particularly concerning your own role. But unrealistically high expectations lead only to blockage as a result of inevitable failure. Therefore, trim your demands a little and enjoy the talents and opportunities that are realistically available to you. That will enhance both your possibilities and your pleasure.

Your attitude has another result also, especially when you try too hard to achieve a sexual goal. Certainly, you are more motivated and determined than most to make your desires come true, but the pressure you put on yourself and your lover to succeed may be self-defeating. Love blossoms more readily when there is no pressure to perform or achieve, and then spontaneous communication can occur more easily. Therefore, in areas that are of most concern to you, take it more easily, and you will probably get better results.

Mars Opposition Saturn

At odd and unexpected times, you may experience periods of sexual inhibition for no logical reason. Thus, at times you may be most willing to try something new sexually, while at another time you simply cannot bring yourself to do so, although the circumstances are the same.

With a relatively understanding lover, this should not present a problem; sometimes you are in the mood and sometimes you aren't, and that's all there is to it. If this causes a problem of satisfaction for your lover, you can solve this by taking the passive role for a time. In that way you can allow your lover a variety of sexual expression without participating actively yourself. This solution may also help if you are occasionally unexpectedly overtired. As they say, relax and enjoy it.

In time, you and your lover will become accustomed to such changes. Then you can use them to enhance any number of sexual fantasies dreamed up in advance to take advantage of your present energy state.

Mars Conjunct Uranus

You should avoid giving in to the temptation to rush headlong into love, either physically or emotionally, until you have taken a second look. Too hasty an approach may be unsettling to your lover, particularly in a new affair, and perhaps destroy its chances of going further.

Emotionally, if you make a commitment too quickly, you may find yourself trapped in a less-than-satisfactory relationship that is difficult to extricate yourself from. On occasion, such a situation can work out successfully with exhilarating results, but in general the odds are against you when you rely on snap judgments.

You may be rather attracted to the more aggressive or even violent styles of loving, which can be most exciting if handled correctly. However, there is a rather broad difference between fantasy and reality, and you must be very careful that both you and your partner are really enjoying it. Frequently a fantasy that seems in imagination deliciously exciting or perhaps agonizingly pleasurable turns out to be painful or frightening in a very nonerotic way. You must pick your partners and scenarios well and monitor yourself fairly carefully during the experience.

Mars Sextile Uranus

You are probably quite inventive and energetic sexually, not in a way that is either offensive or tiresome, but in a style that leads to mutual interest and exploration. Your attitude of eagerness tempered with sensitivity allows you to pick a path of sexual inventiveness that truly suits you and your lover.

You may get involved in a very natural way with styles or techniques that seem quite unusual or far-out to others. But for you and your lover, they are a natural outgrowth of love and imagination, no matter how they fit with the accepted norms of society.

In exploring new avenues of sexual satisfaction, you have a talent for making experimental styles work out well. Where some people would be disappointed or frustrated because of the inherit difficulties of trying something new, you usually manage to avoid the pitfalls because of native talent combined with simple good luck.

So feel free to let your imagination wander in your relationship. Just be sure that your lover is not too inhibited and is willing to go along with your sexual creativity for maximum satisfaction.

Mars Square Uranus

You usually try to cover up your natural impatience, but when the dam breaks, it releases a flood of physical passion that takes a lover by storm. This tendency should be watched rather carefully, however, so that your sexuality is loosed at the appropriate time, preferably when approaching orgasm rather than in the middle of dinner.

There is a very hard inner core to your style of loving. Although it seems to be very tender, underneath it has a biting, pungent quality. You may express this, quite literally, in love bites, scratches, pinches or other sharp and suddenly stimulating movements during very tender loving. Carried to extremes, this can result in a technique of soft caressing followed by sudden pain or vice versa, which can be tremendously exciting if both partners are ready for it.

You show a certain meticulousness in lovemaking, such that not a single stitch is missed in a night's play. But take care not to overload your lover with too much variety or too many details lest the basic drive toward union run out of energy.

Mars Trine Uranus

You have a native talent for sexual innovation that needs to be actively tapped. You tend to be quite open and free in your approach to a lover and to loving in general. However your sexual creativity may come to be based on habit, instead of on true and exciting departures from the norm.

229

Usually the varieties of loving that you choose are original but safe enough to fall within the range of probable enjoyment. In the long run this is the most profitable way to create sexual diversion, but some special peaks of excitement might be missing. Therefore, you might look for a lover who is inclined to go further, perhaps into realms that could be sexually perilous. Here, you can patrol the boundary between what can be done effectively and what is potentially dynamite. This may sound unsettling, but you have the special talent to handle such situations in a way that can bring you both to heights of enjoyment not usually available to others. It might not be a bad idea to at least stick your toe in the water and try it out.

Mars Inconjunct Uranus

You are inclined to take risks in matters of love, pushing on to greater heights of stimulation without regard for the consequences. Admittedly, you can be forcefully inventive in sexual matters, but such restless pressure may prove too much for a quieter lover who likes to be more slow and easy.

Certainly, you have a desire to perfect the products of your sexual imagination. To that extent, you need a partner who is willing to try anything but who can also serve as a governor on your inspirations, so that you act out only those fantasies that can give you both pleasure and will not backfire.

In general, your restless energy can interfere with the smoothness and ease of a sexual situation, particularly when it is somewhat uncertain to begin with. But you can allay such difficulties with a drink or other relaxing techniques, so your energies are more regular and blocked energies have a more creative flow.

You tend to pursue direct or sublimated sexuality rather energetically, so you need a receptive lover who can absorb and transform those energies for maximum satisfaction.

Mars Opposition Uranus

Your sexual inspiration tends to come in sudden spurts, at least if you are the instigator. You may suddenly have a period of boundless energy that needs to be expressed instantly, followed by a time of intellectual fantasizing but little energy for putting your ideas into action.

To a certain extent, an adaptable partner will be a great help to you—someone who can take the active or the passive role, depending upon your physical and emotional state. As each of you learns to play both roles and thus better understand those roles within you, your experiences will be more varied.

You may find that you enjoy going to physical extremes in love, for that can provide the peak of sexual satisfaction and pleasure. However, you should be fairly careful about how you implement it, lest you have misgivings afterward.

Your sexual inventiveness may be quite separate from your energy and desire to implement it, so it might be a good idea to jot down your inspirations, regardless of your mood, so that you can try them out at a more energetic moment.

Mars Conjunct Neptune

Your lover may consider your actions somewhat mysterious and thus find it difficult to figure out just what you mean by them. This is principally because you have a unique and rather sophisticated code of meaning in your movements that requires quite subtle interpretation.

If you and your partner are verbally oriented, you can sit down and discuss the finer points of love so that the delicacy you are capable of may be enacted with understanding. However, it may be rather difficult to put your intent into words. Subtle movements, may be your best mode of expression, but it will take time for your lover to become acclimated to experience without words.

In any case, you need an intuitive partner who can respond to your finer needs and movements with spontaneous and immediate understanding. A particular advantage of having such a partner is that at times you may be unable to decide just how to approach your lover; someone who picks up on this quickly and moves in to make his or her desires known will clear up your confusion.

However, avoid being deliberately mysterious in your actions, at least with your friends, for that will lower the level of communication between you.

Mars Sextile Neptune

You usually approach a lover in a fairly forthright yet not too obvious way. Your ability to size up a situation intuitively enables you to move in tune with your partner's rhythms and needs.

Because of this ability, people think of you as an actively warm, empathetic person. Instead of reacting just to your lover's stated needs, you act without being asked, knowing quite accurately what will please your partner.

You are able to handle a lover who finds it difficult to make his or her wants known; with you, they will be fulfilled anyway. Indeed, spelling out what should be done too explicitly could spoil the loving spontaneity that you are capable of. The warm, mellow, friendly love that is your style is best left unspoken except by mutually understood glances or gestures. Words are often either insufficient or destructive to the flow of communication. All that needs to be said can be said with much greater impact with a single movement.

Make sure, however, that your gestures convey what you mean them to and do not simply assume that your lover will always understand. Now and again a few well-placed words will do much to reinforce communication.

Mars Square Neptune

You may find it difficult to respond confidently to your lover, not knowing exactly what he or she wants or how to go about it. Such uncertainty tends to be compounded when an action taken in error reinforces your doubt about where you stand.

You will gain a great deal by making your needs known to each other clearly and verbally, specifying what they are and when they occur so that there will be no mistake about it. Although this may take away some subtlety, the results, in terms of regular and certain satisfaction for you both, will be worth that small sacrifice.

Naturally, you are happiest with a regular partner with whom you can have a clear and effective arrangement. You find a new partner harder to work with, because you do not know all the ins and outs of his or her needs and do not feel free to express your needs verbally. Thus, you tend to hang on to an old relationship where you are more sure of your ground. This attitude will help you through rough spots in an affair, because you are unwilling to break off a good thing. On the other hand, it can cause you to cling to a truly unworkable relationship.

If you have questions about sexual morality, base your actions strictly on what pleases you and your partner most, not on theories, most of which are outdated and useless.

Mars Trine Neptune

You are probably good at putting your ideals into action, and you can calm the roughest waters in a relationship with your affectionate attentions. This talent stems in large part from your intuitive knowledge of how to please a ruffled partner, as well as from a sincere desire to make your lover happy.

Your inner convictions do much to reinforce your actions, and thus you can act with strength and confidence based on sincere and solid belief. Your treatment of your lover is not dictated by society's outside morality, but by sensitivity to your partner's needs and to what will make your mutual love grow most effectively.

Your ability to accomplish your ideals is also derived from the fact that you see situations realistically rather than through idealized images. Thus, you do not make demands of yourself that you cannot fulfill, and you are pleased with the results that you do achieve.

However, you should avoid the temptation to rest on your laurels once you have brought a given aspect of a relationship to fruition. A relationship is alive only as long as it continues to grow and improve; when that ceases, it becomes stale and flounders. Therefore, enjoy your achievements, but always look to the future for better ones.

Mars Inconjunct Neptune

You may have to work very hard to achieve the goals you have set for yourself in love. Although such high standards are admirable, they can be quite debilitating unless you lower them now and then.

Avoid questioning your performance too much in either a physical or a moral sense. Much of what you consider imperfections or failures are simply your humanity showing through and should not be scrutinized too closely. It is all too easy to kill spontaneity by close inspection, and one's emotional and sexual performance is almost always

232

hindered by heavy monitoring before or during the fact. Wait until all the returns are in before you judge yourself; you will probably come off much better in hindsight.

This will help your lover also, because if you are constantly judging yourself, you may project a certain anxiety that prevents an even flow of communication in love. This is particularly true if you are concerned about sexual morality. It is most important to reserve judgment in that area except concerning pleasure. If you both enjoy something, pursue it; if not, drop it. Do not let preconceived notions about what is sexually right and wrong hamper you, for that would be counterproductive to the relationship.

Mars Opposition Neptune

You may swing from being quite confident and sure in your actions to being very confused about how to approach your lover. In general, you go too far in both directions, and you should modify these tendencies.

You can easily work on solving this problem yourself. In the first case, simply stop and question your self-assuredness before rushing ahead, for you may put your foot in your mouth without knowing it. And when you are in doubt, simply follow a course that seems promising; chances are, things will work out better than you expect.

If you can find a partner who will help temper your extremist tendencies, you should have even fewer problems. Simply trust your lover's advice and adjust your actions accordingly.

If you do make errors in judgment occasionally, avoid self-recrimination, because that will not help you modify your future behavior. If anything, it has an adverse affect on future performance. This is particularly true if you believe that you have made a moral as well as a physical error. In fact, you should eliminate the concept of "moral error," at least concerning sexuality. The only mistakes are those that cost you pleasure.

Mars Conjunct Pluto

You are likely to be quite willful in pursuing your pleasure, and when you have decided to do something, nothing can stop you. Such forcefulness may be quite stimulating to a lover who enjoys being overwhelmed or swept away, but you should choose your partners carefully, because that is not everyone's cup of tea.

Whether you play an active or a passive role, you throw yourself into loving with a will. Sex is not usually a playful matter for you, but quite all-encompassing and total. In fact, it may be a transforming experience.

As an outgrowth of the pleasure you find in going to extremes, you may enjoy lovemaking that is fairly forceful or even violent. Certainly that kind of lovemaking presents great opportunities for uplifting, ego-shattering experiences, but you must be sure that it does not get out of hand. You and your lover must be in complete agreement as to the direction and the extent to which it can be pursued and still fall within the confines of pleasure.

You should be particularly careful not to inadvertently hold too much power either physical or emotional, over your partner, which can happen quite easily. In a way, you don't know your own strength. In order to keep the relationship on an equal basis, you should get regular feedback from your partner.

Mars Sextile Pluto

You have a certain quiet confidence in what you do that rubs off and creates a feeling of trust in your partner or lover. It is not that you have great skill or experience necessarily, but that you are quite sure that your actions will come out well. As a result, they usually do.

To a certain extent this may be true because you don't try to accomplish anything that is beyond your abilities, but that is not always the case. Indeed, you may take on more than you can handle and thus fail, but that will not daunt you or undermine your confidence to try again in the future. Physical or emotional defeat in love or in any other realm of endeavor, for that matter, will never be lasting. You will pursue your goals again and again until you achieve them with a combination of perseverance and faith.

For this reason, you can inspire a discouraged lover, lending support by your demonstrative actions, which are more reassuring than words. At the same time, however, you can take rational, structured steps to overcome obstacles and achieve the goals you desire. You use your strengths to accomplish what you want without impinging upon your lover's freedom, even though you may have considerable power, laced with gentleness, within the relationship.

Mars Square Pluto

You should do everything possible to maintain an equal footing in any relationship you enter into. Avoid becoming embroiled in emotional power plays in which one partner forces the other's hand. It may be difficult to resist the great temptation to do so, and the results of such power plays may be pleasing on a short-term basis. Eventually, however, there will be less and less communication between you and considerable emotional blockage, which will probably bring the affair to an end.

Once you have decided on a relationship, you pursue it with considerable determination until it is completed. If properly used, that is an admirable trait, but you must commit yourself only to those goals that you know realistically you can accomplish. Otherwise you will experience only exhausted frustration instead of glowing success.

If at first you don't succeed, it might be wiser not to keep trying but to go on to something else. In that way you will save yourself a lot of energy and perhaps end up with a lot more pleasure. Forced sexual achievement, even if you reach your goals, does not generally lead to real mutual fulfillment. If what you are doing doesn't come naturally, abandon it and fall into another, easier mode of loving. If stressful loving does give you pleasure, however, you may enjoy playing out high-intensity fantasies in the bedroom.

234

Mars Trine Pluto

You have enough self-assurance to play love scenes in a casual, spontaneous manner and know that everything will come out right. And if things do go awry for some reason, you go on easily to something else without a sense of disappointment or failure.

This ability allows you to sustain a lover who has less self-confidence and needs reassurance that everything is all right. This does not have to be done in words, necessarily, but by your faithful, sure actions in love, which usually makes affection flow easily between you.

Direct sexual expression comes naturally to you and is an important part of any love relationship, serving as a very strong channel of physical communication between you. When other elements of your world are in trouble, the warm expression of sexuality can infuse your life with radiance and confidence and make the rainiest day seem sunny again.

Because of this style, you can show your partner how to have a freer mode of sexual expression. That will give you both great pleasure and possibly untie the knots of inhibition that hold your lover back from some forms of sexuality.

Mars Inconjunct Pluto

You should do everything possible to take the pressure off yourself concerning sexuality. The pressure is mostly internal in that you feel that you must perform and live up to impossibly high standards of sexual expression. Also you may choose a lover who somehow demands this kind of sexuality.

You can channel this kind of compulsion very enjoyably into extensive fantasy role-playing in the bedroom. The more high-powered and intense the fantasy, the more enjoyable it will be to play out. All you need is a partner who is willing to put considerable energy and originality into your sex life, someone who won't neglect you or slow you down through laziness or inhibitions.

However, you need a lover who has a good sense of what you can realistically fulfill and will point it out when you are headed down a dead-end road. In such cases, you should take your lover's word and try a new direction that has more pleasure potential for you both.

In the long run, you will enjoy great sexual achievement if you can fulfill sexual fantasies with your lover. Not only will this provide you with much physical pleasure, it will also reveal your deepest inner workings to you and make you more self-aware.

Mars Opposition Pluto

Your sexuality may be expressed rather fitfully but quite powerfully. At times your sexual feelings may be so repressed that they seem nonexistent, but at other times they well up with such tremendous power that you feel you must put them into action immediately.

The urgency of this drive may lead to difficulties with a more regular lover who is not quite ready for the intensity of your loving. Similarly, your lover may demand attentions when you are simply not in the mood at all.

You may find an enjoyable outlet for your sexual energies in styles of loving that are quite energetic and perhaps even a little violent. This can be the most pleasurable expression of all, as long as you channel these powerful energies so that you and your lover get only enjoyment, with no physical or emotional harm to either of you. You can achieve maximum pleasure without worry by adhering strictly to a previously decided-on fantasy that contains built-in checks. Also, by working out the fantasy ahead of time you can build up very strong excitement, which is repressed at first but assured of fulfillment in the end. That would suit your style very well and give you a wide choice of pleasure possibilities.

Mars Conjunct Ascendant

You present quite a forceful image, and you have a lot of energy on tap to fulfill your own and your lover's needs. You can be a tireless lover, but it might be good to temper your energies at times, because you may seem too formidable or overwhelming to a potential partner.

Sudden, impulsive affairs can be quite stimulating and rewarding, but you should not make a long-term commitment hastily. Spontaneous pleasure will always be a joy, but you should remain uncommitted until you both are sure of where you are going.

You are quick to express your emotions, whether they are joyful, sorrowful or angry. This makes you seem very alive to your lover and a most exciting partner. If you are angry, however, you may unintentionally hurt your lover quite deeply by saying things you don't really mean, which you later regret. A patient and understanding partner who is not easily or quickly put off will help considerably.

Similarly, a long-term partner who knows when you are going to extremes in any direction can help even you out. In any case, you need a lover who will help sustain the relationship at your high level of energy.

Mars Sextile Ascendant

You have considerable control over your energy output, not because you keep a tight grip on it, but because you don't need to struggle to express yourself physically with effectiveness. Indeed, your physical actions usually reinforce your verbal expression, which will make you seem open, honest and sincere to a potential partner.

Knowing that your lover has this image of you, however, you must do all you can to sustain it and not cause disappointment by being less than candid. Indeed, it might be worthwhile to be somewhat mysterious now and then, so that you do not create expectations you cannot fulfill.

You have an even flow of energy, and you are graceful and consistent in the mode and quality of your sexual expression. With your natural style, you can help a lover who is less at ease physically in bed. Even when your lover encounters obstacles, you do not, and thus you can ease your partner back into the mainstream of loving.

Because of your talent in this area, you should be particularly sympathetic and patient with a partner who is less effective in physical expression. Don't assume that others are as talented as you and are putting you off in some way; they may just be having communication problems.

Mars Square Ascendant

Your looks may belie your energy, so that you and a potential partner are at cross-purposes because your true style has been misinterpreted. As a result, you may not always be able to release as much energy in sexual expression as you would like.

This problem requires some patience, and you must avoid acting too hastily in breaking up a partnership that makes you momentarily angry or frustrated. It may have great potential. In general, the longer you know a partner, the more satisfying your sexual expression will become, as you work out how to get the fullest enjoyment together.

You should be particularly careful to keep the pressures of your home or career from getting in the way of lovemaking. If possible, set aside some time for love no matter what else is happening, so that the important sexual communication between you and your partner is not interfered with. It is easy to neglect this when you are busy with other matters, but in the long run it would be very detrimental to do so. Even temporary neglect can cause you to become out of sync with each other, and it will take some time to get back into the right rhythm. It is far better to plan for regular expression that can build and grow in quality and style; in love as in other areas of life, practice makes perfect.

Mars Trine Ascendant

Sexuality is a very natural and healthy outlet for your energies, and you will always be happiest with regular and full sexual expression. Indeed, you are at your best when you have a sexually energetic partner who stimulates your energy flow and keeps you from becoming blocked or frustrated, because that interferes with the rest of your life as well. You may find that sex never tires you out, but rejuvenates you and gives you more energy to work and be creative in other areas.

Lovemaking probably comes rather easily to you, so that you don't need to study to get it right. If you follow your natural inclinations, everything will work out right, even in a physically or emotionally complicated situation. Generally you can make the right move at the right time to pull it all together, even if your lover is not so sure-footed and stumbles now and then. Your own natural rhythm will help to reinstate the flow for both of you.

You are not likely to explore highly technical forms of sexuality, because too much intellectualizing tends to interrupt the flow for you and stultify love's communication. You don't need technical variety for great enjoyment, but for your lover's sake you might try it from time to time.

Mars Inconjunct Ascendant

You may drive yourself rather hard sexually, perhaps putting more effort into it than is really necessary. It would be worthwhile to settle back, relax and let your partner do more of the work. You might find that twice as enjoyable, and it would give you a needed rest from time to time.

Similarly, you should try some of the less physical forms of loving, such as playing out fantasies that don't involve a lot of physical contact. Such fantasies can utilize the mind and imagination to heighten sexuality far beyond what is physically possible. This has the double effect of taking away the pressure to perform and of improving the physical aspects of sex as well.

Fantasy exploration can also reveal areas of yourself that you are not familiar with. If lack of self-awareness is causing you to get less than your full pleasure potential from love, this can help by demystifying love. You are certainly capable of taking the most energetic sexual roles. You may find that expending extra energy on the details gives you a more flowing kind of sexual expression on the physical level without additional thought or pressure.

Mars Opposition Ascendant

Your physical energies may come and go, but when they are low you can take much energy and inspiration from your partner. Indeed, a partner can be very beneficial in a number of ways by sustaining and evening out your sexual expression so that it is regular and pleasurable without going to extremes.

Also, a lover tends to focus your efforts, because you will feel more like doing things in a partnership. Even if your lover is not particularly energetic, you have more energy simply because he or she is there.

You may also find that your lover is the initiator in love and in other activities, although not in an overly active or dominating way. Rather, your partner may stimulate you to expend much energy merely through small gestures or suggestions. Or your lover may be the main energy source in the relationship and regularly take the initiative. In either case, your partner is probably the trigger for your actions, both in and out of bed.

You should try to conserve your energy. You are likely to throw yourself into every activity, which may leave you too exhausted to enjoy the pleasures of the evening, which could be disappointing to both you and your partner.

Chapter Ten

Jupiter

Jupiter in the Chart

Jupiter represents your positive and actively creative attitudes toward sexuality as well as life in general. Its position and aspects reflect the ease or difficulty of your expression of these attitudes.

Easy aspects of Jupiter indicate an even flow of creativity; you can be active without going past the limits of enjoyment. With more difficult aspects, you may go to extremes or overdo some aspect of sexuality. If this is the case, you should be aware of it so that you can have some external control over this tendency. That will help you see more realistically the difference between true enjoyment and too much of a good thing.

No matter what its position, Jupiter encourages activity and creative change in the areas governed by the aspected planets and the affairs governed by its sign and house. It is helpful to know exactly what these areas are, because you may not have had the opportunity to explore them and you may wish to direct your energies accordingly. This is especially likely when Jupiter falls in quite a different category than the rest of the planets in the chart, indicating much unexplored territory that can provide considerable pleasure if given some extra attention.

Jupiter in Aries

You tend to take the direct approach in love, particularly when entering a new affair or trying a new twist in an old one. Often this gives you an edge on others in terms of experience. In affairs of the heart you are the early bird that gets the worm.

However, this same tendency can lead you into affairs that are a waste of time, which you could avoid by taking a second look. In most encounters it will be to your advantage to curb sudden impulses and take the time to be particular in your choices.

For you, love is at its best when it is rather impulsive. If you hold yourself back too long, the excitement disappears. You must learn to balance spontaneity and caution. Only then will you be able to fulfill your relationship potential.

You tend to be clear in expressing your needs and ideas about love, and you become impatient with a partner who dallies too much. Honesty of this kind is its own reward with an open-minded partner, but you might do well to express yourself with more subtlety for one who is not prepared to be so open.

Essentially, you prefer a direct and forceful approach to creativity in love, which eliminates the usual pointless ambiguities that surround the subject. Used tactfully, this special talent will make you particularly desirable to any partner you may choose.

Jupiter in Taurus

A new love affair usually inspires you to great generosity. You see love as ideal when it is surrounded by unlimited bounty and fruitfulness.

You are not likely to enter a new relationship hastily, and once you are involved, you will do everything in your power to make the affair rich and perfect in every detail. The keyword for new love is abundance; you try to provide every chance for a full and tender relationship to blossom.

This can be true physically, also, for you savor every special touch of your lover. You communicate not by words alone but by body language and by the mutual, quiet understanding that this closeness brings.

At times you may need to be a bit more verbal in making your feelings known to your lover, particularly a new love who is not yet totally in tune with you. A few thoughtful words or questions can eliminate any awkward or uncomfortable moments stemming from unfamiliarity. Such foresight can bring you closer intimacy and greater communication in a shorter period of time.

In its most precious moments, love is an intuitive communion that leads you both to new heights by the instinctive movements and age-old choreographies that lie locked within the human body.

Jupiter in Gemini

You have a seemingly endless flow of ideas about love, how it can be made more beautiful, more expressive and more fulfilling for you and your lover. Particularly in a new affair your imagination awakens and stimulates your creativity.

You consider love a subject of mercurial beauty and not something to be hidden away or avoided in conversation. You may be more eager to approach the various aspects of love than others are. In such cases you must trust your own judgment in determining which partners will deal with sex directly and which need a more delicate touch.

You should seek a partner with the same sense of humor and fun about sex as yourself. Much of the hesitancy involved in some forms of sexuality can be washed away by a gentle laugh or loving smile. Generally, you will not find comfortable companionship with those who are too sensitive or take sex too seriously.

You should get along best with a lover who encourages your creativity in developing new and enjoyable expressions of love, one who will not inhibit your fertile imagination. Your physical expression need not fulfill all the details that your mind creates, but you must be free to express your innermost feelings, as this is the mainspring of your love life.

Jupiter in Cancer

You, more than most, have the ability to enjoy the sentimental side of love. You derive great pleasure from the most pure and chaste expressions of affection. This is a great advantage, for you can find fulfillment and personal creativity without desiring more exotic forms of loving. You have no need for lengthy sexual experimentation.

You are able to attach considerable emotion to everyday expressions of love, but you must realize that your lover may not be quite as sensitive. Try not to be needlessly hurt by small sins of omission or forgetfulness; instead, gently remind your lover of the attentions you consider important.

You may devote considerable attention and creativity to providing a lavish atmosphere for intimacy, where you and your lover will not be disturbed. These surroundings give you freedom to let every quiet motion expand in a scenario of love that can develop to its fullest.

Your need for exclusivity in a relationship may become inadvertently confining at times. Learn not to encroach on your lover's freedom so that your intimacies remain spontaneous and meaningful.

Jupiter in Leo

This position indicates great generosity to your loved ones. You don't constantly shower them with specific gifts; you are more inclined to give your lovers carte blanche in choosing whatever they want, as you pick up the tab. This can be a perilous tendency, particularly if you've chosen the wrong partner. Fortunately this susceptibility usually becomes tempered with age and experience. Nevertheless, your innate desire is to throw caution to the winds in order to please a lover whom you are pursuing.

Your approach to love reflects your innate innocence. You view your relationships with a certain childlike simplicity, no matter how tangled or far-out they have become. This attitude may annoy your more sophisticated friends, who insist upon the seriousness of sexual behavior.

In the long run your outlook is the healthier one. Love and sexual enjoyment, however expressed, are of value to you because they are pleasing. For you, the gratification of any desire, as long as it hurts no one else, is worthy in and of itself without further analysis. Nothing can allay arousal and desire as much as tedious psychoanalytic pontification. That's fine for reading about, but not for discussing in bed.

Jupiter in Virgo

You can design and carry out an infinite variety of detailed settings for love, so you should find a lover who can join in the pleasures of playing out these detailed fantasies. For you, the initial performance of an imagined scene is the most pleasurable; with repetition it becomes tedious. Once you have fulfilled a fantasy, it is best to move on to something else, so that you can replay the same scenario another night.

Take care to make your fantasy role-playing simple and undemanding, so that it may be carried out physically with ease and concentration. The mind can accomplish great feats that are much too difficult or distracting to enjoy in reality. A little prudent judgment will help you avoid taking on more than you can handle. Don't be too demanding of yourself or your lover, so that love games stay creative and pleasurable rather than work.

You must make an extra attempt to separate fantasy from the everyday reality of a relationship. If they are too closely entwined, you and your lover may drift apart because you mistake your fantasy roles for the real ones. With a little care, however, you should be able to have a more satisfying sex life than most, if you have chosen a partner of similar desires.

Jupiter in Libra

You do not worry about fixed role-playing within a relationship. On the contrary, you can heighten the interest and be more creative by exchanging a variety of roles with your partner. In this way you both can gain a wealth of new sexual experiences, but be sure that you do not accidentally break your lover's unspoken taboos.

Your open approach to new aspects of sexuality is an asset. You insist on being truthful, and you expect the same from your partner. Take care to respect your lover's privacy and be sensitive to subjects that your partner considers too personal to get involved in or even discuss. This is particularly important in a new relationship.

You may become involved in a number of relationships and tire quickly of an affair that does not offer continuous stimulation. Although no love relationship can survive an excess of boredom, avoid changing partners just because the two of you are emotionally becalmed for a time. These periods can serve as respites before you move on to deeper and more rewarding exploration. Because your creativity is linked to being involved in a worthwhile relationship, you must develop one fully.

Jupiter in Scorpio

You enter new relationships very carefully and with grave consideration. Except under extraordinary circumstances, you begin an affair with your eyes open.

Once involved, however, you want to become totally immersed in love in order to achieve the greatest creativity and satisfaction. You must find a lover who appreciates the generous physical aspects of lovemaking that you desire. Once you have decided to further the relationship, you need a lover who will not leave you wanting more.

Under ideal conditions, sex is a source of strength and balance to you. It can energize your daily life and enable your creativity of expression to flow more swiftly and smoothly. In this respect, your love life controls the style and success of your other activities to some extent.

Avoid overreacting to minor problems that come up in the bedroom, and don't turn molehills into mountains. Take the extra time and effort to understand your lover's feelings and needs. Learn not to use pressure of any kind to gain sexual satisfaction, for that may work against you and even lead to estrangement. It is better to end an unsatisfactory affair than to try to force it into an unnatural mold.

Jupiter in Sagittarius

You are at your best when sexuality is relaxed and open, not beset by restrictions or confining demands. You find that a detailed scenario drains your sexual energies by drawing your attention to performance rather than enjoyment.

A new affair usually starts out robustly without artful technique or subtlety. You require plenty of good spirit and the assurance of warmth and friendship between you and your lover. Later you can develop different approaches to physical love, which you both may enjoy, but first you want to commit yourself to comradeship.

You are happiest with a partner who appreciates honesty, as your direct attitude may unintentionally hurt someone who is more inhibited and sensitive. In that case, you should be more restrained or find a partner who communicates more directly.

Once involved in a relationship, you should make an extra effort to become aware of your lover's specific needs and faithfully fulfill them, even if they seem puzzling or superfluous at times. Although some of your lover's pleasures may not particularly excite you, mutual consideration is essential in building a stable and loving relationship.

Jupiter in Capricorn

You are happiest when a new affair can be guided along familiar paths. Then you can provide your partner with enrichment and fulfillment. In an unpredictable relationship you will spend too much time coping with change to fully unleash your capacity for expression. Your style is solid and substantial; continual fluctuations diffuse your energy and do not suit you. You need a fairly well defined relationship.

For this reason, you will probably be happiest with a lover you know well and can be certain of pleasing, a comfortable companion who also knows how to give you maximum enjoyment.

One technique that may particularly heighten your lovemaking is abstinence, folowed by fulfillment in a very carefully delineated and predictable fashion. In this way, you may reach a special intensity of expression that can't be found in regular sexual release.

On the nonphysical level, it is best if you have the reinforcement of continuous love from your partner. If you can count on love, you are able to keep your creativity flowing in other areas. Similarly, you are most appreciative of a lover who treasures your daily affections and is aware of the variety of your attentions, however small.

Jupiter in Aquarius

You often are attracted to more than one person at a time, and if circumstances allow, you carry on several relationships simultaneously. And if you have only one partnership, this tendency will probably be expressed as a multiplicity of sub-relationships with your partner. You both play a number of roles, depending upon the time and place.

Sexuality is an area of considerable research and discovery for you. At its most exciting, sex continually presents something new and unique to your imagination. To keep your creativity burning, you need to find multiple forms of unusual sexual expression, for you will become frustrated if you continue along a monotonous path for too long.

Such needed variety can be increased if you and your partner play clearly defined but ever-changing roles. Each love scene should be not only a physical but also a mental challenge, in which you both participate fully. To some extent your head may rule your heart, as far as new sexual experiences are concerned. You require more than just a thorough physical experience to find true satisfaction in expressing your sexuality.

An imaginative partner will be an invaluable asset, and the more stimulating nonsexual communication there is between you, the more satisfying your sex life will be.

Jupiter in Pisces

You are happiest when love follows its own course and takes you along for the exhilarating ride. Questioning or examining your motives in an affair tends to interfere with its natural rhythm and direction. Such close examination may cause you to lose the thread of your affections.

Although you are happiest when you follow your intuition and feelings, do not act entirely blindly. Set certain limitations, then stop and take a second look before going on. This procedure still encourages spontaneity but at the same time protects you from occasional predatory lovers who may try to take advantage of your easygoing nature and generous style.

Do not be surprised if letting yourself go leads you into unusual or unexplored areas of the imagination. You should not restrict yourself sexually on the basis of other styles or moralities. Your criterion should be whatever gives you and your lover the most enjoyment.

You may enjoy letting yourself be carried along in a love experience, taking emotional and psychic inspiration from your lover. Your sexuality is not actively aggressive but subtle, uncovering the little-known hidden areas of sensuality. These secret recesses are a reminder to both of you of the infinite complexities to be enjoyed when body and spirit are entwined in the physical and emotional act of love.

Jupiter in the First House

You have a special talent for acting and role-playing within a relationship, and probably you can take on whatever appearance or style seems likely to win over a lover. By developing this tendency, you and your partner can have endless fun and variety in love, as your bedroom becomes a stage upon which to play out exciting fantasies.

Like all actors throughout history, however, you must take care not to get lost in your role. Always keep a good grip on the real you, for if you lose touch with your own personality, so will your partner.

In any case, others are impressed by what they see in you. It is a good idea to lace your image with modesty so that a potential lover won't overestimate and expect you to deliver more than you can or want to.

Your energy level is rather high, and you should find a partner of similar style who will help you maintain your energy rather than feed on it. You need to have plenty of energy left to develop your own creativity and direction, so don't neglect yourself in favor of a too-demanding lover. In a balanced relationship, each of you will stimulate the other to greater heights without excessive demands or dependency.

Jupiter in the Second House

This is a pleasant position for Jupiter, if a trifle costly. You tend to be exceedingly generous to your lover, to the point that you are turned off by any kind of stinginess. The drawback to this tendency is that love sometimes gets lost in all your attentions to the surroundings. A simple, quiet picnic turns into an extravaganza, just because you want to be sure there is enough of everything, with no detail omitted.

When everything is in balance, this position indicates that you have plenty of sexual stamina and a large sexual appetite. Indeed, your expansive physical nature can do well with more than one partner, although the rest of your personality may not be quite ready to cope with the complications.

In general you have a good reputation as a lover among current and former partners. In spite of any emotional complications that arise, good will and generosity are always in the forefront of the relationship.

You feel frustrated only when you don't have enough money and goods to indulge your generosity. But even under such circumstances, you will bring forth whatever you have, no matter how meager, and offer it for the pleasure of your lover.

Jupiter in the Third House

You are likely to have a bountiful sexual imagination and the ability to express your ideas creatively both physically and in words, either verbally or on paper, so that others can enjoy them. You may indulge in ribald humor if the occasion is right, and when alone with a lover you can outline the possibilities of enjoyment in a way that is a pleasure in itself.

This is not to say that talking about sex can be a substitute for the real thing. However, you have enough verbal talent, perhaps not yet fully developed, to enrich your love life with a fullness and variety that those of lesser imagination cannot provide.

For this reason, you prefer a lover who can be stimulated verbally as well as physically. Your partner should get special enjoyment from sharing your new views of love and enjoying your lively imagination, either in direct fulfillment or in flights of fancy that are better savored mentally than attempted physically.

Only take care to do as much listening as talking, and be responsive and sensitive to your lover's imagination, which may be as intense and rewarding as your own, even though less voluble.

Jupiter in the Fourth House

Your most enjoyable times with a lover are not lavish nights on the town or active social occasions with many friends and acquaintances, but intimate evenings at home with just the two of you.

This is not because you are particularly antisocial, but because a quiet intimate experience actually stimulates your imagination more than a situation with seemingly more possibilities for variety. You require a certain quiet and reserve in order to focus your energies, and too much outside activity tends to prevent you from getting into stride emotionally. This is not to say that you don't enjoy a good party now and again, but it is the special times that you share only with your partner that you remember most vividly.

You may have a particular talent for creating a homelike situation in the most unlikely circumstances. With just what's in your pocket and a little imagination, you create a comfortable, intimate atmosphere wherever you pitch your tent. Your natural style is to create closeness, so you can make a new relationship seem like an age-old friendship in a rather brief time.

Jupiter in the Fifth House

You are a natural entertainer who can turn any social gathering into a party just by your attitude. As a result, your happiest times with a lover are probably when you are in the company of good friends. You tend to diffuse your feelings of love for your partner and share them with others.

Conversely, you draw on the good feelings of others in your crowd to enhance and heighten your love for your partner. Your loving style is not overly serious but fun-filled and jovial. For you, love is an experience that is closely linked to comradeship. Its nature is spreading and sharing rather than concentrated and all-consuming.

There may be a close relationship between your love activity and your external creativity, with one encouraging the other. A profitable, active day leads you into a happy, loving night, whereas an argument with your lover slows you down the next day. When there is a hiatus of creativity in your life, loving seems somehow fruitless.

You may have considerable talent in the creative arts, and you will certainly surround yourself and your lover with beautiful music and gracious surroundings. These enhance your relationship and are really quite necessary to maximum fulfillment. Wherever you are, when you are in love you decorate and improve your surroundings, both for your own sake and for the pleasure of your partner.

Jupiter in the Sixth House

In lovemaking you probably think fairly far ahead of what you are doing, so that you lead your lover in previously conceived patterns of expression rather than simply accepting whatever turns up.

For you, a carefully designed sexual exercise lends increasing excitement, like a well-written play, whereas too much offhand spontaneity may diffuse your energies or leave you at loose ends.

This can be a particularly satisfying style of loving as long as you let your lover in on what you are doing, so that he or she knows where you both are going and can enjoy the same gratifying fulfillment of expectations. Otherwise you might appear to be exercising too much control in the relationship or seem too distant and uncommunicative.

You get special pleasure from doing favors for your lover and demonstrating your affections with thoughtful gestures, making your partner's life easier. Take care to let your lover return your favors in kind so that there is a true two-way flow. If you give too much, your lover may feel unable to match the extent of your love and attentions. You should learn to enjoy receiving as much as giving.

Jupiter in the Seventh House

You may rely heavily on your lover as a source of creativity and inspiration, and partly for that reason you choose rather outgoing and active partners.

Even if your partner is not particularly volatile, you receive much of your energy from him or her, which you direct to initiating and developing the relationship.

You prefer an active relationship, and you become restless unless there is continual motion. Until you find just the right lover who can keep you continually interested, you may go through a number of affairs rather quickly, either because you lose interest or, on the other hand, because you discover that you have taken on more than you can readily handle.

A relationship needs to be carefully balanced, because too much intensity and complexity can drain your creative energies from your other endeavors. Conversely, too dull a relationship tends to leave you feeling uninspired.

But relationships are a prime source of learning for you, so an imperfect one is better than none at all. Also, prolonged abstinence will be counterproductive to your own enjoyment as well as to your personality development.

Jupiter in the Eighth House

You may be particularly interested in exploring and shedding light upon the darker and less well-understood aspects of a relationship. Right from the beginning you gravitate toward an affair that seems to have deep undercurrents, as if you share something mysterious that you cannot quite put your finger on. Such a relationship can be a source of inspiration and adventure.

You may enjoy a more casual affair, but you aren't really excited by it. This may lead you into some rather tangled situations, but it will be worth it because you get so much more satisfaction from successfully probing the depths of a really difficult affair.

You may have a reputation for being a particularly insightful or understanding lover, but don't become overconfident, for you might stride boldly into a relationship that proves to be your nemesis. Your accomplishments in love are less important than the knowledge you gain from them and the new areas of exploration that they open up.

Indeed, you may have to sustain difficulties and even heartbreak to achieve these ends, but remember that both joyous and painful experiences are necessary in order to understand the fundamental motivating forces behind the emotional experience of loving. However, you are less likely than most to sustain lasting emotional harm because you know what you're getting into and you have a capacity for quick recovery.

Jupiter in the Ninth House

You look upon a new love as a special adventure, and you are not satisfied with a humdrum affair. You may have to go pretty far to find the partner who pleases you most; the chances are it's not the girl or boy next door, unless your neighbor is an adventurer like yourself.

You are drawn to new and original concepts of love, unique ways of looking at your lover and your relationship. Over the years you may evolve a number of radically different styles of loving, each of which is especially gratifying at the time.

You are not one to be tied down in a static situation, at least in style. Even if you continue indefinitely with a single partner, there will be considerable changes within that one relationship. On the other hand, you may change partners periodically. Your partings are not usually difficult or bitter, however, and you harbor warm feelings for former lovers who have gone their own way.

Generally you are the instigator of change and evolution within a relationship or the one who wants to move on to a new affair. This is an expression of your personal creativity in developing new modes of expression in love.

Jupiter in the Tenth House

You are likely to have strong, although perhaps unrealized professional abilities. Thus you put much of your energy into efforts that are quite apart from any love relationship. Often you either have too little time to develop a love affair or you do not put your prime energies into it as readily as your partner. For this reason, you will be happiest with a lover who is not excessively jealous or demanding of your time, someone who will give you extra attention when you are tired or preoccupied with other necessities.

If you are not concentrating on your career for one reason or another, this same tendency may be reflected in a very thorough and businesslike approach to your relationship, mining it of everything it's got. If your partner has as much energy as you, such a relationship can be extremely dynamic, but for a quieter person, your attitude can be quite wearing. Learn to be aware of when you should slow down.

You are likely to have an excellent but possibly inflated reputation concerning your abilities, both public and private. If you make an extra effort to be modest about your talents, you won't be called upon to demonstrate feats that you are incapable of or disinclined toward.

Jupiter in the Eleventh House

You enjoy mixing with well-thought-of people and leader types; indeed you are, or strive to be, a leader yourself. You are not emotionally self-motivated, but take your inspiration from moving among others of talent and achievement.

Similarly, you want a lover who matches your desired image of beauty and creativity. Probably, this means that you overlook some diamonds in the rough, preferring the more polished gems. This may be just as well, for you are not inclined to put much effort into developing your lover's personality. Such energies are better spent on your own personal growth and striving toward excellence.

It is more likely that you will benefit from your partner's position and skills, rather than the other way around. You will do well to listen to your lover's advice, particularly in matters of image improvement, because in that area, the feedback you need must come from outside yourself.

You may not be particularly verbal or outgoing, but when necessary you can give that appearance at a social gathering. Be careful not to do this too much, however, for you might attract incompatible partners who have misinterpreted your image. It is best just to let your light shine, even if quietly, for the people whose companionship you most enjoy will pick up on it without extra effort on your part.

Jupiter in the Twelfth House

You probably present your best performances behind closed doors, for your style is not public or flashy. You shine in a more private setting with your closest friends, and your favorite audience is usually your lover alone.

Since you are not highly visible to other potential partners, you are likely to pursue a single relationship for a fairly long time, devoting all your freshness and creativity to it. However, you may have other, more casual contacts in which you do not fully let yourself go.

You are particularly good at shedding light on hidden problems within a relationship and turning what might seem to your partner like difficulties or hangups into sources of mutual pleasure and joy.

Your love of secrecy also allows you to carry off a clandestine relationship with positive and happy results. You don't think of secrecy as something dark or dishonest but as a special hiding place where you can express your joy without hindrance from others.

Your talents may not be widely recognized, but your partner will certainly be aware of and appreciate your capabilities. Your lover will know just how much love and happiness you can create within the quiet confines of an intimate relationship.

Jupiter Conjunct Saturn

You may often think that you should have more inhibitions about your sexual desires and your innate inventiveness. As a result, you may do something in bed that you later feel guilty about, or you may refrain from something that you later wish you had done.

To get around this problem, you must construct a complete set of sexual ethics that is uniquely yours, not just borrowed from the dated and usually erroneous concepts about sex that everyone learns during adolescence. To do this, you will have to consider and reevaluate the meaning of every aspect of sex. When you have a clear view, you should stick by it. There is much to be learned from up-to-date books on the subject, especially concerning the physical aspects of sex. However, in the end you must derive your judgments from searching your own heart and mind to decide what is right and wrong for you as well as what is and is not pleasurable.

When you have accomplished this, you will pass up a sexual opportunity only when you know that you wouldn't have enjoyed it, with no regrets about doing so. And the affairs that you do enter into will be of your own choosing, so you can enjoy them fully and creatively. You will no longer be held back by inhibitions that have no basis in reality but that can destroy your enjoyment and even the relationship itself.

Jupiter Sextile Saturn

You probably have quite a good understanding of sexual morality, knowing just what you like and don't like in sexual expression. Thus you are unlikely to have the experience of wanting to try something but feeling inhibited or guilty about it. In general, you feel there's nothing wrong with what you do want, and you have no desire to get involved with any aspects of sex that you feel uncomfortable about.

In this respect, you are quite lucky, because many people feel that they are in a moral bind about what they are doing, but they keep right on doing it, which certainly inhibits the pleasure that can be derived from sex. Keep that in mind when dealing with others, and do not ask a lover to try something that he or she feels wrong about, even though it seems perfectly all right to you. It is not that you must avoid leading others into trouble, but that if your partner is feeling guilty or inhibited, neither of you will get as much enjoyment from the experience.

At times this policy may cut you off from some potential pleasure, and in that case you should think carefully about whether to continue the relationship. Just remember that in time and with patience, your partner's feelings of guilt or inhibition can be overcome, thus saving a good relationship.

Jupiter Square Saturn

For various reasons, you may find it somewhat difficult to balance your sexual inhibitions with your enthusiasm about sex. It may be that your sexual morality is dated and does not conform to today's standards, so that you feel guilty, even though your sex life is quite normal according to most people's morality.

Or you may be very attracted to sexual activities that you know will get you in trouble, such as an involvement with two jealous partners at the same time. The result of this situation will also inhibit enjoyment.

In the first instance, you will have to completely restructure your sexual attitudes to bring your beliefs in line with what you enjoy. That may be easier said than done, since old inhibitions tend to hang on, but the sooner you start, the better.

In the second instance, you simply have to judge in each situation whether the pleasure is worth the risk. Once you commit yourself, don't look back, lest second thoughts detract from your enjoyment of the moment. Your judgment in these matters will improve with age, and the more experienced you are, the more accurately you can choose what will work out and what won't.

Jupiter Trine Saturn

You are likely to have good judgment about what will and will not be pleasurable in sexual expression, concerning not only your own needs but also your lover's.

Thus when you and your lover are in doubt, you should be the one to decide whether to try a particular style or technique or whether to pass it over for something that you know has real pleasure potential.

You are not likely to get involved in sexual situations that make you feel guilty, but that may not be the case with your lover. You should be especially sensitive to the fact that some sexual situations that seem quite natural to you may make your lover feel uncomfortable or nervous. You should take care to notice this and help your partner overcome his or her inhibitions. Because of your ability to handle it, you can gradually free your lover from reservations that prevent you both from fulfilling your maximum pleasure potential.

Although you can help a lover who has inhibitions, you may be just as happy with someone who tends to go overboard or who would take the wrong direction sexually without your guidance. That situation will provide extra sexual stimulus and enjoyment as well.

Jupiter Inconjunct Saturn

You may go through a continuous process of growth concerning your beliefs about sexual morality and freedom. Your opinions will probably not remain static for long, because the experiences that result from your creative imagination continually modify your ideas about what is right and wrong, enjoyable and unenjoyable.

As a result, your sexual views are quite eclectic. You refrain from criticizing other people's views in this area, because you have been through enough changes yourself to realize that it all depends on your point of view. Probably you enjoy experiences now that used to seem uncomfortable or offensive, and you may look back on some of your old habits with distaste.

Over time, your standards will continue to improve, not on the basis of some ultimate judgment but because they work better for you and provide the maximum interest and pleasure in sex.

You need a lover who is adventurous enough to follow you closely and add creatively to the experience, at the same time restraining you from change simply for the sake of change. Such a partner can show you when your current practices are still satisfactory.

Jupiter Opposition Saturn

Your attitudes toward sexuality may swing from the liberal to the conservative, depending on the moment and your degree of inspiration. Thus, when you are in a very loving mood, you may do things with your partner that seem entirely too permissive or far-out to you later. As a result, you may feel a certain guilt or shame afterward.

On the other hand, when you are feeling somewhat withdrawn, you may put the damper on ordinary techniques of love, because you just aren't in the mood.

Needless to say, this attitude can be quite trying at times for both you and your lover. If possible, you should try to take a more even, middle-of-the-road course. One way of modifying these extremes of attitude is to write down, when you are in a detached mood, just what your limits should be and then make a conscious effort to stick to them. This approach can save you some embarrassed recollections and can keep your lover from being unnecessarily frustrated.

You will be most happy with a partner whose sexual philosophy is well balanced, who can modify your extremist tendencies in both directions, so that you do not go too far on either the liberal or the conservative side. Regular and certain sexual expression will certainly add to the enjoyment of the experience for both of you.

Jupiter Conjunct Uranus

You have a talent for creative and unusual sexual expression. While others take the same worn path again and again, you strike out into the unknown and come up with original, sometimes startling ways to enjoy yourself.

This talent is a special blessing that will fill your life with pleasures that others will never know. However, your radical approach will not make you popular with conservative types. Therefore, you need a freewheeling lover who is willing to try anything once, as long as it is within the bounds of physical safety.

You should probably concentrate on actions rather than words, especially if you associate with less liberal people. Although sexual experimentation can be very pleasurable, discussing it can ruin your career and reputation in this society, which doesn't practice what it preaches concerning sexual mores. Besides, in most cases your pleasure comes from doing, not from talking about it.

Don't get so carried away with originality that doing something new becomes a substitute for real sexual communication between yourself and your lover. Sometimes the tried and true methods are the best, both as a physical rest and as a way to allow love to flow without distraction.

Jupiter Sextile Uranus

You have a flair for originality in sex, and no one would ever call you a prude. At the same time, you have a good sense of what works and does not work, so that you don't get involved in new techniques just for the sake of newness.

If a new style of loving holds real promise of enjoyment for you and your lover, you go ahead full steam. But if it does not seem truly promising, you will pass it by, no matter how intriguing it sounds or how many other people are trying it out. You follow your own judgment, which in most cases is quite sound.

You also have a good sense of when to move on to something new and when to keep exploring the old. Too often in lovemaking, a potentially enjoyable technique is abandoned after one or two tries, when with a little practice it could give great pleasure. Or a favorite style of loving is overused and becomes useless as a source of enjoyment in the future. Because you know where the dividing line is between too much and too little, your lover should trust your advice and follow your lead.

Your style is to approach a new experiment gradually and not take great leaps into the unknown where there might be danger of emotional injury. The field of sexual exploration can be covered safely, if taken step by step in an unhurried fashion.

Jupiter Square Uranus

You have a very inventive streak, but you should monitor it carefully, so that you don't get into waters over your head. It is a good idea to examine carefully any new sexual directions that you think of, to determine whether they hold real pleasure potential or whether they are just new and titillating.

In this area you can ask your partner to help you weed out the pointless ideas from the useful ones so that you don't waste time pursuing avenues of sexual exploration that are bound to be disappointing.

This is not to say that following a sudden impulse will necessarily lead you down a blind alley. However, it may turn out to be less than you had hoped, which can be a waste of time. Real pleasure reinforces a relationship, whereas empty experiments tends to wear it down.

Your partner should not restrict your inventiveness too much, for you need plenty of room to breathe in a relationship. However, you do need a second opinion about the

255

feasibility and desirability of the ideas you cook up. With time and experience, you will be an accurate judge of that yourself, but a lover who reflects your ideas will help.

Jupiter Trine Uranus

You are very creative in sexual expression, but even though you may devise some startlingly original techniques, they never seem bizarre or strange. Instead, you make them seem quite natural, the logical outgrowth of proven methods of enjoyment.

Because of this ability, you can explore the farthest realms of sexual experimentation without seeming at all outlandish to yourself or your lover. The certainty and sincerity of your enjoyment transcends the artificially imposed morality of the outside world.

Similarly, you can guide your lover on the path of sexual experimentation in such a way that he or she will not come to harm through lack of judgment, for you are always there for support.

You and your partner will have a most unusual and wide-ranging collection of sexual experiences, which presents a sterling argument for total sexual freedom. Unfortunately, not everyone is so lucky, and you must understand that other people may run a far greater risk of harm in practicing your kind of freedom. Many people are actually protected by their fears and inhibitions, so be especially tolerant of them. Probably you are an object of envy and admiration to them.

Jupiter Inconjunct Uranus

You tend to be extremely inventive in your sexual expression, sometimes to the point of being compulsive about trying out every new idea, regardless of its quality or usefulness. This is not to be frowned on, but it may mean that you waste a good deal of time trying out new techniques that have little real potential for pleasure or satisfaction.

Also, in your impatience to get on with something new, you may pass over some styles of loving that require a certain perseverance. Introducing too much new material into a relationship too quickly tends to be confusing. The result is that you may not carry through on some potentially good techniques, and the real communication between you and your partner may suffer because each new technique demands so much attention.

Thus you need a lover who has a talent for discarding the chaff and keeping the wheat, who can select and distill your ideas so that the two of you spend your time exploring only the best of them. In this way you will have plenty of time to get the fullest pleasure from your inventiveness as well as from each other.

In any case, you probably have more sexual experience than most people, and if you are careful, you needn't give up depth of experience while keeping plenty of variety.

Jupiter Opposition Uranus

Your ability to devise new and unusual methods of sexual pleasure may be quite separate from your inclination to carry out your ideas. Thus, when you are in a mood to experiment, you may have too many ideas to choose from, if you have written them down or remembered them, or you may have nothing to go on except your positive frame of mind.

Indeed, the desire to try something new may come over you quite suddenly, so you will be most happy with a lover who is willing to go along with you at a moment's notice. Certainly you need a free, spontaneous partner who will not try to tie you down or force you into a particular sexual mold. When you feel it is time to move on, you will follow that impulse, and your love should not stand in your way.

With that kind of freedom, you can form very strong relationships founded on true intellectual friendship as well as physical attraction, which are not affected by sudden sexual shifts or reorientations. Fortunately, society is becoming more open to such relationships, as more and more sexual restrictions are removed, allowing people to adopt any style that suits them without much interference.

Jupiter Conjunct Neptune

You have a certain tendency to spiritualize love mentally, attributing to a relationship higher and more fated qualities than it actually merits. However, this does not mean that your relationships tend to be nonsexual; indeed, your affairs may be very gratifying physically, but there is always an overtone that the involvement is a fulfillment of destiny in some way.

This makes a sound and fruitful relationship all the stronger, uniting the two of you with bonds that transcend the physical, which will hold you together when physical problems arise. However, in a relationship that is not basically sound, this feeling of fatedness tends to keep you together in your unhappiness, making it that much more difficult to split up gracefully.

You may find it hard to distinguish a good relationship from an unsatisfying one, because the feeling of creative spiritual union may blind you to differences that make the affair impossible. In that case, you will learn from experience to be more cautious and more discerning before getting involved in a new relationship. Caution is advisable anyway, because a relationship that is spiritually meant to be will happen no matter how cautious you are, and being careful will only make it better. Although you may really enjoy physical love, you are drawn toward partners who you feel are spiritually important to you.

Jupiter Sextile Neptune

You are drawn toward relationships that at their best moments transcend the physical, uniting the two of you on a seemingly spiritual plane. However, you are not compulsive or foolish about pursuing such goals, and you happily receive pleasure from any channels of communication that open up between you.

Thus you let the affair flow and allow the level of communication—physical, spiritual or both—to establish itself, encouraged by a jovial spirit of companionship rather than by a compulsion to seek higher goals. Instead of having to strive to achieve spirituality, you find that time and events bestow it on you. The more you attend to the pleasantries of the moment with your partner, the more this quality of spirituality will grow between you, quite unattended. Indeed, thinking about it too much will slow the growth of this spiritual bond.

You always seek and find true friendship in a love relationship, not necessarily a tremendously deep friendship, but one that is mellow and comfortable. Because of this, you tend to remain friendly with old lovers as well as new ones. If you have loved someone enough to have spent some time together, there will always be warmth between you, even if it is not active at the moment.

Jupiter Square Neptune

You should try not to cling to illusions within a relationship but to enjoy them while they last and be willing to move on when reality intervenes and dissolves them.

Essentially, you must learn the difference between knowingly living in a fantasy world and chasing endlessly after impossible dreams that can lead only to continuing disappointment. The key concept is learning to let go willingly and start anew. At times this may be quite difficult, because your inclination is to doggedly pursue your image of a relationship in an attempt to make it real through the force of will. Unfortunately, such efforts usually fail when reality intrudes, and you find that you have wasted much emotional commitment, time and energy.

In a long-term relationship, therefore, you should learn the art of self-observation and be willing to change your views now and then to sustain it. As time passes, you will have a clearer and clearer view of what you and your partner mean to each other, which will make the relationship increasingly solid.

However, in a short-term affair, you can feel quite free to fantasize in any pleasurable manner, as long as you are willing to let go of the affair when the fantasy is over.

Jupiter Trine Neptune

You tend to become involved in relationships that have strong spiritual overtones and are not based merely on physical attraction, although that may be important too. Indeed, you may be quite sexually experimental, but the solidity of the relationship is guaranteed by the stronger but less obvious spiritual bond between you and your partner.

This bond makes communication at any level much easier and helps you avoid the kind of misunderstandings that can be damaging to a relationship, especially concerning sexual experimentation. The basic trust between you allows you both to make mistakes without recrimination, thus keeping the relationship from being harmed.

Although you may express your love for each other verbally, underlying the words is an unspoken communication that makes your verbal expression more enjoyable for being unnecessary. Words become the playthings of love rather than critical vehicles that can make or break the relationship.

In any case, you are always attracted to lovers who are also friends; in fact it would be hard to prevent that from happening. And the friendship will live on, even if you both move on to other partners.

Jupiter Inconjunct Neptune

You have a certain lofty drive to spiritualize and idealize love, but at times that may throw you onto the rocks of reality. The feeling of "something more" that you seek in a relationship may be more difficult to achieve because of the pressure to achieve it.

Indeed the best way to encourage spirituality in a relationship is to not seek it at all but to let it happen of its own accord. You may find this difficult at times, but you can use the energy that powers this inclination to seek spirituality on your own through various endeavors, which will take away some of the pressure to achieve it through the relationship.

Any relationship tends to become more spiritual as the partners do, so the main emphasis should be on individual spirituality rather than on bringing the relationship to that end. You can actively pursue this goal alone with success, but forcing it on the relationship is likely to be quite counterproductive. At first you may seem to achieve a great deal by pursuing spirituality together, but it is very easy to become involved in mutual self-deception. Then, when the truth of the situation comes out, the affair will fall apart like a house of cards. Better to let the higher qualities of the relationship take care of themselves.

Jupiter Opposition Neptune

At times you may find it difficult to decide how and where to improve on a love affair, not knowing which of the many possibilities that come to mind will be profitable.

The result of your indecision can be paralysis and stagnation, which are definitely to be avoided. It would be better to choose a direction at random and launch into it with gusto; probably the rest will take care of itself. This is particularly important when you are deciding whether a new sexual style or direction will hurt the affair morally or spiritually. Such quandaries are almost by definition unsolvable except by taking action and later analyzing it. If the love between you is deep and sincere, any direction you take will be seen in its best light; if the relationship is ephemeral or temporary, you can feel free to go ahead without worrying about the outcome.

This may seem like a fatalistic approach, but it is not. It is simply that the higher aspects of an affair tend to take care of themselves if you let them develop without interference. Concentrate instead on the physical details of the relationship, making sure that you and your partner are giving each other what you really desire, not simply forming wishful images of each other. Then the more spiritual aspects will fall into place.

Jupiter Conjunct Pluto

Growth and development are very important factors in any relationship that you are involved in, and you willfully seek change and evolution in an affair. The reason for this is that motion and change make you feel more alive and self-aware, while inactivity tends to kill your loving feelings.

At times this approach can lead you to a very deep level of self-understanding and can be a source of real inner satisfaction. However, you must take your lover's personality into account and not force changes when your partner is not ready for or comfortable with them. Change should come through evolution of your feelings for each other rather than being forced by one partner. This may be a problem, because you feel much more comfortable when you are in charge of initiating changes.

But in any affair you cannot always be the leader. Often you must let the realities of the situation dictate the direction for you both. You can avoid the potential anxiety of this circumstance by looking at it as a new opportunity for play and enjoyment rather than as a situation to be conquered and subjected to your will.

Jupiter Sextile Pluto

Continually exploring new emotional and physical territory in a relationship makes you very creative and serves as a basis and motivation for further growth. Change will only reinforce you and make you stronger, as long as it moves at a regular and gradual pace.

Indeed, you may look back on how far you have come in small steps, seeing how without noticing it you have gradually achieved a great deal of positive transformation. Time is very much on your side and is a necessary element for real creativity in a relationship.

You are fortunate in this because you can bring a rather fearful or conservative lover along this path of growth with you. The increments of change that you create are never so large as to be disturbing or even noticeable. But in the end your relationship will be in a better place without having gone through a lot of tumult.

You may even take this process of growth for granted, because it results from your everyday actions and doesn't require a great deal of conscious thought. Instead, it proceeds at its own pace, leaving your love for each other changed and improved.

Jupiter Square Pluto

You should try to resist the temptation to seek change in a relationship just for the sake of change. When you see an area that seems to need major alterations, stop and take stock of the situation carefully before launching into a wholesale renovation.

Frequently, through this kind of introspection you will learn that your motive for making changes is not necessity but your need to be in charge of the relationship. You should keep this motivation in check, because making needless changes will not keep you in a leading position for long. The ultimate result is likely to be a relationship that is torn asunder by too many drastic alterations.

This is not to say that you should sit around and do nothing. Instead, any major changes, either sexual or emotional, in an affair, should be the result of mutual agreement and a plan worked out between you. Very often, the final direction will not be what you had originally thought, but by working on it together, you are much more likely to arrive at a satisfactory solution that will make you both happy in the long run. In this way, great changes can be made in a fairly short time without ill effect.

Jupiter Trine Pluto

You have a talent for being foresighted about new directions that you and your partner should take in love. Thus you can implement changes gradually and with plenty of time for adjustment, without the shock effect of last-minute rearrangements. When you know that you will be taking a new direction in the near future, you won't let yourself be too heavily committed to your present path, so that the transformation takes place easily when the time comes.

You have a kind of luck in choosing the right projects to become involved with, including love affairs. Therefore, when you have some doubts about an affair that cannot be clarified rationally, you can safely rely on intuition and instinct to guide you in the right direction. Some people may consider you rash or careless about where you tread, but in the long run your track record will prove your judgment correct.

This ability puts you ahead of people who require more time to think things through and who can't move ahead with such confidence when they do make up their mind. Your lover may be like that, and you must be patient if he or she is more hesitant about new directions than you are. A show of self-confidence and loving support for your partner, no matter what the prospects, will do much to assuage such doubts.

Jupiter Inconjunct Pluto

The love relationships that you get into may not progress and evolve nearly as fast as you would like them to. This merely reflects a certain restiveness on your part rather than any real need for swift changes.

Certainly any affair that you are involved in will be oriented toward growth, for otherwise you will not remain in it for long. However, you should avoid pressuring your partner for hasty evolution of the relationship. Substantial growth does not take place overnight, and if you push it along too quickly, the affair may collapse of its own weight, as the two of you lose touch with who you are and where you are going.

Before moving ahead on a grand scale, confer carefully with your partner, for you are inclined to take emotional gambles that may be quite risky, especially if repeated often. There is a certain thrill in taking a giant leap into space, but you may not always find sufficient satisfaction when you land, so you are tempted to try it again. Your fear of stagnation in love is mostly unwarranted; you can retreat to a more conservative position and still have plenty to handle emotionally.

Jupiter Opposition Pluto

From time to time you may have a strong urge to rearrange everything in a relationship or to throw it away altogether and look for something new and more meaningful.

In part this trait may stem from an inability or unwillingness to deal with problems in a relationship as they arise, until they pile up so high that they demand a solution. If you are aware of this problem, you can solve it by finding out what's wrong periodically and making adjustments right away. Or you may be fortunate enough to have a lover who will make the observations and goad you into making the necessary changes.

However, if an affair has gotten to the point of needing large-scale repairs, there is nothing to be done but go ahead with it. Very often the easiest solution for both of you is to end the relationship. In that case, you should think carefully about what led up to that state of affairs so that you will not repeat the same mistakes in another situation.

If your partner has a similar style, however, your affair can survive and even benefit from great upheavals. A relationship can lie dormant for many years, then suddenly rise up like a phoenix, transformed into a new form. But don't count on that, for then you won't be disappointed.

Jupiter Conjunct Ascendant

You are probably a fairly open, outgoing person who is usually the initiator in discovering new realms of physical enjoyment with a lover. You enjoy taking the lead in exploring new territory in which love has a merry, friendly quality.

Thus you are not particularly attracted to intricate or far-out forms of sexuality, not because of social or sexual inhibitions, but because they do not allow the easy expression of good feelings that you prefer. Indeed, you are perfectly willing to transgress the usual accepted norms in sexual expression, but only if the experience has a jovial, good-feeling style.

You can play almost any role in a relationship at different times, just for entertainment. However, you have a good sense of the difference between acting a role and living it. You are not likely to get stuck in any one role, but can move from one to another easily, according to your own and your lover's pleasure.

You have a good deal of energy to expend, and it is a good idea to find physical outlets for it, either in love or in other forms of recreation. Sublimating this energy into nonphysical pursuits can lead to a kind of nonspecific frustration and, particularly, overweight. The more openly and physically affectionate you can be in an affair, the better you will feel, both emotionally and physically.

Jupiter Sextile Ascendant

You can coordinate the physical and the mental aspects of love quite well, and you will probably find that each area tends to stimulate growth in the other. Therefore you should make every attempt to implement your creativity on the physical level so that you can derive the most benefits from it. Too much delay may lead to laziness or loss of sexual creativity.

You also have less trouble than most people in communicating what you mean during sexual experimentation. You make your directions so clear, both verbally and physically, to your lover that there is little chance of confusion about what is happening during lovemaking. But remember that your lover may not be so skilled at this kind of communication; by gently probing now and then, you can bring your lover's real feelings and needs to the surface so that you both understand them.

In general, your attitude toward new experiences in love is positive, and you tend to transfer those feelings to your lover, which will go a long way toward easing his or her unnecessary inhibitions. In fact, confronting another's blockages and difficulties can help you understand why you don't have them and can also aid your partner in becoming more free, sexually and emotionally.

Jupiter Square Ascendant

You should be very careful to monitor your actions and reactions to your lover, especially when you are initiating new emotional attitudes or new sexual tecnhiques. It is not that you initiate anything that is wrong, for that is not likely to be the case. But you may tend to overstate your case and spoil the intended effect by getting carried away. Or, on the other hand, you may not make your point strongly enough, so that it goes unnoticed. Your physical energies are not always in tune with your inner intentions, so one can get in the way of the other without your being aware of it.

In a long-standing relationship this problem can be worked out quite easily by having your partner act as a governor on your actions, so that you will know how to readjust your energy level to suit what you are doing. This is valuable, because you will learn through experience to be more in control of your expression, and subsequently you will be able to operate alone more successfully.

If you do not have a long-term partner, ask a friend to fulfill that function, and also make a special attempt to criticize yourself and your actions so that they are effectively tempered. The more self-aware you are, the less of a problem this will be.

Jupiter Trine Ascendant

You are probably quite lucky in your ability to implement your desires physically and communicate your good feelings to your lover. You don't usually have to be too verbally precise in presenting your idea of a good time; a gesture or a general description is all that's necessary to start the ball rolling.

Thus your love affairs tend to be natural and easy, not plagued with so many details in need of attention that you can't enjoy yourselves. If the details get in the way, you take care of them without wasting time or detracting from the general good feelings.

Also, you may feel that whatever you do is fresh and enjoyable by itself without any need for anything more. This may be true from your own point of view, but your lover may need some startling or stimulating touches added to the relationship now and then. If you go along with your partner's need for variety, you may discover something new and pleasurable yourself. It is not your style to concoct such plans yourself, because you would rather just fall into loving situations, but sometimes an arranged scene can be quite exciting and should not be overlooked.

Jupiter Inconjunct Ascendant

You may tend to push yourself too hard physically in lovemaking in an attempt to make it just as good and exciting as possible. In the process you may try things that you simply can't sustain comfortably or that are a bit too much for your lover.

If you have any doubts about where to set your limits, be guided by your partner's judgment and needs and don't feel obligated to do more than that. In fact, do not feel obligated to do anything, because that approach will only hamper your enjoyment of sexuality. Physical achievement means little if you have to sacrifice physical enjoyment.

You may tend to view sex almost as a gymnastic exercise, which can take away from its emotional meaning and almost destroy it as a source of real communication. It is better to relax and do just enough to keep the physical communication flowing without going past the point at which emotional communication falters.

The lesson you must learn is to relax and take love as it comes, remembering that there are many tomorrows in which to enjoy the thousands of potential pleasures that come to mind in a single evening. Let those ideas wait until another day, when they can give you and your lover continuing, developing pleasure.

Jupiter Opposition Ascendant

Your lover may be a boundless source of new emotional directions and sexual innovations, and you should do your utmost to mine that resource. Indeed, your partner can truly be your inspiration.

This may be a problem if your lover is shy or inhibited, for it will be hard to get at his or her inner self so that inspiration starts to flow. One way to do this is to goad or challenge your partner to come out and open up with real feeling and imagination. Much can be gained by gauging the degree of your affection to your partner's spontaneity and creativity, as long as you don't use affection as a power game to gain control over your lover.

On the other hand, if your lover is very spontaneous and open, you may become quite addicted to your partner's creativity, which will throw the relationship into imbalance. Your own sexual creativity tends to come in widely spaced spurts, but with a partner you can work out a good give-and-take arrangement. As the need arises, you can pass the responsibility for a regular flow of sexual expression back and forth between you.

Chapter Eleven
Saturn

Saturn in the Chart

Saturn represents sexual conservatism and, in general, inhibition. It can indicate repression and prudery or healthy common sense that keeps you out of difficulties.

Difficult aspects of Saturn usually lend a negative or self-repressive attitude toward sex in the area governed by the aspected planet or by the sign and house that Saturn is in. This effect is most likely to occur early in life before you make a real attempt to overcome these tendencies.

In easy aspect, Saturn makes for great perseverance and consistency in love, as well as a sense of honesty and honor in the friendship that is part of a long-range love affair. Easy aspects of Saturn mean sexual security, successful habits and the courage to try new directions. Difficult aspects have the opposite effect, making you feel insecure about your current mode of expression but afraid to replace it with something new.

In the long run, Saturn builds courage and character, either through the confirmation of success or through the struggle to overcome emotional difficulties, which are at last conquered. Saturn casts a rather serious light on whatever it touches, but it also lends considerable intensity.

Saturn in Aries

You are probably a fairly demanding partner who does not tolerate an inconsiderate lover. You expect to be treated with respect and affection, and you refuse to let anyone take advantage of you.

This is an asset that can save you much grief and help you avoid exploitative relationships. But be sure you use it well, for you may be quite impatient with a partner who simply needs more tolerance to help bring the relationship to fruition.

Because of your rather high standards, you may have to spend a long time finding a lover of sufficient substance to fulfill your needs. That will be time well spent, for it is better to do without a lover than to waste your time on one who is unsatisfactory.

Although you may not be overtly aggressive, you have a formidable talent for cutting a presumptuous partner down to size. Save this ability for those who truly deserve it, and don't waste your words on minor offenders.

While you are young you may be treated with the respect usually reserved for a more mature person. But oddly enough, as you grow older, you will seem increasingly youthful in style and will attract younger partners.

Saturn in Taurus

You can be particularly patient in judging your partner, giving him or her plenty of room to make mistakes before you get angry or hurt or make any condemnations.

This is an admirable quality, but it must be tempered with insight, for you could be taken advantage of by the wrong partner. However, although you are slow to take offense, once you have been hurt, it is difficult to erase it from your mind. If you want to make up with an estranged lover, you will have to make an extra effort.

Some misunderstandings may stem from forgetfulness or reluctance to let your partner know what seems wrong. You may expect your lover to sense the difficulties without a word from you, which is likely to lead to greater problems. Before being judgmental, make sure your partner understands your problem and how you want to deal with it.

Also you should try to be more amenable to your lover's suggestions, particularly about how to add more variety to your love experience in order to rejuvenate the relationship. In this area you may have considerable capacity for enjoyment, but your partner probably has more talent for initiating the changes.

Saturn in Gemini

You tend to be succinct in telling your partner about your needs and problems in a relationship. Your few words have great intensity and impact, conveying the essence of your thoughts with no need for elaboration.

Depending on how perceptive your partner is, this approach may solve the problem immediately, or it may overwhelm your lover with the intensity of your message. You may even miss your mark entirely by choosing the wrong words to touch your lover's understanding. Therefore, when you realize that your words haven't had the effect you intended, elaborate and define the problem more clearly.

On the other side, you may take your lover's remarks too seriously, interpreting them as being as intense as your own. Before deciding on the seriousness of a criticism, wait to see if it is repeated; that is a more usual expression of emphasis than your intensity.

You tend to ponder matters in a relationship and spend much time clarifying the aspects that seem most critical. Therefore you may be the one who makes the long-range decisions, while your partner handles more of the day-to-day matters.

Saturn in Cancer

This position indicates that you vacillate somewhat about your sexual inhibitions, which can be both an asset and a drawback. Either you flaunt your hangups or you keep them totally hidden from your own and others' sight.

People with this position tend to either come out of the closet with a bang or remain there forever. You are unlikely to be in between. The gradually increasing sexual self-awareness that comes with some other Saturn positions is not usually found here.

The growth of sexual awareness can be most easily attained through erotic fantasies. This should not be done by idle daydreaming about already established turn-ons, but by either imagining or reading about erotic fantasies that seem alien or even upsetting. If they are upsetting they are probably striking a hidden chord in your personality that should be brought to light and examined with your new-found insight. Not only will you have a new supply of erotic stimuli; you will also be able to even out your sexual intensity and have easier access to its expression.

Indeed, the word that best describes this position is intensity—the intensity of reined-in sexual desire and the attendant extremity of its release.

Saturn in Leo

You look at sexual enjoyment more systematically than most. You like to plan a love affair carefully, for you feel more at ease when you are seeking pleasure within a well-defined environment. You may find that you have a special talent for planning festive occasions or special evenings of enjoyment for your lover, for which you take the full responsibility and credit.

You probably have a fairly clear idea of exactly what sexual pleasures you prefer and the techniques to achieve them. But don't let that outlook prevent you from using your lover's imaginative suggestions and new directions. You may not want these ideas sprung on you unawares, but if you have some warning, you may find enjoyment in a good many activities that had never occurred to you.

In general, you pace your pleasures and do not bite off more than you can chew. Although you don't rush to try all the latest techniques, your enjoyments seldom backfire through overindulgence. Also you can spread your pleasures out over a long period so that you never run out of potential good times. Occasionally you may be a slow starter, but you are almost certainly a strong finisher.

Saturn in Virgo

The details of a relationship often seem unduly important to you. Therefore you will be happiest with a lover who bestows affection on you in the areas where you appreciate it most. Although you need this kind of attention, do not make too many demands of your partner or condemn him or her when all your expectations are not fulfilled.

You probably have the ability to make sure that every aspect of a relationship is carried out perfectly. You never miss an opportunity to please yourself and your partner. This is an admirable trait, but it could eventually drive you and your lover crazy. Too much attention to detail can obscure the overall direction of the relationship.

You enjoy sexual variety, particularly if suggested by your lover so that you don't have to provide all the inspiration in that area. However, you want to retain control over the sexual direction of your relationship so that you are not thrust suddenly into an unexpected scenario.

At times you will be jealous of your lover, particularly concerning physical loyalty. You are, however, better off with a partner who wanders occasionally than with one who is not loyal where it counts—in the heart.

Saturn in Libra

You tend to be balanced and stable in settling difficulties within a relationship, and you aren't flustered by temporary turmoil. Generally you can patiently wait out an emotional storm or take steps to calm it down, even to your own disadvantage if you are at fault. You have the foresight to see that the situation will balance out in the end and that you will reach that equilibrium only by keeping your present relationship on an even keel.

Indeed, you are probably better than your partner at coping with problems, at least in your approach to them. But that may be a sensitive issue between you, so avoid reminding your partner of personal failings, particularly when you have successfully handled a situation and your lover has not. In the interests of harmony, let it go at that. Otherwise your partner may be at cross-purposes with you in similar situations in the future.

You may have a special talent for arbitrating problems outside of your own relationship, which can be a creative outlet for you. But you should do this only if requested to, lest others think you are interfering. Or your lover might think you are less interested in your own relationship.

Saturn in Scorpio

Sexual fulfillment ranks high among your physical needs, and you may be quite sexually demanding of your partner. For this reason you should find a sexually active partner who is highly attuned to your urgent special needs.

If you have been significantly frustrated or misused in love at some time, you may become spiteful and resentful, which will adversely affect later relationships. You must work hard to put such experiences behind you and look at a new affair with fresh and unprejudiced eyes.

On the other hand, you have a very long memory for affection and will hold an old lover dear long after you both have moved on to other relationships. When a lover helps you at a critical time, you reward him or her a thousandfold. You consider its real value to you, not just the effort expended by your benefactor.

Because of your very intense attitude toward sexuality, you may tend to go to extremes in love, both physically and emotionally. You seem to seek self-dissolution in sexual experience and find special reinforcement in being swept away in a relationship. This is a reward in itself, but you will benefit from having a cheerful partner who can make you laugh when you become too intense. This will lighten the mood when your intensity fails to accomplish its purpose, which must occur at times.

Saturn in Sagittarius

Your style in a relationship is to be continually in motion, particularly when difficulties arise. Others may face up to a problem and either defeat it or go down fighting, but you manage to avoid the situation or take evasive action until it goes away.

But relying on motion and change only works with problems that are not deeply seated. When a situation refuses to go away, you should rely on your partner to do much of the work. For that you will need a steady, dependable lover.

However, you do have a talent for spotting the specific causes of a problem and pointing them out. Take care not to mistakenly pin the cause of a complex problem on one simplistic source.

When difficulties crop up in your relationship, you can look on the bright side and cheer yourself and your partner. You are sure that between the two of you, you will solve the problem and come out the better for it. By refusing to dignify adversity with gloom, you can dispel sorrow and strengthen your union, not so much by determination as by hope and good cheer.

Saturn in Capricorn

You handle your life in a steady, practical way, and you seldom let problems upset you too much. Instead, you methodically work to clear them up forthwith.

Indeed, your ability to plan ahead helps you avoid many of the major obstacles in a relationship, because in building it you are careful to steer clear of such dangers. For this reason you can sustain a partner who is less stable than you. In fact such a lover is a stimulating challenge, for you enjoy serving as a bulwark to your lover in times of difficulty. Such a role can be a creative outlet for your talents as a friend and lover.

You have enough patience to take the good with the bad and to create a workable long-term affair. You do not rush into an affair headlong just for involvement, preferring to wait for a partner with whom you can have a full and rewarding relationship.

With the help of your lover, you should try to overcome your innate conservatism now and then, for that will bring added spark and excitement into the relationship.

Saturn in Aquarius

In a love relationship, you have the ability to stand back and view your problems from outside, which keeps you from making long-range decisions in the heat of the moment. You should develop this invaluable gift, even if your partner accuses you of being cold-blooded, especially when you have to terminate an affair. In hindsight your objective view usually proves correct, and you will be very glad you followed it.

You have the ability, though not necessarily the inclination, to maintain several strong relationships at the same time without interference. This is likely to be more difficult for your partners, however, and you should carefully consider whether the emotional strain on them will be too great if they are less sturdy than you.

In love, while you are on the move you tend to stay in motion, but once you settle down, you are likely to stay put. This is a matter of convenience rather than preference, and it can be counterbalanced by a partner who provides more or less variety, as needed. Once ensconced in a stable relationship, you have great staying power and the ability to meet all sorts of difficulties with a minimum of fuss.

Saturn in Pisces

For you, the greatest security is achieved through consistent emotional attention from a sensitive and devoted partner, rather than through financial stability. In a way, you feed on emotional communication and will feel starved if you are not involved in an active love relationship.

As a result of this talent plus considerable emotional experience, you may become a good judge of emotions. When you understand what is real and what is not, the false will not suffice. You will demand great sincerity and sensitivity in a partner.

When you find the right partner with these qualities, you will go to extremes of self-sacrifice to keep the relationship going. This is an admirable trait, but it should not be a substitute for the two of you facing your problems together. In an emotionally difficult situation, you should not let love blind you to the need for painful growth; every relationship goes through such phases.

As for more concrete concerns, you will be most comfortable with a partner who is more practical than you are. Before making a physical or financial commitment, consult with your lover, who may be a stabilizing influence.

Saturn in the First House

You are a person who does not become involved in an affair lightly. Once you are committed to a lover you immerse your entire being in the affair with great intensity. You see personal commitment as a serious responsibility, and as a result your own personality is more forceful when you are involved in a love relationship.

You have a good deal of perseverance and will not give up easily when difficulties beset a relationship. Indeed, you are more likely to go down fighting than to abandon your commitment.

You are the pillar of any relationship you enter, but you must not allow a lazy partner to take advantage of your earnestness. In any worthwhile affair, both partners must work together, particularly in times of stress, or there will be little chance of success.

You need a lighthearted lover, for you sometimes take things much too seriously, allowing circumstances outside your control to weigh you down. A partner who can mollify you with gentle fun and affection is an excellent complement to your personality. Although you have tremendous tenacity and durability, you are probably not fully emotionally aware of this. You need a partner who will remind you just how much love and joy you have left inside.

Saturn in the Second House

Wealth and material possessions are not important factors when you choose a partner. You are not looking for monetary reward in your personal relationships, and you may even feel that too many financial considerations taint the affair, preventing both of you from true, open communication in love.

Such a philosophy, though fundamentally honest and pure in motivation, may lead you into some rather financially impoverished relationships. In that case you may not have enough money to take part in activities that you both would enjoy.

Learning balance in this area is something that often comes with age, but it is prudent to recognize early that insufficient physical security can eventually destroy a relationship. This is particularly true when marriage and/or children are involved. A close and powerful relationship can weather all such hazards, but a little foresight can help prevent such unnecessary trials.

On any level you may find that you never have quite enough to fulfill your expectations. This situation arises because your imagination and creativity are well ahead of your means, and before you are through with one project you start another. As long as you have food and warmth, however, your love is free of your physical surroundings and is based on intimate personal communication.

Saturn in the Third House

For you, a verbal commitment in a relationship is a serious matter, and it is very important that you and your lover say exactly what you mean. You should not back out of a previously made commitment or change your mind in midstream. This will result in more carefully thought-out verbal communication between you, talk being the crystallization of your intuitive inner feelings rather than empty banter. Indeed, you should avoid a really loquacious partner, for too much talk confuses you and leads you in contradictory directions. A word to the wise is sufficient; a flood of words is simply foolishness.

Your partner can rely on you to diagnose precisely any problems that arise, and if you can't come up with immediate answers, at least you will have a clear idea of the trouble you are facing.

Your partner should be a very honest person, for you are easily deceived. In your naiveté, you may not recognize a bald-faced lie or intentional misstatement that others would catch immediately. Truth and clarity should be essential elements in any relationship; a muddy, false affair would be quite unfulfilling. It is to your advantage to know where you stand in relation to your partner at all times. Since you take verbal commitments seriously, you should mean them in the first place.

Saturn in the Fourth House

You are most comfortable in a secure and loving relationship in a home environment with a reassuring partner who is sensitive to your emotional needs. A free and easy relationship that comes and goes can't give you the necessary emotional fulfillment and will leave you feeling empty and neglected. You are happier in a harmonious marriage than in a less formal relationship with no definite commitment.

You should be slow to commit yourself to such a relationship, for once you are involved it would be painful for you if it didn't work out. But few relationships are perfect, so once you have entered into one, resist your natural urge to criticize and complain. If all your needs are not attended to, compromise a bit. You both have responsibilities, and you must work together to see that your mutual needs are understood and taken care of.

The physical appearance of your home is less important to you than the emotional warmth and security within it. You need those qualities more than most people.

Your relationship can serve as a shelter from the problems of everyday life. You must offer your partner as much support as you receive, lest the affair become an escape from reality. Instead, try to make it a strong union of two devoted partners.

Saturn in the Fifth House

You are not one to trifle with sex. When a sexual relationship comes into your life, you take it quite seriously. Because you do not enter into an affair just for amusement, you may not gain a wide variety of sexual experience. However, the experiences you do have will be much more intense and you will derive great benefit from them.

It is not necessary to become involved in affairs that you don't really desire just because that is the swinging thing to do these days. Such transient affairs will probably have a negative quality that detracts from your enjoyment of love in general. It would be better to wait for that special person to come along and then devote all of your energies to him or her. That will be much more beneficial and rewarding.

Your partner should be as honest and sincere about the relationship as you are, in order to derive the most pleasure from the experience. A lighthearted lover would balance your own earnestness. Ideally, your partner should recognize your intensity and move with you at the right moment, without trying to diffuse the strength of your motivation by taking you too lightly.

Conversely, you should try not to be too demanding, and learn to adjust to your partner's needs even when they do not coincide with your own. There will be times when you want that favor returned.

Saturn in the Sixth House

You may have an innate desire to play the game of love by "the rules," so you are somewhat at a loss when a lover doesn't follow the pattern you are accustomed to.

Trying the anything-goes philosophy is not the right answer for you, for that would create a great deal of mental confusion about where you stand with your lover.

You should develop a complex and varied set of patterns in lovemaking so that you always have a reference point and can't get lost. By so doing, you can become an extremely skilled and sensitive lover, whom your partner can rely on for direction if the situation becomes confused. It takes a good deal of effort to learn and educate yourself to the myriad possibilities in lovemaking. Fortunately, there is now an abundance of literature on this subject, so you do not have to rely only on your own experience. But at the same time, only personal involvement can give you confidence in using the knowledge you have gained.

You will do well with a lover who has a healthy amount of sexual curiosity and a deep desire for fulfillment, who will support and encourage you in finding complete gratification.

Saturn in the Seventh House

You may be particularly choosy about selecting a partner who can live up to your stringent internal guidelines. Although this finicky attitude can save you many a profitless and time-wasting affair, remember that much of the beauty of a relationship is in its development. Few lasting affairs start off in full bloom. What seems like a weakness or fault in a partner may provide an opportunity for mutual growth and refinement.

Your inner desire for an elevated and accomplished affair may lead you into involvement with older or more experienced lovers who seem to have more expertise than you. If your experienced lover is a sincere person, you can gain a great deal, but take care not to mistake a demanding lover for one who is experienced. In any affair you should receive as much as you give, or you may find that you are being used for your desire to become accomplished in love.

As you advance in age and experience, avoid being too demanding of a younger lover. An inequality of affection may cause one or both of you to become alienated. Patience is a virtue, particularly with a lover, and you can develop that quality fully.

You will learn from experience that an unpressured partnership that develops slowly and surely will give you the greatest feelings of accomplishment and fulfillment.

Saturn in the Eighth House

You may have a needless fear of the unknown in matters of sexual exploration, particularly when you are with a lover for the first time. Some hesitation is natural, since sexuality is held in such awe in our culture, but for you it may mean particular worry and fascination.

You are not likely to avoid any areas of mystery or insecurity in love matters. Quite the opposite, you are drawn to these experiences like a moth to a flame, with a combination of expectation and anxiety.

Your best approach, as Zen teachers say, is to leap into the heart of the flame and have it out on the spot. Real life situations can turn out to be easier and less formidable than your imaginings, particularly if you have an understanding lover. An overly demanding partner or one who is not sensitive to your desires and hesitations can be emotionally harmful, so take great care in choosing and knowing your lover ahead of time.

The dark recesses of love are frequently the most exciting. As you become more experienced, you have the ability to become the focus of all that is mysterious and thought-provoking to a lover. You can develop a kind of gently persistent magnetism that many will envy.

For you, loving is simply a matter of proceeding one step at a time toward those areas that especially attract you, even though at first you have some anticipatory anxiety.

Saturn in the Ninth House

You are not likely to rush into new sexual territory until you have thoroughly explored the old ground. In this respect you know how to conserve your love energy and experience, treasuring every ounce of pleasure from each lovemaking technique.

At the same time, you may be reluctant to move into new areas of technique while you are still enjoying the old. This does not mean you will turn down a sexual experiment; indeed, with an active lover you may enjoy many new approaches to sex. A real, in-depth appreciation of them, however, may come slowly as you climb the ladder of love.

Once you understand the pleasure potential of a particular method, you perfect it in order to bring yourself and your lover to special heights of fulfillment. For this reason, you are most comfortable with a partner who doesn't try to rush you from one experience to another. Such frantic activity could leave you frustrated, missing the depth of experience that you want and need.

While others may become bored or jaded from shallow dabbling in many varieties of sexual experience, your own relationships will continue to grow in depth and intensity. As life goes on, they will become even more rewarding, giving you youthful vitality when others are losing theirs.

Saturn in the Tenth House

You may tend to be quite modest about your abilities in love, but you shouldn't underestimate your capacity for affection. Your talents as a lover are considerable, but you tend to mask them with a certain formality, except with your most intimate partners.

While you are young, this may work against you to some extent by giving you the reputation of being introverted. Although you will thus be spared some unwanted relationships, you will end up sitting on the sidelines when you would rather be actively participating in a relationship.

On the other hand, you will be able to develop particularly strong and lasting ties with a lover, and as a result you will have considerably more control over your partner. This power is desirable if you use it to strengthen the relationship, but watch out for any tendency to deny your partner needed freedom.

You are a particularly persevering and devoted partner, and will spend much time and effort in developing and supporting a relationship, sometimes even setting aside your own interests. In that case, be aware of what you are doing, and don't unconsciously use your self-sacrifice to coerce your partner. Priorities in the relationship should be decided on by both of you so that they will further the growth of a solid, lasting partnership.

Saturn in the Eleventh House

In love you are a realist who does not usually get wound up in the peripheral aspects of a love relationship. You usually concentrate on the essence of an affair, neglecting the extra touches; in matters of the heart, you are a classicist rather than a romantic.

While you are young you may get off to a slow start, because youthful romances tend to be so superficial, which may leave you unenthusiastic about the whole subject. Spending too much time in emotional irrelevancies leaves you bored and yearning for a solid relationship.

You may be part of a small but close circle of friends with whom you have quiet but intense relationships over a long period of time. In a love affair, friendship and honesty are of prime importance, even overshadowing the more physical aspects.

Once an affair is established, it may be easier to move on to the more delicate facets of love that you eschewed earlier. This is just your particular method of growth, which will bring you increasing richness and elegance. At the same time you will maintain the substantial commitment upon which a love relationship must be founded.

Saturn in the Twelfth House

This is a difficult position for Saturn, but its effects are not easily discerned by others.

You are likely to withdraw emotionally at inappropriate times for one reason or another. At the very peak of excitement, you hold back almost involuntarily, resulting in a less than complete pleasure. This may go unnoticed by your partner, who goes ahead heedlessly with no loss of enjoyment, physically or emotionally. But your personal disappointment will make an otherwise joyful experience one-sided.

This results from the age-old fear of flying or letting go; even when you have consciously discarded all outward physical inhibitions, the inner ones still cling, preventing full enjoyment of otherwise ecstatic moments.

There are many traditional remedies for this problem, the most popular being a couple of cocktails or various other relaxation techniques.

Psychologically, the best answer is to find an utterly trusted and understanding lover who knows the emotional pitfalls to avoid, one whose loving hand can break through occasional barriers to total uninhibited involvement.

Saturn Conjunct Uranus

You treat the subtle details of love with particular care and skill, and you do not need a great deal of variety to keep love fresh and full of new discoveries. For you, slight variations hold a wealth of pleasure possibilities that can last you a long time.

You may be able to discover some especially pleasing styles and delicate techniques that your lover may not have been aware of before, since you have devised them yourself. Such discoveries are not made in a flash, however, but developed through careful, sensitive observation of your lover's responses over a long time.

Indeed, you might explore sexuality with an almost scientific method, so that your knowledge is thorough and precise. In that way you can move with confidence, knowing the exact effect that your actions will have. This approach will be more successful if you stay with one partner. People's responses are so varied that it is difficult to establish a reliable set of standards for more than one partner. In a long-term affair, however, you have the time to explore every possible pathway to pleasure.

Saturn Sextile Uranus

You can uncover a wealth of satisfying methods of sexual expression without having to venture into highly unusual or experimental territory. You are more likely to pursue a particular style or technique for some time until it unfolds special pleasures than to hop from one idea to another without exploring each one very deeply.

Since in-depth pleasure is more your style, you need a lover who has the patience to pursue this goal as well, who is not impatient to move on to something else before you have really exhausted the present possibilities. Oddly enough, a sexual adventurer would be a less enjoyable partner for you than a quiet lover who will go with you hand in hand for the extra mile that will produce really satisfying sexual expression.

At the same time, however, you need a lover who from time to time can bring new material to the relationship for you both to explore, someone who will continually refresh the affair with stimulating innovations. These will not be major changes of direction but interesting garnishes that make your loving seem new again, even though the basic style or technique has not been altered significantly. In that way, each approach to love lasts longer and is more enjoyable.

Saturn Square Uranus

You hate to have lovemaking become routine, which makes you somewhat restless in a long-term relationship, where you are likely to get into a rut.

If you are content with being single, this is not really a problem, because your restlessness will just lead you into new and more interesting experiences with different partners. But if you are married or committed to one person, you need to work out this problem if you want the relationship to endure.

First, you must be very honest and tell your lover immediately when you are bored; then you should work to make the situation more lively. In doing this, you may have to experiment with approaches or techniques that go against your inclinations, but it is better to have some doubts or anxiety than to be bored with sex. At least your difficult energies are turned outward and made active instead of being pent-up inside, which would eventually lead to an explosion or the breakup of the relationship.

Although this lifestyle may be tumultuous at times, it will provide you with great sexual freedom and discovery within a single ongoing relationship, so that you can have the best of both worlds.

Saturn Trine Uranus

You are able to feel comfortable with any form of sexual experimentation that you choose, and you choose those that have real substance, not just passing whims. Once you have decided on a new direction, you stay with it long enough to derive the maximum pleasure.

Your lover should let you choose new styles and techniques, because your judgment is so good about which ones have the most potential. You need a partner who will go along with you in your explorations, even though it may take some time and practice to get the most out of each one. Very often, sophisticated sexual techniques require some time to master physically before your minds are free enough of technical distractions that your emotional communication flows easily and without interruption.

Although you do not seem like a sexual adventurer, your style is quite innovative. It is just that your pace is slower, but in time you will have covered as much ground as many others. You do it much more thoroughly, so you know in great detail just what pleasures may be found in the varieties of sexual expression.

Saturn Inconjunct Uranus

Your sexual inhibitions may be somewhat at odds with the areas of sex that seem most potentially satisfying to you. Thus you may be happiest when you are doing something that you feel rather guilty about. If you do not handle this problem carefully, it can be destructive to yourself or to the relationship.

The most practical solution is to be stringently honest with your partner about this and to allow each other considerable leeway for experimentation without harming either of you. In that way you can successfully and pleasurably transgress your inner inhibitions without breaking the rules of your commitment to your lover. You can have your cake and eat it too, but only if you are careful about it.

In a way, you can gain great pleasure and inner knowledge by setting up restrictions and then breaking them down, but be sure that this process does not cause your partner any harm. Breaking an inhibition about a particular sexual approach can be exciting, even if the inhibition was set up artificially. But if you commit yourself exclusively to one partner and then break your commitment, it can be quite harmful to your lover, so don't make that kind of promise unless you intend to keep it.

Saturn Opposition Uranus

You may indulge in sexual experimentation only after a long period of building desire that finally breaks through your inhibitions. You tend to stay with the normal, tried-and-true range of sexual practices and then suddenly venture far afield.

In an ongoing relationship, this may mean a sudden affair with another lover that you throw your body and soul into. Or it may mean doing something extremely daring with your regular partner, or perhaps breaking out of your usual style and establishing a new pattern that will last until another sudden change occurs. In any case, the break from the established norm will happen suddenly through release of pent-up energy.

This pattern could become too extreme for comfort, resulting in long dull periods followed by sudden unsettling changes. In that case it may be wise to methodically bring new ideas into your relationship now and then just to liven things up and relieve the pressure. This may go against your inclinations and seem forced at first, but it can be a useful way to make sexual progress more evenly.

Saturn Conjunct Neptune

You may be quite happy in a restricted relationship that does not allow you much freedom, not because you have no desire to try anything new, but because such a setup gives you a feeling of stability and emotional support.

One reason for this preference is that you yourself tend to construct concrete and demanding ideals in a relationship that can be satisfied only by strict adherence, not wandering off and testing another situation simply out of curiosity.

Once you have chosen a partner, you are extremely loyal to him or her, and you hang onto a relationship through thick and thin when you have made a commitment to it.

Take care not to be too demanding of your partner, however, because your partner's standards may be quite different from yours or less rigid. The changes that must be made will occur slowly and spontaneously, and they will happen in ways that neither of you will perceive at the time. Be patient with your lover's failings as well as your own, for you may look back on them from a totally different viewpoint later.

In relation to your partner, however, following your own ideals will be most rewarding, as long as you are not too hard on yourself when you do slip up.

Saturn Sextile Neptune

You probably have quite a good understanding of how far you can go in implementing your ideals in love and where you must accept reality without trying to change it.

Because of this understanding, you do not have to suffer the heartache of crushed beliefs as much as others do.

If possible, however, you cleave naturally and without strain to the standards you have set for yourself. For instance, instead of trying to force your beliefs on others, you are a living example of what you believe in, which draws the admiration of others.

Probably you are not particularly interested in an overactive or tumultuous sex life, but will fall easily into a simple and satisfying style in which you can count on regular expression. In the long run, you will be most happy with a regular partner whom you are familiar and comfortable with, someone who knows your needs and desires well. Your love takes the form of physically demonstrated affection and friendship rather than flaming bodily passion. You use sexuality as a reliable and enjoyable means of communication rather than merely as an outlet for physical need or personal gratification. As a result, your sexual expression will stay at the same level of interest and ability well into old age.

Saturn Square Neptune

You must try to stand back from your relationship and view it as objectively as possible. You tend to create an idealized vision of the affair, which you confuse with the reality. If that tendency is not checked, it leads to mutual recriminations and disillusionment when you and your partner finally face your problems.

Thus you must take care to be completely honest and straightforward with your lover, with no unproved assumptions, for they may well turn out to be in error. This may require a lot of unromantic, down-to-earth discussions, which are likely to seem trying, but in the long run the rewards will outweigh the bother.

This kind of carefulness will help to defuse the jealousy that often arises with this aspect. Jealousy is largely created in the imagination, and it can be allayed or even dispelled by clearly and truthfully defining where each of you stands.

Not only is it important to make your positions clear, you must then abide by them and not back down or fudge on your promises. Trust is the most important pillar of a love relationship, no matter how unusual the arrangement is, and if that is there, emotional reward will follow.

Saturn Trine Neptune

You definitely prefer a long-term love commitment that is more than just a physical outlet, uniting you and your partner in serving some higher goal, either social or spiritual. Although sexuality may be present, in the long run it will take a back seat to other aspects of the relationship.

Your sexual expression may be quite austere, or it may be a regular and special expression of friendly affection. Sex just for the sake of physical release has little appeal unless it also serves as a channel of personal and spiritual communication.

As a result, you will probably build a very stable, long-lasting marriage or love affair based on love and friendship rather than on momentary passion. Your ideals and expectations are based on real accomplishments, not on impossible hopes and dreams that lead to disappointment.

Sexuality may not even enter such an affair at the outset, but after you have become true and lasting friends, it will develop as a channel of communication between you. In any case, friendship will usually come before your desire or need for sexual expression.

Saturn Inconjunct Neptune

Your ideals and expectations of sexual expression may be quite incompatible with reality. This may lead you to restrict your own or your partner's behavior in a way that greatly inhibits the pleasure of sexual activity. As a result, your sexual tensions and needs may build to such a peak that you are forced to release them in ways that are not truly satisfying and may not even be enjoyable.

One way to handle this problem is to set your sexual standards according to society's accepted norms rather than your own. If you expect no more and no less than that, ignoring the flights of idealism that you would prefer, you will probably meet with much less disappointment in love. Another solution is to let your partner be responsible for all the decisions concerning your sexual direction. In that case, however, you should reciprocate by taking responsibility for another area, such as finances, so that the relationship does not become lopsided.

Under any circumstances, you should relax your rules concerning sexuality. By setting standards that you cannot comfortably adhere to, you only succeed in frustrating and disappointing yourself and your partner.

Saturn Opposition Neptune

At times you may expect much more from sexual expression than you can possibly get, while at other times you are so pragmatic that you expect nothing, and as a result, you sometimes get just that.

In general you tend to go to extremes in both directions, both toward the real and the ideal, which is likely to spell disappointment because you seldom get what you expect. To get around this problem, simply expect the unexpected in love, reserving all judgment until after the fact. You may find it quite difficult to toss away your expectations and inhibitions, but in the long run, the freedom this provides will be its own reward.

This approach may involve walking a tightrope between the ideal freedom that you would like, which will not provide the necessary emotional security, and a secure, tied-down relationship that clips your wings. Try to find a middle ground, where you have freedom to engage in occasional outside affairs, knowing that you are loved and wanted at home. To achieve this, you must have a firm understanding and commitment with your partner, and you must shun jealousy in favor of scrupulous honesty, which will become the backbone of the relationship.

Saturn Conjunct Pluto

You are probably a person who makes life-and-death commitments, and once you have made a long-range decision, you aren't likely to give up. This can be either good or bad, depending upon the wisdom of your commitments, so be sure to take enough time in deciding on a lover or partner, so that you don't lock yourself into a bad situation.

You should be especially careful to avoid restrictive, emotionally smothering relationships. You may find that difficult, because frequently the easiest way to keep a partner is by being possessive. But in the long run, that leads to considerable inequality and resentment, which will probably bring the affair to an end. If your lover is right for you, the partnership will last; otherwise it will naturally end. Being overly possessive will only be counterproductive.

However, in a basically sound relationship, your determination will be very helpful if you express it by being extra tolerant of your partner's mistakes and patient with problems in the relationship. You are able to withstand great adversity, which will make you stronger for having had the courage and tenacity to see it through.

Saturn Sextile Pluto

In general, you can guide a love relationship with an even, steady hand, particularly in areas that require restriction or inhibition. Thus you are not overly possessive of your partner, but you know when to call a halt when a situation gets out of hand.

In this regard, you are fairly secure and not easily threatened, because you know that a substantial relationship will not go on the rocks if you or your partner exercise your freedom somewhat; indeed, a good affair need not and should not be shackled in any way. On the other hand, the most stringent restrictions will not sustain a weak relationship for long, so it is best to let the affair develop as it will.

The only time it is important to step on the brake is when one partner is unknowingly hurting the other. Here it is important to have good communication so that you can nip such problems in the bud. If your lover is causing you sorrow without meaning to, do not suffer in silence, because that will lead only to resentment and retaliation. Express your feelings right away so that the situation can be corrected, and the smooth flow can be reestablished. It may be easier for you to keep silent and wait for improvement, but it is better not to.

Saturn Square Pluto

You must make a point of never trying to force your lover's hand or impose any form of expression that he or she is not definitely sure about. You should discuss this quite clearly, because you may be very tempted to physically or emotionally blackmail your lover into doing what you want if you feel that you are being deprived of some sort of sexual expression.

When you feel that your partner is neglecting you, bring it out into the open verbally and leave it up to your partner. Often this amends the problem instantly. However, if your partner does not want to move in the direction you indicate, you should not on any account try to railroad your lover into it, assuming that it will turn out to be pleasurable after all. The chances are it won't, and almost certainly your partner will resent and distrust you.

If this situation arises often, the two of you may simply be sexually incompatible and should end the relationship. The only occasion where force should exist in sexual expression is in playing out a mutually agreed-upon fantasy that is pleasurable and exciting to both partners.

Saturn Trine Pluto

You have a quality of great endurance that will enable you to go through considerable hardship to make a good relationship succeed. In any affair, time is your ally; the longer you are involved with a lover, the more you both will grow and be positively transformed.

The changes that take place are not usually initiated by you, because once you have settled into a comfortable affair, you are not likely to change it hastily. This is just as well, because reworking a relationship swiftly may cause surface changes, but in-depth adjustments come only with time and getting used to each other.

When you do work for change, it is not your style to force the issue, but to let it work out naturally. In that way both partners are happy, and one does not get all the credit for what has been accomplished.

Make a special attempt to be receptive to your lover's suggestions about new ideas and be willing to go along, even if you are somewhat skeptical. If you keep an open mind, you may have some pleasant surprises and even change your attitudes a bit.

Saturn Inconjunct Pluto

You should avoid putting sexual pressure upon your lover, which you may do without realizing it by speaking openly of your needs when your lover cannot fulfill them.

Only your partner can tell you when that is happening, and you should encourage such communication at every opportunity. You need that feedback to know whether you are being too demanding or, indeed, if your desires are imaginary.

Your desires may actually be imaginary or at least so hard to define that they are impossible to satisfy. This may make you feel neglected in a nonspecific way, but your partner can do nothing to relieve it and therefore should not be held to blame. This feeling frequently originates deep within the sexual subconscious. By exploring your sexual fantasies extensively and living them out whenever possible, you can bring your subconscious needs to light and satisfy them.

For this, you probably need a very cooperative lover, but if your partner is unwilling to participate in a given fantasy, do not force the issue. Instead, rework the scenario into a form that evokes the same feelings for you and is more acceptable to your lover.

Saturn Opposition Pluto

You may unconsciously resist making fundamental changes in your attitudes toward sex and personal relationships. When changes do occur, they cause considerable upheaval, because you have resisted the pressure to change until it has built up to the boiling point.

Therefore you should listen to your partner's advice and others' suggestions about how to make such changes gradually and less destructively. You have to face problems in yourself that you would rather turn away from, but that is quite necessary unless you are prepared for the much less pleasant prospect of occasional major character upheaval. Therefore, make an extra attempt to deal squarely with the not-yet crippling problems that are secretly troubling you. Discuss them with your lover; if your problems concern particular techniques of loving, confront the issue by trying the things that bother you and then discussing your feelings with your lover afterward. This will give you much more insight into yourself, and it can head off the little problems that can build into serious blockages if you are afraid to face them and dispose of them in the early stages.

Saturn Conjunct Ascendant

You are a person of quiet determination who keeps at something until it's complete, particularly in personal relationships. You may not get intimately acquainted with a potential lover right away, but you are persistent and will not give up on a desire until you are sure it is beyond your reach.

Because of this style, you seem to be older and more mature than your years even at an early age. Once you are really mature, you blossom into a sort of agelessness. This tends to attract two kinds of people: those who intend to get seriously involved on a mature, adult level and those who are seeking a parent figure to lean on.

You may be very tempted to have a fling with a lover who sees you as a parental figure, especially since you have so much control over such a person. However, it is wise to avoid that kind of entanglement. Once in, you will find it rather difficult to get out, and if you try, your partner may undergo a crisis like the crisis of leaving home for an adolescent, for such a person is still an emotional adolescent.

It would be better to find an older, more serious partner, even though you may find it hard to keep up at times. The results will be more rewarding.

Saturn Sextile Ascendant

You are probably not very talkative in matters of love, and you prefer to make your desires and intentions known with as few words as possible. This is reinforced by your ability to communicate effectively without overdoing it, making talk unnecessary.

Basically, you would rather get down to the real pleasures of loving than talk about it. But even in loving, your style tends to be laconic. Although you are capable of great endurance, you prefer not to overdo pleasure so that it doesn't get worn out.

What you are seeking is quality of enjoyment rather than quantity. Thus, many of the more experimental styles of sexual expression have little physical appeal for you. The traditional styles give you more latitude for developing quintessential pleasure, particularly concerning communication within sexual expression. Love should be something special, not just a form of recreation to satisfy bodily needs.

At times this attitude means that you will do without sex for a while, but that is not a real hardship, because inferior affection is not very meaningful to you, and truly rewarding love is worth waiting for.

Saturn Square Ascendant

You may be hesitant in your approach to a potential lover, which makes it more difficult to make your desires and intentions known. Essentially, your partner may think you are saying no when you really mean yes.

For this reason you are happiest with a lover who knows you well and can sense your desires without your having to make them too explicit. If you are fortunate enough to have such a partner, you would be unwise to reject him or her in favor of playing the field. If your lover is committed to you, be particularly caring and generous with material gifts. You may sometimes be inclined to withhold yourself, either personally or financially, which can make you seem, unintentionally, rather cold to your partner.

You may have to doubly emphasize your messages of love, because what seems emphatic enough to you may seem insufficient and insincere to your partner. If you want your partner to see your real intentions, you will have to overcompensate for that. An observant partner or friend can be a great help, cluing you in as to when to change or add to your presentation so that your intentions will be interpreted correctly by those around you.

Saturn Trine Ascendant

You exude an air of stability and reliability, which may make your lover feel that he or she can lean on you for support. That is a nice image to project, but it may attract partners who are not self-sufficient, whom you have to support emotionally. You may or may not want that in a relationship.

Probably you are not as sexually assertive as some people, but once committed to an encounter, you can sustain a high level of sexual expression. In general, that is not your desire, however; you prefer sex to be a reinforcing expression of friendship and communication rather than a physically gratifying end in itself.

For this reason you may not always have as much sexual expression as you would like, because you are quite particular about the circumstances. It is always harder to find something special than to settle for something commonplace or run-of-the-mill.

But once you have found a satisfying partner, you are likely to stick to that relationship so that you can explore the in-depth loving that you seek. That experience will make you more secure and more self-aware.

Saturn Inconjunct Ascendant

At times you may be so anxious to make the right impression that you defeat your own purpose by putting too much pressure into the effort. Sometimes just contemplating the effort that will be required cripples the will and therefore weakens your self-presentation.

Essentially, the solution to this problem is to think positively and not worry too much about how others see you. Just be simple and honest and let the circumstances take care of themselves. The less self-conscious you are, the better off you will be. Naturally, that is easier said than done, but various relaxation aids or techniques can do wonders. As a result you will become more aware of the flow of communication between you and your partner and less self-conscious about your own conduct in the situation.

Certainly, you will be happier with a steady partner who is sensitive to your needs and your kind of communication. Playing the field will add needless anxiety to your life, so if a steady partner is available, stay with him or her. This will allow you to take your time and enjoy what you are doing. Then sex will be a relaxing, enjoyable activity rather than a task that you have to work at.

Saturn Opposition Ascendant

You may be attracted to partners who restrict you in some way or who are or appear older than you. Although this may limit your sexual possibilities in some instances, in others it will stabilize you, if your partner can provide effective guidelines as to what will be most pleasurable in the long run.

However, there may be certain barriers of communication between you, stemming from a certain coldness and unwillingness on your lover's part to communicate openly. In part, this problem may be of your own making because you have chosen such a person in the first place.

In some ways, it would be better to remain unattached than to lock yourself into an unsatisfactory relationship. You may find it more convenient and more rewarding to take lovers, not limiting yourself to a permanent partner until the right person comes along.

Once the right partner does come into your life, however, you will stick to that partner like glue. When you understand the scarcity of truly compatible people in this world, you will value your lover twice as much. For that reason, you will allow such a partnership to limit your lifestyle a bit if necessary, because the knowledge and certainty of a continuously satisfying relationship will be worth it.

Chapter Twelve

Uranus

Uranus in the Chart

Uranus represents the principles of discovery that lie within us all, and in sexual expression it represents the quest for new and different styles of sexuality.

Uranus is rather sudden and forceful in nature, and the discoveries it brings tend to strike like lightning, particularly when it is in difficult aspect. The areas it touches will be characterized by upheaval and change. If the aspect is difficult, the changes will be upsetting; with easy aspects, the changes bring freshness and stimulation.

The sign that Uranus is in has much to do with the attitude of everyone in your age group toward sexual exploration, since Uranus remains in each sign for a period of seven years. Depending on the aspects of Uranus in your chart, you may either accept or reject these generational attitudes. If your attitude toward sexuality differs in some way from the accepted norm, you should consider it not as a problem but as an opportunity to explore and enjoy realms of sexual expression that aren't available to your peers.

The motive behind the Uranus effects is to discover the absolute truth about sexuality, which may be found right in your own backyard or after an endless search, or it may never be found at all.

Uranus in Aries (1927–1934)

Along with others in your age group, you are inclined toward sexual discovery through active commitment and involvement. Instead of just letting events take their own course, you prefer to shape them, finding special personal enrichment in relationships that you instigate yourself.

This attitude results in part from a belief, shared by your peers, in taking fate into your own hands and shaping it by the force of your will. You have an inner drive to be self-sufficient or willfully self-reliant.

It would be wise to question this generational attitude, particularly if you find that it does not suit your own personality. Any attempts to aggressively change or control your environment, especially a love relationship, should be done cautiously with special concern for adverse effects on your partner.

If you find that change comes easily to you in affairs of the heart, your relationships may become stepping stones to growth. Though these liaisons are often fairly simple and well defined, they represent an increasingly complex pattern of personal growth that is the result of continually taking matters into your own hands.

You may find that your style and philosophy change radically over the years. You will retain your sincerity and commitment while becoming increasingly aware and respectful of other people's differences.

Uranus in Taurus (1934–1942)

You may find that your patterns of learning and self-discovery within a relationship are nonverbal and direct, related to physical rather than intellectual experience. You probably picked up this trait from others of your age group who take quite a direct approach to problem solving, preferring to use sheer force of personality instead of intellectual persuasion.

For many people this can be a most rewarding path to self-discovery; it may or may not be an appropriate or profitable style for you. Your ability to use this approach successfully depends on other facets of your personality, but because it is familiar to you, it may be the easiest direction for you and your partner to follow.

You may find it easier to express your sexuality effectively in an earthy and physical fashion, with few words spoken. To be effective, this kind of communication requires natural style and talent; body language is not easily learned, but develops from within. For you, love is best when it comes naturally, with enough time for your talents to unfold, instead of actively creating the learning experience.

Uranus in Gemini (1942–1949)

This position marks those who were born between 1942 and 1949, who approach sexual experimentation in a deliberate and intellectual way. This group introduced "swinging"as a lifestyle, which emphasizes planned sexual experiences rather than those that happen spontaneously. The head leads the heart and body, rather than the other way round.

Not everyone in this age group is a soulless swinger, by any means, but this generation does tend to overintellectualize new sexual experiences, which sometimes stifles the benefits.

On the other hand, this attitude enables many who might otherwise be restricted by oppressive and archaic sexual mores to relate to new partners and techniques. Being able to reduce sexual hangups and inhibitions and accept or reject them rationally is the touchstone of sexual liberation. This generation has been able to let the sexual taboos and repression of generations out of the closet and into the light of day.

Because of the intellectual interest in sexual discovery, people with this placement enjoy all kinds of lighthearted fetishism. Unfortunately, individuals from other age groups simply cannot relate to these head trips.

Uranus in Cancer (1949–1956)

Like many others in this generation, you probably seek to express your love through the stalwart and traditional values of home and family. You tend to be less than adventurous in forming love relationships.

A secure home and family-style love relationship can be very rewarding and enjoyable. But that may not be the most profitable direction for your particular personality. At any rate, you will profit from understanding these motivations. Probably your own self-discoveries result from personal and private experience rather than from larger group situations.

Your growth will be heightened by creating a very special, intimate world for yourself and your partner, protected from other people's thoughts or influences. You may find that sharing your inner feelings with others diffuses them, thus slowing their development.

On the other hand, by keeping your personal life very private, you can take all the credit and rightful pride in the emotional relationships that you develop. Their success or failure will be the major factor in how you develop or change the patterns of your emotional expression.

Uranus in Leo (1956–1962)

You will probably get the most out of a relationship that has plenty of room for growth, one that does not complete its development or define its direction too precisely or too quickly.

Many people in your age group prefer wide-open, ever-changing relationships that cover a lot of emotional territory. This style may or may not suit you personally, but it is important for you to understand it and participate in it to some extent.

This does not mean that you have to continually change your attitude or your partner, but probably you will be happier with an unrestricted, open-ended relationship. The larger the canvas upon which you paint your life, the more rewarding and actively creative your love relationships will be.

Naturally you risk some emotional injury by being so open-handed, but the more scope there is for you and your partner, the warmer and more beautiful the relationship will become. Arranging particular channels of growth in advance tends to be counterproductive; if you allow the relationship to develop naturally, it will eventually bear the fairest flowers and the richest fruit. Your best expression will come from freely nurturing its growth, rather than directing it.

Uranus in Virgo (1962–1969)

Probably you will learn much from trying out a variety of detailed expressions of love. You treasure affection not so much for its principle and motivation but for the actual forms it takes.

Certainly that is the basic orientation of people in your age group, who seem to emphasize the whats and hows of love rather than the whys. This may also be the most rewarding path for you personally, in which case you may comfortably rely on those around you to provide direction in pursuing this path.

But if this direction does not come naturally, don't force yourself to take it. If your love expression differs from that of your peers, do not curb your own inclinations unnaturally. The accepted expressions of love and affection may not have the same meaning for you, so feel free to develop your own.

In order to know what to accept and what to reject, you should become familiar with the contemporary procedures of love and courting. You may find that you can transmit real affection by attending to the special details and mannerisms that particularly please your lover. Pursuing that goal can significantly heighten the intensity and creativity of a relationship.

Uranus in Libra (1969–1974)

You will probably find that personal self-discovery lies in understanding and becoming involved in other people's lives, either directly or indirectly.

That is quite evidently the direction taken by many others of your age, at any rate. In general, relationships tend to be quite volatile and not very private, resulting in less stability than might be desired.

You must decide whether you want to go along with this view of life and how much of yourself will be on view or open for change by others. Your contemporaries are likely to be somewhat active and changeable in love, which may not fit your personality.

But whether or not it does, you should explore and understand this view of life, so that a lover's changeableness or curiosity will not be seen as fickle or prying, necessarily. Conversely, you will find it particularly rewarding to try out various social and sexual roles in relation to your lover. You can gain considerable insight from learning about your partner's personality and motivations in detail.

Indeed, it may be important for your development to understand that an emotional situation can have many facets. Learning to stand aside and see yourself as others see you can be most beneficial.

Uranus in Scorpio (1974–1981)

Direct and sometimes adventurous sexual experiences are probably a key to your emotional and personality development. Indeed, you may take some risks to obtain the clarity and understanding that come with first-hand experience. Admittedly, you can get hurt, both personally and socially, by searching for this knowledge too actively or indiscreetly, but the rewards of the search surely outweigh the perils.

In this respect, you will be encouraged by your peers, many of whom are similarly motivated to explore the sometimes mysterious depths of human sexuality. On the other hand, if you are not personally inclined to take this direction, you may feel that others are pressuring you to try experiences that you do not want or are not ready for. Take the responsibility of knowing your own mind and having control of your heart in order to avoid such difficulties.

In any case, you will learn a great deal through pursuing the deeper currents of your consciousness, particularly in respect to love and personal relationships. If you are willing to honestly confront and explore your inner feelings, no matter what their nature, your social and sexual experiences will be most rewarding.

Uranus in Sagittarius (1981–1988)

You may be able to convert your sexual energy into very active physical expression, particularly when pursuing adventure or a challenging new experience. Similarly, exciting new situations often stimulate your sexual and emotional drives, which may be rather sluggish when things are slow.

Others in your age group are likely to have a particularly simple and romanticized view of love that may or may not fit in with your own. If you share their idealized concept of love, you will be most content with lovers in your own close age range. If your view of love is more complex or realistic, you may be happier with a partner who is either quite a bit older or much younger.

You should understand your generation's attitude toward relationships, even if it differs a bit from your own. There is much beauty in an honest, energetic approach to love, and the qualities of earnestness and ingenuousness are well suited to pure love untainted by baser motivations. If you can sustain a relationship on this level, tremendous fulfillment is possible, but often such success is easier to achieve in a movie script than in real life. However, this general direction is worth the effort; tempered with realism, it can be most rewarding. Certainly this is one of the most sought-after styles of loving.

Uranus in Capricorn (1988–1996)

You will find unusual rewards in pursuing love in the face of adversity. Difficult circumstances may even favor the development of a love affair. For you, love is not something to be given or taken lightly, and once you make a commitment, you defend it, so its value grows proportionately.

Naturally, if your judgment is poor, you may defend a lost cause to the death. You should not let your peers pressure you to hang onto a relationship that you honestly believe has no real future. There is a proper time to abandon a sinking ship, even if you are the captain.

On the other hand, if your partner is in your age group, he or she is likely to be similarly determined, and the two of you will treasure your relationship more if you have spent a lot of effort in ironing out the difficulties.

An easy, unchallenging relationship may be rather boring, but don't trouble calm waters just to keep your interest up. In time, circumstances will provide plenty of challenges. Later you will treasure the quiet times in your relationship. Think of these times as moments when you can enjoy the fruits of your efforts and prepare for further growth ahead.

Uranus in Aquarius (1912–1920 and 1996–2004)

Change may be the essential ingredient for self-discovery in your love relationships. As you look back upon your life, you may realize that you have played many different roles for various reasons, because of circumstances and the need for personal growth at the time.

But you may also find that your peers pressure you to change in areas where you feel it is inappropriate. In that case you should stick to your convictions and avoid the ambiguousness that you may see around you. Change should be made according to what seems right and loving to you, not according to convenience or short-term advantage.

When you do decide to make a change, you are likely to do it cleanly and without hesitation. However, you should always keep the newer roles in context with the old. Don't lose respect for your earlier activities, even though you may now be far from your old self. Anything that develops from sincere effort or belief is worthy and to be treasured, however dated or superfluous it may seem later. What you do is essentially *you*, and that is of constant value. If you downgrade your past, you cripple the impact of your current direction on the future. You would do best to stay on an even course, but one that is characterized by variety and change.

Uranus in Pisces (1920–1928 and 2004–2012)

You are likely to be very loyal to your ideals. Much of your creative ability comes in devising methods of putting your ideals to good use. When you and your lover are entwined in working for a common goal that transcends you both, your relationship is that much richer.

You may derive particular pleasure in delicate, sensitively emotional forms of expression. Some people might consider this sentimental, but you will find a wealth of meaning and communication in it. If your partner is similarly inclined, that will cement the bond between you.

Although you may be quite adaptable in your modes of expression, your peers may expect too much of you in fitting your own convictions to a group cause or project. That is a general characteristic of your age group, so you should understand it and go along when it doesn't interfere with your convictions. When something really counts, however, you should resist any peer pressures to change. Even though your stubbornness will seem externally disadvantageous, it will lead you to considerable internal understanding and growth.

On an emotional and personal level, you will probably learn most by being pliant and adaptable to your lover, for subtlety of communication is paramount in bonding the partnership.

Uranus in the First House

You have a flair for the original and unusual, and through your dress or attitude you often appear rather different from the people around you. Similarly, your approach to the opposite sex is not ordinary, and you can expect that potential partners will consider you something of an enigma.

Your energies may be rather irregular; either you throw all your effort and attention into a relationship, or you neglect it entirely. Although this means that you are capable of great intensity at times, it would be better to make your energy cycle more even to avoid alternately overwhelming and neglecting your lover.

In lovemaking you are often the one who initiates and invents new directions; certainly you will leap at them when presented. But you should avoid pursuing originality for its own sake. Use new techniques primarily to heighten the excitement of love and intensify the resulting communication. It is easy sometimes to become preoccupied with the newness of an idea and to lose perspective of its effectiveness in a relationship.

You will probably leap into and out of relationships quite suddenly and spontaneously. This taste for variety creates stimulating affairs, particularly in the beginning, but be careful not to duck out of an affair too quickly. You might look back and realize that you have lost a good thing forever.

Uranus in the Second House

In a love affair you are quite fond of unusual surroundings and possessions. You value objects of special interest, but once you have enjoyed them, you do not cling to them. Thus you may pass on valuable possessions to a lover quite spontaneously, just because he or she fancies them.

You should find a lover who does not depend on money and possessions for emotional security, for this side of your life is likely to go through many unpredictable ups and downs.

You should be very careful to discuss your values and ethical beliefs with your partner. In this area you may be rather unusual, and you would not want your partner to inadvertently tread on something that is meaningful to you. You may attach a special and unique meaning to something that others consider mundane or unimportant, so you should warn your lover in advance.

In order to keep in good shape for loving, try not to overindulge in special repasts for which you have suddenly acquired a taste. You may enjoy throwing yourself into a new-found pleasure, but that may wear it out too soon. Also it may throw your constitution out of balance.

Uranus in the Third House

You have a very inventive mind, but it proceeds in irregular leaps and spurts. When you try to communicate or explain a problem, your mind may run ahead of your lover's understanding. You should take special care to explain and make sure that your true intentions are not misinterpreted because of haste or incomplete expression.

You probably bring many new and original ideas to your lovemaking, some of which may be so imaginative that they are unworkable. But you can get pleasure just from creating fantasies without having to fulfill each one. You should find a lover who is adventurous enough to help put some of your ideas into action, since you may toss them off without making any effort to realize them.

You will enjoy a partner who can stimulate you intellectually, someone whose mind is quite unique and different from yours, who can show you a fresh new way of looking at the world.

You seek clarity and truth in a relationship and will value a partner who is both scrupulously honest and able to express feelings with precision and insight. A muddy relationship would be frustrating, and in that situation you should follow your immediate impulse to end it.

Uranus in the Fourth House

You are not likely to make your home permanently in one place. Your home is where your heart is, and changing location now and then or even unexpectedly will notupset you. But if your lover needs the security of an unchanging physical place of abode, your sudden moves could be unsettling to the relationship. You should find a partner whose security is internal, as yours is.

Even if you do settle down for a longer period, your home will probably change in nature or decor and not be average in taste or construction. Your partner should be open to your changes and let you express your inspiration and creativity freely, however unusual it may seem to others.

You will be happiest when living with your lover, because an intimate relationship can be a major source of inspiration and learning in all aspects of your existence.

You must resist the temptation to suddenly end an affair when it does not seem to be going well. Creativity in a relationship often comes in leaps and spurts, and some resting time is necessary for future growth.

Uranus in the Fifth House

You are quite inventive and spontaneous in lovemaking and will be most compatible with an enthusiastic lover who is willing to try out new methods of enjoyment at any time. Your inventiveness may come and go, however, so your lover should not expect you to always be a source of amusement, but rather should be ready when the inspiration strikes.

You may have a taste for more unusual forms of love, and you should not let an outmoded morality or a prudish partner hold you back from new experiences. Do consider, however, that your lover may simply be less interested in variations and not be as enthusiastic as you would like. Be sure to maintain a basic foundation of love communication so that affection does not get lost in complexities of technique.

You appreciate physical beauty as much as anyone, but a lover's special emotional vibrations may be just as important as looks. When a lover creates a unique excitement that touches your own inventiveness, the main requirement for a relationship is met, especially for physical expression.

Uranus in the Sixth House

You are most creative in teaching and in learning the arts of love and in devising particularly enjoyable methods of pleasing your lover. You need a partner who can return the favor and can learn some subtle techniques for pleasing you.

Your specific tastes may change quite sharply and suddenly from time to time, so you need a lover who is sensitive enough to follow along quickly. Do not hesitate to express your needs verbally, for that will make your mutual adjustment much easier.

In spite of changes in your sexual needs or approach, your external life should not reflect the vicissitudes of the bedroom. Often you may be playing quite different roles in the different areas of your life. If you can keep the roles separate, this duality will lead to greater growth and personal understanding for both you and your partner.

Your view of physical sexuality is quite realistic and not overly intellectual. You gravitate toward fantasy fulfillment that has a real physical basis in pleasure, not drifting off to more abstract eroticism that appeals primarily to the imagination.

Uranus in the Seventh House

You may have a certain talent for choosing unusual partners, at least ones who are quite different from yourself. For you a partner is a source of discovery and learning in all areas of your life. Only a person who can help extend your emotional frontiers will provide the richness and variety you seek.

In your search for these qualities, you may find that a love affair begins quickly and enthusiastically and then ends just as suddenly when you have taken all that it has to offer. Or, you may become involved in off-and-on relationships, either because of changing emotions or because of external factors such as finances or location. At any rate, your partnerships tend to be quite uneven and unpredictable, although not necessarily unrewarding.

It is wise, however, to think twice before abruptly ending a relationship that does not seem to be giving immediate satisfaction; it may just be in a dormant period. By acting hastily you might lose a very rewarding relationship.

You should look for a directly expressive lover who, although perhaps not particularly verbal, is very clear and honest about your relationship. As long as you are on firm ground together, you can work out your differences, but if there are barriers between you, the relationship may fall apart because it is no longer creative for both of you.

Uranus in the Eighth House

You tend to be strongly attracted physically to a lover and to have affairs that take you by storm. Very possibly, they will also take you into waters over your head. These affairs have a certain fated quality, and you feel almost powerless to stop them.

You may derive greater long-term satisfaction in a more easygoing relationship, but a whirlwind affair can be a special source of knowledge and sexual self-understanding, teaching you about needs and desires that you may have been unaware of.

Even in a slower and steadier affair, however, you are the prime mover in bringing to light problems or hidden motivations between you and your partner, often through experience and insight gained in earlier, briefer affairs.

Exercising this ability can be quite important in a relationship, as your own sexual interest in your partner may pivot quite directly on actively positive emotional relations. If things are not going well, you may swiftly lose any desire for your lover. Therefore, the two of you should probe your problems with dispatch and solve them before they become too ingrained. Otherwise the physical side of the relationship may go sour.

Also any illness or health problems may have unhappy emotional repercussions, which will vanish when the illness clears up.

Uranus in the Ninth House

You probably learn the most from relationships that are free and on the move, without too many ties holding you down. This does not mean that you should limit yourself to brief or shallow love affairs, but you will be most comfortable with a partner who does not try to tie you down or keep you from choosing your own direction.

Physically and emotionally, you get special enjoyment from not staying put but continually exploring new territory and finding new ways to express love and sexuality. Indeed, simply moving to a new place now and then will help considerably to keep your love fresh and original.

You may often be the initiator of both physical and emotional changes. Take special care to see that your lover has time to adapt, however. If the changes are too sudden, communication between you might be lost. Although you need someone who is not too conservative or incapable of change, your lover may not share your talent for periodically reshaping an affair. He or she may need to be gently led by the hand instead of being catapulted into it by your enthusiasm in a new discovery. Here, timing is everything, so make your changes gradually, so that you and your partner remain in step at all times.

Uranus in the Tenth House

You may acquire a reputation for being rather original in all areas of life, including lovemaking, even if you don't feel that you actually merit it. It is not that you are interested only in the new or unusual aspects of a subject but that others pick up on it when you do touch on something new.

Thus, you may discover or invent ideas and concepts in love that others subsequently adopt. This may give you quite a reputation and perhaps make you seem more of a trend setter than you really are, since your discoveries seem to happen by chance rather than choice. You have a talent for stumbling on enjoyable pursuits or techniques before other people discover them.

For this reason, you should find a lover who is fairly adventurous and will happily follow you into your chosen realm of exploration. What seems like creativity in loving to you may be a great adventure to your partner, so you don't want someone who lags back or cramps your style.

To some people, you may seem like a demanding partner, for you usually settle for nothing but the best. Excellence in loving will be paramount to you and your partner, and in order for a relationship to be fulfilling and long-lasting, it must have a high degree of creativity, both emotionally and sexually.

Uranus in the Eleventh House

Whatever your own inclinations toward sexual experimentation, with this position the actual suggestion or opportunity will probably come from your lover. Thus when the two of you are trying out some far-out variation in bed, you should consult with your lover about your next move. In that way you will be certain that you agree, and you can discover the most promising possibilities together. If you want to have more control of the sexual direction, you can offer a series of possible directions, allowing your partner to choose the one to follow.

You should find plenty of opportunities and partners who would like to share your experiments; it is only your willingness to pursue these opportunities that will determine whether your sex life is as broad and interesting as it could be. With an understanding lover, you can try anything once, as long as it is not physically harmful. If you don't seize the opportunity, it may be gone forever, leaving you with unfulfilled fantasies. This position lends itself to sexual experimentation guided, in general, by your partner.

Uranus in the Twelfth House

You have a strong talent and inclination for making sudden leaps into the unknown, and you may try out something new on the spur of the moment without investigating it beforehand.

Although this habit will lead you into many interesting and rewarding paths of sexual exploration, it can also get you into situations that are not as pleasant as you had anticipated. Before committing yourself, you should gather as much information as you can, so that you won't run into unanticipated difficulties.

You enjoy ferreting out little-known or hidden motivations and drives in sexuality, which you should feel free to uncover, explore and enjoy. You will be most comfortable with a lover who is similarly inclined, someone who takes pleasure in confronting long-repressed and perhaps disapproved feelings. There is nothing like the light of understanding to chase away the demons of sexual disapprobation.

It may be that these discoveries will remain hidden from the world, that they will be known and enjoyed only by your lover and yourself, retaining a certain secrecy and mystery. At times this may be for the best because your discoveries are usually sudden rather than systematic. It is just as well not to tie down your revelations with too many external ties. Verbalizing them may detract from their spontaneity.

Uranus Conjunct Neptune (1993)

On the one hand, you may be inclined to dive headlong into sexuality, raising it to an almost spiritual ideal and transforming you in union with your lover. On the other hand, you may become so involved with nonsexual spiritual goals that sexuality takes a back seat in your life.

The direction you choose will be largely determined by your basic attitude toward your body. If you consider it a special gift whose energies you can use to better achieve spiritual understanding, then you will steep yourself in physical pleasures in order to achieve universal discovery. In that case you need a lover who is committed to the same goals and is closely in tune with you. Without such a partner, this goal of higher understanding through sexual expression will be largely unattainable, because both partners' energies are required for success.

If, on the other hand, you reject the physical path to deeper universal understanding, you may achieve a great deal, either on your own or with others who need not be so perfectly in tune with you. But if you make that choice, you must cut yourself off from the pleasures of the flesh, which otherwise will impede you.

Neither of these two paths to spirituality is easy, but you don't have to pursue either one to its most extreme conclusion. You can go just as far as you want in either direction.

Uranus Sextile Neptune (1966–1968)

Your fantasy world may be a source of great discovery and insight for you. The more you explore it, the more you will learn about yourself and the human psyche in general.

Essentially, you can pursue your fantasies as far as you want without risk of real psychological or emotional damage. The forces that you uncover will not usually be troublesome; in fact, they will probably be inspirational and revealing.

Remember, however, that this may not be true for partners who are much younger than you. Internal sexual revelations may be much more troublesome and difficult for them to handle. Therefore, in choosing a lover with whom to explore your inner sexuality, pick someone who is close to your own age or older, for he or she will be better suited to accompany you successfully on your inward journeys.

This is not to say that all your sexual realizations will be sweetness and light, for bringing them to light may require some struggle and understanding, and they may not be entirely pleasurable. But probably you will not encounter anything that you can't handle or that would cause sexual problems, as might happen with someone much younger.

Uranus Square Neptune (1953–1956)

Externalizing sexuality in a healthy way may be the best way for you to derive pleasure and self-understanding in this area. The more direct, open and uncomplicated you can make your sexual expression, the more enjoyable it will be.

Although this does not entirely shut out realizing your fantasies, you may tend to get lost in the intricacies of your sexual dream world and lose touch with the more enjoyable here and now. This can be a particular problem if excessive fantasizing causes you to feel uncertain about your sexual identity, contributing to sexual problems or feelings of insecurity.

The problem, in part, is that you identify so closely with a fantasy-created role that it becomes entwined with daily reality, and as a result the two worlds interfere with each other. Successful fantasy role-playing requires that you define and separate fact and fantasy, which may be difficult for you to do. This is not to say that you shouldn't work out your fantasies, because that can be a most enjoyable pastime, but don't do it to excess. If you carefully define what you are doing, you can learn from the experience by contrasting it with reality. Otherwise, if reality and fantasy are too closely paired, the result is turmoil and confusion instead of the desired self-understanding and inner knowledge.

Uranus Trine Neptune (1939–1943)

Your most important and stimulating sexual experiences will come from living out your sexual fantasies. The more successfully you can do that, the more sexual pleasure you will obtain. You have a wealth of pleasure potential inside your mind, and you should not hesitate to let it become reality for a while.

This does not mean, of course, that you should run your life according to your sexual fantasies, but that you should try to make them come true within the confines of the bedroom, separate from the realities of everyday life. In so doing you will gain more than immediate pleasure. By contemplating the meanings of the sexual roles you choose, you will understand what motivates you in many areas and also gain more insight into what makes people act as they do, particularly when motivated by sexuality. Indeed, your discoveries may radically rearrange, for the better, your view of life as a whole.

In choosing a partner with whom to share all this, you should find someone who is your age or older, because younger people do not benefit so much from this method of sexual exploration. An older partner, on the other hand, may pursue it even more energetically than you do.

Uranus Inconjunct Neptune (1893–1896 and 1924–1927)

When you deal with implementing your sexual fantasies or ideals in reality, you may find that you have let a maddening, if enjoyable, cat out of the bag. When you and your lover live out a fantasy in the bedroom, instead of being a simple pleasure, each time it uncovers a wealth of new ideas that you hadn't been aware of before. Each new possibility just begs for similar exploration.

This kind of sexual chain reaction can be quite exhausting if you are too eager to follow up every lead to pleasure and self-understanding that is offered. Instead, it may be profitable to categorize the material you come up with and then approach it systematically. This will save you endless time and confusion in running from one element to the next and will allow you to experience and understand the feelings of each category without having to live out everything your fertile imagination comes up with. This approach will also give you a good overview of human sexuality, for that is the approach used by sex researchers today.

Each of us must do our own research to achieve real personal understanding, and the more clearly it can be done, the deeper that understanding will be.

Uranus Opposition Neptune (1906–1910)

Your ideal fantasized sexual situations may not match up with the concrete realities of sexual expression as much as you would like them to. All too often you must learn to appreciate the dream for its own sake and then enjoy reality as it comes.

This happens for two reasons. First, when your fantasy world was created, during your formative years, sex was not talked about and was dealt with only in fairy-tale fantasy fashion. Thus, you are imbued with images that are impossible to realize in the concrete world of sexual expression. Probably you can live out these fantasies only vicariously, through movies or novels.

Second, when you create new sexual ideals based on your intellectual feelings, you are in a constant battle with the old feelings and inhibitions that were instilled in everyone of your age. That conflict makes the emotional transition to better sexual habits quite difficult. However, if you have enough determination to change and see your principles enacted in reality, you can eventually attain the sexual status described by your own beliefs. It will not come easily or quickly, but few goals that are really worthwhile and satisfying ever do.

Uranus Conjunct Pluto (1965)

Deep inner sexual discovery may not come to you easily or often, but when it does occur, it comes all at once in an overwhelming flood. In fact, all your inner subconscious forces tend to be like that, so that you suddenly burst forth with an extreme expression of joy, anger, ecstasy or sorrow.

It is a good idea to find a way to channel these forces and express them more gradually and regularly. One way to do this is by regularly choosing an area of sexuality that causes you some anxiety and confronting your partner with it, thus releasing the pressure that would otherwise build to the bursting point. This can be a very effective way to defuse fears and blockages that start small but may grow out of all proportion to their real importance if neglected.

Doing this will not change your basic style, which is one of rather sudden and explosive inner discovery. But it will take away the negative charge, so that your flashes of insight can bring on positive leaps of growth rather than turning to anger or grief and thereby destroying what you already have. It is easy for you to sweep problems under the rug, where you think they will remain forever, but you are courting disaster if you do so. It is far more profitable to face your problems and find solutions to them.

Uranus Sextile Pluto (1943–1945 and 1994–1996)

You have a talent for effectively digging deep into your subconscious in search of inner discoveries. You are able to do this in such a way that you do not risk emotional injury caused by uprooting long-buried problems.

Thus you can confront even the most mysterious inner taboos in sexuality without fear or worry. In fact, doing so will bring you a wealth of inner knowledge that will enhance your sexual enjoyment through a better understanding of the fundamental motives and drives behind sexual pleasure.

These primitive drives in themselves, unmasked by complex fantasies, can be a source of direct pleasure and wonderment for you if you take the time to explore them. Most of the rituals and intricacies of lovemaking are derived from the most basic but hidden drives of procreation, power and territory. When you understand these drives better, they will greatly enhance your ability to use the details of love more effectively, because you understand their source.

This kind of exploration may sound like a lifetime of work, and it is, but you don't need to wait until the project is over to reap its rewards. Every day that you are engaged in it you will derive increasing benefits in heightened sexual pleasure and understanding.

Uranus Square Pluto (1932–1934)

You will find that fundamental changes in a love relationship do not come easily but are accompanied by considerable upheaval and difficulty for both you and your partner. For you, transformation is a process of destruction and rebuilding, rather than growth.

You do not usually fade slowly and gracefully out of one relationship and into the next, at least if the two affairs are significantly different. Instead, as the first relationship becomes less satisfying, it becomes more of a battleground, until it is finally wrecked by the strife and abandoned. Then you take up the next relationship joyfully, because of the new world ahead and the release from past emotional pain.

This kind of transformation can occur in a relationship without changing partners, if the basic commitment is sufficiently strong or if finances or social pressure prevent you from separating. In that case you will go through a period of great strife that destroys the original fundamental assumptions of the relationship. Then you and your partner can pick up the pieces and start over, with a new understanding of each other.

Uranus Trine Pluto (1921–1923)

You have a basic natural understanding of your inner drives and motives, which you use unconsciously to make yourself more attractive to and successful with potential lovers and partners.

This does not mean that you spend a great deal of time in deep inner exploration, for you don't need to do that. You are in contact with your inner self enough that you do not need to go through a painful process of digging to find out what is causing your problems. Instead, you use your natural self-understanding in more external ways for your own and other people's benefit.

You may never become a very deep thinker in a verbal way, because you intuitively understand what such a person goes to great lengths to find out. When you need inner support, you can call on that deep understanding.

However, you should be tolerant of those who are less fortunate, especially those who are younger, for whom inner change and development come more tumultuously and less gracefully. You may go through periods of strife within a relationship, but never at a basically painful level, which you should be thankful for.

Uranus Inconjunct Pluto (1892–1894 and 1911–1912)

Your life may be a series of basic changes in direction and attitude as the direct result of your inner discoveries. Certainly you will go through at least one change so great that on looking back you will hardly recognize your earlier self.

This change may cause you to move to a different place or take up an entirely new career. Circumstance alone will not force this; rather, deeper inner motivations will trigger this transformation, almost as if you were trying to live more than one life in your allotted span of years.

This kind of change may happen on the sexual level as well, which may mean changing from one deep relationship to another or at least radically rearranging the relationship that you already have. Again, you may look back on your former self and wonder how you could have been that person, but be sure to avoid self-recrimination. Sexual attitudes are strictly relative, and you are probably no better or worse off now than you were before, only different and hopefully happier.

In any case, you will probably have a more varied and interesting life than most people, if perhaps not the most peaceful.

Uranus Opposition Pluto (1901–1902)

You may see a pattern in your life of considerable effort over a long time with few results and then sudden reward when you had almost given up hope of success.

This pattern, which can show up internally as well, may be a good argument for staying with a good partner even if the relationship is not going well because of the prospect of future transformation. That does not mean that you should remain in a miserable marriage in hopes of sudden deliverance, but if the relationship is basically sound, it is worth pursuing. In the long run, needed improvements may happen all at once.

This also applies to your own inner problems and sexual blocks, which may not respond to pressure or efforts to solve them for long periods of time, so that they seem much deeper and more mysterious than they really are. But with time and regular attention, they will vanish one day, almost as if they had never existed, and you will feel like a new person, both emotionally and sexually.

Uranus Conjunct Ascendant

Although you may not see yourself this way, other people consider you very unusual. Your approach to a potential partner is out of the ordinary, which you can use to great advantage if you are aware of it.

In order to use this talent effectively, you should definitely avoid staid establishment types who may be put off by your originality. If you can find a crowd that appreciates a fresh approach, you will always be in the vanguard.

Some people may feel that you have a rather curt or brusque approach, so you might consciously soften that effect so that you appear refreshingly new but not harsh. You simply want to get right to the heart of the matter, but in social situations that is not always the best strategy.

Once involved with a lover, you prove equally original in your style and approach to loving. Probably you are willing to try anything that promises mutual pleasure, even when others would be inhibited by something so unusual. You are more concerned with the end, which is pleasure, than the means, so there is a much broader range of enjoyment open to you. Ideally, your lover should be someone who does not curtail your flights of fancy but who can offer some stability if you go to extremes.

Uranus Sextile Ascendant

You have a very original mind, which you can use to dream up creative and sometimes unusual methods of sexual enjoyment. You may not have had an opportunity to utilize this talent, but when you do, don't let it go to waste.

In addition, you have a good sense of judgment, which many people lack, concerning which of your fantasies are practical and which should remain in fantasyland. Thus, in a relationship you can continually refresh the styles and techniques of sexual expression that you and your partner enjoy without causing new ideas to seem forced or inappropriate. A new idea, instead of being an end in itself that distracts you from the true expression of affection, is a means to enhance the basic communication of loving.

Your environment will encourage this way of thinking to a certain extent, because you are likely to move in a circle of friends who also lean toward the creative and original.

You can learn much from these people. The lovers you meet are likely to be similar in this respect and will easily move along with your changing styles of sexual expression. Certainly you do not want a partner who clings too closely to the old, for you tend to leave that behind, and you do not want to hurt a more cautious lover in the process.

Uranus Square Ascendant

You should spend some time and thought in making your social style smoother and sweeter, even though you sometimes find that approach stifling. In the long run, you will be better off if you are less outspoken about your feelings, even though you do this out of concern for the truth. Often what you say to a lover may seem clear and necessary at the time, but your words may cause emotional harm unintentionally, which you will regret later, possibly because you have lost the friendship.

Similarly, in a sexual situation, you may enjoy expressing your great talent for originality, but you should rely on your lover's judgment about how far you can go before experimentation gets in the way of communication. Once involved in an experimental situation, you may go to extremes without thinking, which can kill the kind of pleasure that comes with a more even and sustained type of loving.

Although you yourself can do much to consciously control this tendency, a stable partner whom you can trust will be of great value in pointing out where you tend to go overboard. Particularly while you are young, such a partner will have a tempering influence on you. In time you will become much more self-aware and mellow.

Uranus Trine Ascendant

You have a talent for making a seemingly unusual or even worrisome form of sexual expression seem like the most natural, pleasant pastime in the world. This is a truly remarkable gift that can lead you and your partner to some truly unique experiences.

Instead of intellectually planning such situations ahead of time, you seem to just fall into them spontaneously. You can feel quite safe in trying out anything that seems workable and promises real enjoyment for both you and your lover—it will probably work out very well.

Of course, for this you need a lover who is relatively free from inhibition, who will not cramp your style or be upset by your modes of expression. You are quite capable of handling a partner whose ideas are as unusual as yours but less practical. You can temper those wild ideas and save the situation when things go wrong.

Your love life will probably be in continual motion, not because you have many different partners but because your flow of creativity is so consistent. You seldom repeat the old, and you are always uncovering some new source of pleasure.

Uranus Inconjunct Ascendant

You may tend to be physically restless in a way that encourages continual changes in your physical mode of sexual expression. Because of this, you will probably have a wide variety of sexual experiences, which can be positive or negative, depending on how compulsive you are and how much time you take to pursue each one to its fullest.

Your first impulse may be to get in and out of a situation as quickly as possible, for the urge to move on to another experience is kindled almost before the first one is over. This does not necessarily mean that you will move from lover to lover, although that may happen, but you may move quickly from one sexual technique or emotional mood to another.

If this style is not modified, it may deprive you of much depth of sexual expression. It is better to stay with one method long enough to get the most pleasure from it and establish good communication with your lover. In a word, relax and settle down a bit. There is plenty of time in life to enjoy everything you can dream up, if you take one thing at a time and in depth. The result will be the richest possible variety of sexual experience, as well as the most meaningful.

Uranus Opposition Ascendant

You may be particularly attracted to partners who are somewhat unusual, either physically or intellectually. Thus you may find yourself in a relationship with a lover who is quite different from you in stature, attitude, social upbringing or behavior.

Learning to share intimately with someone who is very original can provide a particularly enjoyable and broadening experience; indeed, your partner may serve as a real source of learning and inspiration. To a certain extent, this unusual quality will rub off on you as well as on your other friends, who will enjoy the company of you both.

However, your partnerships may form and dissolve rather swiftly, so you should not be overly possessive nor become involved with someone who is very possessive. If you do, you will both suffer emotionally in the long run.

Your usual reason for splitting up suddenly is that you discover that you have nothing left to learn from your lover and that the relationship is no longer causing creative changes. When you do settle down with one person, it will be because you have found someone who changes as much as you do, so that you can keep the process going indefinitely.

Chapter Thirteen

Neptune in the Chart

The position of Neptune reflects your inner ideals and expectations of sexuality. These can be either confining or fulfilling, depending on the aspects involved and your willingness to deal with these matters.

The greatest problem that Neptune brings, especially when it is in difficult aspect, is that of expectations that are so high and unrealistic that they cannot be fulfilled, thus leading to disappointment. In easy aspect, however, Neptune indicates strong personal reinforcement and security through continuing success and achievement, which can lend much to a happy love relationship.

You share the sign that Neptune is in with everyone in your age group, since Neptune remains in a sign for almost fourteen years. The sign represents the ideals and romantic ideas about love that are held by your generation. Those ideals may not be totally realistic, however, and they apply differently to each individual. Each person must come to an understanding of how much of the generational sexual mythology is acceptable and workable and how much is unrealistic or overdemanding. In the long run these tendencies are regulated by experience more than by conscious effort.

Neptune in Aries

This placement will not occur in this century.

Neptune in Taurus (1874–1889)

Your age group has a long-range desire for love that is solid and concrete. As part of that group, you share this inclination to some extent.

This means that however much you may appreciate a partner who expresses love very verbally, you will place the most value on tangible deeds as evidence of affection.

This does not mean that you need physical goods or possessions for the sake of security, although that may enter into it. Instead you have a basic need for more physical expressions in love and for the emotional commitment that is thus reflected.

Although beauty of expression is an enriching aspect of a relationship, you need more than that for a really meaningful, long-range affair. Your mutual love is based on

313

gut-level bodily communication and expression rather than on intellectual considerations. You give and receive love through physical attention and commitment, and if that is lacking in a relationship, you may be somewhat insecure. This will happen even if such forms of communication are not focal to your personal approach.

Neptune in Gemini (1889–1902)

Your age group has a special talent and inclination for verbalizing emotional issues and problems in order to better understand them. Regardless of your own verbal abilities, this generational characteristic means that the clear expression of ideas is an essential part of a fulfilling love relationship for you.

But remember that words are not everything; much of the communication in a love affair is nonverbal, and its exact nature may never be pinned down. Verbally crystallizing the emotional state of an affair may be counterproductive and may even result in stagnation if each partner feels obligated to play only the role that has been defined.

Nevertheless, you will be happier in a relationship if you can get a fairly clear idea of its nature and extent so that you can define it verbally. This may be very important if there are physical or financial commitments that you have to depend upon for security at a later date.

Words have considerable power, and you may find that verbal expression somehow makes the relationship more concrete and gives it an added dimension of reality.

Neptune in Cancer (1902–1916)

People in your age group have a great fondness for home and family. The ideal relationship for your generation includes a snug, secure little cottage, surrounded by children and even grandchildren.

Depending upon your own personality, this ideal may or may not appeal to you. However, it will certainly affect your subconscious evaluation of your success in love in comparison to the relationships of friends and acquaintances.

If you are interested in physical security, this generational attitude will cause you to value emotional conformity to some extent. You will fit yourself into a more or less standard family mold, which can provide great satisfaction as long as the mold remains intact.

But if you are independent or a lone wolf in emotional matters, you will probably disdain your peers' security-oriented fearfulness, for your own strength is internal. However, those around you will always feel some disapprobation or even pity for you, believing that you are missing out on something, even though that is not the case.

At any rate, you probably won't escape the home and family orientation to which you have been exposed. Of necessity it will always be a factor in your emotional self-judgment, for better or for worse, depending on how you handle it.

Neptune in Leo (1916–1929)

Your age group tends to look at love quite sportively and to idealize the fun-loving couples who always have good times together.

As a result you will subconsciously judge your own success in love by this standard, which may or may not be beneficial. If lighthearted love is your natural style, then you will feel quite accomplished and on the right track in your relationships.

But if you are more serious and intense about relationships, you may regard your peers as overly foolish in love. Or, because you aren't a "good-times" person, you may judge yourself to be somehow lacking as a lover.

Of course, neither extreme is the right one; a succcessful relationship depends on creatively expressing the personal styles of both partners, whether or not they resemble society's norm. Naturally, it is easier to follow an external pattern, but that is not always the wisest course. It can lead you to alter your own inner positive potential.

In any case, your ability to handle this generational attitude will be increased if you are aware of it. Then you will know when you are judging yourself by your own standards and when you are going by others' guidelines.

Neptune in Virgo (1929–1943)

People in your age group are quite particular about what they demand of a partner and a relationship. They tend to search endlessly for the "perfect match" instead of growing and changing within a relationship.

This has resulted in a rather high divorce rate because couples find that they can't fit the mold of a perfect match without significant personal change. Thus, you might do well to avoid this generational attitude, although it is necessarily an ingrained part of your upbringing.

Thus, you may feel impatient if a relationship does not seem to be working out, or if it seems that you will have to reshape your own personality to make it viable. Few marriages are made in heaven, however, and mutual change and growth are necessary in almost every relationship. Expecting your partner to fit you exactly, or vice-versa, is a folly that is encouraged by movies and romantic novels. Often it is hard to completely get away from that attitude. You tend to feel that somehow, it's just not right if the relationship doesn't go smoothly all the time. "Perhaps we really weren't meant for each other," is the feeling that surfaces, even though that may not be the case at all.

However, understanding this prejudice that is part of your upbringing is half the battle in overcoming it.

Neptune in Libra (1943–1957)

This position marks the generation of men and women who founded the current struggle for sexual equality. For the first time, a woman's enjoyment of sex has become as important as a man's to both partners. This change in attitude has resulted in a host of joys and complications.

This generation is primarily concerned that both partners understand each other's feelings. Sex should be more than just a chore and obligation for the woman and more then an insular act of self-pleasuring for the man. This means that sex cannot be truly pleasing or successful for either partner unless it is satisfying for both, which is the triumph of liberated sexuality.

However, when the desire for equality and mutuality is carried too far, it can present problems. This is exemplified by pursuit of the myth of mandatory simultaneous orgasm. Equality does not come from each partner giving the other exactly matched doses of pleasure, but from each one reaching sexual fulfillment in the manner that he or she finds most enjoyable, according to personality and physical preferences. This is a much harder bill to fill, for it requires each partner to be intimately aware of just what pleases the other and to do the utmost to achieve it without neglecting self-pleasure in the process.

But this goal is worth every minute of learning and caring, for with Neptune in this position, it is the only path to real satisfaction.

Neptune in Scorpio (1957–1970)

Your age group puts a premium on sexuality in love relationships, and that attitude is bound to affect you, whatever your personal feelings may be. The previous generation had a more easygoing and freewheeling attitude toward sex, but your generation's do-or-die attitude toward sex does not lend itself to relaxed relationships.

If total intensity in love is your style, you may feel quite at home with this trend. However, if it is not, you will encounter much peer pressure, often unspoken, to throw yourself head-over-heels into stormy and tumultuous affairs just to make love seem real and significant.

Indeed, if your relationships seem quietly amicable and not stressful, you may subconsciously feel that something is missing. This is not necessarily the case, depending upon your personal style, and too much intensity may actually wreck a relationship for you. You should follow your own inner guidelines, separating them carefully from the attitudes toward love and sex that surround you. In the end, it is you and you alone who can make love work.

Neptune in Sagittarius (1970–1984)

You have grown up in an age group that has fairly uncomplicated, simplistic ideas about love and sexuality. But these ideas may not apply to you personally if you are involved in a very complex or subtle relationship. Love cannot always be approached directly and straightforwardly, but you may subconsciously feel that something is amiss in an affair that gets too tricky or involved. The problem is that it does not fulfill the relationship ideal that you have grown up with.

Thus, you should think quite carefully about your peers' idea of a good relationship and then decide whether that suits your personal style. If it does not suit you, reject it; otherwise you will be striving to achieve what is impossible for yourself.

However, you may be very much in tune with the feeling of those around you in this respect. The straightforward notion of enthusiastic and exciting romantic love may be rewarding and uplifting to your relationships. In that case you should find a partner of like views rather than someone who will slow you down with too many extraneous details or causes for self-doubt.

Either way, you should carefully compare your own style and expectations in love with those of your peer group before judging your own relationships.

Neptune in Capricorn (1984–1998)

In general, your contemporaries have a rather negative view of love and personal involvement, a certain expectation that disappointment and loss are necessarily involved in any commitment.

Naturally, that does not have to be the case, but it is certainly more likely if you go into an affair with a defeatist attitude. Love can certainly restrict your personal freedom in certain respects, particularly a permanent relationship. However, that restriction should be taken on joyfully and willingly, not as a sacrifice that will be regretted later.

You may find that your attitude toward love is quite different from this negative approach. In that case, you should follow your own direction and take on love without hesitation or worry that it will somehow turn out badly. However the affair proceeds, it does not happen because of the nature of love itself but because of the problems and joys you and your lover develop on your own.

You should thoroughly investigate your peers' preconceptions about love and sex, for they will certainly color and perhaps distort your own attitude. If you understand this, you can be true to yourself and can develop relationships in your own way, unhindered by others' prejudices.

Neptune in Aquarius (early twenty-first century)

This placement is beyond the scope of this book.

Neptune in Pisces (well into the twenty-first century)

This placement is beyond the scope of this book.

Neptune in the First House

You have a rather dreamy, intangible quality, which will certainly add to your romantic appeal. However, it may also tend to confuse the situation if you try to define a relationship too carefully.

Therefore, you will be most comfortable with a lover who does not try to pin you down too much or force you into a permanent commitment with little room for change or creativity. Love is quite tenuous and changeable for you. If your partner tries to trap it in a specimen jar for close inspection, your love is likely to flee altogether.

Do not let these feelings prevent you from forming a solid relationshp in which you and your partner can depend on each other. A durable relationship that will not founder in mutual misunderstanding requires a certain amount of definition.

It is particularly important to express your true feelings clearly to each other. Your partner may see you in the light of his or her imagination rather than as you really are. This idealistic attitude can result in working at cross purposes and perhaps unintentional neglect of your real needs. Therefore, make sure that your lover is aware of who you are and what you want. That will dispel the clouds of mystery that have gathered.

Neptune in the Second House

Your idealistic values may sometimes come into conflict with physical reality or necessity in a love relationship. This may be a problem especially if money is an issue, for you want love to remain pure and untainted by financial considerations.

Physical and financial stability, however, can be very important in maintaining a relationship on the emotional level, particularly if there are other problems as well. Therefore, one partner should have a good grip on financial management. If you are not the person to do that, entrust the responsibility to your lover and then go along with his or her provisions. Although this may make you feel somewhat helpless, it will free you to spend more time perfecting the emotional side of the relationship. You will then be able to work on making the affair fulfill your high standards. Indeed, you can attain your emotional standards with ease and satisfaction, so that is the most profitable area to attend to.

If you have to become involved with the financial side of the relationship, think of it as a necessary evil, but don't let it influence your emotional life.

Neptune in the Third House

You put a great deal of emphasis on understanding love intellectually, even to the point of overlooking the noncerebral aspects. As a result, you may take a lover who talks knowingly about love but is somewhat disappointing when it comes to physically realizing it. In fact, because of the nature of love, with this placement you are not likely to find any concrete answers, although you will expend many words in the attempt.

This intellectual approach may be a problem if you try to explain why a specific form of sex is arousing, particularly if it is an unusual form. It is far better simply to accept the fact that it is enjoyable; if you debate it at length, you are likely to kill the enjoyment.

The best way to handle this inclination is to simply experience love without question in a sexual situation, and then intellectually explore the details. The subject of sex lends itself to all kinds of fascinating discussions, but preferably after the fact.

Neptune in the Fourth House

You tend to look at your childhood through rose-colored glasses, and you may pattern your love affairs after your parents' relationship.

Ideally, this attitude can give you a very stable foundation upon which to build. On the other hand, if your parents' relationship was less than ideal, you may just repeat their mistakes. Also, you will probably have conflicts with your lover, who may want to play quite a different role because of a different upbringing.

You should think very carefully about your childhood home life and decide just how much of it really applies to your adult relationships. Such retrospective sorting-out will help you understand your motives in an affair so that you can change any negative traits that you were previously unaware of.

While you reflect your own upbringing, you also place great value on maintaining your own well-run home environment. In that area you will do your utmost to fulfill your high standards. To a large extent, your understanding of your own foundations will determine your ability to fulfill these expectations, both for yourself and your partner.

Neptune in the Fifth House

You may have high expectations of love, and your sexual encounters may not always give you as much as you want. For this reason, you would be happiest with a physically expressive lover who can turn lovemaking into a true art form. At the same time your lovemaking should retain an innocent, childlike quality, for the jaded world of the swinger is definitely not for you. Although you want your lover to have a good deal of experience and technique, these are not ends in themselves but rather tools to express physical love in a more refined form.

You should learn to look at sex with some humor as well, for the details of physical love sometimes get fouled up. When that happens, you might as well enjoy it and not worry about your romanticized ideals. Taking sex too seriously is a problem if your plans go slightly awry, and being able to laugh at yourself can defuse a situation that would otherwise be frustrating or disappointing. Then you can turn it to your advantage and mutual pleasure.

You will develop a romantic style of loving that transcends the physical and allows you to express sexuality at a highly developed emotional and spiritual level, which will elevate your partner and yourself.

Neptune in the Sixth House

You may find that concentrating on sexual technique is less than rewarding because it tends to separate you from the emotional fulfillment that you seek. That reaction is quite natural and should not be a source of worry. Although successful lovemaking requires some skill, the emotional communication between you and your partner is more important. If you leave the technical direction of love to your partner, your own feelings may flow more easily.

Your lover should be someone who does not insist on elaborate lovemaking, who can integrate his or her own skills without interfering with the ease and intensity of your affection. You can help by being very understanding of your lover's technique and tolerant of any foibles.

You will probably gravitate toward a warm, devoted relationship in which both of you go out of your way to see that the other is happy. This is a very enjoyable style of loving as long as it is not one-sided. At any rate, you will find great reward in the care and feeding of your lover, and the more ways you both find to do this, the richer your love life will become.

Neptune in the Seventh House

You tend to idealize your lover, which makes you an ideal partner in the classically romantic fashion. A strong and satisfying partnership is very important to you, and your standards of what is desirable in an affair are rather high.

To a certain extent, you should modify your expectations with patience and understanding, for no lover can measure up to your standards in every category, no matter how hard he or she tries. If you expect too much, you will be disappointed and may even break off a relationship that could become very rewarding.

The fact is, nobody's perfect. But you can find more reward in gently changing a lover to fit your desires than in making love an all-or-nothing proposal. Indeed, in time your needs will change to more closely fit your partner's abilities. With that kind of give and take, the relationship will grow increasingly more ideal.

Your love relationships will always be a source of motivation for you, and as a result they will be more carefully wrought and attended to than most. Others will look up to you as someone who is especially blessed and successful in love.

Neptune in the Eighth House

You appreciate an intense love affair that increases your self-understanding, shows you new aspects of yourself and unearths strong feelings. Indeed, unlocking internal mysteries in yourself and your partner may be very rewarding, but it should not be too relentless. If the affair is too tumultuous and intense, inner knowledge becomes a substitute for more simple, gentle loving. Satisfaction results from a blend of intense exploration and relaxed knowledge.

You should always make an effort to be tender and understanding with your lover to soften the necessarily intense nature of your love. Otherwise, some feelings will certainly be bruised by the encounter. If you can be intuitive about your lover's feelings, you both can gain a deeper understanding of each other's strongest motivations without emotional injury.

You will not be happy in a relationship that dodges honest feelings. In a long-term relationship, you and your partner will expend considerable effort to understand each other's innermost feelings and needs.

Neptune in the Ninth House

You are likely to have rather varied and inventive ideals about what you want out of a love relationship. However, you may have some difficulty expressing your ideals or bringing them down to specific reality.

In this respect, your mind may race far ahead of your ability to put your feelings and ideas into action. You will seldom get everything you want all at once, and you may not fulfill your early expectations until later in life.

On the other hand, when you do succeed in fulfilling your desires, you will do so in a much fuller and more accomplished manner because you have had plenty of time to plan. The experience will be the more enjoyable for the long period of anticipation.

In general, your needs are quite internal and generalized. You will fulfill them through a kind of character development that brings personal satisfaction in and of itself. This process may be accompanied by external signs of achievement, but that is secondary.

In love you are an idealist. Physical satisfaction and enjoyment will come only when your inner self is in balance and you have achieved a personal sense of self-worth and accomplishment.

Neptune in the Tenth House

You may have a reputation for being somewhat mysterious concerning love. This may work either for you or against you, depending upon how you use it. But you should try to see what is happening and get other people's candid opinion of you so you are not working in the dark. Then you can take steps to improve your reputation.

You probably have fairly high standards concerning your outwardly recognizable achievements. As a result you may be overly critical of yourself. In this respect, if you can live one day at a time and give yourself credit for each daily success, you will feel better about your progress and be able to move more surely toward your goals.

In love, as well, you should proceed on a moment-to-moment basis. Too much planning for the future can restrict the development and immediate enjoyment of an affair. It should grow almost entirely on its own, with you following rather than shaping its course.

This advice must be taken in context, for life requires some design and continuity, if only for the security of knowing what might happen tomorrow. A good combination of supple planning and internal freedom will result in a relationship that is a joy and an achievement.

Neptune in the Eleventh House

You probably spend much time thinking about how to achieve higher status in your own and others' eyes. You want to do this, not through external achievements, but through proving to yourself that you are an admirable person of high character.

Because of this striving, you may be your own harshest critic, endlessly driving for self-improvement. As a seeker after excellence, you refuse to take second best.

Similarly, you have very high ideals in friendship, seeking and finding the most loyal people as your friends. But you should not let your desire for perfection prevent you from forgiving a friend or lover who fails you. In fact you will probably fail your lover from time to time, as we all do. It is just as admirable to admit and correct your errors as it is to be always right.

While you are young, your search for excellence in all things may lead to some disappointment, both in yourself and in those you love. In time you will learn to be tolerant. Also you will find that you have achieved much of what you are striving for and that you can recognize and accept what cannot be attained. Then you will receive the admiration you have been seeking. You won't enjoy this wantonly, but will share it with a close circle of loyal friends and lovers.

Neptune in the Twelfth House

Your most valued goals and achievements in life will be very personal and private. You may well realize all your dreams without anyone else knowing about it. One of your most important goals is to understand the hidden facets of your personality, which will bring you great satisfaction. To do this, you must expend considerable effort in psychological exploration. You need a partner who can help you discover your inner motivations. In the end, however, it is your own self-knowledge that has real meaning, and you won't necessarily share that totally with your lover.

Because your goals are likely to be quite deep and hidden, they may not be immediately apparent, even to you. To find out what you really want in life will require much self-exploration. The effort will be more than worthwhile when your vision clears and you get a good view of your purpose in life.

Do not be surprised if in retrospect the direction of your fulfillment seems obvious. Sometimes things that seem the most difficult and profound are the simplest when penetrated with real understanding.

Aspects of Neptune to Pluto

Since the late 1800s, there have been only three Neptune–Pluto aspects: the conjunction of 1891 and 1892, the semisquare of the 1930s and the sextile, which began in the late 1940s and will continue into the 1990s. These aspects last quite a long time, and because it is difficult to get an accurate perspective on long time periods, they are not well understood. The sextile has been going on for so long that it is hard to separate its effects from those of other elements and indications. Until this aspect is over, any discussion of its effects would be totally speculative.

Neptune Conjunct Ascendant

Other people may find it difficult to put their finger on what your personality really means, which you can use either to your advantage or to your disadvantage, depending upon how aware you are of it. You can use this talent to fool, charm and otherwise cajole a potential lover into doing almost anything you desire, because others easily see their own fantasy images in you, which makes you a particularly desirable partner.

But this trait may backfire on you, because the longer you allow your partner to set your personality, the harder it will be to communicate your real personality. If your lover's image of you becomes too ingrained, the disillusionment of discovering the real you may be too much for the relationship to bear, or at least very disappointing. Thus, it might be better to use your powers of deception on a social level, but once involved with a partner, to doff the cloak of unreality so that you can achieve real, meaningful communication.

Once you establish real communication in a love relationship, you can be an excellent partner in sexual fantasy, for you can slip easily into and out of your lover's fantasy roles as well as your own. For you, that is a very rich and rewarding area of sexuality to explore.

Before getting into such forms of expression, however, you and your lover should be sure you understand each other's real nature, so that you do not become lost or confused about what is reality and what is fantasy.

Neptune Sextile Ascendant

In communicating with a lover, you may find words unnecessary, relying on your intuitive feelings to make communication flow between you. This will make for very easy love affairs, as long as your partner shares this ability. Otherwise, your own needs may be virtually ignored, while you intuitively sense how to satisfy your partner's needs and desires.

For this reason, you should not become too dependent on your intuitive ability, because the more complex problems in a relationship must be dealt with in clearly spoken words. Although intuition is probably the best way to deal with the positive aspects of loving, it may only confuse the situation when difficulties or conflicts arise.

You may not require sexual expression in order to become quite close to semeone. A long-lasting platonic relationship may prove richly rewarding and in some ways much closer than any sexual relationship that you are involved in at the same time. Friends of your own sex or brothers and sisters may be much dearer to you in a special way than the person whom you are living with.

Whatever the nature of your relationships, in the long run you will have the most success if you let your inner feelings and intuition guide your decisions in love.

Neptune Square Ascendant

The image of yourself that you transmit to others may often be illusory and not get across exactly the meaning you intend. This may result from a hesitancy to assert yourself or simply from misinterpreting how others are responding to you, so that feedback does not alter your presentation to produce the effect you want.

You can clear this up by making your messages quite verbal and not communicating just with gestures or eye contact, for these are too easily misinterpreted. Insist that people respond to what you say, rather than just to what you do, and you will have a much clearer idea of others' reactions to you.

Because of this situation, you may feel somewhat insecure about whether your lover's responses to you are sincere and dependable. Chances are, your doubts are unfounded. Here again, put your confidence in words rather than deeds, where your motives may be uncertain or misinterpreted. If you establish a clear policy of openness and honesty between yourself and your partner, you can depend on your verbal communication more than on feelings, which may be based in insecurity. But if you are anything less than strictly honest, the relationship will fall into a quagmire.

Neptune Trine Ascendant

You tend to romanticize and idealize love in a very spiritual way, but not to the point of being unrealistic. Instead of seeking a relationship that can't be attained in reality, you use your natural talents to make your current affair much more romantic and ideal.

Throughout a love affair, you are more concerned with spiritual communication than with the technical aspects of sexuality. But you do this in a natural fashion so that the flow of physical sexuality is not interrupted but infused with the higher qualities of loving communication.

At times, if your partner shares these qualities, this tendency may lead into affairs in which sex is not at all important. In any case you will not seek sexual expression for its own sake, unless you know there is something higher to be gained from it, either immediately or in the future.

Probably you will retain a certain innocent and playful quality that makes sexuality airy and gentle rather than hard and tense. Indeed, this trait will enable you to soften a partner who is less at ease and reestablish the flow of sexual communication when it has been broken because of your partner's problems.

Neptune Inconjunct Ascendant

You tend at times to seek spiritual qualities in a relationship to the exclusion of everything else, which may limit your partner's choices severely and also confuse others as to your real intentions. Once involved in a relationship, you want to elevate it continually, which may be exhilarating for you but difficult for your partner.

On one hand, with the right partner you may become totally involved in the spiritual aspects of sexuality in a very positive way, exploring such paths as Tantric yoga, in which sexuality is used to achieve spiritual goals. On the other hand, if you do not have such a partner, you may become rather asexual or, if your sexuality is more intense, quite frustrated. Or you may sublimate your sexuality in other activities.

You should relax your standards in this area to a certain extent and enjoy the more down-to-earth aspects of sexual expression, if only to keep your sexual energies from becoming too knotted inside you. It isn't necessary to work toward an ideal sexual experience every time. You can gain a great deal by waiting and letting your lover produce whatever he or she is capable of, which in the long run may be much more than you had thought.

Neptune Opposition Ascendant

You may tend to idealize your partner to the point that he or she is more a concept than a real person. You may heap praise and adulation on your lover, which can be very flattering, but it can lead to great difficulties later if your lover fails to live up to your high expectations. At that point you both may be in for an unpleasant and rude awakening.

You may be the victim of a similar tendency, for you gravitate toward partners who are as idealistic as you are, who may mentally frost over your character and come up with an image of you that is not very realistic.

Getting down to brass tacks is an important part of any successful relationship, so that you can get to know each other for what you really are, instead of creating shadow images of each other based on what you would like to see. This doesn't mean that you must settle for less than you would like, but that you must be aware of what you and your partner are working with. Then you can work concretely to build the relationship into the shape that you both will enjoy. The only effective road to reaching your ideals is through first recognizing reality.

Chapter Fourteen

Pluto

Pluto in the Chart

The position and aspects of Pluto have to do with the deep underlying motives and fears that propel you toward inner transformation and force you to come to terms with the basic issues of life and death.

On a more mundane level, Pluto governs the power motive in sexuality, the impetus for one partner, perhaps because of personal insecurity, to dominate the other. Difficult aspects of Pluto can cause serious problems in a relationship by preventing real intimacy through an irrational fear of personal invasion. Easy aspects, on the other hand, create a fundamental inner faith and security that will stand up in the face of repeated difficulties or even defeat. It can give sexuality an almost religious quality that is elevating and transforming.

You share the sign that Pluto is in with an entire generation, for it is in the same sign for at least twenty years. The sign reflects the sexual issues that each generation works to transform in order to make sexuality relevant on an individual basis.

The house position of Pluto indicates the areas in which you seek power and have a positive reforming effect on others, including your lover.

Pluto in Aries and Taurus

These placements will not occur in this century.

Pluto in Gemini (1882–1912)

Your generation has great esteem for the written word and for the mind's ability to unravel man's inner mysteries. This same style is applied to sexuality and love, resulting in a tremendous volume of writing, much of it highly perceptive, about what makes our emotions tick. Much can be learned and transmitted this way, but it is possible to rely too much on the mind's ability to understand and control love.

This may or may not be your own attitude toward love, but you will certainly encounter it in general among others of your age. Too often, unspoken problems are ignored, and when they are, they may take on larger dimensions.

On the other hand, if you analyze each problem, even those that are rather subtle and not easily described, they can be clearly identified and consequently cleared up.

This ability to relate to the world mentally will bring you closer to those of your age, but it will also separate you from the generations before and after yours, which can't look at life that way. Thus, your ability, or lack of it, to fit this particular mold will determine the age group with which you feel most comfortable.

Pluto in Cancer (1912–1938)

You will probably find that your generation is quite security-conscious and home-oriented, partly because security was rather hard to come by as you were growing up, mostly for external economic reasons.

This attitude may or may not rub off on you personally, but you will have to deal with it continually among your peers. One result of this attitude is an undertone of conservatism in the social structure that does not fit well with changeable or volatile relationships.

In fact, if your style is more freewheeling, you may relate more easily to people in the younger, much less conservative generation or to your parents' generation, which was just as revolutionary but in a more intellectual way.

At any rate, you are part of a generation that puts a premium on the security of physical possessions and the privacy of relationships. To that extent it is less liberal in love and sexuality. As a general rule you will have to step carefully in these affairs so as not to upset or offend your partner, particularly if your own style is somewhat different.

Pluto in Leo (1938–1957)

This position marks the generation born between 1939 and 1956 that brought sex out into the open. They are the *enfants terrible* of sexuality. This whole generation suddenly decided that sex was something to have fun with, a wealthy storehouse of pleasure at everyone's beck and call.

When the first members of this generation came of age in the 1960's, they flaunted sex everywhere, as if it were a brand-new discovery. The discoverers rolled and reveled in it, which changed the whole world's attitude toward sex. This is still going on, but perhaps less flamboyantly.

The precocious sexual innocence of the 1960's is gone, but those in this generation still look upon sex as something joyous and sportive, something to be enjoyed for its own sake and not for any ulterior motive. Without doubt, this is the best position for Pluto next to Scorpio, its own sign. If there is any disadvantage to this position, it may be that you sometimes put too high a value on sex, neglecting the myriad pleasures of the mind and other faculties.

Pluto in Virgo (1957–1971)

As a rule, your generation is more demanding and particular about what is required in a relationship than earlier generations have been. Thus, committing yourself to an affair can be unusually difficult and require a great deal of attention.

This attitude results in part from the fact that this generation must consolidate and bring down to earth the previous generation's changes in the nature of relationships. But at the same time, insisting on so many conditions in a relationship may make it difficult or impossible to fulfill them.

This can be a particular problem if your personal style is rather relaxed and undemanding; you may feel that you are quite different from others in your generation. In that case you must learn to attend more carefully to the details of a relationship so that your needs and those of your partner are fulfilled as much as possible. If you are a careful person anyway, this will not be difficult and will surely enhance the affair.

If your style is at odds with that of your peers and an affair becomes just too nit-picking, you may have to give it up. In that case you may find the company of your elders more enjoyable and closer to what you want in relationships.

Pluto in Libra (1971–1984)

Your generation may seem to be obsessed with relationships that change continually. Constant change may make you more creative in dealing with changing roles in life, but it can be rather unsettling for those whose style of loving is more regular and consistent.

Certainly, it is possible to gain greater equality and wider experience, both emotionally and sexually, in this way. However, if you prefer fairly direct and steady communication with your partner, with unchanging images of each other, the pressure to change your way of relating may be unnecessarily trying.

You will encounter this attitude quite generally, so you should either learn to enjoy it or simply avoid it. This generational point of view is not one that can be easily resisted.

You are part of a generation that is making the greatest possible contribution toward real balance and equality between the sexes. Although that is not an easy or always pleasant task, it will make relationships far easier and more fruitful for generations to come. If you are heavily involved in this movement, you will eventually derive much reward and credit for being in the vanguard, reforming the nature of male-female relationships for generations of future lovers.

Pluto in Scorpio (1984–1995)

You may find that your generation puts a premium on intensity in a relationship. Love, like other aspects of life, is considered an all-or-nothing proposal. If this is in line with your personal style, you will feel catapulted along by the times you live in. Your love relationships will be both very stressful and very rewarding, often at the same time.

However, if you are more easygoing, then you may find that your partners expect more energy and conflict in a relationship than you want or can deliver. In that case, you should look for a lover whose temperament is similar, even though you may be attracted to those who are very different from you. In the long run, you will be happiest with someone who keeps your pace and does not run you ragged emotionally, even though that may seem like the most exciting direction.

No matter what kind of relationship you are in, however, the level of intensity will be heightened just by the attitudes and expectations of those around you. If this is not your preference, it might be better to postpone a permanent relationship. Those in the next generation, about ten years younger than you, will approach love in a radically different and much simpler way. That style may be more to your liking.

Pluto in Sagittarius (1995 into the twenty-first century)

Your generation has a very robust, simple, almost pioneering approach to love, a direct but rather romantic way of looking at people. This is an innate point of view, but in part it is a response to the last two rather turbulent generations. They did not look at love as a pure concept that needs no tampering to make it more whole or perfect.

In general, the potential partners in your age group prefer to let a relationship take its own course; if it is headed for the rocks, they let it happen. They won't alter the pattern of a relationship for better or worse, except to abandon it altogether and start anew.

If you are more introspective, this will seem like a disastrous attitude. You may feel that a viable relationship should not fall apart for lack of correction or restructuring. There is not much you can do about this generational point of view, however, except to find an older partner or someone of your own age whose style is like yours. If you have a flair for the romantic, you will be right in tune. For better or worse, love will sweep you along into, and sometimes out of, relationships that are very powerful.

Pluto in Capricorn, Aquarius and Pisces

These placements will not occur in this century.

Pluto in the First House

This position can, if ill-used, lead you into a domineering egocentricity. If handled well, it can help shape a forceful personality with a thousand exciting sexual spin-offs.

Your relationships tend to be extremely intense, seeming to arise almost outside of the will or influence of either partner. You will be greatly tempted to get involved in emotional games of personal dominance or confrontation on a mental or spiritual level. You should avoid such games if you hope to have a fruitful relationship.

On a sexual level, however, it is all right to pursue these interests with vigor if both of you understand exactly what is happening. This is an ideal position for planned, out-of-the-ordinary bedroom games and other aggression outlets, which can provide the most explosively high-powered sex. As with any other high-energy source, you must be very careful to keep it a game, so that neither of you is accidentally hurt.

These diversions can be successful and enjoyable only when strictly confined to the bedroom. In your everyday social life, you and your partner should maintain absolute equality. Then, a creative relationship may flower, and every trip to the bedroom can be a fireworks display.

Pluto in the Second House

A steady source of income may be particularly important to you. If you aren't sure where your next dollar is coming from, you feel quite insecure. For this reason, you may be attracted to a lover of substantial means who can provide both financial and emotional security. Although it is tempting to settle for this solution to your insecurity, financial dependence can have many pitfalls; money will surely become a sore point between you and result in an unequal relationship.

On the other hand, you may want to be the sole provider in the relationship. Although this attitude seems generous, it gives you a certain power over your lover, which can potentially drive an emotional wedge between you. Love should not be subjected to the power of money, and when these areas are too closely associated, affection may become forced or even wither entirely.

It is better for both partners to be either financially independent or mutually involved in your financial support. Probably you will have more talent for controlling money or at least be the more concerned about finances. In this area, you may be the leader, but to preserve harmony and affection in the relationship, you should allow your partner to make an equal contribution.

Pluto in the Third House

You probably have a talent with words, an ability to speak effectively as an extension of yourself. This enables you to make your ideas clear to others and also to gain influence or control over them.

In a love relationship you should use this talent with care. It will certainly help you to state more forcefully your view of any problems that arise, but if your lover is not as skillful at argument, his or her views may be suppressed by your force. Therefore, you should take care to listen well to everything that your partner says, to keep the affair from becoming unbalanced.

You should try to spell out the details of your relationship quite clearly, for unspoken disputes are more likely to cause problems than difficulties that are hotly debated. You have a certain power over problems that are expressed verbally, which you cannot have over unspoken complaints.

At any rate, you have a strong desire to understand a relationship and to delineate all its details. You want to have an intricate and profound understanding of what makes you and your lover tick so that you know what qualities are expressed as a result of the relationship.

Pluto in the Fourth House

You probably derive great comfort from the security of your most intimate surroundings, your home and especially your bedroom. Making sure that your home environment is secure is very important to you. Naturally, you will be happiest with a lover who respects these values rather than someone who feels that home is where you hang your hat. Because of this quality, you can care for a truly fine home for yourself and your family, spending great energy in improving it.

If carried too far, this tendency can lead you to imprison those you love in a close and restricted atmosphere without freedom to come and go as they wish. It is fine to provide a secure place where your loved ones feel protected, but it should be a refuge, not a prison. Sometimes it is difficult for you to see the line between the two. If you follow your lover's inclinations about the situation, any such problems will be overcome.

Probably you are the partner who is more qualified and interested in maintaining the home you share with your lover. However, its uses should be decided by both of you. Otherwise the management of your home could become a tool of control over others, which would defeat its purpose as a place of personal security and refuge for you both.

Pluto in the Fifth House

The physical expression of sexuality may be very important to you and quite intense, but you may not be able to find a regular outlet for sexuality. Because of this problem, internal pressures may build so much that when you do find an opportunity for release the experience may be overwhelming from your partner's point of view.

Try not to pressure your lover into any sexual situation for which he or she feels unready. If you do, you might get your way at the time, but you run the risk of ruining the relationship by denying your lover necessary breathing room.

When you do find the opportunity for sexual expression, you will be happiest with a lover who can share the depth and intensity of the experience as much as you do. Such a partner will suit you much better than a lower-keyed person who is not able to fully participate in or understand your intensity.

Carefully matching your rhythms with your partner's is quite important; in this way your pressure-building and release will more or less coincide, and neither of you will feel the frustration of being out of sync.

Pluto in the Sixth House

Your sense of responsibility in sexual matters can, if properly handled, help you become a most thoughtful lover. You feel bound to provide everything that will please your partner when it comes to loving and sexual technique.

But if you carry this service too far, satisfying the demands of your lover's pleasure may eclipse your own; in the long run that will put the relationship out of balance.

On the other hand, you may feel that your lover must always do specific things in order to give you real satisfaction, which is likely to limit your own sexual potential.

You should discuss with your partner exactly what you really want of each other and then take care to fulfill each other's needs equally. You may find a certain reward in playing out bedroom fantasies that involve sexual obligation or even control and dominance. However, it is very important to keep such games confined to the bedoom; otherwise, the inequality of respect and love within the relationship can cause your mutual affection to erode.

Probably you prefer to have your own and your partner's needs fairly well delineated, but you should not let these roles remain static. Be willing to change your respective parts in a structured way to give you both the greatest potential satisfaction.

Pluto in the Seventh House

One of your main concerns in life is having a partner, and that need may sometimes outweigh all others in your life. This basic need is stronger in you than it appears to be in many others.

Although you are likely to form very strong long-lasting partnerships, an unscrupulous lover may take advantage of your overwhelming need. Therefore, you should not let a lover gain too much control over you through your fear of being abandoned if you don't do everything to please. If this situation occurs, it will be your fault for permitting it as much as your partner's for playing on your weakness.

This same motivation may cause you to try to control or tie your lover down with unnecessary commitments in order to assure yourself that the relationship will continue. You can do this up to a point, but in the end your attempts at control will be counterproductive, for mutual freedom is essential to an enduring partnership.

Rather, give your lover maximum freedom, even if that is worrisome at first. Time will bring you the security you long for, as the relationship grows increasingly stable. This goal can be accomplished with the help of your strong will in these matters, and in the end you will have a firm and lasting partnership.

Pluto in the Eighth House

In relating to your partner, you may have to learn how to relax and let things flow, even if nothing exciting comes of it. You very much want a high degree of involvement in a relationship, so you usually throw yourself into it, exerting every effort to heighten the feelings.

But that kind of intensity may make your lover feel emotionally pressured to produce. Instead of becoming more involved, he or she may just back off. The deepest and most intense commitment within a relationship usually evolves in time through getting to know each other's feelings and habits, without prompting from either partner. Too much pressure to produce may thwart the relationship or force it in a direction it would not normally take, which in the end will be destructive.

An affair may ramble on for a time with no apparent action, but there may be a lot happening below the surface that will appear in time if you give it the opportunity. Indeed, that kind of uncontrived growth is frequently the strongest and most important to a relationship, resulting from the true inner workings of the evolving partnership.

Pluto in the Ninth House

You may find that you need to keep your love in motion with frequent changes in order to feel that something is happening, that your emotions are active and in play. This makes you a skilled lover who is well able to please a partner, but it can also lead you to miss some deeper involvement. Your impatience and restlessness may push you on to new things before the old are really played out.

For that reason, you should slow down from time to time and give extra attention to the emotional details of an affair, even if nothing much seems to be happening. A slow period in a relationship may be covering up much that is going on underneath, which will blossom later if you hold on to the relationship.

When physical activity is at a minimum in the relationship, take that opportunity to explore the emotional bonds between you or find new intellectual interests to share and enjoy together. Not only will this profitably take up your leisure time, but being close in other areas will also restimulate the physical side of the relationship and allow your partnership to take a series of important steps forward.

Pluto in the Tenth House

You may often be presented with opportunities to use or manipulate a lover for some ulterior motive, which is a temptation you should resist strongly. It goes without saying that love should not be tampered with or used to gain your own ends in other areas. More important, if you give in to the temptation to manipulate, it will certainly be noticed by others, and you may gain an unwanted and perhaps undeserved reputation, for the distortions of gossip will not be in your favor.

Since you are someone who highly values your reputation, you will want to be extremely careful to protect it. One easy way of avoiding situations that are invitations to manipulation is to keep your business and your love life thoroughly separated so that they do not come into conflict. In this way you can freely develop your talent for forcefulness in your career without affecting the tenderness and honesty of your love relationships.

If you do become involved with someone emotionally as well as financially, be sure your interests are so thoroughly entwined that neither of you will want to take advantage of the other. In that way you will avoid any hint of mistrust. Such relationships, though more difficult, can be stronger than most and yield even greater rewards.

Pluto in the Eleventh House

Excellence in a relationship in every respect is a strong driving force for you. In fact, you will go out of your way to alter any aspect of an affair in order to improve it. This motivation can lead you to very harmonious relationships that others will envy, but getting to that point will require considerable care and experience. You must learn just where and when a relationship can be successfully changed and when too radical an alteration will lead to the demise of the affair.

This is particularly important for you to learn, for the responsibility for growth in a relationship is likely to fall on your shoulders. You will be the one to make the first move to improve the situation or, if that is impossible, to break up the partnership. Remember, although certain aspects of a relationship can be altered by mutual agreement, you cannot alter your partner's nature; trying to do so will prove frustrating and ultimately counterproductive. Only time and experience can change people, and if your partner's personal style doesn't fit your ideal, move on to someone else. You'll be happier, and so will your partner.

Although your standards of a good partnership may be very demanding, don't lower them. In the end, you will see great rewards for adhering to your concepts of excellence.

Pluto in the Twelfth House

It is quite important for you to be completely honest in a relationship, for if you or your partner keeps secrets from each other, your relationship will be damaged much more than someone else's would.

You both may have to make a considerable effort to understand each other's personality in depth, for some areas of your character or your partner's may be unintentionally hidden, coming to light only after the harm has been done.

Similarly, you may deliberately hide something from your partner in order to spare him or her harm or embarrassment, but in your case that is not wise. When the secret is revealed, as it eventually will be, its negative impact will be even greater.

However, you will develop excellent personal insight into your own and your lover's character, as well as into people who are not quite so honest with themselves. For this reason, you can help those who cannot resolve their problems because they can't see the hidden roots of their difficulties.

Just be careful never to use your knowledge of others' weaknesses to take advantage of them. In your case, they would be likely to turn around and do the same to you. If you cannot actively help someone, just enjoy your special knowledge as a widening of your experience.

Pluto Conjunct Ascendant

Your personality has a strong impact on others in one-to-one situations, which can be a tremendous asset if you are careful in the way you use it. You can overwhelm people quite easily, which will not lead to successful relationships unless you learn when to pull back and give your partner freedom for personal assertion and communication.

The lesson you must learn is to use the power of your personality for the good of both partners in a relationship and not merely to serve your own goals. You may need to watch yourself carefullly, for it is easy for you to step in and take control of the situation, especially if a less assertive partner seems to accept it at the time. But you may be stepping on your partner's toes without realizing it. The unspoken resentment that builds up will eventually explode and destroy the whole relationship.

You must be very careful to give your partner plenty of room and enough time to make decisions uninfluenced by you, even if you feel an urgent need to step in and make the decision yourself.

If power games or attempts at domination must exist in the relationship, it is better to fulfill this need through bedroom fantasies. In that way both you and your partner can learn more about your inner needs and drives without interfering with the external course of the affair.

Pluto Sextile Ascendant

You may have a compulsive need to verbally express and thereby control your deepest sexual motives and feelings. This is an admirable goal,but one that is not easy to reach. It requires not only that you be able to plumb your own depths, but that you have a loyal partner who is willing to accompany you and tell you the truth, even if it hurts.

With such a partner you can have a relationship that continually changes and evolves as you get to know each other's inner workings better. The changes are not usually swift or tumultuous revelations, but rather slow, long-term evolutions, although in the end they may be quite revolutionary.

Throughout your journeys in the realm of sexuality, you will be consistently reinforced by a belief that you will get where you are going. You won't worry if your progress is not fast or if you seem to be going nowhere for a time, because you know that great changes take time and that they continue subconsciously even when nothing seems to be happening on the surface. Thus you are not likely to suffer from sexual dysfunction caused by psychological problems, because you have faith in your body as a reliable vehicle for sexual expression and inner learning.

Pluto Square Ascendant

You should restrain yourself from overreacting to sexual situations, especially if it is a question of personal control, either emotional or physical, by you or your partner. You may feel that if you do not control the relationship, your partner will control you.

In such a situation, it is better to end the relationship than to engage in power struggles, for they will bring grief to both of you in the long run and certainly prevent any meaningful communication. If you decide to end it, however, wait until you are sure that your partner intends to dominate you. You may be quite mistaken about your lover's intentions, and there is no point in ruining a good relationship, if it is good.

This is particularly important in the area of sexual performance, where you or your partner may feel pressured to act in a particular way. Love under pressure is not love at all. You both should try very hard to give each other the freedom to achieve maximum pleasure, taking responsibility for your own pleasure, but not for your partner's beyond the limits of comfort. If there has to be domination or obligation in the relationship, it is healthier to express it through ritualized fantasy role-playing, rather than in earnest through your everyday lives.

Pluto Trine Ascendant

Probably you have a deep inner confidence and pride in your body, which makes you an excellent, consistent lover, whether or not you fit the popular social image of one. In sexual expression it is inner strength, which you have plenty of, rather than physical appearance, that determines your impact.

To this extent, you can help a lover who is less aware of bodily pleasures, who has not learned how lucky the soul is to have a body to enjoy. You can reassure a shaky or hesitant partner who may be uncomfortable with the externals of sexuality and thus be inhibited or have more serious problems.

In a way, such a partner would be very good for you by reminding you of the great variety of assumptions and attitudes that people have about the body. You tend to take your physical being on faith with few questions, which means that intellectually you could learn something about this subject, so you can communicate with others better.

This does not mean that you will never have any sexual problems. However, they will not be inner or basic problems, but ones that are caused and resolved by circumstances. Your mental relationship to your body is all right as it is.

Pluto Inconjunct Ascendant

You should do everything you can to lessen your conscious control over sexual expression, because the more you try to push yourself, the less successful you will be. This does not mean that you won't have conquests, for you certainly will, but using sexual conquest and achievement as a gauge of your personal power over someone else is counterproductive to real love and communication.

Under such pressure, the body is the first component to fail, and bodily spontaneity is essential to good lovemaking. Trying to control your body for too long will only result in failure at some point and possibly sexual dysfunction because of insecurity.

The reason behind your attempts at control is a strong need to achieve internal transformation through physical sexuality. It is quite possible to achieve that goal, but you must go about it by different methods. If power or domination must be expressed in the relationship, it should be done through fantasy role-playing in which you both are committed to what's happening. In that way the electricity and dynamism of both partners can flow together instead of in crosscurrent. The result can be intense transcendence through sexual experience, instead of a merely temporary respite from inner pressure.

Pluto Opposition Ascendant

You may seek partners who are quite dominating and powerful, not so much from a need to be dominated as from a desire for struggle and transformation within a sexual relationship. This can lead to very intense forms of sexual expression, but it can also lead to knockdown drag-out affairs that can take quite a lot out of you.

If you want this tendency to be sexually useful and not too interfering, you should not express it in your daily life but reserve it for the bedroom, where it can provide much pleasure. When conflict is confined to the sexual arena and ritualized, it can become a tremendous agent for transformation, making sexuality much more than just a pastime. It must be stressed that neither of you should force your fantasies on the other, even if the fantasies are very forceful. The scenarios should be mutually agreed upon, so that each of you can express fully your needs for aggression and power, while maintaining equality in all other areas. If this is done effectively, it can defuse competition in your daily life, and you can use the transforming power of sexual energy for better self-understanding and closeness.

Chapter Fifteen

The Ascendant in the Chart

The Ascendant represents how your physical body appears to others, so it is quite important in the discussion of sexuality. The sign on the Ascendant at your birth colors your style of presentation to a lover and the image you first project to others.

Your image may or may not be consistent with your inner personality. It is important to understand the relationship between these two areas of yourself so that you will be able to tell when others are misinterpreting you because they are judging only by superficial appearances. At times you may want to consciously alter your image to suit your inner intentions or, on the other hand, you may just wish to be aware of the impression that you make so that you can work within it.

Aspects to the Ascendant have a significant effect on your physical energy and timing in sexual and social situations. If there are difficult aspects to the Ascendant, you may have to modify your approach to others in order to become more in tune with them. Reinforcing aspects can provide valuable clues to why you are as successful as you are and what reputation you may have to live up to.

Ascendant in Aries

With this position you are likely to be quite aggressive in relationships; you are usually the one who makes the first move in an affair. Even if that is not the case, you do take the lead in exploring and developing the relationship.

Your main concern is to get to the essence, physical or emotional, of the affair, without bantering and beating about the bush. Physical foreplay is not so important to you, but you should try not to be impatient with your lover in this, for you might miss the intensity of passion that you seek, which you value most highly.

This position makes you stand out in a room full of people; you can't help but be the center of attention, socially. But for a permanent partner, you should find someone who is quieter and more reticent in order to balance your dominant tendencies. You are likely to be quite competitive socially, but if you choose a lover of similar temperament, your bedroom will turn into a battleground.

You are best suited to someone who will let you take the initiative, ideally a person with Venus prominent in his chart. Such a partner would soften intense feelings, which would make for a lasting, loving relationship.

Ascendant in Taurus

This Ascendant position lends an unusual physical beauty, not superficial beauty, but more of an earthy animal magnetism. Thus, although you are concerned about how you appear to others, you do not judge your appearance by external details, but by the total physical ambience. You are just as attractive in casual clothes as in formal dress, which few others can manage. Your mood rather than your clothing determines your attractiveness, although you very much enjoy rich or sensuous attire.

In beginning a relationship you are most interested in honesty and tend to be bored by social formalities. You prefer a down-to-earth partner who speaks directly from the heart, and once you find such a person, you lavish affection on him or her.

Similarly, your lovemaking style is likely to be direct and physical—you like to do it, not talk about it. You appreciate a sensual partner who is aware of every caress, but who does not dally too much in the peripheral aspects of lovemaking. Much of your pleasure in sex comes from the physical comfort and security provided by your partner. More indirect or intellectual forms of sex tend to leave you cold and somewhat mystified that anyone can enjoy them at all.

Your ideal lover is one who will capture your heart immediately, someone whom you can trust with your life.

Ascendant in Gemini

With your Ascendant in Gemini, you have a talent for variety in personal relationships, and you can enjoy many different kinds of lovers. Above all else, you want variety in your love life; a stick-in-the-mud partner who liked the same thing every time would be very boring.

You prefer the more delicate and intricate styles of loving, involving a good deal of foreplay. Indeed, in some instances your enjoyment of that aspect of sex outweighs everything else. Since you are an inventive lover, you need a very sensitive partner who can respond to your delicate touch and lively imagination. In fact, imagination is the keyword to your style. To that extent, physical love is almost a mental exercise for you, and you seek a lover with whom you can intertwine in mind as well as body. You have the capacity to invent and enjoy all kinds of unusual love games, but their success lies in the communication you achieve with your partner thereby.

You are able to achieve great physical satisfaction from techniques that would leave others only half-fulfilled, while more ordinary styles may leave you bored and wanting more. In the end, you will achieve lasting fulfillment through exercising your sexual imagination and through communion with your partner.

Ascendant in Cancer

For you, probably the most important aspects of a relationship are integrity and security. You do not rush into an affair helter-skelter, and when you do commit yourself to a lover, you expect it to be a lasting relationship. You will persevere through many trials and tribulations in order to make an affair work out, as long as you feel that your partner is equally committed.

If there is any problem with this position, it is oversensitivity, a tendency to take remarks made in jest too seriously. You can overcome this difficulty in part by choosing your lover carefully. Then you should watch your emotional reactions and be discriminating about what you take to heart.

This position makes you a very faithful lover, but in the liberal climate of today, an incident of unfaithfulness will be very traumatic for you. You should avoid being overly possessive in the physical sense; faithfulness belongs more to the heart than to the body. If you can keep this in mind, you can avoid much unnecessary emotional injury.

Physically, what is most meaningful to you in sexuality is love and devotion; sincerity in a partner far outweighs technique. For a truly happy and fulfilling long-term relationship, sex and love must be synonymous.

Ascendant in Leo

With this Ascendant, you have an affable, affectionate nature, emphasizing physical expression. The physical love you seek is rather playful and childlike, and others see you as outgoing and friendly, rather than inward and intense, like some other signs.

You seem to have an open, straightforward nature without too much complexity   self-confident and charming, with an honest natural social grace. This may reflect your inner nature, but as often as not, your cheerful, outgoing appearance hides a much more complex and inward-turned personality. The camouflage of this Ascendant allows your inner personality to operate more freely.

However, the disadvantage of this duality is that you may feel pressured to sustain an image that you don't truly feel within. In any lasting love relationship you should emphasize the inner qualities of your Sun and Moon positions so that your lover will have a real personal understanding of you. People with Leo Ascendant are usually physically attractive, which promises sexual enjoyment. However for true and lasting communication, you must establish inner rapport with your partners; that will determine the success of the relationship.

Ascendant in Virgo

This position makes you a very attentive lover, and your sexual enjoyment is limited only by your imagination and the means to implement it.

You should find a partner who knows exactly what pleases and displeases you. At the same time, you will go to great lengths to find out precisely what turns your lover on, and then you will do just that with love and care.

The only suggestion is to not linger too long on any one facet of lovemaking, lest it obscure the overall spirit of the occasion. You may tend to get into a rut physically, so from time to time you should discuss with your lover what you most enjoy so that you can add some variety to your relationship.

You derive great pleasure from the props and surroundings of your lovemaking, from a well-appointed bedroom to all kinds of playful fetishism. In general, you should go by a predetermined scenario, for too many surprises may prevent you from fully entering into the spirit of the occasion.

It is rather important to have a partner who conforms physically with your image of a good lover, and it is wise to discuss ahead of time your preferences in bed to avoid running into problems later. You will be happiest with a lover with whom you can work out a mutually exciting scene ahead of time and then play it to the hilt.

Ascendant in Libra

With your Ascendant in Libra, you have almost an addiction to physical beauty and grace in sexuality. You are happiest when surrounded by all the props that make lovemaking more sensual and beautiful — fine clothes, incense and perfume, elegant sheets, anything to set the stage for a ballet of love.

If there is a disadvantage to this position, it is that you idealize love so much that it is difficult for any partner to live up to your expectations, both physically and emotionally. Ocasionally you must come down to earth, for otherwise you may set your sights too high for any realistic relationship.

In most relationships, you are the one who develops ideas rather than the one who thinks of them. Your talent lies in turning a love affair into an artistic mode of self-expression for both of you. However, you must give your lover plenty of room for personal development and avoid the temptation to be manipulative in order to get your way. Although you may modify and refine the relationship, you cannot choreograph it all yourself; that requires an equal effort and contribution by both partners.

If the relationship is well balanced, you can shape and articulate it to the point that others will see you both as "beautiful people."

Ascendant in Scorpio

With this position, you are likely to be quite secretive about your emotions at first; you do not tip your hand to anyone on first meeting because that would allow a mere acquaintance to have too much of a hold on you.

You reserve the disclosure of your true feelings for those who are close to you, those whom you can trust with the full intensity of your emotions. Once involved with a lover, your physical passions are very strong, so you must choose your partner carefully to be sure he or she can go along with you measure for measure.

Sexuality at its best totally involves and overtakes you. For this reason you may be attracted to some unconventional kinds of sex in which you control or are controlled by the situation. Delicately handled, this can be a powerful expression of sexuality. It may be better to handle this need directly through sex than to sublimate it through games of personality control, which you may be drawn to.

Once involved in a relationship, you commit yourself totally. Your feelings are very intense, but that can backfire if the affair does not work out. If that happens, try not to hold a grudge against your former lover — some affairs just don't work out, and neither of you is to blame. If it does work out, no one can enjoy it more intensely than you.

Ascendant in Sagittarius

For you, love is an opportunity for endless sport, mirth and enjoyment, to be taken in generous helpings and with gusto. Because of this tendency, you should choose a lover with an equally jovial attitude toward sex rather than someone who is overly sentimental about it.

It is not the method or technique of loving that turns you on as much as the sheer joy of mutual participation with your partner. Instead of spending time exploring the sex manual, you are more likely to do whatever comes naturally at the moment, without too much thought or design.

Remember, you probably have much more stamina than most, so you may inadvertently wear your partner out with your abundant energy. Find out just what your lover likes and dislikes, so that you do not stray into forbidden territory unintentionally, thus spoiling your mutual pleasure. In fact, it may be easier to let your partner arrange the details of your lovemaking, so that you just follow along at the right time. Whatever your lover devises, you will doubtless enjoy, and that takes the worry out of preparation.

People with this Ascendant are the most innocent and enthusiastic about sex, an attitude that lends itself to wholesome and joyful relationships without personality hangups.

Ascendant in Capricorn

You tend to take any personal relationship quite seriously and generally don't get involved unless you are fairly sure it will be permanent. In that case you throw your whole self into it. If you can't find anyone who measures up to your standards, you will go without sexual release for long periods of time. Frivolous one-night alliances just aren't your style.

When you do choose a partner, you provide a calming, stabilizing influence. Ideally, you should find a volatile lover who requires your soothing. Such a lover will have a stimulating effect on you, leading you into new and interesting forms of sexual expression.

It would be wise to follow your lover's lead in lovemaking. Your own tendency may be to become sexually repetitive, so that the experience is a bore. Learn to open up and try out new ideas to get the spark going again; once you are afire, few lovers burn with such steady intensity.

347

If your relationship is not going well, avoid using sex to control your partner. That is likely to make the situation more oppressive and ultimately destroy it. Instead of clinging to a dying affair, make an active effort to change it or dispose of it. Be sure that the relationship deserves the intensity of your affections.

Ascendant in Aquarius

As far as sex is concerned, you have two distinct personalities: one that becomes physically involved with a lover and one that stands back and watches with a rather clinical eye.

This kind of self-awareness gives you quite a bit of control over your sex life, but you may have trouble with a more passionate lover who accuses you of not being "all there" during lovemaking.

You should seek a partner who is as aware as you are rather than one who rushes blindly into love without a second look.

Because of your ability to stand off and observe yourself in a situation, you may derive great pleasure from the more intricate lovemaking techniques that require your kind of self-control. In general, the more you experiment and use your imagination, the more creative and enjoyable your sexual experiences will be. Try not to repeat yourself, because for you the simple act of sex is not enough and may indeed turn you away from the whole experience.

You should consciously try to involve your mind and your imagination in lovemaking, as well as your body. In that way you can achieve a full and satisfying panorama of sexual expression.

Ascendant in Pisces

You are highly empathic, and your physical involvement with a lover is directly geared to your emotional and psychic involvement.

You happily participate in any kind of sexual expression that your lover desires, not for the experience alone but as a vehicle for becoming closer to your partner.

Once you have found the partner you want, you are the most willing and supple lover, but you must take care that your own personality does not get lost in the process. Because of selflessness and generosity, you may be taken advantage of on occasion by even the most honest and decent lover. It's better not to offer that temptation; be gentle and giving, but retain your individuality and independence.

In general, you will be happiest with a lover whose sexual consciousness is rather highly developed. You can easily transform physical sex into a highly spiritual experience, but only if your lover is willing to go in the same direction. Sexual mysticism, such as Tantric yoga, is well worth trying; it will sharpen your sexual expression to a keen and delicate edge, which can turn lovemaking into an almost religious experience.

Appendix

We are currently witnessing, in the media and pop culture as well as in world politics, a resurgence of interest in sado-masochism. Movies with heavily sexual sado-masochistic (henceforth referred to as s/m) themes, such as *The Night Porter* and *The Story of O*, pack the cinemas and are reviewed by major news magazines. Women's liberation groups protest the sexual exploitation and debasement of women by men. On another level, organizations such as Amnesty International are ripping the veil off the rampant use of torture as an instrument of political oppression in many countries. Statistics on violent sex crimes in the U.S. continue to skyrocket. In addition, hundreds of people have begun to openly admit their interest in sexual sadism and masochism and their desires to sexually dominate or be submissive to others. The most important forum for such people is the Eulenspiegel Society, the first and most prominent sado-masochists' liberation organization in the country.

As Pluto and Uranus pass through Scorpio in the coming years, we can expect that these two outer planets will reveal the most tumultuous side of Scorpio in man. Just what kind of behavior will we witness in ourselves when the Christian era reaches an Orwellian 1984 years of age, with Saturn and Pluto in Scorpio, and Uranus aligned with the Earth on its south polar axis? We as astrologers should look closely at the traits in the human personality that will surface then, in ourselves and in others.

It was with this lofty goal that I attended my first meeting of the Eulenspiegel Society in 1972. I went with some trepidation, fearing that I might be seized by a band of savage Huns and tortured to death for sheer fun. Anything can happen on the Lower West Side of New York, near the bleak abandoned piers and warehouses.

But the group that greeted me was far from uncivilized—quite the opposite, in fact. A majority of its members were in "intellectual" trades—writing, music, art, photography, teaching—and all were considerate, polite and very concerned with not impinging on anyone else's personality, probably because they were meeting to discuss and explore just such impingement, in the sexual sense.

When one hears the term sado-masochism, one tends to think first of Torquemada, Hitler and other evil geniuses who, throughout history, have managed to inflict pain and misery on their unwilling fellow creatures. Most of these men have eventually been crushed under the weight of law or history (an exception was Genghis Khan, the most notorious murderer of all). But this is not the kind of evil discussed by members of the Eulenspiegel Society. In fact, they feel that what they speak of is not evil at all but self-fulfilling, and for some it is a means to attain the heights of spiritual ecstasy.

What is s/m? A brief working definition might be: the use of dominance techniques, including bondage, humiliation and/or pain, for the purpose of sexual arousal among consenting partners. The final phrase, "among consenting partners," excludes most acts that are generally thought of as sadistic, such as rape, political torture and the like, because we are speaking solely of *sexual* sado-masochism. To create any significant sexual arousal among participants in s/m, consent and indeed trust are essential. (Nonconsensual acts of sadism, including rape, rarely provide any sexual satisfaction to anyone involved; such acts allow the aggressor to temporarily release or transfer political and social pressures to the victim.)

Few will deny that the trappings of s/m are an extension of animal dominant-submissive sexual patterns. In an age when men and women are being touted as equals, and sex is said to be a matter of mutual sharing and respect, why should dominance and other s/m manifestations be associated with sex? Precisely because sexual equality in the modern sense seems to contradict biological and social history. Throughout animal and human history, it has been the stronger male that has always "won" the female, first by dominating his rivals, then by dominating her. This process is basic to the evolutionary law of natural selection. Modern society, by attempting to hold back and/or alter these basic instincts of survival and evolution, is at odds with some several billion years of life development on the planet.

But if life on the planet is not to snuff itself out through overpopulation during the present technological era, we must indeed radically alter our basic instincts, at least for a time. The aim of most legal structures has been to prevent the strongest individuals from controlling everyone else; however, in an overcrowded world fraught with personal frustration and future shock, people must find new ways to attain individual equality and redirect our animal instincts, or we will perish all too soon. The next twenty years will probably be critical years for the planet in these respects.

On the individual level, astrology can help spot and channel s/m tendencies so that they play a creative and nondestructive role in society, but in using astrology for this purpose, one assumption must be made: that s/m tendencies are not uniform in all of us but vary according to the individual and are indicated in some fashion in the birth chart. Only a statistical survey suggesting the presence or lack of some significant s/m indicators in the charts of people with s/m interests can clarify the issue. This hypothesis inspired me to undertake some research to discover whether there are any such indicators.

If s/m were manifested in individuals only later in life—say, after puberty—then we would have reason to believe that this tendency arises through middle-childhood conditioning (in other words, the time when the child is learning social responses to dominance, aggression and sexuality). Certainly, the channeling of s/m tendencies is learned during this period, but there is evidence that it develops even earlier. According to the testimony of most s/m enthusiasts, s/m fantasies often occur in very early childhood, indicating an early, if not natal, predisposition. Whether the tendency begins with preverbal conditioning or is actually natal in origin is not clear.

What does an s/m sexual encounter entail and how does it affect the participants? It has been said that the perfect orgasm washes away the personal ego and allows the individual to become one with the spiritual whole of the universe. This concept, indeed, is the basis of Tantric yoga. To a greater or lesser extent, this is also the goal of s/m sex.

The basic quality that all s/m sex shares is *ego destruction*. Through the techniques of pain, bondage, humiliation and other physical and verbal methods of domination, the sadist (dominant participant) seeks to make the personality of the masochist (submissive participant) seem less worthy of existence by restraining, beating down and generally trampling the personality out of existence until, in sexual orgasm, it becomes totally nonexistent; the masochist's ego is diffused into the cosmic whole. Of course, this occurs only under "ideal" circumstances.

Such masochistic ecstasy is reminiscent of the motivations of early Christian martyrs and flagellants, who sought to become one with Christ by taking the paths of pain, deprivation and death. Many letters still in existence, written by Christian martyrs, describe in eager detail the torture they expected to go through on the way to death and reunion with Christ—not an easy path to God, but the one upon which the Christian Church was founded.

In such a relationship, how does the sadist benefit from what seems to be exclusively the masochist's pleasure? He or she benefits primarily through vicarious participation. The sadist is participating in—indeed, *causing*—the transcendence and union of the masochist (who may seem like a Christ figure) with the One. Just as the religious follower receives the experience of Christ and the martyrs empathically through worship and communion, so the sadist, although physically dominating the masochist, is transfigured by empathizing with the masochist's experience. The parallel between s/m and the early Christian martyrs is too close to ignore. They are, in essence, the same.

This is not to say that the average s/m enthusiast or any other person performing the rituals of ecstasy-seeking is consciously doing it for religious reasons. Many do it for reasons of guilt, lack of self-worth or mere show. But, in its ideal form, s/m uses a combination of sex and other ego-destroying devices to cause a temporary death of the personality, enabling the soul to experience momentarily the union with the One that it will ultimately experience in death.

Some may find the identification of death with sex and the procreative act a bit morbid, if not positively twisted. But it is not in any way abnormal to associate sex with death. The two concepts have been associated throughout history in many cultures. S/m brings together the themes of sex, death and transcendence in a unique and delicate fashion—by consent, not by force. Surely the quickest way to the "other side" is a .45 automatic or some other weapon. But the idea of transcendence is to get there and live to tell the tale. Therefore the s/m experience must be conducted with the greatest care, knowledge, commitment and trust; without these elements, it will fail and simply degenerate into disappointment and perhaps injury.

Before attempting to collect current data on s/m, I explored what was already available in traditional astrology. What I found was rather inconclusive, because most older authors have understandably identified sado-masochism with sexual "perversions" and have equated sadism with physical cruelty. These theories are not without some

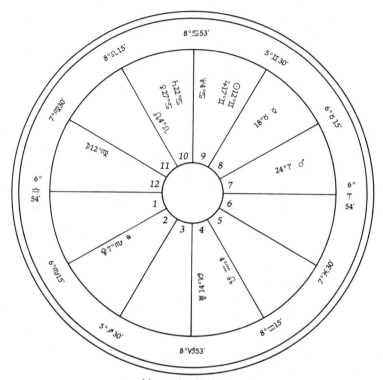

Marquis de Sade
June 2, 1740, Johndro Location Chart

validity, however. The kind of hard Uranus contacts often associated with deviant sexual behavior might indeed be likely in the chart of an individual who is adventurous enough to indulge in sex acts considered unusual or taboo by society. Similarly, the repression and tension engendered by hard aspects of Mars, Saturn or Pluto could easily give someone the motivation to become involved in an s/m relationship.

To illustrate, I include here the charts of three famous men whose sex lives have been topics of much discussion. The Marquis de Sade was an 18th-century French writer. He was notorious at the time for his scandalous and licentious conduct, for which he spent about twenty-seven years in prison. He believed that because sexual deviations exist in nature, they are therefore natural, which challenged the views of his time. The term sadism is thus derived from his name. While in jail, de Sade wrote numerous sexual romances, including *Justine* and *La Philosophie dans le Boudoir*. Leopold Von Sacher-Masoch was a successful 19th-century Austrian author whose popular works were noted for their theme of sexual pleasure through pain. Adolf Hitler, of course, is well known for his destructive role in 20th-century political history, and many people have speculated about the nature of his private sex ife.

De Sade's and Hitler's charts have many similarities, particularly the hard Mars-Saturn-Venus relationship, with both having Saturn, Venus and Mars in the seventh and tenth houses, angular and southern hemisphere (representing that which is projected

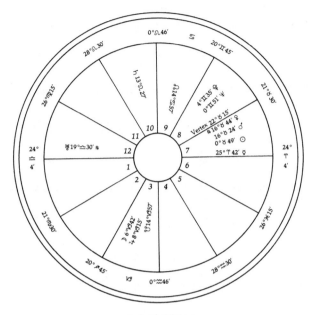

Adolf Hitler
April 20, 1889, Braunau, Austria

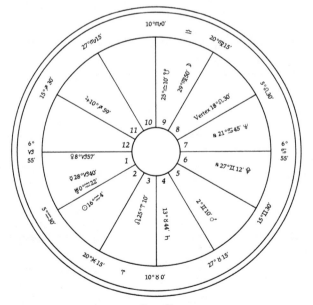

Eva Braun
Feb. 6, 1912, 5:31 AM, Munich, Germany

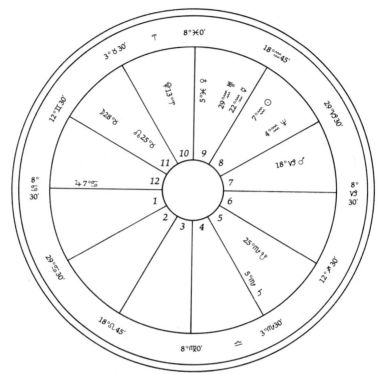

Leopold von Sacher-Masoch
Jan. 27, 1836, Johndro Location Chart

externally and which interacts with the world). Both also have Libra rising, the sign that bestows on one the social graces that make it easy to manipulate others into doing what the individual wants, while letting others think that they are getting the better end of the bargain. Both charts have great tension, especially Hitler's, since he lacks the grand earth trine that allowed de Sade his easy wealth until his incarceration. Both men were involved with more than just sexual s/m. They were men of great cruelty and obsessed with death to the extent that they practiced their fantasies upon others against their victims' wills. It is of particular interest that, in his private sex life, Hitler was strictly a masochist, at least according to the Allies' secret psychological profile drawn up at the beginning of World War II (see *The Private Life of Adolf Hitler* by E.A.P. Braun; London, Aldus Publications, Ltd., 1950).

Hitler's mistress, Eva Braun, was a gymnast, dancer, athlete and model. When she was in her twenties, she met Hitler through one of his bodyguards. Their relationship was very private; he kept her a virtual prisoner in his mountain retreat at Berchtesgaden, where she remained completely out of sight of the world. Apparently Hitler did not want anyone to know that Eva dominated him sexually, playing the sadist to the Fuehrer's masochist. Hitler's previous lovers never revealed anything about their affairs with him, because after he was done with them, each one died suddenly and mysteriously. Hitler and Eva lived in Berchtesgaden from 1936 to 1945. In that year they went together to Berlin because the Allies were closing in. On April 30, 1945, Hitler had one of his aides marry them, three hours before they committed double suicide, with Hitler first giving Eva lethal pills, then shooting himself. Soon after, they were cremated together in the back yard; their bodies were never found.

Eva's natal Saturn-Sun square ties in very prominently with Hitler's natal square from Saturn to Mars and Venus. Other close contacts between their charts include the conjunction of Eva's Mars with Hitler's Neptune and her natal Uranus exactly squaring his natal Sun. One of the nicer ties was her natal Venus conjunct his natal Jupiter.

Sacher-Masoch's chart, on the other hand, indicates a very passive person. This is shown in several ways; it is highlighted by Neptune conjunct the Sun, Venus in Pisces and the Moon in Taurus, with the Moon being the personal ruler of the chart. He appeared to be a likable person, which one would expect with Cancer rising and the Moon in the eleventh house in Taurus. His masochism was highly involved with the spiritual aestheticism of his day. His Saturn in Scorpio in the fifth house in square aspect to the Sun-Neptune conjunction in the eighth house is enough by itself to indicate an individual whose ego would be dissolved through love and sex.

These people have been considered classic cases of s/m, but not everyone follows their pattern. In fact, their cases are extreme. So, in order for the astrologer to study this subject we need more current data to go on and, in particular, a more up-to-date definition of s/m. For this reason, with the help of the Eulenspiegel Society, I collected the birth data, including exact time of birth, of fifty s/m enthusiasts born over a period of forty years. Each person filled out a form outlining his or her sexual preferences in order to categorize them further if possible. This group was then matched by age and sex with a fifty-person control group from the same geographical area (the New York tri-state area). These were the basic statistics of the s/m group:

Male	35
Female	15
Homosexual	14
Heterosexual	25
Bisexual	11
Masochists	22
Sadists	19
Switchable (S or M)	9

The accompanying graphs here show how much the two groups differ from the expected norm and from each other. The s/m group is most significant in Virgo, Aries and Scorpio; the control in Leo, Libra and Capricorn. By house, the differences are more significant: the first, third and fourth are favored by the s/m; less inhabited are the eighth, ninth and tenth. Very little emphasis is given to the fifth as well. The s/m house and sign positions signify that s/m is truly a matter of ego-concern (first house) and rather more cerebral (third house) than basically sexual (fifth and eighth). The additional fourth house flavor also suggests its development in early childhood.

The prominence of Virgo may have dual significance. First, s/m deals with the natural subservience of that sign and second, Virgo is significant in the particularly baroque attention to fetishistic detail indulged in by most s/m fanciers—elaborately wrought costumes and paraphernalia and carefully constructed and ritualized fantasies. Another important finding of my research was the predominance of Jupiter in direct motion among the s/m group, indicating the ability or inclination to act out fantasy.

Other pertinent data:

	Control	S/M
Earth	77	69
Air	77	74
Fire	72	69
Water	69	79
Cardinal	95	95
Fixed	103	93
Mutable	102	112
Feminine Signs	142	157
Masculine Signs	158	143
First Quadrant (NE)	123	154
Second Quadrant (NW)	110	123
Third Quadrant (SW)	117	92
Fourth Quadrant (SE)	150	143

The s/m group concentration is in the feminine, mutable and water signs. This is definitely in agreement with the high proportion of Eulenspiegel members who are artists, writers and the like; perhaps only those with artistic qualities can be aware enough of their fantasies to actualize them. Also, the planet Neptune lends the impulse and the shortage of earth signs lends the lack of inhibition required for straying into the socially forbidden area of s/m.

Placement of particular planets by sign and house does not differ enough between the two groups to have much significance, contrary to my earlier statement in an article in *The Astrological Review*. Of note, however, is the fact that although the Sun and Mercury run high in Virgo in the s/m group, Venus does not; it falls evenly into Leo and Libra, showing that the need to dramatically express one's desires and to relate emotionally must be emphasized in s/m activities.

In the charts of the s/m group, easy contacts from Venus to Saturn, Uranus and Neptune are quite common, as are Venus-Uranus oppositions and Saturn-Moon sesquiquadrates, but not the classic Moon-Uranus conjunction referred to by Charles E.O. Carter.

Another factor pertinent to the study as a whole is the predominance of bowl charts of people born during World War II, when the outer planets were in summer signs. That generation was concerned more with the inner self than with external goals.

Interestingly enough, there were few differences between the charts of heterosexuals and homosexuals, sadists and masochists, males and females. This confirms the belief that s/m is a two-way affair; the sadist contains within himself the masochist, and vice versa. Certainly this is consistent with the personal experience of many s/m enthusiasts, and few people remain in an s/m relationship for long without playing both roles.

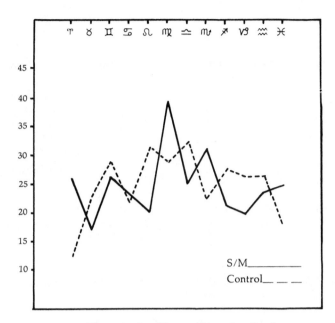

Planets in Signs (Sun-Jupiter)

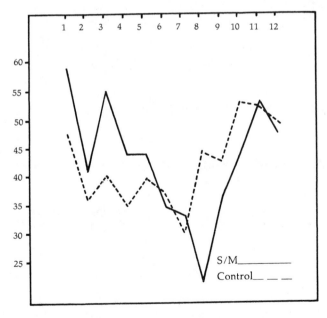

Planets in Houses

359

Astrology students should be warned not to use the results of this study to spot people interested in s/m. Statistics are noted for their ability to mislead, and that could easily happen here. In my own astrological practice, I have seen a far greater emphasis on Leo planets and on the second house in s/m charts than this study indicates. Group studies are full of traps for the interpreter of an individual chart and for those who try to generalize from a group of fifty persons and make statements about the rest of the world.

The famous s/m madam Monique Von Cleef says she numbered among her masochistic clients a large number of judges, lawyers, doctors, politicians, priests and other professionals—people who are not at all likely to be retiring. Why would a person who is well known for his stability and authority in public life pick the pleasures of bondage and the lash in private life? These public-service professionals are considered to be among the most-respected people in our society. Perhaps they find release in balancing the inflexibility of their public life with this kind of uninhibited private expression.

In the natal horoscope, how can the astrologer be sure that an individual is an s/m enthusiast? The answer is that he cannot. One can speculate about the potential for s/m in a chart, both through traditional aspects and through some of the more surprising indicators that have turned up in my study, as well as others that undoubtedly will turn up in future studies. But every aspect in a chart has a hundred different possible manifestations, and their actuation depends entirely upon earlier conditioning, present circumstances and opportunity.

A person may have been brought up with attitudes that violently prejudice him against any form of "perverted" sexual expression, to the extent that he would rather perish than stray from the sexual straight and narrow. But the aspects will find expression in some way, perhaps in more social forms: the domineering boss, the fawning employee and the like. But these people might enjoy much greater life expression and spare the world a lot of grief if they would express their tendencies with a willing partner in the bedroom instead of in their everyday life. Indeed, the Eulenspiegel Society has on various occasions suggested in its publication, *Pro-Me-Thee-Us*, that one can spot a potential s/m person by observing how he or she sublimates tendencies of dominance and submission in otherwise acceptable social behavior.

On the other hand, the astrologer may stumble on someone with no s/m chart indications who has inadvertently found himself in a formidable s/m relationship. In any case, it is the astrologer's responsibility to find out what kind of relationship the client really is involved in and then counsel him accordingly.

When dealing with the overt expression of s/m, the astrologer must keep in mind that this is a very complicated subject, further confused by its long history of social repression. There are many manifestations of s/m, from the high-school football jock who lords it over a fluffy cheerleader to the dominatrix who whips her willing male slave until he bleeds, with a thousand permutations in between.

Compounding the confusion of the many varieties of s/m expression is the extreme guilt that most people feel when they admit that they have these tendencies. Where s/m tendencies are more or less in accord with socially accepted attitudes as with a woman

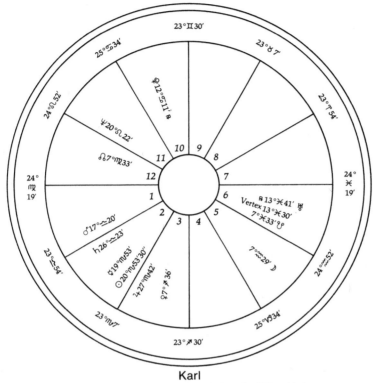

Karl
Nov. 14, 1923, 2:00 AM, Atlantic City, N.J.

who desires to be dominated by a man, there is less difficulty, unless the man is frightened or threatened by the extent of the woman's need or desire for s/m expression. But people whose desires run counter to social attitudes, such as homosexual s/m partners and male masochists, often have tremendous, bottled-up guilt feelings, which make full and open expression and fulfillment practically impossible. The result is a frustrated, knotted personality whose latent masochism may be expressed in repeated career failure, frequent illnesses, etc. In such cases the astrologer should be tactful, only gently suggesting that the client open up, until full trust is established.

When a client is involved in some kind of s/m relationship, the astrologer may be called upon to analyze it or recommend changes, etc. From a glance at the study, which showed no real difference between sadistic and masochistic types, one might conclude that it is impossible to make such recommendations, but that is not always the case.

In individual chart comparisons, the sadist is likely to have Saturn, Pluto or other dominant planets touching the personal points of the masochist. Roger Hutcheon pointed this out to me in the belief that he had found a definitive formula for s/m relationships. Naturally, in the interests of general troublemaking, I went back to my files and found several s/m relationships that did not fit that formula. But as a general rule, this holds true, especially if the s/m tendencies have not found creative expression

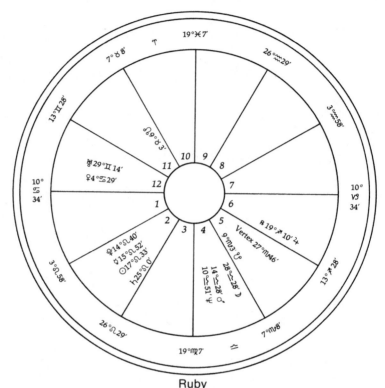

Ruby
Aug. 10, 1948, 2:00 AM, Bayshore, N.Y.

and self-awareness; instead the relationship is characterized by the sullen dominance of one person over a rather resentful partner. "Enlightened" s/m does not entail these kinds of feelings and does not require the corresponding heavy planet crossovers to come to fruition.

There is, of course, another way of looking at relationships in astrology, through the composite chart, which consists of the mutual midpoints of two charts. However, in the long run, no patterns have been consistent enough for me to believe they represent s/m tendencies in a relationship, although for a while I did believe I had some clues. Perhaps the usual clues to s/m inclinations in two individual charts simply cancel each other out in a midpoint construction.

The following three charts are from my original study of fifteen members of the Eulenspiegel Society in New York. I include them to illustrate some of the points I have made about s/m charts so that readers can interpret them and draw their own conclusions.

Karl, a professional photographer, is very active in the Eulenspiegel Society. Although he is married, he spends most of his time with his set of "slaves" and other partners who come and go. Striking in appearance, Karl looks like the classic dominant type, with a deep voice and commanding presence, although he has a good sense of humor.

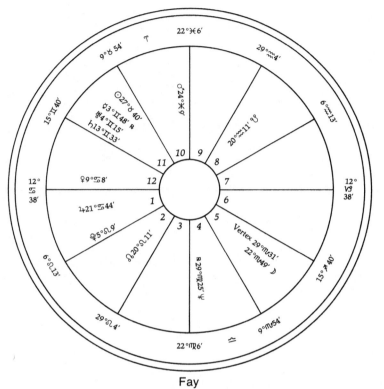

Fay
May 19, 1943, 8:30 AM, New York, N.Y.

Ruby is one of Karl's current lovers, actually his head slave. Their relationship is more one of play than of heavy bondage and pain. Fay, a co-founder of the Eulenspiegel Society, was heavily into the slave trip, wanting her partner to destroy her ego with pain. She was one of Karl's lovers until her demands became too much for him.

In this field, other researchers are collecting their own sets of data, so in the future there will be even more information. Much of it may be very different from mine because of regional bias and because of the changing nature of s/m as it comes out of the closet and into the public. A good example of this change is the difference between the first fifteen charts that I collected, all of Eulenspiegel founders, and the charts in the final study of fifty people. The first fifteen showed a remarkable number of inconjuncts (over two to a chart, using narrow orbs)—far beyond any possible chance; yet in the larger study these were lost in the matrix, and the inconjunct appeared to have no overall significance. I attribute this to the fact that the first fifteen were the "leaders of the pack" (the inconjunct occurs ten times more often then normal in the charts of U.S. presidents, Mien were the "leaders of the pack" (the inconjunct occurs ten times more often than normal in the charts of U.S. presidents, Michelsen found) and the restless, driving quality of the inconjunct was responsible.

This example illustrates the pitfalls that haunt small-scale astrological research of the type usually done in the U.S. because of data-availability laws. For this reason most truly ground-breaking research (e.g., Gauquelin's broad data base) will probably be done in Europe until American astrologers can become plugged in to the university system and its benefits.

From the little that has been written here, the astrologer may have a better idea of what to expect in an s/m chart and how to approach the s/m personality and experience in general. I have spent at least as much time on description of the phenomenon itself as on its known astrological reflections, which can be set down in a few paragraphs. The s/m experience can range from a brief, titillating experience with light bondage to heighten sex for a novice, to an arduous and painful road to spiritual transcendence for the devotee. In between lie peaks of esctasy, swamps of guilt, deserts of loneliness, depths of devotion and every other emotion on which one could pin a metaphor. The s/m experience is so complex and diversified that it cannot be adequately described, even by the many volumes that have been written about it already. Many remain to be written. Unless the astrologer is familiar with the subject itself, all the calculating and chart-casting in the world will be of little aid; in fact it is more likely to be harmful to the client. What the astrologer has to work with is the real world and its phenomena. Because the horoscope is only one filter through which the real world may be seen, it must be used in careful conjunction with all the other factors if it is to be constructive.

Index

This horoscope is about love, sex ...and *you*

How To Order Your Love Portrait

Use the order form on the opposite page or, if you prefer, use another piece of paper. Send the following information plus $12 for each Love Portrait to Para Research, Dept. 2, Rockport, Massachusetts 01966. The price is subject to change.

Name, Address, City, State, Zip Code

The address to which the Love Portrait(s) should be sent.

Time of Birth

Accuracy to the minute is important. Don't rely on parent's memory. Consult hospital records or birth certificate. Midnight and noon are neither A.M. nor P.M.; A.M. is between midnight and noon; P.M. is between noon and midnight. To avoid confusion, if you are submitting a noon birthtime, please write "noon." If you are submitting a midnight birthtime, please write "midnight" and two dates: the day that was ending and the day that was beginning. For example: "June 19/20, 1947, 12:00 midnight."

Please do not convert from daylight saving time to standard time. Just send us local clock time and we will convert. Or if you cannot do this, please explain. If you do not send birthtime, we will use 12:00 noon.

Date of Birth

Month, Day and year.

Place of Birth

If you were born in a small town that may not be on our maps, please give us the name of the nearest city.

Please Print Clearly

Keep a copy of the birth information you send us for comparison with the computer printout. Notify us in case of error.

Guarantee

Para Research guarantees every horoscope. If for any reason, you are dissatified, please return the Love Portrait for a full refund.

Please allow two weeks for processing and delivery.

Para Research, Inc. Dept. 2, Rockport, Massachusetts 01966

Please send me the horoscope offered in *Planets in Love.* ☐ I enclose $12
☐ Charge $12 to Master Charge ☐ Charge $12 to BankAmericard-Visa.

Name _____

Address _____

City _____ State _____ Zip _____

Birth Information

Date of Birth: Month_____Day_____Year_____

Place of Birth: City _____ State _____ Country _____

Time of Birth: _____ AM _____ PM
☐ unknown, use 12 AM (noon)
Note: Price subject to change.

. . . .

Para Research, Inc. Dept. 2, Rockport, Massachusetts 01966

Please send me the horoscope offered in *Planets in Love.* ☐ I enclose $12
☐ Charge $12 to Master Charge ☐ Charge $12 to BankAmericard-Visa.

Name _____

Address _____

City _____ State _____ Zip _____

Birth Information

Date of Birth: Month_____Day_____Year_____

Place of Birth: City _____ State _____ Country _____

Time of Birth: _____ AM _____ PM
☐ unknown, use 12 AM (noon)
Note: Price subject to change.